WITHDRAWN FROM
TCC LIBRARY

CENTER FOR TEACHING EXCELLENCE
TALLAHASSEE COMMUNITY COLLEGE

TALLAHASSEE
LIBRARY
COMMUNITY COLLEGE

Key Works

on Teacher Response

D0887605

Key Works

on Teacher Response

An Anthology

EDITED BY RICHARD STRAUB

Boynton/Cook Publishers
HEINEMANN
Portsmouth, NH

Boynton/Cook Publishers, Inc.
A subsidiary of Reed Elsevier Inc.
361 Hanover Street
Portsmouth, NH 03801–3912
www.boyntoncook.com

Offices and agents throughout the world

© 2006 by Boynton/Cook Publishers

All rights reserved. No part of this book may be reproduced in any form or by any electronic or mechanical means, including information storage and retrieval systems, without permission in writing from the publisher, except by a reviewer, who may quote brief passages in a review.

The editor and publisher wish to thank those who have generously given permission to reprint borrowed material:

"The Effect Upon Student Composition of Particular Correction Techniques" by Robert Stiff. From *Research in the Teaching of English*, 1.1. Copyright © 1967 by the National Council of Teachers of English. Reprinted with permission.

"Students' Response to Teacher Comments" by Thomas C. Gee. From *Research in the Teaching of English*, 6. Copyright © 1972 by the National Council of Teachers of English. Reprinted with permission.

"The Effects of Between-Draft Teacher Evaluation Versus Student Self-Evaluation on High School Students' Revising of Rough Drafts" by Richard Beach. From *Research in the Teaching of English*, 13.2. Copyright © 1979 by the National Council of Teachers of English. Reprinted with permission.

"The Message of Marking: Teacher Written Responses to Student Writing at Intermediate Grade Levels" by Dennis Searle and David Dillon. From *Research in the Teaching of English*, 14.3. Copyright © 1980 by the National Council of Teachers of English. Reprinted with permission.

Acknowledgments for borrowed material continue on page 383.

Library of Congress Cataloging-in-Publication Data
Key works on teacher response : an anthology / edited by Richard Straub.
    p. cm.
ISBN-13: 978-0-86709-528-9
ISBN-10: 0-86709-528-8 (alk. paper)
  1. English language—Rhetoric—Study and teaching.   2. Written communication—Evaluation.   3. Grading and marking (Students).   I. Straub, Richard.   II. Title.

PE1404.K488 2006
808′.042071—dc22   2006013121

Editor: Lisa Luedeke
Production: Elizabeth Valway
Composition: TechBooks
Cover design: Joni Doherty Design
Manufacturing: Jamie Carter

Printed in the United States of America on acid-free paper
10 09 08 07 06   VP   1 2 3 4 5

No man could have been a more devoted son than Rick Straub. In honor of the special bond he had with his family, I would like to dedicate this book to Rick's parents, Eileen and Joseph Straub.

—Ron Lunsford

Contents

Preface

Although it has been over four years now since Richard Straub's tragic death, I seldom respond to a student paper without hearing Rick's voice somewhere in the back of my mind. I have never known any teacher who was more supportive, or more confrontational, in responding to student writing than Rick. Rick never saw a piece of writing that couldn't be improved. And so he challenged every student whose writing came under his scrutiny to make their writing better. If he found the student responsive to this challenge, he would be absolutely supportive of his or her efforts. If he found the student resistant, he would confront. But the thing that made his confrontation palatable was the fact that he brought the same high standards to his own prose that he brought to the prose of others. In fact, Rick's work in student response grew out of his feeling that his responses always needed to be revised themselves. So when I'm tempted to write a sloppy time-saving response to a piece of student writing, I see that impish look that Rick would give when he cocked his head ever so slightly and said, "Ah come on, you can do better than that." He's right, of course, and so it's back to the drawing board to frame a better response that will help the student produce a better piece of writing.

I first met Rick when he appeared as a student in my introductory composition theory course at Clemson University. He was a confident, some might have said brash, young man who challenged any and all received truths about the teaching of writing. It didn't take us long to find that we shared a passion for teaching writing in a way that could make writing matter for our students. After Rick completed his master's at Clemson, he did doctoral work at Ohio State and then joined the English department faculty at Florida State University. My relationship with Rick continued, and evolved, as he began his career at Florida State, and the teacher/student dynamic began to give way to one of mutual support in our frequent conversations about our teaching.

It was in one of those conversations that Rick wondered aloud about the possibility of getting a group of well-known writing teachers to respond to student writing and then writing a book in which we would present and analyze those responses. When I understood that he meant this as a serious proposition, my first answer took the form of a question: Why would anyone expose themselves like that? After several other answers that weren't "yes," Rick finally convinced me that we should try to undertake such a project. To my amazement we—I should say he, because it was his persuasive powers that made it happen—were able to find twelve brave (and generous) souls to accept our challenge. The result was *Twelve Readers Reading: Responding to College Writing*. After that book was completed, Rick's genuine interest in what students really wanted to say in their writing led him to continue studying the ways in which teachers respond to student writing until the day of his untimely death. His work includes numerous scholarly articles on the subject and two additional books, *A Sourcebook for Responding to Student Writing* (1999) and *The Practice of Response: Strategies for Commenting on Student Writing* (2000).

When Rick died, he had nearly completed this, his fourth book dealing with response to student writing. In fact, several days after his death I received drafts of its introduction and the chapter that we were to write together about *Twelve Readers,* along with a note saying that he looked forward to my responses to each piece. My responses will have to stand as the final word since Rick left us before he could receive them. However, had he lived, those responses would have been only the beginning of our conversation about what the final product should be. To Rick, that's what a teacher's (or anyone's) response should be: the beginning of a conversation. How I wish he had lived to continue that conversation with me! Since he did not, this book will be his final contribution to a topic that engaged him for so much of his professional life. Our lives as writing teachers are so much richer for those contributions. My life is richer in all ways for having been fortunate enough to have had a student who came to be a most cherished colleague and friend.

Ronald F. Lunsford

References

Straub, Richard. 1999. *A Sourcebook for Responding to Student Writing*. Cresskill, NJ: Hampton Press.

_____. 2000. *The Practice of Response: Strategies for Commenting on Student Writing*. Cresskill, NJ: Hampton Press.

Key Works

on Teacher Response

Introduction: The Emperor (Still) Has No Clothes

Revisiting the Myth of Improvement

They say a bitter pill is best swallowed in one gulp, so here goes. The essays collected in this volume represent the dedicated efforts of two generations of composition specialists, over the course of half a century, to make the case that response to student writing is a meaningful pedagogical activity. . . . and the results are inconclusive. Gulp. How odd to think that a practice as intuitively sensible as commenting on student texts in order to facilitate more and better writing should have occasioned such a labor of scholarly justification. And how disconcerting to find, after all the theorizing, the case studies, the controlled experiments, not to mention all the dutiful and well-intentioned scribbling of millions of teachers in the margins of billions of student essays over the same half century, that the matter remains unresolved. Yet that appears, at least to us, to be the state of things. We find nothing in our own experience as teachers, and nothing in the accumulated research, to alter the fundamental impressions we formed twenty-five years ago in our own contributions to the literature (Knoblauch and Brannon 1984). First, there is scant evidence that students routinely use comments on one draft to make rhetorically important, and in the end qualitatively superior, changes in a subsequent draft, although students will make limited, usually superficial corrections in order to comply with overt or tacit instructions. Second, there is still less evidence to show that they change their practices from one assignment to the next in ways that measurably represent or affect their development as writers. And third, the very possibility of acquiring such evidence is compromised by the imperfect assessment instruments available for the task.

We suspect that not every contributor to the volume would endorse these disquieting assertions, and that most writing teachers would, in fact, reject them. Scholars and teachers alike might wish instead to accept one or both of the claims with which George Hillocks concludes his 1982 essay, that "teacher comment, when positive and focused on particular aspects of writing over a series of compositions, can be effective," and that "contrary to what has become almost accepted dogma, . . . significant gains in writing skill are possible over short periods of time" (277). The trouble is, within the framework of the sorts of questions that Hillocks, among other researchers, is asking, his optimistic conclusions are unmistakably at odds with the preponderance of the evidence, and reveal a peculiar disjunction between what scholars, no less than teachers, want to believe about the benefits of responding to writing and what they see in front of their eyes. The response literature is reminiscent of the old folk tale "The Emperor's New Clothes," where, despite ample cause for skepticism, there is powerful incentive for everyone to participate in sustaining an illusion. In this version of the tale, a reassuring narrative about the "improvement" of writing ability as a result of teacher commentary belies a persistently unconvincing demonstration that it occurs. The more speculative and theoretical scholarship gives lip service to the concept of improvement, tending to evade direct questions about changed performance while subtly invoking "development" as the dividend from some recommended instructional change. The empirical research, meanwhile, bravely puts the issue of changed performance at center stage but then repeatedly finds itself obliged to settle for local, mostly cosmetic or mechanical revision of student writing as its best case for the value of commentary. What passes for "development" in student writers, in this research, is little more than their willingness to follow a teacher's directions for correcting errors.

The root of the problem, we believe, is precisely the narrow focus on performance that has dominated the literature, and we will argue, momentarily, for a more productive way to frame the issues. There is a perfectly sensible retort to the morose conclusions with which we opened: *Of course*, learners respond superficially to teacher comments, draft to draft, and of course they change little as writers, if at all, from one assignment to the next. That's why they're called *learners*. If people were willing to adopt a more patient attitude toward learning, the result could be a new infusion of common sense in the discussion of what students and teachers can reasonably achieve in the course of three or four months of instruction. Only writers who are already mature and accomplished (including, of course, some students) will self-assuredly sort through reader reactions, choosing some, rejecting others, allowing the best to influence substantive revision. The less mature, including most students, need time to grow. In any case, commentary doesn't create better writers; at best, it may create better writing—and then only when the writer is already skilled enough to take advantage. Unfortunately, however, lots of people aren't comfortable with such a sensible (they might say, "defeatist") point of view. Some teachers aren't comfortable because, having put a lot of sweat and tears into the burdensome task of grading essays, they would prefer to think that their efforts will be reliably compensated. They point to anecdotes of dramatic change (successes do certainly occur) and extrapolate to the conviction that "most" students routinely learn to write in their classrooms. Some scholars aren't comfortable either, because, if prompt and steady improvement can't be observed as an index of instructional success, then what defines "effective" pedagogy? Why should one pedagogical regimen, or writing assignment, or style of commentary, be preferred over another? Taxpayers and public officials, meanwhile, aren't the least bit comfortable, because, if short-term improvement isn't measurable, then how can anyone know that something useful is going on, how can there be accountability in schools? Surely, a lack of improvement in students must mean poor teaching, poor curricula, and/or poor use of resources, and surely there are ways to engineer learning in visible increments to assure everyone that schools "work." Not surprisingly, then, no matter what the research has been able or unable to confirm, there is substantial pressure to stifle any frank concession that students seldom improve quickly as writers. As a result, educational public policy, literacy instruction, and even, to some extent, the research literature itself all continue to insist that the emperor is clothed.

Janet Emig (1983) explored this durable public self-deception more than twenty years ago, calling it "magical thinking," essentially a belief that what teachers teach reliably determines what students learn. We have referred to it elsewhere (Knoblauch and Brannon 1984) as the "myth of improvement," by which we mean a belief that particular teaching activities cause identifiable advances in learning in a smoothly upward trajectory over specific increments of time. Educational research has recognized the myth for a long time, but the public generally accepts it as true, so that arguments about educational effectiveness continue to be framed in its terms. There's a well-established, two-part response to the question, why is the myth of improvement a myth? The first part, thoroughly documented, is that human development is unpredictable, irregular, and time-consuming; the second, similarly documented, is that, while no one doubts that it occurs, and that teachers can help, it is difficult to measure in small increments. We recall a pointed anecdote from Jimmy Britton, the renowned British scholar-educator, who once likened the American preoccupation with educational measurement to an empirically curious gardener who plants a new seedling. The gardener digs a large bed, fills it with rich earth, loads it with nutrients, inserts the tree, waters it daily, protects it from the elements—and then digs it up every six months or so to see how its roots are doing! The romantic metaphors of organism and growth may not suit the taste of the contemporary analytical palate, but Britton's story draws attention to something obsessive in our zeal to identify small increments of development over short periods of time in human behaviors as subtle as the practices of language. On the one hand, just as the gardener uses recognized techniques to nurture a plant, so there are no profound mysteries regarding the appropriate strategies for supporting the development of reading and writing abilities: students need frequent opportunities to read and write; they need supportive responses to their efforts; they need chances to analyze their misreadings or to revise their writing; and they need time, commonly years of time, for these experiences (not to mention many others outside the classroom) to have cumulative impact. On the other hand, there is nothing *but* mystery regarding the subtle developmental pathways and timetables involved: readers and writers don't all progress in the same ways, or at the same rates, or at the same times, or in response to the same specific instructional stimuli. The curious gardener, of course, is luckier than teachers are because she can at least discover a lengthening of the roots. Her problem is a lack of faith in her work and a neurotic inquisitiveness that, once satisfied, does more harm than good to the

growth of the plant. One could say as much about the mania for writing assessment, but the problem is even worse in education: we know what we need to
do in order to develop literate practices, but we don't have fully reliable ways
to measure the results. And the shorter the time interval, the less reliable the
measurement.

Identifying improvement has always been, and remains, a dubious enterprise in the language arts. Thirty years ago, Paul Diederich (1974) of the
Educational Testing Service explained what can and cannot realistically be
accomplished in writing assessment. Nothing in the considerable research
effort since then has shown Diederich to be significantly incorrect in his conclusions. To be sure, he observed, raters can be trained to evaluate written
texts. With appropriate preparation, and assuming a limited range of evaluative
options (good, average, poor), they will make roughly similar judgments. But
there are two important caveats. First, evaluation instruments cannot be freed
from some degree of subjectivity. Raters may believe they are looking through
a textual window at the writer, but in fact they are looking in a textual mirror
at themselves: what they see derives from the values and predispositions they
bring to the reading. The degree of subjectivity is proportionate to the subtlety
of the feature being evaluated. Raters can usually agree about a sentence fragment; they are less likely to agree about an effective use of irony. Second, sup-
posing that evaluation can provide a crude snapshot of a writer's competence
at a given moment in time (a reasonable presumption if the protocol is sound),
nothing in that success implies an ability to distinguish "progress" between
two such moments if the interval between them is as short as the duration of a
course or academic program. In other words, even if it seems reasonable to
assume that a writer has "matured" (or at least changed) between the first and
last assignment of the semester, we don't have instruments sufficiently refined
to detect, let alone identify, the maturation. Given that reality, why should anyone be surprised that research hasn't been able to identify the effectiveness of
teacher commentary?

Despite the efforts of a generation of scholars—Emig, Britton, and
Diederich among many—to "expose" the truth about the emperor's clothes,
the myth of improvement remains alive and well in educational culture,
impressively resistant to challenge. If sustaining the myth had no more serious
consequence than to motivate teachers and students to persevere in the rich
variety of reading and writing activities that, over the long haul, do indeed
enhance competence, there would be little harm in it. Teachers regularly and
wisely cook their books, grading more sternly at the start than at the end of a
term, giving extra points for multiple revisions or bonus assignments, rewarding effort because they appreciate that learners need to believe they're making
progress. No harm, no foul. More seriously, however, and less consciously,
teachers, mistaking obedience for development, sometimes trick themselves
into rewarding students who are merely canny enough to write in the ways that
School requires. That's acceptable for the students who guess correctly, but

less so for those who don't or won't. Most seriously, the myth has broad consequences for educational public policy. For one thing, it stimulates a voracious public appetite for educational "results," where the instant gratification that American culture has come to expect from credit cards, cell phones, and fast-food restaurants carries into the classroom as well, now as early as prekindergarten. It encourages impatient politicians, their reelections riding on promises to fix things, who eagerly mandate "value-added" testing as though making it a legal requirement were sufficient to make it meaningful. The myth guarantees additional power—and profit—for a rapidly expanding assessment industry, which offers, through the quantifying of teaching and learning, a positivist mirage about the feasibility and benefits of an engineered society. Driven by assessment mandates, curriculum designers have discovered the advantages of concocting programs of study that are best able to deliver measurable results—by emphasizing what Ann Berthoff used to call "muffin tin" forms (like the five-paragraph essay) and mechanical correctness (like avoiding the comma splice), because multiple observers will be better able to agree on whether students have incorporated such recognizable features into their texts and assess their performance accordingly. The myth of improvement is not benign, and it needs to be challenged.

To be sure, laying all this sociopolitical baggage at the door of the composition teacher writing "awkward" in the margin of a paper, or at the door of a researcher trying to figure out whether the student writes less awkwardly as a result, would smack of hysteria. But the point we want to make, against the backdrop of the myth of improvement, is that the issue of responding to student writing is properly regarded as a synechdoche for all the tangled themes—pedagogical, cognitive, curricular, ideological, political—that comprise the narrative of literacy education today. We believe that the stubborn strength of the myth is what accounts for the peculiar sleight of hand that we find in the response literature, its persistent framing of recommendations and criticisms in terms of improvement or the lack of it. Instead of discarding the questions ("which responses are most effective?" "how much development do they stimulate?"), as we will shortly propose, researchers seem to want to continue tinkering with the answers in the hope that something that hasn't been successfully identified in half a century will eventually come to light. That persistence represents more than a waste of valuable research effort. It also represents a squandering of whatever political capital the educational community may have to challenge the mechanistic curricular and assessment schemes to which misperceptions of development have given rise. If educators half-believe, or just carelessly, or even metaphorically, employ the myth themselves, how do they challenge it when and where it is doing the most damage?

Broadly speaking, there are three, often overlapping, argumentative aims running through the literature. The most common aim is hortative, proposing what teachers *should* do when commenting on student writing. A second, closely allied to the first, is descriptive, seeking to identify what teachers actually do. A third is experimental, setting out to investigate whether response of one kind or another makes any difference in student performance, either from draft to draft or from assignment to assignment. Each of these narratives typically offers the assurance that teacher commentary is or can be valuable, provided that it follows some set of appropriate criteria, and each advances that view by linking it, tacitly or directly, to the development of writing ability. We want to review a small number of representative examples simply to note the persistence with which some notion of improvement, however artfully disguised, is invoked. And ruefully, we need look no further than our own earliest contribution to the research (Knoblauch and Brannon 1981) to find the first illustration. While defending a particular style of response, we offer the undocumented assurance that "intervening in the composing process, by allowing students to write successive drafts immediately responding to facilitative commentary, can measurably improve student writing, provided that a teacher adequately supports revising efforts" (289). No doubt, a heartfelt leap of faith impelled this implausible contention, but its assurance is hollow, an insubstantial rhetorical move to encourage the practice of facilitative response. Commenting on student writing has always been, and remains, a valuable instructional activity, and we'll renew our faith in it momentarily. But the argument is not well framed when it's based on an illusion about predictable development.

Hortative arguments offer plausible, albeit speculative opinions about the importance of responding to student writing, and about how best to do it, theorizing (or sometimes only presuming) the good it accomplishes but rarely posing the alleged gain as a question for analysis. Nancy Sommers (1982), for instance, reasons that, since skilled writers look for thoughtful commentary on their work, students who have not yet recognized the role of readers in their composing processes can learn from the dramatizing of reader feedback represented by comments from students and teacher alike. Her explanation for why students should respond to each other's writing is that "ultimately, we believe that becoming such a reader will help them to evaluate what they have written and develop control over their writing." In short, "we believe" they will improve, although questions about when, how, or how much are sidestepped. She offers a second "belief," as well: that teachers need to offer assistance to student writers "when they are in the process of composing a text, rather than after the text has been completed" because comments create "the motive for revising" (170). She concedes that "we don't know how our theory squares with teachers' actual practice" (or, we might add, with students' revising practices either), and goes on to conclude, based on some preliminary case-study research, that the teacher commentary she has analyzed fails to give students content-centered advice (as opposed to error corrections) or clear direction for revision, therefore falling short of her model (173–74). This finding encourages her to exhort teachers to respond in more useful ways—that is, by commenting with detailed specificity on textual meanings rather than on trivial issues of form or mechanics—"as a means for helping students to become more effective writers" (176–77). Sommers' argument is explicitly hortative: comments "need to be suited" to particular texts; teachers "need to sabotage" student belief in the completeness of their first drafts; comments "need to be viewed" in classroom context; teachers "need to develop" appropriate responses. But the "need" in each instance is a theoretical conviction unsubstantiated by her available case-study evidence. The insinuation of improved performance hovers like a ghost over an argument that, generally speaking, knows better than to summon it.

Hortative rhetoric is neither uncommon nor inappropriate in pedagogical argument. It's part of the self-critical, ongoing conversation in which teachers no less than scholars regularly engage—imagining a reasonable instructional possibility, taking oneself (or the profession) to task for not having done it sooner or better, and contending, with an inextinguishable hope peculiar to teachers, that students will benefit from the new approach. Our point is only that the hortative literature finds adroit ways to link proposed teaching activities, as cause, to "improved" writing, as effect, presuming that the only way to justify the first is somehow to invoke the second. Richard Straub (1996), for example, commends a disciplined "discussion" between student-writer and teacher-reader, criticizing the "one way line of communication" (375) that too often typifies response. He claims confidently that this active dialogue "will engage students in looking again into their writing . . . and continue their work as writers" (394). His claim is theoretically plausible, but he doesn't offer to document it or certify any alleged result in student performance. Instead, his carefully wrought statements about students' "looking again" into their writing and "continuing their work" convey the obligatory, if vague, suggestion of improved practice as a result of the dialogical effort. Thomas Gee (1970) offers the intuitively sensible contention that praising students creates better motivation to write than merely correcting their errors. At the beginning of his study, he expresses, but does not attempt to explain, his belief that "a great part of student improvement may be attributed to composition teachers" (212). And at the end he claims that students' "continued improvement apparently comes from recognition of what they do well in addition to what they do not do so well" (219). Between beginning and end, however, his documentation extends no further than the soliciting of student opinions about whether they feel better after praise or after criticism, a question whose no-brainer answer, we submit, says little about the effectiveness of teachers or the development of writers. Hortative arguments seek to reflect on teaching activities, and explore alternatives, by reference to (perfectly legitimate) standards of theoretical plausibility and practical classroom experience. But they don't set a high bar for demonstrating the results, employing instead a rhetorical sleight of hand ("continued improvement apparently comes from . . . ") to suggest the power of their recommendations to affect student learning.

Descriptions of current response practices, the second argumentative aim of research, are typically hortative in intent but dressed in an ostensibly more neutral rhetoric. They seek to identify what teachers are actually doing, but they virtually never just report the state of things as though such information were intrinsically useful. Instead, they depict the observed practices against a backdrop of assumptions and values found in the hortative literature. The description frequently sets the stage for critique, where observed practices are shown to ignore, or only minimally accommodate, the recommendations of pedagogical scholarship (correcting errors, for instance, rather than facilitating content revision). Commonly, there is an implication that teachers will need to change their means of intervention if there is to be any real progress in student writing. Descriptive arguments work, then, from a deficit theory of improvement, suggesting that students fail to profit from what teachers are currently doing. Hence, Searle and Dillon (1980) set out to document how teachers actually respond to students in order to determine "their criteria for good writing" and their understanding of their "role in improving student writing" (233). The study finds that nearly two-thirds of teachers' responses are of the "didactic/correction" type, that most of these responses are at "the mechanics end of the continuum," and that content statements are typically very brief and generalized ("good job," "excellent") (239). Searle and Dillon are clearly disappointed with the lack of emphasis on content, noting that "the participating teachers did not operate with the view that a focus on the meaning and purpose of language is basic to language development." They find "little evidence" of teachers working to develop students' ability to think, and they conclude that "the message about language which seemed to be communicated was that it doesn't matter what you say; what matters is how you say it" (239–40). Searle and Dillon are plainly aware of "theoretical views on how writing develops" (242), and they are just as plainly critical of teacher-response practices that don't reflect these views. Logically, their conclusion must be that teachers do not currently understand their "role in improving student writing" and would be more successful in developing writing ability if they did.

Connors and Lunsford (1993), similarly descriptive in their aim, survey 3,000 student essays in order to catalogue types of response, concluding that teachers are not as relentlessly preoccupied with mechanical errors as Searle and Dillon imagine, but also finding that teachers do not "communicat[e] their rhetorical evaluations effectively, over-emphasize isolated problems on individual papers without regard for patterns, and are too preoccupied with "giving students standards by which to judge finished writing"—in other words, explaining grades rather than promoting revision" (462). They are somewhat more generous than Searle and Dillon are, presuming that teachers might prefer more facilitative and less evaluative commentary but that they face institutional constraints (like large class sizes or curricular mandates) that enforce unproductive practices. But they parallel Searle and Dillon in commending an alternative set of practices (emphasizing clarity of response, pattern recognition, and the revision of successive drafts), and in presuming that a change would represent more successful pedagogy. Moving from descriptive to hortative rhetoric, they claim that we "*need* a rhetorical context for every disruption we make in a student text," and that we "*need* to start putting into programmatic practice what we've learned about effective teacher commentary" (463, our italics), insinuating but never quite explaining what the terms of "effectiveness" are supposed to be. They are careful to say nothing directly about improvement in student performance as a result of the changes they commend, but they also give no alternative reason to commend them so forcefully.

"Experimental" arguments play for the highest research stakes and are, historically, the most disappointing: they look for evidence to document the success of teacher commentary, where "success" means that students follow the advice they get from a discerning teacher-reader, measurably change their practice, and enhance the quality of their work as a result. These arguments often target a specific commenting strategy to see how it affects student performance, sometimes measuring it against an alternative tactic (as in marginal versus end comments or mechanical versus content responses) or analyzing one group of students, the experimental group, against a control. The conclusions have been bleak indeed, those of Robert Stiff (1967) the bleakest (and earliest) of all: "there appears to be no significant improvement in any large group from pre-test to post-test writing" (60). Experimental arguments sometimes make modest headway when they focus on commentary comprised of straightforward directives regarding grammatical, lexical, or stylistic change, emphasizing correction of drafts in a single assignment. But they make less headway when they focus on subtler aspects of organization or content, and they fail, for the most part, to show carryover from single-essay revision to improved performance across assignments. Yet most of them also conclude, with more confidence than their findings justify, that student writers have "improved," offering the obligatory qualifier of all scientific investigation—that "additional research needs to be done"—as a tease for more promising findings in the future. At the center of experimental rhetoric lies the word *significant,* surely the most overworked adjective in the lexicon of empirical inquiry. It is a usefully ambiguous term, employed carefully in statistics to refer to a finding whose occurrence is more than mere chance, but understood in common parlance to mean "arresting and consequential." Hillocks' (1982) leap, in our earlier reference to his research, from the modest, if vague, observation that specifically focused comments "can be effective" to the enthusiastic assertion that *significant* gains in writing skill are possible over short periods of time, gets full value out of just this ambiguity.

Earl Buxton's often cited 1958 dissertation marks an early foray into empirical research on teacher commentary, and we mention it optimistically in our own earliest work. The central discovery of his study is that students who receive written responses on papers "improve significantly" in word choice and the organizing of sentences (83–84) from one draft to the next. In short, they dutifully follow teachers' directions when told to correct an error. But a corollary finding, elaborately discussed in his conclusions and a good deal more interesting, is that students appear to make "negligible" progress in "critical thinking," "originality," "transition," and "general coherence." He notes, with unintended irony, that, "It may be important that the categories [of response and attempted revision] which show . . . non-significant gains are categories that assess a student's ability to think" (83). But he then proceeds, knowing full well how important these non-gains are, to invoke studies showing that "critical thinking" can be directly taught, leading to "significant improvement in pupils' ability to see relationships, to avoid superstition, to understand the nature of valid evidence, to solve . . . problems, and to recognize logical patterns of reasoning" (92). Without examining the claims in these studies (including an unselfconscious rhetoric in which the pejorative, "superstition," is intended to oppose such positive terms as "valid evidence" and "logical patterns"), he assures readers that the findings show there is "little validity to the implication that students cannot be taught to think critically and to relate critical thinking to their writing of essays" (93). Buxton speculates on explanations for his own poor results: some students were writing for "aesthetic impact" and weren't trying to think critically, a possibility that he is obliged to reject (94); the students improved but the readers of the essays were unable to detect the improvement (94); improved critical thinking takes longer to manifest itself than the sixteen practice essays the experiment allowed (97); the readers failed to "concentrate sufficiently upon direct instruction of the requisites of critical thinking" (99); the readers (all of whom he characterizes as "potential teachers") weren't sufficiently trained to help students think well in writing (100). The one option we can think of that Buxton doesn't address is that comments simply don't have the power to cause the meaningful short-term cognitive development that he wants to attribute to them. Understandably so, perhaps, since that explanation would sabotage the most important finding he offers in his investigation, "that the assigning and correcting of . . . essays . . . resulted in a significant improvement in students' writing" (86–87).

Writing a quarter of a century later, George Hillocks (1982) undertakes a similarly empirical inquiry and claims greater success. His central conclusion is that students perform effectively in response to comments that are offered according to the particular requirements he proposes, which include teaching to specific objectives, consistently highlighting the same textual features through teacher comments, and directing revision persistently toward those features, which he titles "focus," "specificity," and "impact," never explaining what they mean. His study goes further than any other in the literature with an aggressive assertion that, if instruction (we would call it "drill") is sufficiently focused on "particular goals or skills" and sufficiently repetitive, it can "affect writing skills as displayed in subsequent new pieces of writing, and not simply in subsequent revisions" (276). No doubt, in the context of a narrow behaviorism, Hillocks is correct about what students can be trained to do. The question, however, is what relationship this training bears to the more complicated matter of stimulating the development of writing ability. Hillocks' writing class seems analogous to the art class that sets children to painting by numbers or the dance class that invites students to move their feet according to the footprints etched into the floor of the dance studio. In each case, the demonstration of a limited technical mastery counts as success. But whatever one might call the mechanical process of matching the student's feet to the footprints, and however successful the performance may be, no one would think to call it dancing. From our perspective, Hillocks has "succeeded" where virtually every other researcher has failed, only by first translating subtle textual features like "focus" or "impact" into mechanical values (though, again, he never actually explains what they look like in a text), and then deploying a training regimen designed to achieve given behavioral results. In doing so, he has simply created a higher-order grammar for teachers to correct, showing that, just as students can be obliged to follow directions that plainly insist on the replacement of one word or syntactic or punctuation choice by another, so they can be obliged to obey similar instructions regarding focus and impact. One could use the same protocol for organization, insisting that students follow the format of the five-paragraph theme, or for argument, insisting that they write in syllogisms. Either Hillocks has failed to engage the question of whether responses can lead to mature writing, settling instead for showing that they can coerce a mechanical performance, or else he doesn't believe there is a difference between the two.

It seems clear to us, in sum, that the literature has never come forthrightly and candidly to terms with the myth of improvement as a problematic justification for advocating response to student writing or for preferring one kind of teacher commentary over another. The empirical research has been unable to identify meaningful development, falling back on the "significance" of error correction, while the advocacy scholarship has been disinclined even to try, preferring instead to offer vague and unexamined assurances that a preferred method will produce beneficial results. Neither has directly confronted the myth as a myth. This is not to say that the research has been naïve about the issue and therefore inclined to make extravagant promises. For the most part, researchers are cautious to avoid promises, especially the suggestion that response causes immediate gain in fluency, knowing well what they can't deliver. They don't champion the myth, but they don't repudiate it either; for the most part, they simply allow it to hang in the air, a concession to the public appetite for results. Only occasionally are there exceptions to the pattern, arguments that seek new ways to explain the value of commentary without appeal to magical thinking. Chris Anson (1999) suggests, for example, that the response literature has moved on in recent years from the preoccupations of the '80s with "single method[s] supported by empirical research" or "key method[s], informed by theory and predictable in outcome" (375). His argument sets out to identify a different way to understand the usefulness of teacher commentary, framing it in the context of a "more principled practice" (379) grounded in what he refers to as "reflective" teaching (375). The substance of his reasoning is that teachers must bring to their practice "an overarching disposition or educational theory that guides [their] choices" (375) matched with an alert flexibility of approach that takes into account different classroom contexts, learning styles, teaching aims, and student needs. What seems to matter most to Anson is the impact of commentary on the quality of the relationship between teacher and student, as well as the quality of the writing experience itself, rather than specific revisions in a subsequent draft or on a subsequent assignment. This seems to us a promising change of focus, emphasizing a self-conscious articulation of educational priorities and values, as well as a concern to personalize the interaction between teacher and student, rather than an effort to shape or control immediate changes in student performance. Indeed, his argument forces discussion away from traditional understandings of pedagogy that valorize "what works" and toward understandings of pedagogy that privilege social, ethical, and philosophical considerations— the representation of teaching as a cultural project, a narrative of values—more than the pursuit of short-term results. "What works" is an illusory ideal, however it may seek to pass itself off as a pragmatic standard. In teaching, whether responding to student writing or engaging in other classroom activities, virtually everything either works, fails to work, or works inconclusively with some students some of the time in the short term.

Anson's shift of emphasis is important to literacy education generally, not just to the local question of responding to student writing, because it shows how arguments about pedagogy can be redirected toward values and away from illusions of instantaneous progress. But we also think that the myth of improvement will need to be directly addressed and repudiated before such value arguments can have any impact on educational policy. As long as the myth of improvement prevails at any level of public consciousness, there is every reason for the public to prefer curricula and instructional activities that appear to "cause" the most conspicuous changes over the shortest period of time—a tidy exchange of educational value for taxpayer money. It is, after all, a relatively straightforward exercise to train students to avoid dangling participles, write topic sentences, and put the correct sorts of information into the boxes of a five-paragraph theme. Behaviorist pedagogies, focused on measurable short-term results, are currently favored because, in an educational environment driven by an assessment ethos, they offer an illusion of learning through the achievement of artificial performance objectives that are reasonably susceptible to evaluation even though they have no compelling relationship to the development of writing ability (that is, one can avoid dangling participles, write topic sentences, and master essay formats while learning little or nothing about purposes, genre awareness, audience sensitivity, strategies of reasoning, political intelligence, ethical perceptiveness, register and tone, stylistic effects, or any of the subtleties characteristic of mature discourse). These pedagogies are now the centerpieces of federal legislative mandates with ideologically freighted titles like "ABC's of Public Education" and "No Child Left Behind," one artfully encouraging the "fundamentals," the other evoking Orphan Annie as a poster child for basic skills instruction. And because educational scholarship remains ambivalent about the myth of improvement, its voice is compromised in circumstances where public policy, curriculum design, and teaching practice alike continue to pursue a fantasy of quick and measurable instructional gain.

By contrast, if the myth were effectively shown to be a myth, the intellectual (even if not immediately the political) scaffolding of behaviorist pedagogies would cease to exist, and the debate about educational practice would be obliged to look beyond simplistic cause-and-effect formulas as justification for preferring one practice over another. Competing vantage points would have to make their cases by reference to other values—values that might look very like those that Anson suggests in his concern for the quality of the learning environment in schools. Questions about "better" curricula and pedagogies could not be resolved empirically; instead, answers would have to emerge in the way they should, out of community debate, where contrasting representations of educational ideals struggle on a level playing field to enlist public support. The ongoing debate between phonics and whole-language approaches to literacy instruction, for example, would resemble the struggle between Democrats and Republicans for the hearts and minds of the American electorate. The issue in American political debate is not really how to solve the Medicare crisis, or eliminate the national debt, or create more effective schools. The issue is, what kind of a country do people want to live in? What values should underlie problem posing and problem solving? Which political narrative more effectively appeals to the electorate's hopes and aspirations? In the case of the two poles of literacy instruction, the issue is not the technical details of teaching children to read and write. It is, rather, what ideal of literacy animates the enterprise of teaching, and what kinds of classrooms do people want for their children? Should the ideal image underlying the construction of classrooms, for instance, be an image of the home? A factory? A hospital clinic? A college dorm? A corporate office? A reformatory? In short, the debate about schooling would no longer be fundamentally about performance, but rather would be about ideology—the domain where philosophy meets politics in order to articulate aspirations, develop agendas, and compose representations of success. Here lies, it seems to us, the only plausible ground on which to compare and argue competing educational practices, once the myth of improvement is dispelled.

Our own ideological representation of literacy instruction looks like this. We reject behaviorist pedagogies because they offer learners so much less than what they are capable of achieving, and deserve an opportunity to achieve. For us, a "better" classroom brings all the complicated intellectual, rhetorical, logical, emotional, stylistic, ethical, political, and other dimensions of language practice into play at once in an environment rich in both reading and writing opportunities. We think that dancing is a more gratifying activity for human beings than just matching feet to footprints on the floor. We suspect, therefore, that learners might be more motivated to do it, even if, for awhile, they do it badly. If we must concede that no evidence can be marshaled to show that this classroom "causes" students to develop more efficiently, quickly, or fully than another, we are also entitled to insist that no evidence will find it less successful in supporting development. And we would further insist that, once arguments for "what works" are shown to be superficial or illusory, the quality of an educational experience becomes the most legitimate standard by which to evaluate instructional alternatives. Our ideal classroom is the kind in which we, as teachers, would prefer to work, and we believe it is also the kind in which students would prefer to learn. Since human beings have more capacity to learn than, say, pigeons have, they are entitled to education that aims to promote learning, in all its mysterious complexity, and not just behavior modification, even if the latter can happen faster. If that classroom also complicates the project of learning to write by incorporating additional values (for instance, the importance of a social conscience, and not just workplace skill, as part of the ideal of literacy), then the classroom becomes, for us, more congenial still, a place where the grandeur of the aspiration makes the effort worthwhile. Nevertheless, our educational perspective, like any other, is "only" a narrative about values, with no privilege to claim glamorous outputs. It is a "representation," competing for public attention.

What, finally, can be said for the embedded issue of responding to student writing, the local activity that has occasioned so much learned discussion and so much disappointment in the essays collected here? The obvious first point is that it is one of many available practices in the writing classroom, one tile in the mosaic, neither more nor less significant than others, hardly the magic wand that opens doors to literacy. It resides in the small print of the literacy debate, raising the same questions about what teaching seeks to accomplish, and what results it can hope to achieve, that swirl around larger pedagogical and curricular representations. The literature has demonstrated, beyond anyone's determination to reject the results, that commentary, however defined (as in facilitative versus directive), however categorized (marginal versus end, global versus local, complimentary versus critical), has limited meaningful impact on draft-to-draft revision and virtually no demonstrable effect on performance from assignment to assignment. But the more important point is that there's no reason to expect that such an effect would occur, any more than there's reason to expect that other pedagogical activities—small-group discussion, revising, practicing in a particular genre—will have concrete and immediate impact. Everything in teaching is part of something larger: one response in the margin of a draft is situated in a context of classroom communication, one assignment in a context of assignments, one classroom in a context of classrooms, one academic year in a context of others, and school experiences in a context (ideally) of all sorts of other reading and writing experiences. Clearly, people become competent readers and writers over time as a result of their immersion in this web of influences, even if no one can pinpoint when, or how, or why.

Discussions of the role and significance of commentary are ideological narratives, just as are similar discussions about writing-center tutorials, practicing the sonnet form, and diagramming sentences. In our own narrative, what gives teacher commentary a particular importance in the classroom is the simple fact that it constitutes individualized teaching. Specifically, at its best, it makes explicit to one student at a time, text by text, what a teacher's values are. It orients students to what the teacher thinks is important in the practice of writing, focuses their attention, encourages them to keep trying, makes them think (if the teacher is lucky), reveals an interested reader, offers advice about how best to accomplish some end or effect, and maybe, occasionally, serendipitously, provides this student or that just the insight needed at a particular moment to make some small, gratifying advance. In part, commentary is a modeling activity, offering the teacher a chance to dramatize the presence of a reader whose needs and expectations can and should influence writing. In part, it's a form of instructional emphasis, most useful when it offers the same message about writing on an individual essay that the teacher seeks to deliver in the course as a whole. It is least useful, by contrast, when it contradicts a teacher's self-professed values and goals, for instance when an exaggeration of technical decorum in responses to drafts runs counter to a syllabus emphasis on purposes, audiences, and lines of reasoning. But more than anything, it is, connotatively, the teacher's personal statement about the relationship she wishes to create between teacher and student, and about what matters in the process of becoming a writer. As such, the statement echoes from the individual classroom through the entire enterprise of literacy education. That's our "story." If it isn't sufficient to dignify the activity, we can add two cents, or two sentences, more, having taught long enough to see the eventual maturation of our own former students, perhaps despite the impediments we erected on their behalf. We've come to understand that, whatever one teacher says in commenting on student writing, however local the context, however unreliable the recommendation, and however uncertain the consequence, in the end, the teacher is working meaningfully, not alone but in good company, to advance a process of verbal maturation that is always, already, underway, and that will ultimately prove successful if only the learner is as motivated as the teacher is. When former students tell us that we made all the difference, we don't believe it, but we smile.

Cy Knoblauch
Lil Brannon

References

Anson, Chris M. 1999. "Reflective Reading: Developing Thoughtful Ways to Respond to Students' Writing." In *Evaluating, Writing,* edited by Charles R. Cooper and Lee Odel. Urbana, IL: National Council of Teachers of English.

Buxton, Earl W. 1958. "An Experiment to Test the Effects of Writing Frequency and Guided Practice upon Students' Skills in Written Expression." Unpublished Ph.D. Dissertation, Stanford University, Stanford, California.

Connors, Robert J., and Andrea A. Lunsford. 1993. "Teachers' Rhetorical Comments on Student Papers." *College Composition and Communication* 44 (2):200–23.

Diederich, Paul. 1974. *Measuring Growth in English.* Urbana, IL: National Council of Teachers of English.

Emig, Janet. 1983. *The Web of Meaning.* Portsmath, NH: Boynton/Cook.

Gee, Thomas. 1970. "Students' Responses to Teacher Comments." *Research in the Teaching of English* 6 (2):212–21.

Hillocks, George. 1982. "The Interaction of Instruction, Teacher Comment, and Revision in Teaching the Composing Process." *Research in the Teaching of English* 16 (3):261–77.

Knoblauch, C. H., and Lil Brannon. 1981. "Teacher Commentary on Student Writing: the State of the Art." In *Rhetoric and Composition: A Sourcebook for Teachers,* edited by Richard Graves, 285–91. Portsmath, NH: Boynton/Cook.

———. 1984. *Rhetorical Traditions and the Teaching of Writing.* Portsmath, NH: Boynton/Cook

Searle, Dennis, and David Dillon. 1980. "The Message of Marking: Teacher Written Responses to Student Writing at Intermediate Grade Levels." *Research in the Teaching of English* 14 (3):233–42.

Sommers, Nancy. 1982. "Responding to Student Writing." *College Composition and Communication* 33 (2):148–56.

Stiff, Robert. 1967. "The Effect Upon Student Composition of Particular Correction Technique," *Research in the Teaching of English* 1 (1):54–75.

Straub, Richard. 1996. "Teacher Response as Conversation: More Than Casual Talk, an Exploration." *Rhetoric Review* 14 (2):374–98.

1

The Effect Upon Student Composition of Particular Correction Techniques[*]

Robert Stiff

This study is a logical extension of the Buxton Study, which found, among other things, that student composition improves when it is corrected.[1] The present study, sponsored by the Research Foundation[2] of the National Council of Teachers of English, attempts primarily to determine the effects upon composition of particular parts of the most common correction technique.

Procedure

In both the summer and fall portions of the study, three instructors, three readers, three raters, and a statistical analyst were needed. The summer portion of the study was very helpful in working out several problems of procedure, control, and analysis. The results of the summer study were somewhat less crucial than the results of the fall study, particularly because of the shortness of the summer session and the consequent difficulty of returning papers before the succeeding papers are written. The entire study was much tightened for the fall portion, the results of which are therefore more valid, although most of the final results seem to be reinforced by the findings of the summer portion.

[*] This is a report of the first project concluded with the support of the NCTE Research Foundation. Because space limitations prevent publication of some of the original data on rater reliability, the reader should be informed that Mr. Stiff uses "rater reliability" in a different sense than others may. He is referring to the correlation of the mean score of all grades assigned by one rater to the mean score of all grades assigned by another rater. That, of course, is quite different from a correlation of raters' scores on individual themes.

1. E. W. Buxton, *An Experiment to Test the Effects of Writing Frequency and Guided Practice Upon Students' Skill in Written Expression* (Doctor's thesis. Palo Alto: Stanford Univer., 1958).

2. I would especially like to thank Mr. Paul Farmer, who constantly offered me help and encouragement.

The students were somewhat homogeneously grouped in the course. Almost all of the students in English 1a, the transfer level Freshman English course, score between 66 and 99 on the English Cooperative Test, which has been used for years at the College of San Mateo to separate students according to general English ability. A small group of students come to this course through English A, a remedial course, or through English 50, a terminal course; they come with the recommendation of their instructors. In the fall, only nine of the seventy-seven students studied came to the course through recommendation.

After the students were registered in the course, the placement scores were obtained for all the students. Students coming from English A or English 50 and other students for whom we had no placement scores were asked to retake the test; thus, all placement scores were recent ones. Each of the three *classroom* sections was divided into three groups, each group to receive different kinds of corrections on compositions. Group I, for example, was thus made up of eight students from *each* instructor's class. This division was meant to reduce the variable of instructor difference. In order to reduce standard deviation and study the effect of correction techniques upon particular *kinds* of students, each of the three groups was then further divided into ability subgroups, also according to scores on the placement test.

77 Students in Project

Group I—24 students (papers marked marginally only)

Group II—28 students (papers marked terminally only)

Group III—25 students (control group, papers marked both marginally and terminally)

Placement Score Averages

Group I—73%

Group II—72.7%

Group III—76.3%

Number of Students in Subgroups

	Below 69	70–79	80–100
Group I	8	8	7
Group II	8	11	9
Group III	7	10	9

As a further check on the equivalence of these groups, an outside paper was assigned *before* the class had met for discussion. No changes seemed necessary, although it is difficult to judge student placement on the basis of such evidence as one paper provides.

The instructors (all comparably experienced in the teaching of Freshman English) met in late summer to discuss the course in general and to decide upon particular topics for pre-testing and post-testing. The topics decided upon (appended to this report) are matching topics; each pre-test topic is matched by a somewhat similar post-test topic, similar in that they both elicit a particular kind of writing and even perhaps suggest similar possibilities for organization and support. Students wrote on the pre-test topics during the first week of the semester, before classes had met for discussion. Each class was given 50 minutes to write on each topic in class, on three successive days. Students were given no time outside of class to prepare; the topics were handed them as they arrived in the classroom. These papers were collected and kept (with only a name and code number on them) until the end of the semester when they were mixed in with the collected papers from the post-testing week, during which exactly the same process was followed. The results of this study come from comparisons made of pre-test and post-test papers.

During the course itself, instructors met once a week to discuss controls, paper topics for outside class, in-class discussion, and assigned reading (upon which most of the assigned writing in the course centered). The same text was used in each class, *Inquiry and Expression*, by Martin and Ohmann; identical readings and composition topics were given each section; and, as much as is humanly possible, class discussion followed somewhat the same pattern.

All papers in the course other than pre-test and post-test papers (3,000 words) were written outside of class (total of 5,000 words) and were corrected in the following manner. Students in Group I had their papers corrected with only marginal comments, students in Group II with only summary comments, and students in Group III with both marginal and summary comments. (Examples are appended to this report.) The three readers were experienced lay readers who had read for previous Freshman English classes. The readers met with the investigator before the course began and agreed upon what constitutes "typical" marginal and summary comment. The instructors also read the corrections closely during the course in order to guarantee consistent, typical, and accurate correction.

In order to reduce another variable, that of grade-motivation, no grades were given to papers during the course. Students were told, if they wanted the information, that they were doing satisfactorily or unsatisfactorily, although most students seemed content to rely upon the tenor of the corrections themselves. At midterm time, students were given grades of "C." (They did, of course, receive a final grade.) Student conferences were kept to a minimum to reduce still another variable, and when such conferences were necessary, instructors kept a record of time spent which eventually was very nearly the same for each instructor.

During the post-test week, three raters, all experienced in the teaching of Freshman English, met to discuss the criteria and rating scale to be used in evaluating pre-test and post-test compositions. They decided to use very nearly the same criteria and rating plan that had been used in the summer (a modification of the Diederich and University of Iowa scales, employing the four categories *conception, organization, expression,* and *literacy*), but only after a period of practice-rating with the scale and a serious discussion of the problems involved. These three raters then evaluated the papers on three successive days, six hours a day. After jointly reading and discussing a trial paper, the raters individually evaluated twenty papers, jointly rated (and then discussed) another paper—whose joint scorings were later used to measure rater reliability—rested briefly, then resumed the same process once again. Any significant variations were thoroughly analyzed by the raters, although the first impressions were, of course, the scores used in computing the rater reliability.

The results were then submitted to a statistician[3] who analyzed the data and offered help with their interpretation.

Although an earnest attempt was made to control the experiment, certain variables were impossible to control, like the effect upon student composition of an instructor's casual comment, the effect upon composition skills of other, related, course work, and so on. Nevertheless, research has to begin somewhere, and investigation of English composition has too long been intimidated by the fear of subjectivity.

Results

Specifically, the study attempted to answer the following questions.

1. What overall improvement in writing, if any, can be seen in Groups I, II, and III (this to be determined by comparing pre-test papers with post-test papers)?

2. What improvement, if any, can be seen in Groups I, II, and III within the separate categories (conception, organization, expression, and literacy)?

3. What overall improvement, if any, do students within the subgroups show?

4. What improvement in writing, if any, can be seen in students within the subgroups, in separate categories?

5. What is the degree of rater reliability?

6. Which pair of topics received the highest total scores? (This was an attempt to determine whether students can handle certain kinds of writing better than others when writing under pressure).

7. On which pair of topics did the students show the greatest gain from pre-test to post-test? (An attempt to determine the effect, if any, of semester work upon the ability to handle particular kinds of writing.)

8. Do students within subgroups score higher on particular topics?

---

3. Mrs. Sharon Mangold, University of California at Davis.

Table 1–1 MEAN SCORES, GROUPS AS WHOLES, ON RATING CATEGORIES

Group I Topics		Group II Con.	Group III Org.	Exp.	Lit.	Total
C		17.04	16.73	12.39	2.95	49.13
K	Pre	17.50	15.40	13.13	2.95	49.00
Z		15.27	13.68	11.81	2.63	43.40
O		16.13	16.43	13.91	3.30	49.78
F	Post	16.43	16.43	13.69	3.00	49.56
M		16.73	14.91	13.26	2.95	47.86
C		17.59	17.59	13.45	3.07	52.24
K	Pre	15.69	13.76	12.07	2.90	44.38
Z		14.97	16.41	13.79	3.28	48.45
O		17.86	18.34	13.62	3.10	52.93
F	Post	17.75	18.34	13.79	3.27	53.17
M		18.58	16.41	13.44	3.24	51.69
C		18.67	17.21	13.96	3.04	52.88
K	Pre	15.40	14.00	12.40	3.00	44.80
Z		14.84	15.40	13.60	3.08	46.92
O		14.84	17.08	13.40	3.16	48.48
F	Post	16.52	17.08	12.80	3.32	49.72
M		15.68	15.12	13.00	3.28	47.08

9. What relationship, if any, exists between placement score and final grade; between pre-test score and final grade; between post-test score and final grade?

10. How do students regard the different methods of correction?

Summary and Interpretation

What follows is a summary and interpretation of the data compiled by the fall portion of the study, answers to the questions enumerated above. The first statement in each case is summary; the other comments are interpretations and conclusions.

1. There appears to be no significant improvement in any large group from pre-test to post-test writing (probably because of the wide variance of ability when the groups are taken as a whole). We found the same thing after the summer portion of the study, but we decided that, because of the ability-variance, an

Robert Stiff

Table 1–2 MEAN SCORES, SUBGROUPS, ON RATING CATEGORIES

| Subgroups | Con. | S.D. | Org. | Exp. | S.D. | Lit. | S.D. | Total | S.D. |
| Group I | | | Group II | | | Group III | | | |
Pre		Post	Pre		Post	Pre	Post		
80–100	17.33		17.33	13.57		3.14		51.38	
70–79	16.62		14.71	12.71		3.00		47.04	
–69	15.46		13.42	11.46		2.62		43.46	
								47.29	
80–100	18.67		17.00	15.00		3.24		53.90	
70–79	16.92		17.21	13.96		3.38		51.46	
–69	14.00	5.05	13.42	12.08		2.71		42.21	
								49.19	
80–100	17.89		16.59	13.70		3.26		51.44	
70–79	16.33		16.76	14.09		3.24		50.42	
–69	14.26		14.52	11.30		2.70		42.78	
								46.21	
80–100	19.96		18.66	14.63		3.37		56.63	
70–79	16.33		16.97	13.33		3.24		49.70	
–69	18.93		17.11	12.41		2.89		51.33	
								52.55	12.43
80–100	17.11		17.37	15.00	3.92	3.19		52.67	
70–79	19.10		15.40	12.50		2.90		46.90	
–69	13.61		12.83	11.39		2.83		40.67	
								46.75	
80–100	15.81		17.33	13.70		3.37		50.22	
70–79	16.33		16.56	13.30		3.33		49.53	
–69	14.39		14.39	11.67		3.00	.91	43.44	12.92
								47.73	

The data in Tables 1–1 and 1–2 represent the most important and most easily under-stood statistics. (Other data can be found appended to this report.)

examination of the subgroups would be much more conclusive. Group II, which only received terminal comments, seemed not to suffer at all from that method of correction; rather, they progressed slightly faster than did the other groups. Although the gain was not statistically significant, it may be important to point out here that the greatest gains within that group were in the 69-and-below sub-group (from 42.78 to 51.33), which indicates that at least some students of lower ability may profit greatly from terminal comments. It is also somewhat important to point out that all of the large groups *did* improve their overall scores, and to about the same degree as did the summer groups.

2. There appears to be no significant improvement in Groups I, II, and III within the separate categories. Again, the wide range of abilities makes this finding of little help to teachers of English. The figures do show, as might be expected, that students in the 80–100 subgroup achieved the highest total scores, followed by the 70–79 group and then the 69-and-below group; these data support what most of us probably already assume—that students with greater abilities in English (reading comprehension, vocabulary, expression) write better under pressure.

3. There appears to be no significant improvement in any subgroup from pre-test to post-test. This finding, like that of #4, is a crucial one for the study. We are forced to conclude from this data that class discussion, outside reading, outside writing, and *various methods of paper correction* all appear to have only a slight effect upon the ability to write spontaneously. We are, of course, not able to determine what effect, if any, the different correction techniques have upon outside-of-class writing. We do know (see #10) the effect of these techniques upon student morale, which would suggest that subgroups in Group III should progress much further since they received full correction; this improvement did not take place. Student morale seems to have little effect upon the ability to write in class, even at the end of a semester under an unpleasant system of marking.

4. There appears to be no significant improvement on the part of students within the subgroups in the separate categories. This finding merely confirms in a more detailed way what was discovered about the writing in general. The interesting point here is that even in Group II subgroups, in which compositions received no marginal comments relating to sequence of ideas, organization of paragraphs, or faulty diction, students nevertheless progressed at the same rate as students receiving very close attention to matters of conception, organization, and expression.

5. Rater reliability was 95%. This finding is very encouraging. It repeats the high degree of reliability we found during the summer portion of the study (when we achieved over 99% reliability) and provides, of course, more validity for the entire study. I attribute this high degree of rater reliability to three things: the experience and competence of the raters, the joint rating before and during the rating sessions, and the share the raters had in formulating the criteria and rating scale.

6. Paired Topics C and O received the highest total scores, but not enough higher than the other pairs to allow certain interpretation. It *may* be that C and O were more interesting to write on, since they both asked the students to put themselves in very unusual circumstances.

7. Students showed the highest gain from Topic Z to paired Topic F, a gain twice as large as from K to M and three times as large as from C to O. This gain suggests that students perform somewhat better on topics which require an open mind *after* they have been exposed to a semester of liberal education, for these topics dealt with a society of the future which might be fully automated or completely automobile-less.

8. There seem to be no significant differences between the scores of students within the subgroups on particular topics. Students in the 80–100 subgroup have slightly higher *total* scores than do other students, but there is no consistency to their scores on particular topics. It appears that low-ability students are occasionally capable of writing a good paper, just as high-ability students are occasionally apt to write a weak one.

9. There appears to be no clear relationship between placement score and final grade, between pre-test score and final grade, or between post-test score and final grade. (Only Group *I* was evaluated, but Groups II and II would undoubtedly produce the same conclusions.) It appears that neither an objective test, nor writing samples (the pretest papers) offer much clear information as to how well a student will perform in Freshman English. Perhaps the most these tests can do is to predict that the students who do reasonably well on them will probably survive in the course. That there is no clear relationship between post-test scores and final grades suggests there may be a real difference between a students' performance on outside writing assignments during a course and his ability to write well under pressure, even at the end of a course.

10. At semester's end, each project student was asked for his attitude towards the method the reader used to correct his papers. We asked the student what he particularly liked or disliked about this kind of marking; whether he was, in general, stimulated or discouraged by the corrections. Students almost unanimously preferred their compositions to be corrected both marginally and terminally; students in Groups I and II complained that they had not been given full correction, while students in Group III seemed generally pleased with the type of correction their papers received. Since students in all groups and subgroups progressed at about the same rate regardless of correction system, one might conclude that students (like many of us, I suspect) have a conception of an ideally corrected paper, a type of paper correction that may affect student composition no more than do other methods of correction. However, student morale is undoubtedly important, and even if student attitudes toward correction seem not to affect in-class writing, we do not yet know to what extent these attitudes may affect class work or writing done outside of class.

Implications for Teaching and Further Research

Certain implications of this study seem inescapable. In connection with findings discussed in 1–4 above, perhaps we teachers of English should now be able to occasionally return, without great remorse, a set of compositions with just a few terminal comments, or with only a few succinct marginal comments, since a full correction (both marginal and terminal) seems to have no more effect upon student composition than do what we have usually considered partial corrections. Perhaps both students and instructors are clinging superstitiously to a stereotype of the "completely corrected" paper. More research should be conducted to determine the effect of student morale upon writing done outside of class; indeed, it would be very helpful to know the effect of the different parts of the common correction technique upon outside-of-class writing. It is difficult, of course, to establish controls upon outside-of-class writing. Perhaps students could be asked to write in supervised two-hour periods and permitted the use of certain reference works.

Since in-class writing does not improve during a semester, perhaps more in-class writing should be required in the standard Freshman English course. Some study should be made to determine whether or not in-class writing improves with practice and whether it improves more with close or with minimal supervision and correction.

Divisions of English that place a heavy emphasis upon in-class performance on final examinations would do well to consider the findings of this study. Even three writing samples at the end of a semester did not seem to give much indication of a student's general performance in the class as indicated by final grade, although it still may show what some instructors refer to as "the naked truth."

This study seems to raise serious problems regarding the placement of students, since the placement test used here, the English Cooperative Test, and the three pre-test writing samples appear to have so little predictive value when compared with final grades in the course. Of course, it is possible that instructors base their final grades on skills other than those measured by placement test and in-class writing; perhaps serious departmental evaluation of the course *and* the means of placement would ease the problem. Incidentally, the discrepancies between placement score, topic scores, and final grade probably produced the wide standard deviations. Another possibility that may contribute to the wide standard deviations is the fact that a rater must choose from 1–5 and then multiply by a given factor. Possibly, if there were a continuous scale, say, from 1–55 for every category, instead of 7, 14, 21, 28, or 35 points, the standard deviations would be smaller.

If the rater reliability was as high as it seemed to be in both the summer and fall portions of the study, that suggests that English staffs should be able, if they so desire, to move toward greater departmental consistency in the grading of papers. Perhaps a general set of criteria to follow would be helpful, especially to new instructors. An occasional rating session, with opportunity for instructors to share in formulating the criteria and rating scale to be used, would be a productive means of insuring proper standards and consistency of grading for the entire English staff.

Three more parts of the composition process in Freshman English courses still require further study. First, work should be done to determine the effects upon student composition, if any, of student-instructor conferences. More work needs to be done to determine the effects of revision upon student writing. Finally, study should attempt to answer two familiar questions regarding the content of Freshman English: What effect, if any, do particular kinds of reading have upon writing? Of what importance to student writing are the different number-of-words-requirements for the course?

Mean Scores, All Groups, on Particular Topics

Topic C (Pre-test)	51.41
Topic O (Post-test)	50.39
Topic K (Pre-test)	46.06
Topic M (Post-test)	48.88
Topic Z (Pre-test)	46.26
Topic F (Post-test)	50.82

Topics

Each topic sheet contained the following instruction at the bottom:

> Use pen, single space, and stop writing directly on the hour. Endorse (on the outside of your folded paper) *with only name and code number.*

Topic Z (pre-test)

Social scientists presently predict that our culture will be, in a very few years, fully automated. The major feature of this kind of society will be one that all men have dreamed of: escape from work. But as the time of the automated society comes closer, there has been an accompanying growth of concern over the "problems" of life without work. What will be the advantages of the "workless society"? The disadvantages?

Topic F (post-test)

Some social scientists have predicted that in twenty-five or thirty years our society will be *literally* choked by the automobile; they have, therefore, suggested that we think seriously about abolishing the automobile. What would be the advantages of an automobile-less society? The disadvantages? Should persons be allowed to drink at age 18?

Topic K (pre-test)

Should students be allowed to dress as they please on college and university campuses?

Topic M (post-test)

Imagine that you are the president of a small but distinguished college. Last week—at the request of a student group—you agreed to allow the chairman of the state "Get-Out-of-Vietnam Society" to speak on campus the first week in October. When the announcement of the speech appeared in the local newspaper, a millionaire oilman, an alumnus of the college who had offered to donate several hundred thousand dollars to your building fund, publicly denounced you and threatened to withdraw the donation if you refused to cancel the address.

Topic C (pre-test)

If you cancel the speech, you will break your promise to the students and you may jeopardize your commitment to Academic Freedom. If you approve the appearance of the speaker, you will break your promise to the donor, who offered the funds on the condition that the college administration "support and uphold the highest ideals of Americanism." Too, approval may jeopardize your job.

Reporters from the major news services have asked for your reply. Prepare a formal statement for the press in which you express your reaction to the threat, your decision, and the principles governing your decision.

Topic O (post-test)

Imagine that in the not-too-distant future a cosmic cataclysm will destroy the earth. You—along with a few others—have been chosen to board an interplanetary "ark" to start a new world on an uninhabited planet. The authorities have given you a choice: you may take with you as a memento of this world a wad of bills, a lock of hair from someone you love, or a war medal. Write a paper explaining which you would take and why.

Rating Scale

	Rater .....
Conception: Quality of Thought	$12345 \times 7 =$ .....
Organization	$12345 \times 7 =$ .....
Expression	$12345 \times 5 =$ .....
Literacy	$12345 \times 1 =$ .....
	Total Grade $=$ .....

Some Questions to Help Define the Categories

Conception: Quality of Thought

Is it possible to understand clearly the central idea of the essay?

Does the student discuss the subject intelligently?

Are the ideas relatively free of stock attitudes?

Does he avoid errors in logic?

Does the essay offer evidence in support of generalization?

Does the reasoning appear to be at all organic, i.e., is there evidence in the writing of an alert mind at work?

Organization

Is the central idea of the paper as a whole sufficiently developed through the use of details and examples?

Are the individual paragraphs sufficiently developed?

Are all the ideas of the essay relevant?

Are the ideas developed in some sort of logical order? (Both from paragraph to paragraph and from sentence to sentence.)

Are shifts in thought sensible and fairly easy to follow?

Are ideas given the emphasis required by their importance?

Is the point of view consistent and appropriate?

Expression

Is the diction generally concise, precise, and specific?

Is the language relatively free of cliches and hackneyed phrases?

Is the sentence structure effective? For example, is there *appropriate* variety in sentence structure, *appropriate* use of subordination and coordination?

Are the sentences free of gross errors that interrupt the flow of thought? Are they *reasonably* free of fragments, run-ons, faulty parallel structure, mixed constructions, errors of agreement, case and verb forms?

Literacy

Are the sentences idiomatic and grammatically correct?

GROUP I,
MARGINAL
CORRECTION

A DECLARATION OF INDEPENDENCE

*Pretty general
and overstated
to be believable*

In the very near future the automobile is
going to be the master of the human race. Human bondage to the car is not a fantasy, but
a reality is *that* grim in its outlook of the future.   *awkwardly stated*

needlessly

repetitive

Right now anyone who owns a car is a slave
to it. If the car is financed through a loan
company, then he is literally tied to the car
for a specific length of time. To drive the
car requires gasoline, tires, oil, and a few
other needs which must be supplied if the car
is to function. This is more money which comes
out of the publics pocket to keep these mechanical monsters alive. Of course, to drive
on todays high speed freeways is out of the
question with out adequate protection against
mans love of fellow man. This protection comes
in the form of insurance. Depending on wether
you are young, old, single, married and your
past driving record, for better or worse, you
are required to pay what is sweetly called a
premium.

*Why the
pronoun
shift?*

Poorly constructed

*Weak
constr.*

But the best part of owning a car is yet
to come! Aside from the money angle there are
also many more dividends to owning an automobile which society is aware of, trying to
correct, but getting no where in its fight.

*Are you veering
off your theme
statement of
your opening
paragraph?*

*(Human bondage.
The car.)*

*Has your tone
shifted?*

One extremely important dividend is the high
number of deaths each year due to car accidents. More people are killed on streets than
in wars and the wonderful thing about this
is the fact that the number of drivers (each
year) increases by one half.   *Poorly placed
modifier*

Although the automobile certainly helped
mankind it has also been quite a hinderance.
Crime has climbed to new heights with the aid
of cars. Cars used in crimes for fast retreats

are the ideas co-ordinate? Do they belong in the same sentence? Why connect them with "and"?

by the criminals is nothing new (and) the number of cars used for this purpose each year is un-countable. Since most of the cars used are stolen, the car is usually a crime-before-the-crime.

This is a money argument and seems to belong closer to your second ¶, pg. 1.

With the large number of people reaching driving age each year, and most of these people do drive a car eventually, where are they going to drive? The roads built thirty, twenty and even ten years ago will not contain todays traffic. Therefore new larger free-ways are constructed. Of course who pays for this? Thats right! You, the tax payer! This is more cost which can be added to the enormous amount paid yearly for car maintainance.

Air pollution, scoffed at by many at one time is now a very large and dangerous reality. Smog, as it is called, is a major problem in many large citys today. The solution to the problem? There is only one, quit driving. However with todays clinging need of the car for transportation to fulfill all needs, this is impractical. Smog devices have been installed but their effect is negligible. This is just another problem faced by this and future generations.

Wordy

You seem to be hitting your topic with a scatter gun. Lots of feathers are flying but you're not bringing down the bird.

Where do old cars go? Since a cars has no old age benefits most retire to a junk yard. This is a pleasing view to the eyes of the junk dealer but an eyesore to the majority of the public. The problem of this and a few others took the time of congress last year, and required the passage of legislation to aid in the correction of these eyesores.

your account seems to lack a clear, controlling idea.

What happened to your initial theme statement? You got on your horse and then rode off in all directions.

Money could be saved, accidents cut out, air pollution stopped, needless deaths and the nuisance of unsightly junk years and cluttered high ways could be eliminated by abolishing the automobile.

GROUP II,
TERMINAL
CORRECTION

[No title]

A famous case of a Sympotomatic murder is
the case of Richard Loeb and Nathan Leopold in
1924; this case paved the way for scientific
investigation of murders related to mental illness.
These two boys murdered another boy for no
other purpose than to try to commit a perfect
murder. From the investigation it was found
that both boys came from well-to-do families
and that both boys had fairly high IQ's. It
was also found that the parents of both boys
had mental illness at one time or another.
Both boys had governesses who were very
strict. Richard Loeb had dreams of becoming
a master criminal. Nathan Leopold had vivid
fantasie s of being a slave to a king. He also
worshiped his mother and later became sexually
impotent; although he boasted to his friends
of having many love affairs he really had none.
Both had homoerotic tendencies and, because of
their personality makeups, were perfect for
each other, with Loeb being the stronger and
Leopold the slave. Because of the grotesque-
ness of the crime and the way the victim was
buried the investigation of the case stated
that their might have been sexual overtones
involved. Leob: died in prison; Leopold, after
serving forty years, was finally paroled. Dr.
Abrahamsen believes that it would be remote
for Leopold to commit another murder because
the biological sex drive has decreased because
of his age. This case showed that not only the
poor can commit murder but the rich as well.
They do have their problems and the poor are
not the only ones with environment problems.

"The Making of A Boy Killer", is the case
of a boy named Salvador Agron who at the age
of sixteen was part of a Puerto Rican gang in
New York that attacked six "gringo youths", in
a playground. Argon stabbded to death two of

the "gringos" and seriously wounded a third.
He was covicted of first degree murder but the
sentence was later commuted to life imprison-
ment by Governor Rockefeller. Although Argon
had been labeled, "a Dracrla," he actually was
a weak, timid boy on the boderline of insanity
who had been grotesquely deprived of parental
affection and community care. Salvador Argon
had been born of illiterate parents. After his
parents were divorced he lived with his mother
at a Catholic asylum which sheltered the poor,
the aged, the sick and the homeless. Because
of the mother's long hours she was able to see
Argon only once a week. He later lived with
his father who had ten wives, both legal and
common-law. One of the wives committed sucide
by hanging herself, which had a profound shock
on Argon. It was during this time that he began to skip school, collect razor blades and
stay out late at night. He later went through
two reform schools and while there, it was
discovered that he showed homosexual tendencies and heard strange voices. The recommendation at that time was that he obtain psych-
otherpy for "schizoid traits", but such help
was unavaible. After his release he lived
with a married sister and between time lived
on the streets. In time he joined a Puerto
Rican Club and was in constant trouble inci-
ting riots in school and gany wars on the
streets.

This case might have been prevented if this
boy had the psychotherapy care needed and
help in education. He is now serving his sentence and has a chance to be paroled. According to the warden, Argon has learned to read
and write and has matured spirtually as well.
The warden also thinks that if Argon continues
to make good progress he will have a good
chance of being returned to society in a
short time.

According to warden Riggs of Minnesota the parolee would have a better chance of successfully returning to society if the following could be accomplished! The changing of prisons to hospital rehabilation centers for prisoners that need long term treatments, the increase of pay for Parole Officers, psychotheaputic personnel and related personnel so as to attract the college educated and public support in employment and acceptance in the neighborhood. The period of rehabilation should be used to prepare the individual- vocationally, physically, mentally and spiritually.

I have tried to show two concrete examples of cases, both showing childhood environmental situations, that induced the person or persons to commit their respective murders. I also have try to show that rehabilation and the time can mature a person so he can abide by society's laws and mores.

Your paper shows that you have studied your subject and illustrated it with concrete examples. In your closing paragraph you should have repeated your conviction against capital punishment, using your arguments for rehabilitation and possible causes of crime to support it. This would have made your paper more forceful.

Refresh yourself on the proper use of the comma and semi-colon. These are two punctuation marks which you misuse most frequently.

GROUP III   PRO or CON BENJAMIN
MARGINAL
AND
TERMINAL   Lawrence, in his essay "Benjamin Franklin",
CORRECTION   makes his opinions known very clearly. His
                       thoughts and statements are understood because
                       of the words he uses. *and the way he uses them?*

isn't he pretty direct?   Lawrence begins his essay ridiculing in-
                       directly the people who have attempted to set
                       up a basis by which a man can become perfect.

              "The perfectability of man
              Ah, Heaven, what a dreary theme.
              The perfectability of the Ford Car."

                       He compares a human being to a car. He is
                       angry over the fact that man is looked upon as
                       a machine that can be perfected if all the
                       parts are checked regularly and are oiled with
develop more clearly— the best quality of oil. The basis mentioned
Where? not clear.   previously is compared to the check list that
you have an excellent point here! would be made on a car.   *F's check list?*

              "Anyhow, I defy you, oh socity,
              to educate me or to suppress me,
What is the logic behind your fling?   according to your dummy standards."
                       He seems to believe that if one attempts to
                       perfect himself, he will destroy the many
                       facets of his personality, or as he calls
                       them: " A miltitude of conflicting men." Much
                       sarcasm is revealed. *—show exactly how.*

Why all alone?   It is at this point that Lawrence makes it
                       obvious that Benjamin receives most of his
                       anger.

                       Here bitter sarcasm appears aimed towards
                       Franklin. He was foolish enough to try to set
                       up standards for perfection.

"But a man has a soul, though you
can't locate it within his purse
or his pocketbook or his heart or
his stomach or his head. The whole-
ness of a man is his soul."

He, Lawrence, becomes serious and shows his
strong belief in the soul as an integral part
of the body which can not be separated as
Franklin has tried to do. This change to seriousness is successful because it makes the
reader realize that they are to take very
seriously what will be said shortly.

tr. abrupt.

Lawrence, brings in admiration and defense
even concerning Franklin which is surprising.
He alternates between Phrases of reverence
and defense:

*But what is
total effect
of section?*

"I admire him. I admire his sturdy
courage."

and phrases such as:

"I do not like him"

This last sentence immediately follows Lawrence's praise of Franklin. Then he defends
Franklin with the following lines:

"Of course he did it perfect good
faith, as far as he knew. He simply
thought it the true ideal."

Lawrence seems to be in douby as to
whether Franklin derserves punsihment or
praise. Thus, he teeters back and forth. It
is not difficult to notice when he becomes
angry with Franklin nor was it difficult to
tell when he was in favor of what he did.
Lawrence seems to have a command of tone.
However, he changes so often it is difficult
to understand his point.

good use of example.

"Old daddy Franklin will tell you.
Hé'll rig him up for you, the
pattern American. Oh, Franklin
was the first downright American.
He knew what he was about, the
sharp little man. He set up the
first dummy American."

tr. abrupt

is he classified along with?

Because Franklin is classified along with
the typical American, he, who dared to set up
a standard for perfection, must have this
ideal in common with his fellow Americans. In
other words, all Americans must have tried to
achieve perfection. Franklin is refered to as
a sharp, little man, leading the reader to
believe, once again, through sarcasm, that
Franklin was not a sharp but a confused man.

You haven't made a previous change clear.

Lawrence's tone changes again when he re-
views Benjamin's creed. He now shows his
resentment toward Franklin's conceit. He
quotes the creed and adds his comments.

But what is point L. is making here?

"That there is one God,
who made all things."
(But Benjamin made Him)
"That He governs the world
by His Providence."
(Benjamin knowing all about
Providence)

Franklin is showed to have believed he was
perfect.

tr. good here.

Once again, Lawrence changes tone and he
becomes sincere and drops his sarcasm. He
seems to have found a subject which needs
serious consideration-the soul. Franklin,
Lawrence says, attempted to fence in the
soul and to contain it within a certain area
in one's body.

"Benjamin fenced a little tract that he
called the soul of man" Then Lawrence says:

What you have here is a very interesting series of notes and examples needing to be welded into a unified essay around a central thesis. Your transitions are abrupt, adding to the jotted down effect of the paper.

Despite some very good moments — see notes, you have not written a unified, coherent essay focusing on the tone, devices and related assertions of Lawrence.

2

Students' Responses to Teacher Comments

Thomas C. Gee

Writing is a bore. Who needs to write if he can show and tell? The desire to write well, perhaps the wish to learn anything at all about writing, may well be steadily declining as the oral-aural and visual media flourish. What can be done to increase or, for many students, to create the desire to write? In his research, Mr. Gee hypothesizes that the carrot, praise, might increase motivation more than the stick—a most reasonable psychological assumption. This report is an object lesson for the red-pencil school of theme markers. It suggests that further investigation might make many converts.

—Reviewed by F. I. G.

Good writing skills do not happen by chance, nor do they flower solely as a product of growing up. A great part of student improvement may be attributed to composition teachers. Teachers provide models, demonstrate techniques, and provide time for supervised writing. Teachers also spend countless hours writing comments on students' papers in the belief that their comments will bring about improvement in students' writing skills.

In marking papers, English teachers are aware that their comments do affect students. The students' reactions are sometimes quite different from those that the teacher had expected or hoped for. For example, writing *awkward* in the margin of a student's composition may provoke more than a student's careful revision for clarity and sophistication. Students often interpret a marginal notation like *clumsy, poorly written,* or *illogical* as personal indictment or as almost total disparagement of their skill. A student who receives no marks may interpret the dearth of comments as a subtle way of telling him that his paper was so bland, so unworthy as to merit no comment. Whatever the teacher's marks, the student will respond. The teacher can be assured that his comments influence the attitudes the student has about a particular composition, and his comments will likely contribute one way or another to the expectations the student has about becoming an adequate writer.

Selection of Students

As part of a doctoral study, I conducted an investigation of the effects of praise, negative comment, and no comment on expository compositions of eleventh grade students.[1] The study was designed to test what is normally assumed as fact, that praise is more effective than criticism or no comment in building attitudes. The effects of teacher comments on quantity, on quality, and on the attitudes of students toward writing were measured. One hundred thirty-nine students from junior English classes were divided into high, middle, and low ability groups on the results of the California Short-Form Test of Mental Maturity. The IQ scores ranged from 70 to 141. The students' scores were arbitrarily divided into three ability groups as shown in Table 2–1. One-third of the subjects in each ability level were then randomly assigned to one of three treatment groups so that within each ability level, one-third were praised, one-third were criticized, and one-third received no comment.

Collection of Data

Data were collected over a 4-week period. Classroom teachers helped select topics which they thought were equivalent in motivational interest and difficulty. Topics which students had discussed in class or on which they had written compositions during the year were eliminated. (See Appendix A.) No instruction in composition was given and no discussion of the compositions in the experiment was conducted by the classroom teachers during the time of the experiment. Only the experimenter introduced the four writing trials, one each week. Students were given 50 minutes to write on each topic.

Before the topics were given to the students, standardized instructions regarding the experiment were read to them. After the first composition had

Table 2–1 DISTRIBUTION OF SUBJECTS BY ABILITY

Group	Number of Subjects
Low Ability (IQ's 70–91)	47
Middle Ability (IQ's 92–113)	46
High Ability (IQ's 114–141)	46
Total	139

1. T.C. Gee, "The Effects of Written Comment on Expository Composition" (Doctor's thesis, North Texas State Univer., 1970).

Table 2–2 EXAMPLES OF COMMENTS FOR EACH TREATMENT GROUP

Criticized Group	Praised Group
1. This doesn't make sense.	1. You raised some interesting questions.
2. You did not follow the topic assigned.	2. Cleverly said!
3. This is awkward and unclear.	3. Your grammar and sentence structure are much better in this paper.
4. Use your imagination. Most of your ideas are trite.	4. This paragraph is a vivid description.
5. Please proofread! Your grammar and spelling are poor.	5. This paragraph establishes good unity for your essay.
6. Choose fresh, effective words instead of these.	6. This is interesting! Keep up the good work.
7. Stringy sentences, illogically connected!	7. A very original approach to the topic!
8. You contradict this idea in your next paragraph.	8. These ideas show a keen insight into the problem.
9. You ramble. Please organize more carefully.	9. The precise vocabulary that you use here makes your writing fresh and enjoyable.
10. You over-simplify the problem.	10. I hope your grammar and usage are always this good.

been written, the experimenter read all papers and wrote comments appropriate to the treatment group to which the student was assigned. Table 2–2 offers examples of the kinds of comments that were included on the papers of the praised and criticized groups.

Students in the No Comment group were given only a check mark to indicate that their papers had been read. No standard number of comments was made on each paper, but the number of comments ranged from five to eight for each paper in the Praised and the Criticized groups. The Criticized group's papers were marked for specific errors in grammar, spelling, organization, and usage. Suggestions were also made to improve content and style. Only errors and suggestions for improvement were recorded on the papers; good aspects of writing were ignored. The Praised group's papers were complimented for their good points. Originality, sound and thoroughly developed ideas, good grammar, etc., were praised. Errors were ignored, and no suggestions for improvement were made. No grade was marked on any paper.

One week from the time the first papers were written, they were returned to the students. Students were asked to reread their papers, noting any comment that had been written on them. They were asked to consider how they might improve their next essay. Students who had received no comments were instructed to reread their papers, looking for ways to improve their writing.

After students had reviewed their compositions, they were given the second topic and asked to write on it. The same procedure was followed for the remainder of the writing experiment. Each writing day, students were given their previous compositions and were asked to reread them, considering any comments that had been made.

At the end of the experiment, students were given a questionnaire to determine their attitudes toward the writing experiment. (See Appendix B.) The questionnaire was adapted from one used by Taylor and Hoedt.[2] Eleven questions which could be answered negatively or positively were developed. For the purpose of this study, any student who responded positively to six or more questions was considered as having generally favorable attitudes toward the writing experiment. Any student who responded negatively to six or more questions was considered as having negative attitudes toward the experiment. If a student responded "yes" to any statement except statements 3 or 7, his response was considered as reflecting a positive attitude. A "no" response to statement 3 or 7 was considered as reflecting a positive attitude.

Analysis of Data

After the last writing trial, the first and last compositions were analyzed to determine if the student had increased the length of his compositions. First and last papers for each student were also compared by a panel of three English teachers to determine if the students had improved the quality of their writing, but, as might be expected, no significant differences in quality of writing were found over such a short time as a 4-week period. Unfortunately, no provisions had been made either to measure the effects over a longer period of time when significant improvements might have been expected or to measure the effects of both praise and negative comments as a combined marking procedure.

Hypotheses had been formulated to predict where significant differences among the treatment groups would appear for total subjects, high ability subjects, middle ability subjects, and low ability subjects. In addition, data were analyzed to test differences between sexes. Analysis of Variance and Duncan's New Multiple Range Test were used to establish the statistical significance of differences in quantity and quality.[3] Fisher's t-test and chi square were used to test for significant differences in attitudes. Once data were compiled, each of the hypotheses was tested, and the following conclusions were reached:

2. Winnifred F. Taylor and K.C. Hoedt, "The Effects of Praise Upon the Quality and Quantity of Creative Writing," *Journal of Educational Research*, 1966, *60*, 80–83.
3. D.B. Duncan, "Multiple Range and Multiple F Tests," *Biometrics*, 1955, *59*, 108–12.

Teacher Comment and Length of Composition

Negative criticism and no feedback caused students to write less than students who were praised. Although length of composition alone is not necessarily of value, lengthier compositions may be an indication that students are confident enough of their writing to extend their thoughts on paper. Students who refuse to write, students who manifest great anxiety on composition days, and students who mechanically compile a catalog of simple sentences (or other constructions which they feel confident of handling well) may have had readers who intimidated them by their proofing marks. For these students, self-assurance and interest in writing have been killed. The results of this study seem to indicate that teachers can easily kill whatever it is that allows the student to believe in his ability to write.

Table 2–3 illustrates the results of the treatment procedures as they affected composition length. When Praised students were compared with those who were Criticized or those who had received No Comment, the Praised students maintained approximately the same number of T-units while those of the other groups deteriorated considerably. (For a discussion of T-unit, see Hunt.[4]) Consistent negative criticism or lack of feedback obviously inhibited verbal performance more than did praise. In comparing the mean losses in number of T-units between the Praised and Criticized groups, the Praised group had significantly less loss, as indicated in Table 2–4. The results shown in this table support basic learning theories which advocate using praise in preference to negative criticism or no comment in reinforcing behavior.

While the Praised group had a mean decline of 1.79 in number of T-units thoughout the experiment, the Criticized group had a mean decline of 5.88 T-units, and the No Comment group declined by an average of 4.71 T-units. High and low ability level subjects were more sensitive to the treatments than were average ability subjects. Apparently the average ability level subjects maintained their performance level in spite of the treatment, while higher and lower ability level subjects' performances reflected disgust, apathy, or defeatism. As a group, the high ability and low ability students reacted more strongly to the comments than did the average ability students. (See Table 2–5.) One high ability student

Table 2–3 MEAN NUMBER OF T-UNITS FOR THREE TREATMENT GROUPS

	Trial 1	Trial 2
Praised Group	16.57	14.78
Criticized Group	18.88	13.00
No Comment Group	18.40	13.69

4. K.W. Hunt, *Grammatical Structures Written at Three Grade Levels* (Champaign, Ill.: NCTE, 1965).

Table 2–4 DUNCAN'S MULTIPLE RANGE TEST OF SIGNIFICANCE BETWEEN PAIRS OF MEANS FOR NUMBER OF T-UNITS FOR TOTAL SUBJECTS[**]

Initial Groups	Ranked Means	Mean Difference	Range Product
Praised-Criticized	(–1.81)–(–5.83)	4.02	3.45*
Praised-No Comment	(–1.81)–(–4.71)	2.90	3.31
No Comment-Criticized	(–4.71)–(–5.83)	1.12	3.31

* Significant at the .05 level of confidence.
** The mean decline in number of T-Units (Table 5) and the mean number of T-Units (Table 3) were computed by dividing the sum of the raw scores by N—1 while the ranked means (Table 4) were derived by dividing the sum of the scores by N.

who had received only negative comments wrote, "I thought the essays were a good idea. I enjoyed writing them, but I didn't like the way they were marked. I felt angry. I felt that my work was worth nothing. I think I would have tried harder and written better if the grader had given me encouragement."

There was no significant difference in the effects comments had on male and female students. One previous study by Sweet found that ninth grade boys were more affected by teacher comments than were girls.[5] In my study with eleventh grade students, neither males nor females seemed to be more significantly affected.

Attitudes Toward Composition

Students' attitudes toward writing and their self-concepts as capable writers are significantly affected by teachers' written comments. In this study, Praised students had more positive attitudes toward writing than students who were Criticized or students who received No Comment. A chi square test for difference in attitudes between those who were Praised and those who were

Table 2–5 MEAN DECLINE IN NUMBER OF T-UNITS

	High Ability	Middle Ability	Low Ability	Total Decline
M Decline for Praised	–.44	–1.00	–3.94	1.79
M Decline for Criticized	–8.33	–1.69	–7.63	5.88
M Decline for No Comment	–4.40	–2.80	–6.93	4.71
Total M Decline	–4.39	–1.83	–6.17	

5. R.C. Sweet, *Educational Attainment and Attitudes Toward School as a Function of Feedback in the Form of Teachers' Written Comments* (Madison, Wisconsin: Univer. of Wisconsin, 1966).

Criticized established a chi square of 19.23, which was significant at the .001 level of confidence. That is, those who were Praised had significantly more positive attitudes than those who were Criticized. Similar results were found when comparing the attitudes of those who had been Praised and those who received No Comment: a chi square of 20.41, also significant at the .001 level of confidence, was established. On the other hand, no significant difference in attitudes was found to exist when comparing the Criticized and the No Comment groups.

Conclusions

Students seem to have more patience in working on their compositions if they think they will be rewarded for what they do well and if they are encouraged along the way. This study indicates that to assist the building of positive attitude, teachers must give a pat-on-the-back for the improvements that the student makes. To withhold praise until the student has achieved an ideal performance is educationally unsound. It is an easy thing for teachers to mark a set of papers by correcting errors in grammar, usage, spelling, and punctuation and by making suggestions for improving organization, transition, and clarity. It is often somewhat harder to find several points to commend, but students need encouragement and rightly merit praise for things well done. Their continued improvement apparently comes from recognition of what they do well in addition to what they do not do so well. Certainly their confidence and pride in their efforts, and their enjoyment of writing, are enhanced by a teacher's assurance that they are beginning to master the skills required for good writing.

Appendix A: Essay Topics

I.   Most teen-agers have at least one problem that gives them considerable concern. With some, dating is a problem. With others, getting money or a job is a problem. Some teen-agers worry about their appearance or being popular. Still others worry about their future career or a major problem facing the nation or the world.
What is your main concern at this time? Explain why your concern became important to you and why you consider it worth overcoming. You might also explain how various people or situations contribute to the problem.

II. Newspapers, television, and even popular records keep saying that there is a "generation gap" in the world today. What they mean, of course, is that the younger people and the older people cannot or will not understand one another.
Do you think there is a lack of understanding between younger and older people? Cite some examples to back up your opinion and explain why you think the gap exists.

III. People today are working fewer hours, and some experts predict that by the year 2000, most people will work no more than twenty hours a week. With more free time people must find new and better ways to spend their time.
What are your suggestions? Explain several ways you think people could spend their time profitably and enjoyably.

IV. Happiness has been defined by many great writers. Perhaps you could not accept any of their definitions because what makes one person happy doesn't necessarily make someone else happy.
What do you feel is necessary to make you a happy person? Explain why each point is important.

Appendix B: Questionnaire

Please respond yes or no to each of the following statements by placing a check in the appropriate blank.

	Yes	No
1. I enjoyed writing the essays.	—	—
2. At first I didn't like writing, but I changed my mind and learned to enjoy writing.	—	—
3. Comments on my paper, or the lack of them, made me feel angry with the grader.	—	—
4. Comments on my paper, or the lack of them, made me feel like trying harder.	—	—
5. Comments on my paper, or the lack of them, made me feel good about my work.	—	—
6. Comments on my paper, or the lack of them, made me feel angry with myself.	—	—
7. The comments overlooked the best points of my writing.	—	—
8. I would like to continue writing for this experiment.	—	—
9. I feel that my writing improved because of the comments that were written on my paper.	—	—
10. The comments on my paper, or the lack of them, are the kinds I would like all teachers to make on work that I hand in.	—	—
11. In general, I liked the way my essays were marked.	—	—

3

The Effects of Between-Draft Teacher Evaluation Versus Student Self-Evaluation on High School Students' Revising of Rough Drafts

Richard Beach

Experienced writers often testify that they revise their drafts extensively until they are satisfied that their writing communicates their intended meaning (e.g., Murray, 1978). These experienced writers have developed an ability to critically assess their drafts so that they themselves recognize the need for change. They may also rely on other readers' responses to their drafts to ascertain whether or not those readers understood their intended meaning. The fact that these writers use their own and others' evaluation while they are writing drafts encourages further revising.

In contrast, inexperienced writers in secondary and college courses engage in little substantive reworking of the content and organization of rough drafts; revising often consists of "polishing up" minor editorial matters (Squire & Applebee, 1968; Emig, 1971; Beach, 1976).

One reason that students often do not engage in substantive revising of rough drafts is that teachers generally assess only the final drafts. If teachers focused their evaluation on the content and organization of a rough draft, then students might recognize the need to make substantive changes at that stage. Students might be willing to critically assess and revise their papers at the rough draft stage, particularly if the teacher's evaluation helped them recognize the need for substantive changes.

Since teachers burdened with large classes often do not have the time or energy to evaluate both rough and final drafts, one option might be for students to assess their own rough drafts, using guided self-evaluation forms. These forms could include open-ended questions or self-rating scales that require students to articulate their intentions, describe and judge their writing and then predict appropriate changes. These questions and scales might be particularly useful for students who have difficulty in critically assessing their own writing.

A number of studies have indicated that the use of self-rating scales or questions results in gains in writing ability (Sager, 1973; Lamberg, 1974; Wolter, 1975). However, these studies measured the effects of self-evaluation in terms of pre- to post-essay improvement rather than examining the effects of self-ratings on measures of change or improvement from rough to final drafts. Moreover, the studies did not compare the effects of students' self-evaluation with the effects of teacher evaluation on outcome measures. Because teachers may be able to be more critical of rough drafts than students are, teacher evaluation may result in more extensive revising of rough drafts than if students used guided self-assessment forms or did not receive any evaluation of rough drafts.

On the other hand, neither teacher evaluation nor guided self-evaluation may result in any more revising than with the typical practice of no between-draft teacher evaluation or guided self-evaluation. Students may simply not be capable of using their own or a teacher's evaluation to define and then make the appropriate revisions. Students may change their rough drafts, but change does not necessarily result in improvement. Students may also improve more in some areas than others. For example, if teacher-evaluation or self-evaluation focuses more on organization than sentence structure, students may improve more in overall organization than in sentence structure.

Differences in the type of evaluation could also affect the fluency of rough and final drafts, as determined by the total number of words in each draft. Additions to rough drafts may, in some cases, enhance the quality of final drafts, since some research indicates a correlation between fluency and quality (Rosen, 1969; Page, 1968).

Factors such as topic, grade level or sex could influence the degree to which students revise, or these factors could interact with treatment variables to influence revising.

Students who are more familiar with the subject matter of one topic than another may be able to extend their thinking on that topic to a greater extent than on another topic, resulting in more revising. For example, when a student is writing about a friend as opposed to a general idea about which he/she is less familiar, he/she has a reservoir of material or information about the friend to draw on for adding new material to a draft or for rethinking existing material.

Students at a higher grade level may be more capable of critically assessing their writing than students at a lower grade level, resulting in more extensive revising for higher than lower grade-level students.

Sex may also influence revising, particularly differences between final and rough draft quality. Williams (1972) found that females in an urban secondary school wrote compositions rated as significantly higher in quality than those of males.

Students' apprehension toward writing as measured by an attitude inventory (Daly & Miller, 1975) is another factor which could influence revising. Students with high apprehension towards writing may interpret teacher assessment as implying negative judgments of their writing ability, inhibiting their incentive to revise. Or, highly apprehensive students may not be confident about their ability to assess critically or to revise their writing.

Purpose of the Study

The purpose of this study was to determine whether either teacher evaluation or guided self-evaluation of rough drafts results in more extensive revising of rough drafts than the usual practice of students' revising rough drafts without teacher or guided assessment. Differences in the effects of teacher evaluation (abbreviated as TE), guided self-evaluation (SE) and no evaluation (NE) on revising of rough drafts was determined both in terms of the extent to which subjects changed their rough drafts as rated by judges on a "degree-of-change" scale and the extent to which the quality of the subjects' final drafts differed from the quality of their rough drafts as rated by judges on quality rating scales.

Research Questions

Given the lack of research on the effects of between-draft teacher evaluation or guided self-evaluation on revising, this study examined the following questions:

1. What are the effects of *treatment* (teacher evaluation versus guided self-evaluation versus no evaluation between drafts), *topic* (within expository discourse types—writing about a generalization about people versus writing about reasons for liking or disliking another person versus writing about one's own strengths and weakness), *grade level* (10th grade versus 11th/12th grade), and *sex* on:

    a.   the mean degree of change from rough to final drafts ("extensive" versus "little") as judged by separate raters?

    b.   the mean number of words for final drafts across three writing assignments with mean numbers of words on rough drafts and scores on an apprehension inventory as covariates?

    c.   the mean quality ratings for *focus, sequence, support, sentences, language*, and *flavor* as judged by separate raters for the final drafts across three writing assignments with mean quality ratings on rough drafts and apprehension scores as covariates?

2. What are the effects of interactions among treatment, topic, grade level, and sex on mean degree-of-change scores, final draft fluency, and quality ratings for final drafts?

3. What is the relationship between teacher ratings of *focus, sequence, support, overall quality* and ratings of *need-for-change* for rough drafts of subjects in the teacher evaluation treatment group? What is the relationship of

these variables on student ratings for rough drafts of the self-assessment treatment group?

Procedures

The subjects in this study were 103 students in three 10th grade and two 11th/12th grade classes at a high school located in a predominantly working-class neighborhood in Minneapolis. (Only a small percentage of the graduates of this school pursue some form of post-secondary education.) Students in the 11th/12th grade classes had received instruction on revising in their 10th grade composition classes.

In order to minimize any potential differences across classes, the study was conducted in the very beginning of the school year. Subjects were randomly assigned to three treatment groups: those receiving only between-draft teacher-evaluation (TE), those completing guided self-evaluation forms (SE), and those who received no evaluation between drafts (NE). Subjects were also randomly assigned to three different topic assignments for each of three writing sessions.

Three expository writing assignments involving writing about people were devised. The primary differences between the topic assignments was the familiarity of the subject matter and the level of abstraction of the thesis. The three assignments were:

1. "'Most people are out for themselves.' Do you agree or disagree with this statement? Give reasons why you agree or disagree with this statement."

2. "Write about a well-known person, television/movie star, or friend that you like or that you dislike. Give reasons why you like or dislike that person."

3. "Write about one of your strengths and one of your weaknesses. Give reasons why you chose these as your one strength and one weakness."

Subjects received these assignments and instructions on each of three consecutive Fridays and wrote rough drafts during a fifty-minute period. They were told that they could engage in prewriting prior to writing the rough draft and that the rough draft had to be completed by the end of class. Over the weekend, a person who had taught high school composition (but was not a member of the school staff and did not know the students) read the rough drafts of subjects in the TE group. This outside "teacher" was employed in order to eliminate any bias due to familiarity with individual students.

The "teacher" completed a Teacher Evaluation Form containing the following open-ended categories: (1) specific aspects that the teacher liked about the draft (a means of providing positive reinforcement), (2) inference(s) as to the subject's intention, (3) clarifying questions (cf. Kelly, 1973) about the draft and responses to the draft, and (4) ratings on five-point scales of the *focus, sequence, support, overall quality*, and *need-for-change* of the draft. Drafts and Teacher Evaluation Forms were then returned to subjects in their Monday classes.

Subjects in the SE treatment group received their drafts and were asked to complete a form containing the same categories as the Teacher Evaluation Form. Subjects had to list aspects they liked about their draft, to state their intention, to pose questions about the draft as if they were a reader, to make suggestions for change, and to rate themselves on *focus, sequence, support, overall quality* and *need-for-change*. Subjects in the NE group were asked to simply rewrite their drafts. All groups were told that their final drafts would be evaluated. Subjects were given Monday and Tuesday class periods to complete the final drafts. It was observed that subjects in the SE group were able to complete the self-evaluation form and their final drafts in approximately the same time period as subjects in the other groups.

During the Wednesday and Thursday classes before each of the writing assignments, subjects in all classes engaged in identical writing activities devised by the investigator. Before the first writing session, subjects received instruction only on terminology necessary for understanding the forms; subjects did not receive training in methods of self-assessment or revising. After the three writing assignments were completed, subjects were administered the Apprehension of Writing attitude inventory (Daly & Miller, 1975).

Three judges received approximately thirty hours of training in the use of the degree-of-change scale and the quality rating scales devised by the investigator. The degree-of-change scale employed in previous research (Beach, 1976) with high inter-judge agreement involved rating the extent to which subjects changed rough drafts on a three-point scale: (1) little, (2) some, and (3) extensive.

The criteria for the quality rating scales were *focus, sequence, support, sentences, language*, and *flavor* rated on scales from 1 (low) to 5 (high), criteria considered by the investigator to be important in expository writing. *Focus*, was defined as the organization of the draft around a main thesis; *sequence*, the development of ideas in a logical, sequential order; *support*, the use of reasons, evidence, and examples to clarify, represent, or support ideas; *sentences*, the maturity and effectiveness of the sentence structure or use of syntax; *language*, the clarity and originality in word choice; and *flavor* (derived from Diederich, 1974), the degree to which a writer is employing his/her own unique writing style.

The rough and final drafts from the three writing sessions were mixed together and batches were randomly assigned to the three judges. The judges first rated the quality of drafts. The rough and final drafts were then paired and these pairs were randomly assigned to the judges who re-read the drafts and rated the pairs on the degree-of-change scales.

Prior to rating the drafts, the drafts were not typed, because a small portion of the rough drafts were written in such a manner that they could not have been typed without changing the content of these rough drafts. The investigator had to weigh the cost of altering the rough draft data against the possibility the handwriting would influence the judges' ratings of quality. When asked to distinguish the rough from final drafts on the basis of appearance, judges could not detect differences between drafts, with a few exceptions.

The inter-judge reliability for the three judges' ratings for all drafts on the degree-of-change and the quality ratings was determined by ANOVA (Godshalk, Swineford, & Coffman, 1966), using the formula:
$$\frac{\text{MS subjects} - \text{MS error}}{\text{MS subjects}}.$$
The following inter-judge reliabilities were obtained: (first number = rough drafts; second, final drafts) *focus .87, .90; sequence .86, .90; support, .90, .91; sentences, .91, .92; language .90, .90; flavor .89, .90;* and *degree-of-change* (from rough to final draft) .84.

In order to determine the fluency of rough and final drafts the investigator conducted a word count, checking his own count against others to determine accuracy.

Analysis

Separate one-way ANOVA's were run in order to determine if the sessions in which the students wrote over a three-week period (first versus second versus third sessions) had any effect on subjects' degree-of-change scores or the quality ratings of both rough and final drafts across the three topics; the sequence of sessions had no significant effect on any of these outcome measures.

The means of the three judges' ratings for each version were submitted to separate $2 \times 2 \times 3 \times 3$ mixed factorial analysis of covariance for each dependent measure with S's nested in Grade level by Sex by Treatment combinations and crossed with the repeated measure, Topic. For mean fluency scores on rough and final drafts and for ratings of *focus, sequence, support, sentences, language,* and *flavor,* final draft scores served as dependent variables with rough draft ratings and writing apprehension scores as covariates. In order to focus attention on systematic differences between final drafts, version (rough versus final drafts) was not treated as an independent factor, but rather rough draft scores were employed as covariates in adjusting final version ratings. This technique has the advantage of statistically controlling for inter-subject variation in rough drafts, a factor not of interest, and testing for differences among groups due only to variation in final drafts induced by deliberate intervention (see Campbell & Stanley, 1963, p. 23). Writing apprehension was used as a covariate in order to reduce the influence of differences in subjects' writing apprehension on their experience with teacher and/or self-assessment treatments and their writing of final drafts. Because the degree-of-change rating scores involved comparative judgments between rough and final version, these scores were adjusted only for writing apprehension. Following significant F tests on main or interaction effects, the Sheffé procedure was employed, where appropriate, to determine significant comparisons between adjusted cell means.

The teacher's ratings of the TE group subjects' rough drafts on *focus, sequence, support,* and *overall quality* were correlated with that teacher's *need-for-change* ("extensive" versus "little") rating scores; the SE subjects' ratings for the same quality rating scales were also correlated with their *need-for-change* rating scores.

Results

Degree-of-change ratings: The analysis of covariance on degree-of-change ratings resulted in a significant treatment effect [F $(2,70)$ = 7.33, p < .001; $\bar{X}_{SE}$ = 1.55, $\bar{X}_{TE}$ = 1.84, $\bar{X}_{NE}$ = 1.52]. A Sheffé procedure indicated that the TE group had significantly higher degree-of-change scores than either the SE or NE groups. In addition to a significant treatment effect, the interaction between treatment and topic was also significant [F $(4;142)$ = 2.78, p < .05]. Testing of all pairwise contrasts using the Sheffé technique indicated a significant difference (alpha = .05) only between TE subjects' scores on the essay topics involving writing about their strengths and weaknesses and NE subjects' writing about another person. A final source of significant variation was a Sex × Grade Level × Topic interaction [F $(2;142)$ = 4.14, p < .05]; pairwise contrasts between means revealed only that 10th grade females writing about their strengths and weaknesses exhibited significantly higher degree-of-change scores than did 11th/12th grade females writing about the topic, "most people are out for themselves."

Fluency: The analysis of covariance for fluency indicated significant main effects for treatment [F $(1,69)$ = 17.66, p < .001; $\bar{X}_{SE}$ = 163.49, $\bar{X}_{TE}$ = 193.99, $\bar{X}_{NE}$ = 145.51]. As was the case for degree-of-change scores, a Sheffé procedure indicated that the TE group scored significantly higher than both the SE and NE groups. There was also a significant main effect for Sex [F $(1,69)$ = 9.44, p < .01; $\bar{X}_{male}$ = 154.34, $\bar{X}_{female}$ = 176.81]. A significant Grade Level by Topic interaction was also found [F $(2;141)$ = 3.20, p < .05]. Testing of all possible pairwise comparisons indicated only that for 11th/12th graders, writing about another person resulted in higher fluency than writing about their own strengths and weaknesses.

Quality ratings: No significant main or interaction effects emerged from the analyses of the quality rating scores for *sequence, sentences, language,* or *flavor.* There were significant main effects on *focus* ratings due to differences between grade level [F $(1,69)$ = 6.09, p < .05; $\bar{X}_{10th}$ = 3.17, $\bar{X}_{11th/12th}$ = 3.06] and among topics [F $(2;141)$ = 3.10, p < .05; $\bar{X}_{generalization}$ = 3.05, $\bar{X}_{another\ person}$ = 3.20, $\bar{X}_{strengths\ and\ weakness}$ = 3.10]. Pairwise contrasts among the topic cell means indicated that writing about another person was judged to be significantly more focused than writing about the "most people are out for themselves" topic.

A significant treatment effect occurred for ratings of *support* [F $(2,69)$ = 3.03, p < .05; $\bar{X}_{SE}$ = 2.94, $\bar{X}_{TE}$ = 3.26, $\bar{X}_{NE}$ = 2.94]. Sheffé tests indicated that the TE group *support* ratings were significantly higher than either the SE or NE ratings.

Table 3–1 CORRELATIONS BETWEEN TEACHER RATINGS ON EACH OF FOUR QUALITY RATINGS OF ROUGH DRAFTS AND RATINGS OF "NEED FOR CHANGE" COMPARED WITH THE CORRELATIONS BETWEEN SELF-EVALUATION SUBJECTS' RATINGS ON THE SAME QUALITY RATINGS AND RATINGS ON "NEED FOR CHANGE"

Scale	Teacher's Ratings of TE Subjects' Rough Drafts	SE Subjects' Ratings of Rough Drafts
overall quality	.804	.770
support	.783	.085
sequence	.648	.661
focus	.547	.583

The correlations between the teacher's ratings of TE subjects' rough drafts' *focus, sequence, support, overall quality* and their ratings for *need-for-change* and the correlations between SE subjects' ratings for the same criteria are presented in Table 3–1.

The correlations indicate that both the teacher and the SE subjects tended to conceive of *overall quality* as most directly related to their perceptions of the need to change the rough drafts. The teacher ratings of *support* were highly correlated with *need-for-change* while the SE group subjects *support* ratings bore no relationship with their *need-for-change* ratings. Both the teacher and the SE group subjects' ratings of *sequence* and *focus* correlated in a similar manner with *need-for-change* ratings.

Discussion of Results

The fact that the TE subjects showed significantly higher *degree-of-change* scores, *fluency* scores, and final draft *support* ratings than either the SE or NE subjects indicates that between-draft teacher evaluation resulted in more revising than either the guided assessment or the usual practice of having students revise on their own. The teacher's evaluation gives students another reader's perspective on whether or how well the intended meaning has been communicated. Without that external perspective it may be difficult for students on their own to recognize whether their intended meaning has been communicated. Without any response, a student simply assumes that the writing has communicated the intended meaning and perceives no need for critical self-assessment or revising.

The fact that the TE subjects differed from the SE and NE subjects in both the *degree-of-change* and *fluency*, but only in one of six areas of writing quality— *support*—indicated that while subjects changed their rough drafts, those changes did not necessarily result in differences between rough and final draft quality in a number of different aspects of quality. One reason that the differences occurred only in *support* may be that the teacher focused more attention on matters of *support* in the rough drafts than on *focus* or *sequence*. As Table 3–1 indicates, the correlations between teacher ratings of *support* and *degree to which the draft needs to be changed* were higher than for *focus* or *sequence*. In contrast, the correlations indicate that the SE subjects' self-ratings on *support* had little relationship with perceived need for change correlated with *degree-of-change* ratings.

The teacher may have devoted more attention to support and less attention to sentence structure or wording because she assumed that attention to these matters would be more appropriate for assessment of the final draft. This suggests that further research needs to examine the focus of an evaluator's assessment at different stages of the composing process, differences representing the evaluator's assumptions as to what type of assessment is most appropriate for each stage of the composing process.

Another finding was that the SE subjects did not differ significantly from the NE subjects—that completing the self-evaluation forms did not result in any more revising than the usual practice of doing no formal evaluation between drafts. Subjective analysis of the SE subjects' forms indicated that many subjects had difficulty in identifying their overall intention, strengths and weaknesses, or necessary changes. This difficulty in knowing how to employ certain self-assessing strategies may have been due to the fact that the subjects received little prior instruction in methods of self-assessment. Subjects were also not accustomed to critically detaching themselves from their writing. Further research needs to be conducted on developmental differences in the ability to self-assess and the effects of instruction in self-assessing strategies on revising.

Another possible reason that the SE subjects did not differ from the NE subjects is that there may have been little incentive for the SE subjects to critically self-assess their drafts. This suggests the need for combining guided self-assessment with teacher assessment with both students and teachers using the same criteria. Students could then compare their self-evaluation with the teacher evaluation, noting discrepancies between the two. If a student states an intention for a draft but a teacher describes the draft as doing something quite different from that stated intention, the dissonance between intention and realization could result in further self-assessing and revising. In research now in progress, the investigator is determining differences in the effects of a combination of self- and teacher-evaluation treatment versus a teacher-evaluation-only treatment versus a self-evaluation-only treatment on various outcome measures of revising.

The significant main effects of topic on *focus* ratings for writing about another person as opposed to writing about a general opinion statement may be a function of the subjects' ability to focus material about which they are more familiar (writing about a friend) as opposed to writing about an opinion dealing with subject matter with which they were less familiar.

The significant treatment by topic effect on *degree-of-change* (which further analysis indicated was due to the difference between TE subjects' higher *degree-of-change* ratings in writing on their strengths and weaknesses than the NE subjects writing about another person) may be due to the fact that the teacher's evaluation for the TE subjects was especially helpful for that particular topic.

These findings all suggest that differences in topic, even within one discourse mode (expository) affect revising. Further research that measures subjects' familiarity with or interest in a topic could provide more empirical data to explain topic effects on revising.

In summary, the essential finding of this study was that students who were provided between-draft teacher evaluation showed a greater degree of change, higher fluency and greater differences in support on final drafts than students employing guided self-evaluation forms and students receiving no evaluation. If composition teachers want to encourage revising of drafts, they need to provide evaluation during the writing of drafts. They also need to consider the possible effects of topic assignments on revising.

References

Beach, R. 1976. "Self-Evaluation Strategies of Extensive Revisers and Nonrevisers." *College Composition and Communication* 27: 160–64.

Campbell, D., and J. Stanley. 1963. *Experimental and Quasi-Experimental Designs for Research.* Chicago: Rand McNally College.

Daly, J. and M. Miller. 1975. "The Empirical Development of an Instrument to Measure Writing Apprehension." *Research in the Teaching of English* 9: 242–48.

Diederich, P. 1974. *Measuring Growth in English.* Urbana, IL: National Council of Teachers of English.

Emig, J. *The Composing Processes of Twelfth Graders.* 1971. Urbana, IL: National Council of Teachers of English.

Godshalk, F., F. Swineford, and W. Coffman. 1966. *The Measurement of Writing Ability.* New York: College Entrance Examination Board.

Kelly, M. 1973. Effects of Two Types of Teacher Response to Essays Upon Twelfth Grade Students' Growth in Writing Performance. Unpublished doctoral dissertation, Michigan State University.

Lamberg, W. 1974. Design and Validation of Instruction in Question-Directed Narrative Writing, Developed Through Discrimination Programming. Unpublished doctoral dissertation, University of Michigan.

Murray, D. 1978. "Internal Revision: A Process of Discovery." In *Research on Composing: Points of Departure,* edited by C. Cooper and L. Odell. Urbana, IL: National Council of Teachers of English.

Page, E. 1968. "The Use of the Computer in Analyzing Student Essays." *International Review of Education* 14: 253–63.

Rosen, H. 1969. An Investigation of the Effects of Differentiated Writing Assignments on the Performance in English Composition of a Selected Group of 15/16-Year-Old Pupils. Unpublished doctoral dissertation, University of London.

Sager, C. 1973. Improving the Quality of Written Composition Through Pupil Use of Rating Scales. Unpublished doctoral dissertation, Boston University.

Squire, J., and R. Applebee. 1968. *High School English Instruction Today: The National Study of High School English Programs.* New York: Appleton-Century-Crofts.

Williams, G. 1972. An Evaluation of the Writing Performance of Students in Grades Seven Through Ten in an Urban Junior and Senior High School Using the Diederich Method of Cooperative Composition Rating, with Attention to Performance of Selected Subgroups. Unpublished doctoral dissertation, Syracuse University.

Wolter, D. 1975. Effect of Feedback on Performance of a Creative Writing Task. Unpublished doctoral dissertation, University of Michigan.

4

The Message of Marking

Teacher Written Responses to Student Writing at Intermediate Grade Levels

Dennis Searle
David Dillon

Abstract

Since teacher expectations for good writing, as communicated in written responses on student compositions, may influence the nature of student writing and since little is known about how teachers respond to student writing, this study was designed to investigate the written responses made by intermediate level teachers to their students' writing. Responses were classified as focusing on content or form of student writing. Classification on another dimension dealt with types of response (evaluation, assessment, instruction, audience response, or moving outside the writing). Findings show that teachers responded overwhelmingly to form. Specific types of responses tended to be of two kinds: (1) evaluation, which was usually of a general nature (e.g., "Well written" or a mark) and (2) instruction, which usually focused on specific language structures by correcting all mechanical errors.

A major finding of language study is that social factors are the primary determinants of verbal behavior in any given situation (Labov, 1969; Stubbs, 1976), The classroom is one social setting in which children produce language, and we might expect that teachers' responses to children's writing might shape their language behavior by giving them indications of teacher expectations.

While research has been conducted on (1) the effects on student writing of particular kinds of responses, (2) the degree of reliability among teachers' evaluations of student writing, and (3) the characteristics of student writing that correlate with teacher evaluation or marks, there is very little information on how teachers actually do respond to student writing, especially beyond the narrow notion of response as evaluation. The value of such a study lies in what it reveals about the teachers who do the responding, particularly their criteria for good writing and their perception of their role in improving student writing.

Review of Related Research

A review of the few studies which describe teacher response to student writing reveals the small amount of attention given to this question and the wide diversity of ways of classifying teacher responses to student writing. Each of the following studies analyzed teachers' written comments on student papers.

McColly (1965) discovered that the comments of high school English teachers possessed general internal properties or dimensions which, in order of importance, were (1) a content-style factor, (2) a tone factor, (3) a visual format factor, and (4) an appropriateness factor.

Marshall (1971) discovered that high school English teachers tended to comment on technical errors in student papers, that their comments on student compositions were limited to symbols and abbreviations, and that there were differences in the nature of comments on grade 10 and grade 12 compositions. Aside from these general conclusions, there seemed to be substantial differences among individual teachers in how they commented on student writing.

Kline (1976) asked college composition teachers to rank order what he called their marking priorities. The focuses, listed in order of frequency of selection, are as follows: errors in use of words, representation of experience insufficiently precise, data not taken into account, inappropriate tone of voice or point of view, unclear thesis, lack of coherence, inaccurate or doubtful assertions, and inconsistency in reasoning or judgment.

Jones (1977) studied the responses of high school English teachers and utilized the work of Diederich, French, and Carlton (1961) which classified responses under one of five headings: ideas, wording, organization, mechanics, and flavor. Jones found that her subjects responded in all five ways with responses being fairly balanced proportionately among the five types.

Purpose and Procedure of the Present Study

The purpose of this study was to describe the nature of teacher written responses to student writing at the intermediate grade levels. Since previous descriptions of such responses had taken place only at the secondary and post-secondary levels, we felt that investigation at the elementary level was necessary. It was also our intention to describe the responses by means of a categorization framework firmly founded on theoretical advances in the nature of language and language learning. Finally, it was our intention to note any variability among the response patterns of individual teachers. Only Marshall (1971) had done that previously.

Twelve intermediate level (grades 4–6) teachers in five elementary schools were asked to submit three different pieces of writing from each of five randomly selected students in their classes (a total of 15 pieces from each teacher). The student writing was to be writing upon which they had already made their usual written comments. Two of these teachers did not make written comments on student writing and one teacher did not submit student writing during the one-month data collection period. Thus, 135 pieces of student writing were collected from nine teachers.

Each of the 12 teachers was also asked to fill out a written questionnaire dealing with their purpose in responding to student writing, other ways in which they responded, any ways in which they followed up on their responses, and their criteria for good writing. This questionnaire was utilized to provide a larger frame of reference within which to investigate each teacher's written responses on students' compositions.

Each written response was then categorized according to the two-dimensional framework shown in Figure 4–1. A major division in the focus of teachers' responses was made between content and form (discourse structure, sentence structure, spelling, punctuation, etc.) of a student's written composition. This division was determined by conclusions reached in the study of language acquisition which indicate that while both language learners and their audience focus primarily on meaning or content, form is learned also. The child's focus, as Halliday (1973) points out, is "learning how to mean." While meaning and purpose of language use is the language learner's central focus, the form of language is learned by means of an actively structured, inductive process on the child's part which can neither be observed nor directly manipulated by others (Fillion, Smith, & Swain, 1976). While much of the research on language acquisition has been based on oral language, recent work (e.g., Read, 1975; Goodman, 1978; Doake, 1979) indicates that the acquisition of literacy may be a similar process.

In addition to the focus of a teacher's response (form or content), five major types of responses seemed to account for all possible responses that a teacher would make: (1) Evaluation is any response that judges worth, (2) assessment determines a student's knowledge and/or ability, (3) instructional responses attempt to teach through explanation, correction, encouragement, etc., (4) the audience category involves the response of an interested reader to the writing, and (5) moving outside the writing goes beyond the writing itself to a further step or stage.

Findings

The results of the categorization of teacher responses appear in Table 4–1. An important explanatory comment that needs to be added to the results is that, in many instances, it could not be determined from context whether comments focused primarily on form or content. In such cases of doubt, the response was categorized as focusing on content. The great majority of responses listed as evaluation or assessment of content are of this ambiguous nature. Examples of

Type of Teacher Response	Focus of Teacher Response	
	Content	Form
Evaluation	Good story! Excellent! Poor ideas! Your best work!	Well written! Good word choice. Poor sentence structure.
Assessment	I see that you know the subject.	You are beginning to use paragraphs.
Instructional (a) didactic/correction	The way people treated the boy is an example of prejudice.	You have several spelling mistakes. Use indentations to signal this new idea.
(b) encouragement	This was very exciting. You should write more.	You used a good variety of sentences. Keep up the good work!
(c) comment on attitude	You haven't researched this very well—try harder.	Don't be so careless with your spelling and handwriting.
Audience (a) clarification	I don't understand what happened here. Can you explain.	Misplaced modifier. Where is your topic sentence?
(b) elaboration	What would this feel like?	Use more descriptive vocabulary.
(c) reaction	I enjoyed that. I felt what you would feel if that happened. I think that should be in the class paper.	You have beautiful handwriting. I'm impressed by your vocabulary.
(d) taking action	Change a classroom procedure in response to a written request.	Have a lesson on quotation marks after seeing that most students in class could not use this in their stories.
Moving outside the writing (a) extension	Tell me more! Have you considered what Bill says?	This anecdote would make a good starting point for a play.
(b) addition	Let me tell you what happened to me. I disagree with what you say.	Your work reminds me of the poetry of e. e. cummings.

Figure 4–1 Classifying Teacher Responses to Pupils' Written Work

Table 4–1 TOTAL RESPONSES OF INDIVIDUAL TEACHERS

Content

	#1	#2	#3	#4	#5	#6	#7	#8	#9	Totals
Evaluation	10	53	87	36	22	8	39	8	22	286**+
Assessment	0	2	1	7	3	4	1	5	5	28
Instruction	3	2	3	5	2	1	1	0	0	15
Audience	4	1	9	5	3	1	2	0	1	26
Moving Outside	0	0	1	0	0	0	0	0	0	1
Unclassified	0	0	0	0	0	0	0	0	0	0
Totals	17	58	100	53	30	14	44	13	28	356 (31%)

Form

	#1	#2	#3	#4	#5	#6	#7	#8	#9	Totals
Evaluation	1	4	0	1	8	6	1	0	0	21
Assessment	2	4	1	2	8	47	0	2	2	68
Instruction	37	100	225	29	210	43	12	2	33	691***+
Audience	2	0	2	0	2	0	0	0	0	6
Moving Outside	0	0	0	0	0	0	0	0	0	0
Unclassified	1	2	0	0	1	0	0	0	0	4
Totals	43	110	228	32	227	94	13	4	35	790 (69%)

*233 of these were marks or checkmarks which is 65% of all content responses.

**685 responses in this category are didactic/correction types of response which is 86.7% of all form responses and 59% of all responses.

+Marks or checkmarks plus didactic/correction responses to form account for 80% of all responses.

such comments include: "Very well done," "Good work," "Good composition," "OK," and "Excellent."

Categorization of Responses

Notwithstanding this fact, the overwhelming focus on form and the predominant use of evaluation and instruction types of response by the teachers in this study is clear from the results. Just as clear is the lack of use of the audience and moving outside the writing categories.

Individual teachers showed relative similarity in their content responses, but greater diversity in their form responses (with totals for individual teacher's responses ranging from 4 to 228). The number of form responses made by individual teachers, however, seems to have been determined in large part by (1) quantity of their students' writing and (2) how mechanically correct the students' writing was. It seemed apparent that almost all teachers tried to correct all mechanical errors (spelling, usage, punctuation) in their students' writing. Thus, teachers whose students made many mechanical errors made many form responses and vice versa.

Because the writing abilities of students affect the nature of response, comparisons among individual teachers are deceptive.

Results of Questionnaire

The participants in the study agreed that their major purpose was to praise or encourage students' efforts. This intention may have accounted for the relatively large number of general comments which were difficult to categorize on a form/content basis (e.g., Well done, Very good, Excellent, etc.). Other major purposes stated by the participants were to diagnose mechanical errors for planning future instruction and to provide the response of an interested reader. The former purpose may be a major reason for the overwhelming focus on form in the students' writing, although few of the teachers' responses assessed student ability. The latter purpose seems at odds with the very small percentage of audience responses made by the teachers. The type of purpose acknowledged most infrequently was to respond to the truth or accuracy of students' statements, which seems to match the minor emphasis given to the content of student writing in the teacher responses.

Participants reported using a variety of formats to provide feedback to students: oral review with the class of an assignment, individual conferences with students, classmates commenting on each other's work and students evaluating themselves. However, the most frequently used format was teacher written comments on student papers, accounting for approximately half of all teacher response to students.

Despite great diversity in follow-up procedures, the most frequently used procedures were (1) teaching based on diagnosis of common group needs in writing and (2) encouraging some sort of "publishing" of student writing (e.g., bulletin board, class newspaper, reading aloud to others).

The criteria for good writing at the intermediate grades listed by the participants were numerous, but relatively uniform. Criteria could be classified in three major categories; mechanics (legible handwriting, correct spelling and punctuation, etc), language structure (correct sentence structures, proper use of tense, good use of topic sentence and good paragraph construction, etc.), and style (interesting style, good variety of sentences, different ideas divided into different paragraphs, imaginative and precise use of vocabulary, good organization, use of connectives, individual style, use of dialogue, etc.). All three categories deal with forms of language. Only one comment by one participant dealt directly with content ("There must be *content* to share with a reader/listener."). The participating teachers' criteria for good writing were accurately reflected in their responses to their students' writing.

Discussion

A small study such as this one, which takes a first look into an area, is useful to the extent that it raises further questions for investigation and provides a foundation for further investigation.

One purpose of this study was to test and refine a classification system for teacher responses. It was found that the system did accommodate teacher responses. Further, it was found that the breakdown of response did provide insight into the teacher's view of composition and method of teaching writing. However, the findings indicated several areas of concern which ultimately led to a refinement of the classification system. These concerns are discussed below.

The Role of the General Comment

There was a body of teacher responses which did not the make the major distinction between form and content. This body of responses included checkmarks, marks, and comments which referred presumably to the piece as a whole. Because the comments apparently included a reference to content they were scored as responses to content. However, this procedure gave an inflated picture of responses to content. In fact, 302 (84%) of the 356 responses to content were of a general nature. Those comments primarily served a "pat-on-the-back" function, as if a kind word would encourage the pupil to improve. These comments did not direct the writer's attention to what in the work had evoked the response. Instead, "good" or "excellent" appeared as a summary response. The remarks tended to be stereotyped according to each teacher. We often wondered what interpretation the pupils put on these comments.

The Concentration of Form-Correction Response

As reported, 59% of all responses were classified as didactic/correction-form. Such a heavy concentration caused us to question the classification system and to examine the items placed in this category to see if refinement were possible. This examination revealed three quite different areas—mechanics, structures, and style—all related to form.

We saw these focuses falling along a continuum from mechanics to style. Two summary statements reveal the nature of the continuum.

1. In moving from mechanics to style there is a movement from *mechanics*, which relates to smaller elements such as words, through phrases, sentences, and paragraphs which we called elements of *structure*, to larger discourse considerations which we called *style*.

2. In moving from mechanics to style there is a movement from more clearcut rules for right and wrong with little room for pupil choice to more openended principles from which the writer has considerable choice in determining how to achieve his purposes.

Examination of teacher responses also suggested that teachers handled these aspects of form differently, allowing the following generalizations.

1. Most responses are at the mechanics end of the continuum and progressively fewer as the focus moves toward style.

2. Mechanics errors are corrected ("Should be *their*"). Structural errors are noted and are seldom corrected ("Watch your tenses"). Style concerns receive a more general comment and are rarely corrected ("Limited dialogue").

3. At the mechanics end of the continuum the comments are cognitive and negative ("*Mars* should be capitalized"). At the style end of the continuum the comments are most likely to be positive and affective ("Your ideas are well presented").

It would seem that teachers correct at the mechanics end because that is where the corrections are most apparent and correspond to some well-established standard.

The Role of Responses to Content

The limited number of responses to content suggested that the participating teachers did not operate with the view that a focus on the meaning and purpose of language is basic to language development. The majority of responses were to form, and, the great majority of responses to content were general comments or marks. In fact, from 356 responses, only 28 were clearly related to specific aspects of content. This low number of responses to content indicated clearly that the teachers saw writing as practice in mastering forms of writing,

the what Content fewer	Style	the how Structure	Mechanics greater number of
responses generalizations		errors noted	responses specific correction of
evaluation made no correction		not corrected	all errors little assessment
affective and			cognitive and
positive responses			negative responses

Figure 4–2 Teacher Responses

beginning with a mastery of mechanics and developing a mastery of large structures. There was little evidence of teachers attempting to develop thinking through writing. The message about language which seemed to be communicated was that it doesn't matter what you say; what matters is how you say it.

In the preceding discussion a continuum of teacher responses to aspects of form, ranging from responses to mechanics to responses to style, was proposed. This continuum could be extended to include responses to content as in Figure 4–2.

Assessment of Errors

A final insight into the kinds of responses made by the teachers in this study was the limited use of assessment. Assessment can be considered as looking for generalizable features of pupils' writing which may note stages of development or basic sources of error and difficulty. The tendency was to treat each error as an individual problem in need of individual correction.

Although a preliminary look at the responses of the teachers involved in the study suggested diversity in response, closer examination revealed that there was great commonality. In light of our data, a typical response would include the following: (1) a grade clearly displayed, (2) correction of whatever mechanical errors appeared, (3) a comment on structural concerns and (4) a general comment of encouragement. This typical response corresponds to Squire's (1975) picture of the typical North American treatment of writing as a "write-correct-revise syndrome of instruction."

Revision of the Classification System

The need to accommodate general comments and to differentiate among varied responses to form led to a revision of the classification system, which appears in Figure 4–3.

Type	Focus			
	Content	Form		
Evaluation		Style	Structure	Mechanics
Assessment				
INSTRUCTIONAL (a) didactic/correction (b) encouragement (c) attitude				
AUDIENCE (a) clarification (b) elaboration (c) reaction (d) taking action				
MOVING BEYOND (a) extension (b) addition				
GENERAL COMMENT (a) Grading (b) Impression				
UNCLASSIFIED				

Figure 4–3 Classification of Teachers' Responses to Children's Written Work

A separate entry for general comments includes a place for general grades and for overall impression. On occasions, teachers give grades explicitly for content or mechanics. In such instances, the response would be classified as specifically stated. Other grades would be placed in this general entry.

The revised form also includes a breakdown of form categories for evaluation, assessment and instructional types of response. This breakdown was not extended into audience and moving beyond types because data obtained do not demand such refinement for those types of response. Rather than clarifying the nature of response, confusion could be created through the establishment of several possible responses which would exist in theory only.

Further Research

A preliminary study such as this one raises questions for further study and provides directions for answering those questions.

A first concern is to develop more data. The teachers who participated in this research were atypical in that writing was a regular part of their classroom activity. Many other teachers were unable to provide writing for us. It would seem, therefore, that some pupils may, in fact, receive no response to their writing. We need to broaden our study to look at the amount of writing done, to include more schools and more teachers. We need to look at writing across the curriculum to determine if content receives greater emphasis in some subjects. We need to extend the study to include lower elementary classrooms and junior and senior high classrooms.

We also need to establish a total picture from which to view the data. This would include observing the larger framework of instruction, in order that teacher response can be related to what happens before writing and after work is returned. We need to look at what is communicated in feedback to the class, in student-teacher conferences, and through peer interaction.

Further attention should be given to the criteria used by teachers in making judgments. What do teachers consider to be "good writing"? How do they communicate this to their pupils? A part of this question would involve a comparison of teacher responses to pupils' writing with the responses of other groups, such as parents, preservice teachers, and professional writers.

A final, central, and most difficult consideration is the question of how responses affect pupils. We need to determine what effects specific types of responses have on pupils' writing. We need to know how pupils interpret the responses they receive. We need to test the assumption that a primary focus on content can be viewed as a means of improving form.

The classification system gives us a way of observing particular features of the teacher-pupil dialogue. It relates responses to theoretical views on how writing develops. Perhaps it can help teachers become aware of the nature of their own responses to students' writing.

References

Deiderich, P. B., J. W. French, and S. T. Carlton. 1961. *Factors in Judgments of Writing Ability.* Princeton, NJ: Educational Testing Service.

Doake, D. Reading: A Language Learning Activity. 1979. Paper presented at IRA/University of Victoria Research Seminar on Linguistic Awareness and Learning to Read, Victoria, British Columbia.

Fillion, B., F. Smith, and M. Swain. 1976. "Language 'Basics' for Language Teachers: Towards a Set of Universal Considerations." *Language Arts* 57: 740–45.

Goodman, Y. 1978. Personal communication.

Halliday, M. A. K. 1973. *Learning How to Mean: Explorations in the Development of Language.* London: Edward Arnold.

Jones, B. E. 1977. Marking of Student Writing by High School English Teachers in Virginia in 1976. Unpublished doctoral dissertation, University of Virginia.

Kline, C. 1976. "I Know You Think You Know What I Said." *College English* 37: 661–62.

Labov, W. 1969. "The Logic of Nonstandard English." In *Tinker, Tailor . . . The Myth of Cultural Deprivation* edited by N. Keddie. Harmondsworth: Penguin.

McColly, W. 1965. *The Dimensions of Composition Annotation.* Oswego, NY: State University of New York at Oswego.

Marshall, B. 1971. A Survey and Analysis of Teachers' Markings on Selected Compositions of Average Students in Grades 10 and 12. Unpublished doctoral dissertation, State University of New York at Buffalo.

Read, C. 1975. *Children's Categorization of Speech Sounds.* Urbana, IL: National Council of Teachers of English.

Squire, J. 1975. "Composing—A New Emphasis for the Schools." In *The Writing Processses of Students* edited by W. Petty and P. Finn. Buffalo, NY: Department of Elementary and Remedial Education, State University of New York at Buffalo.

Stubbs, M. 1976. *Language, Schools, and Classrooms.* London: Methuen.

5

Teacher Commentary on Student Writing

The State of the Art

C. H. Knoblauch
Lil Brannon

Arguably, nothing we do as writing teachers is more valuable than our commenting on individual student texts in order to facilitate improvement. We know that successful writers achieve their communicative purposes by correctly anticipating the needs and expectations of intended readers. We also know that inexperienced writers find it especially difficult to imagine audience responses in advance or to use them as a guide to composing. Accordingly, we comment on student essays to dramatize the presence of a reader who depends on the writer's choices in order to perceive the intent of a discourse. Thoughtful commentary describes when communication has occurred and when it has not, raising questions that the writer may never have considered from a reader's point of view. The aim of repeated cycles of writing, teacher response (perhaps peer response as well), and more writing is to enable students gradually to internalize this Questioning Reader so that they can better realize their intentions. Presumably, the more facilitative voices people hear in response to their writing, and the more often they hear them, the more quickly they will achieve that internal control of choices which our teaching strives to nurture.

At any rate, so the theory goes. The depressing trouble is, we have scarcely a shred of empirical evidence to show that students typically even comprehend our responses to their writing, let alone use them purposefully to modify their practice. This is not to say that we have never sought empirical support. Over the past 25 years, from J. H. Warmsbacker in 1955 to Searle and Dillon in 1980,[1] better than two dozen studies have looked at diverse modes of teacher intervention, and compared their effects, within student populations ranging from grade school to college age. Nina Ziv's recent study of the relevant literature[2] shows the diversity, but also the futility, of this completed work. Some research has contrasted responses offering praise with others offering criticism, for instance, Taylor and Hoedt in 1966[3] or Earl Seidman in 1967.[4] Not surprisingly, this research concluded that students who are praised tend to write longer essays and to have better attitudes about writing. But it also found no necessary connection between higher motivation and a higher quality of performance. Other researchers have contrasted oral and written comments, including McGrew in 1969, Coleman in 1973, and Miller in 1978.[5] Again, attitudes seemed better among students who received taped oral responses than among those who received only comments written on their essays. But neither group wrote demonstrably better essays because of the commentary they received. In 1972 Evelyn Bata contrasted marginal and end comments but found no important differences in their impact.[6] Marzano and Arthur, in 1978, wrote varying types of comment to students in three different groups, one group receiving abbreviated grammatical responses ("awk," "sp"), one receiving actual corrections of mechanical errors, and the third receiving substantive commentary "designed to foster thinking," Once again, no significant differences in the quality of student writing could be discerned.[7] The morose conclusion of their study could well summarize a dominant impression to be gained from all the research cited here: "different types of teacher comments on student themes have equally small influences on student writing. For all practical purposes, commenting on student essays might just be an exercise in futility. Either students do not read the comments or they read them and do not attempt to implement suggestions and correct errors."

Actually, Marzano and Arthur overlooked the drearier possibility that students simply fail to appreciate what teachers are trying to tell them. Jean King approaches this conclusion in a 1979 study of certain types of grammatical intervention.[8] King discriminated three varieties of comment, one an outright correction of errors, a second only naming kinds of error (*e.g.*, "lacks subject-verb agreement"), and a third offering rules (*e.g.*, "singular subjects take singular verbs"). She found that students rarely understood directly corrective commentary and that, even when they did understand comments in the other two categories, they were not necessarily aided by either, or by one more than the other, in making corrections on their own. The implications of her research, to the extent that they can be generalized, are as plain as they are troubling: (1) students often do not comprehend teacher responses to their writing; (2) even when they do, they do not always use those responses and may not know how to use them; (3) when they use them, they do not necessarily write more effectively as a result. In light of these findings, the question whether one type of comment might be more or less helpful than another is conspicuously irrelevant.

Is there reason to persevere in the time-honored practice of commenting on student essays in the face of all these unpromising empirical studies of its relevance to writing improvement? Seemingly, either that practice is deficient and the available research has proven it so, or the research is somehow deficient and has failed to reveal the true promise in teacher commentary. We would argue that responding supportively to student writing is indeed central to enlightened instruction, despite the apparent weight of evidence to the contrary. But we would also implicate both previous research assumptions and certain traditional commenting practices in the repeated failure of studies endeavoring to show its value. One problem is methodological: it concerns the habitual focus of these studies on types or modes of commentary, which has led researchers to expect too much from isolated marginal remarks on essays and to reflect too little on the larger conversation between teacher and student to which they only contribute. A second, more important problem concerns the actual practice of commenting, its peripheral and largely judgmental role in conventional teaching. If research efforts have failed to show the use of teacher commentary, one reason may be the larger ineffectiveness of the instructional format within which it has been evaluated. In other words, those efforts may say more about the limitations of a widespread and traditional teaching method than about the potential value of our intervention in student composing.

Consider, first, the matter of research focus. Nearly every study has distinguished types of comment and then tried to evaluate the impact of one type against another. We have already noted the implausibility of attempting to determine degrees of effectiveness amidst such gross uncertainty about the value of *any* kind of commenting. But the problem of focus goes beyond its present impracticality: even when we can finally show the positive effect of intervention under certain conditions, we will not necessarily be able to prove a qualitative difference in types. For the implicit assumptions of such an undertaking are, first, that the process of commenting can be isolated from the whole environment of oral and written communication between teacher and student, and, second, that categories of response can be further isolated according to the intrinsic merits of their superficial features (such as, statement versus question, or marginal comment versus end comment, or abbreviated reference versus extended reference) and thereby ordered as a hierarchy. It is hard to imagine that any experienced writing teacher would find intuitive validity in either of these assumptions. The first one in particular seems demonstrably false.

The flaw in both assumptions lies in their reductive view of the dialogue between teachers and their students. A single comment on a single essay is too local and contingent a phenomenon to yield general conclusions about the quality of the conversation of which it is a part. Any remark on a student essay, whatever its form, finally owes its meaning and impact to the governing dialogue that influences some student's reaction to it. Remarks taken out of this context can appear more restrictive or open-ended, more facilitative or judgmental, than they really are in light of a teacher's overall communicative habits. Potentially facilitative questions ("Is this really the best word to use here?"; "Can't you be more specific?") may be implicitly judgmental if an instructor's posture in the classroom tends to be judgmental. Grammatical references ("See Harbrace, p. 53"; "Comma splice") can be facilitative, not merely evaluative, if the teacher has previously shown ways to respond to them. Therefore, the difference that Kelley introduces in her 1973 study of "clarifying" versus "directive" responses,[9] or that Ziv offers between "explicit" and "implicit" revision cues, or that Seidman describes between praise and blame comments, is probably illusory, since individual teachers can make superficially similar comments bearing vastly different connotations. Other surface features such as the location of comments or their oral versus written form are certainly distinguishable, but their difference seems largely irrelevant to the issue of communicative effect. We suspect that, if it ever becomes possible to separate modes of teacher response, the starting point will be, not the superficial features of comments, but the attitudes, postures, and motives that teachers communicate both through and apart from their reactions to particular texts. Perhaps we will discover commenting styles, such as the Harsh Grammatical Critic, the Kindly Question-Raiser, or the Old-Fashioned Nitpicker, rather than commenting "types."

In any case, the problem of research focus is secondary to a larger difficulty concerning our typical practice as responders to student writing, a practice that has conditioned the persistently negative findings accumulated over the past quarter century. Most studies have accepted, as a "given" of the research setting, the view that commenting is essentially a product-centered, evaluative activity resembling literary criticism. Conventionally, students write essays and teachers describe their strengths and weaknesses, grading them accordingly. The essays are then retired and new ones are composed, presumably under the influence of recollected judgments of the previous ones. Our assumption has been that evaluating the product of composing is equivalent to intervening in the process. Teachers concentrate on retrospective appraisals of "finished" discourses, so that students seldom rewrite in direct response to comments. Rather, they only notice the critical reception of earlier work and strive to do better next time. The recent *RTE* study by Searle and Dillon shows how pervasive this procedure is: they categorized 59% of the responses to student writing in their survey as "didactic/correction form," that is, summatively judgmental in their intent. By contrast, they found practically no responses in the category "moving outside the writing," that is, anticipating eventual revision (p. 239).

We suspect that intervening in the composing process, by allowing students to write successive drafts immediately responding to facilitative commentary, can measurably improve student writing, provided that a teacher adequately supports revising efforts. Certain studies already bear out parts of this surmise. The earliest of them dates, in fact, from 1936, when John Fellows showed that students receiving mechanics corrections with the chance to revise improved in grammar and punctuation[10]—not a startling conclusion but perhaps a suggestive one. A more contemporary, and more broadly conceived, study is Ziv's, in which students rewrote essays in response to both technical and rhetorical "revision cues" ranging from "explicit" directives to "implicit" suggestions for development. Her results show that intervention can affect writing improvement in multiple-draft assignments. Apparently, students found explicit technical and rhetorical advice more helpful than merely suggestive comments, as we might expect. But even her implicit cues stimulated rewriting, although the expanded statements often featured new grammatical and organizational problems. Ziv suggests, ingeniously, that teachers gradually adjust their emphasis from explicit to implicit cues as students grow more comfortable with their expectations and more adept at anticipating them. In any case, her research supports the potential of teacher intervention as a central activity of workshop instruction concerned with stimulating and directing revision. It successfully argues the advantage of making our commentary facilitative rather than merely evaluative.

However, an important limitation in this positive research is that it fails to consider the natural impediments to revising that we can assume in most inexperienced writers, a resistance that grows more acute as more radical rewriting is suggested. As a result, few of the studies that have included direct student response to teacher comments have shown the happy results that Ziv achieved. In a 1963 study, for example, Louis Arnold asked one group of students to revise with reference to teacher comments while a second group did not. After a year, he could find no difference in the performance of the two groups, suggesting that the chance to rewrite did not affect growth.[11] Kelley reached a similar conclusion in 1973, finding no difference in writers' maturation as a result of opportunities to revise in light of "clarifying" or "directive" commentary. But the deficiency in these studies, we believe, is their assumption that revising is a spontaneous, self-initiating activity for unskilled writers, requiring no explicit support from teachers beyond simply focusing attention on errors or development possibilities. The experience of countless writing teachers argues the inadequacy of this expectation.

Our own experiences in workshop classrooms, where students revise through several drafts, has been that unsophisticated writers ordinarily limit their revising to changes that minimally affect the plan and order of ideas with which they began, readily making only those adjustments that place least pressure on them to reconceive or significantly extend the writing they have already done. Often, their revised statements are actually poorer than the first drafts because of their reticence to change anything that has not attracted specific attention, even when a recommended change in one place implicitly necessitates changes elsewhere. The motive for this resistance seems more complicated than laziness. We think the resistance is natural, rising out of the anxiety that even experienced writers feel at having to reduce an achieved coherence, however inadequate, to the chaos of fragments and undeveloped insights from which they started. Practiced writers overcome their anxiety through habitual success in rewriting, but no such comforting pattern of successes exists to steady the resolve of the apprentice. Hence, we should not be surprised that revision, which entails repudiating what we may have struggled

mightily to say in the mere hope of saying it better, represents a more sophisticated compositional habit than the young writer may yet have developed.

Nor is this natural psychological resistance the only barrier to self-initiated
revising. Even assuming that our commenting language is clear (and obviously
it is not always), another barrier is the ordinary student's inability to perceive
alternatives to the choices that have already been made, choices that lie reified
as a document. The temptation is strong, even among experienced writers, to
forget the arbitrariness of so many initial decisions about what to say and where
or how to say it, imagining in retrospect an inevitability about the patterns and
connections that make up the existing discourse. Seeing through that apparent
inevitability in order to recover additional options requires an intellectual discipline and a rhetorical awareness that beginning writers frequently lack, even
when their writing suggests a fairly mature verbal competence. Writers with
underdeveloped verbal skills will have all the more difficulty conceiving what
else might be said when herculean effort may already have been required to say
anything at all. We must concede the fact that commenting on drafts will not,
by itself, inevitably assure effective follow-through in revision efforts.
Additional support must attend the stages of rewriting.

Minimally, that support would include helping students to understand the
comments they receive, both by defining our commenting vocabularies in
advance and by discussing plans for revision before students actually attempt
to rewrite. Once rewriting has occurred, we might also wish to review the new
choices, emphasizing the positive value of changes, deletions, and additions in
revised essays. But a different kind of assistance may be the most valuable of
all: it involves preparing students to appreciate the potential for development
implicit in their writing and to tolerate the pressures that accompany extensive
revision in the effort to realize that potential. This is, of course, no easy matter. Frequent efforts to rewrite paragraphs or short paragraph sequences, which
can be done rather painlessly, and then discussing the changes, might help to
create a receptive attitude about the advantages of rewriting. But however we
undertake to stimulate the habit of revising, we should bear in mind that it
entails learned skills requiring some conscious nurturing and guidance before
it is likely to assume a substantial role in the typical student's composing
process.

We have found only one study that includes, at least embryonically, all the
features of effective instruction that might enable researchers to show the real
value of teacher intervention. In 1958 Earl Buxton asked one group of students
to revise essays in response to extensive commentary while another group,
which also received comments, did no revising. The "revision group" rewrote
their essays in class as raters went from student to student answering questions
and giving advice. A statistical analysis of pre- and post-test scores suggested
that writers who revised their work improved demonstrably compared to those
who did not revise.[12] One study hardly makes the case for requiring guided
rewriting following teacher commentary. But it may offer a prototype for

additional, more restrictively designed research based on the teaching model that Buxton implicitly recommends and that we have been describing. The model includes these features: (1) an emphasis on writers' performance rather than exclusively on their finished products; (2) a facilitative rather than judgmental view of our commenting practices; (3) a preference for multiple-draft assignments so that teachers can intervene directly in their students' composing and so that students can respond directly through revision; (4) a concern for actively educating students, perhaps through short, acclimating exercises, about what rewriting involves (and how it is different from editing), what it can accomplish, and how it can be done; (5) a concern for supporting revision by insuring that students understand what comments mean, by discussing possible changes and additions before rewriting begins, and by reviewing completed revisions, perhaps in conference, to see what they have achieved. Assuming this teaching environment, new research might profitably seek, not to discriminate comment types by their presumed intrinsic merits or deficiencies, but rather to study the full teacher-student dialogue accompanying efforts to shape writers' performance. Knowing more about this dialogue, the unspoken motives and agendas on each side that make communicating such a delicate enterprise, ought to improve the subtlety as well as the purposefulness of our more local commentary on student writing. Research that aspires to such a knowledge may enjoy a double effect, in showing the positive value of teacher intervention as it occurs in the best classrooms, but also in revealing ways to improve it through a richer understanding of the larger conversation in which it plays a part.

Notes

1. J. H. Warmsbacker, 1955. A Comparative Study of Three Methods of Grading Compositions. Unpublished Master's Thesis. University of British Columbia. Dennis Searle and David Dillon. 1980. "The Message of Marking: Teacher Written Responses to Student Writing at Intermediate Grade Levels." *Research in the Teaching of English* 14 (October):233–42. The fact that most of the empirical work on teacher commentary is in the form of graduate, usually doctoral level studies suggests a critical need for additional research by more experienced professional investigators.

2. Nina Ziv. 1981. The Effect of Teacher and Peer Comments on the Writing of Four College Freshmen. Unpublished Ph.D. Dissertation. New York University.

3. Winnifred F. Taylor and Kenneth C. Hoedt. 1966. "The Effect of Praise Upon the Quality of Creative Writing." *Journal of Education Research* 60:80–83.

4. Earl Seidman. 1967. Marking Students' Compositions; Implications for Achievement Motivation Theory. Unpublished Ph.D. Dissertation, Stanford University.

5. Jean B. McGrew. 1969. "An Experiment to Assess the Effectiveness of the Dictation Machine as an Aid to Teachers in the Evaluation and Improvement of Student Compositions." Report to Lincoln Public Schools, Lincoln, Nebraska (ERIC 034776). V. B. Coleman. 1973. A Comparison Between the Relative Effectiveness of

Marginal-Interlinear-Terminal Commentary and of Audio Tape Commentary in Responding to Student Compositions. Unpublished Ph.D. Dissertation. University of Pittsburgh. T. E. Miller. A Comparison of the Effects of Oral and Written Teacher Feedback Only on Specific Writing Behaviors of Fourth Grade Children, Unpublished Ed.D. Dissertation, Ball State University.

6. Evelyn J. Bata. 1972. A Study of the Relative Effectiveness of Marking Techniques on Junior College Freshmen English Composition. Unpublished Ph.D. Dissertation, University of Maryland.

7. R. J. Marzano and S. Arthur. 1977. "Teacher Comments on Student Essays: It Doesn't Matter What You Say." Study at University of Colorado, Denver (ERIC, ED 147864).

8. Jean Anne King. 1979. Teachers' Comments on Students' Writing: A Conceptual Analysis and Empirical Study. Unpublished Ph.D. Dissertation, Cornell University.

9. Marie E. Kelley. 1974. Effects of Two Types of Teacher Response to Essays. Unpublished Ph.D. Dissertation. Michigan State University.

10. John E. Fellows. 1936. The Influence of Theme Reading and Theme Correction on Eliminating Technical Errors in the Written Composition of Ninth Grade Pupils. Unpublished Ph.D. Dissertation. University of Iowa.

11. Louis V. Arnold. 1963. Effects of Frequency of Writing and Intensity of Teacher Evaluation Upon Performance in Written Composition of Tenth-Grade Students. Unpublished Ph.D. Dissertation. Florida State University.

12. Earl W. Buxton. 1958. An Experiment to Test the Effects of Writing Frequency and Guided Practice upon Students' Skills in Written Expression. Unpublished Ph.D. Dissertation. Stanford University.

6

The Interaction of Instruction, Teacher Comment, and Revision in Teaching the Composing Process

George Hillocks, Jr.

Abstract. This research examines the effects of three treatment conditions: 1) observational activity preceding writing, or assignment only; 2) regular revision or no revision; and 3) brief teacher comments or extensive comments. Two pre-tests and two post-tests (all writing samples) were collected from 278 seventh and eighth graders in twelve classes taught by three teachers in two schools. These compositions were coded, mixed randomly together, and scored by three raters who achieved intraclass rater reliabilities for three raters from .95 to .98. Results show significant gains for each instructional set: observational activity with revision, observational activity and no revision, assignment with revision, and assignment and no revision. As predicted, the assignment/no revision group made the least gains, significantly lower than the observational activity/no revision group. Analysis of covariance of mean gain scores with IQ as a single covariate revealed significant two-way interactions between instruction and revision and between instruction and comment type.

This study examines the effects of stressing three phases of the composing process in the teaching of composition. Two of them, feedback (especially in the form of teacher comments and marks) and revision (as implied in the assignment to write first and second drafts) have been assumed for years to be efficacious. The third, observation of data, is related to invention, which has witnessed a revival of interest over the past two decades. These three variables and their control conditions require explanation.

Feedback: The Effects of Teacher Comment

Audience response or feedback is ignored in popular studies of the composing process (e.g., Emig, 1971; Pianko, 1979; Perl, 1979). Conditions and goals of the research, namely the necessity for writers to express thoughts aloud as they write in the presence of an observer or recorder, prohibit explicit feedback. Rhetoricians have long been aware of the importance of both predicting probable audience response and attending to actual response. Teachers and pedagogical theorists (e.g., Moffett, 1968) have attended to the need for feedback, and at least one has incorporated attention to audience response as an explicit element in a model of the composing process (McCabe, 1971).

Audience response may be conveniently divided into three types in school settings: teacher comment, response from peers, and audience response predicted by the writer in the course of writing. Most available studies have been concerned with the effects of teacher comment, and for good reason. An important question about composition teaching is whether or not the time spent in commenting on compositions makes a difference. A number of studies have examined the effect of teacher comment alone. Gee (1972) studied the effects of praise, negative criticism, and "no comment." Four compositions written in four weeks were not preceded by instruction. Nor were the topics linked for instructional purposes. Although he was able to find no differences in the quality of writing, Gee did find that students receiving negative comment and no comment wrote significantly fewer T-units and had significantly more negative attitudes about the four writing experiences than did the praised students. Taylor and Hoedt (1966), Stevens (1973), and Hausner (1975), have all shown that students receiving negative comments display less desirable attitudes toward some facet of writing than do those receiving positive comments. None, however, has shown differences in the quality of writing.

Stiff (1967) and Bata (1972) studied the effects of marginal, terminal, and mixed marginal-terminal comments on the writing of college students over the period of a semester. Both writers report no significant differences among the various groups, and more interestingly, no significant differences from pre-test to post-test.

Other studies have examined the effects of teacher comment in relation to such variables as frequency of writing and revision. Burton and Arnold (1964) examined the effects of frequent writing (one 250 word composition per week) vs. infrequent writing (three 250 word compositions per semester) and the effects of intensive evaluation (marking every error and writing detailed comments) vs. moderate evaluation (grading only an occasional paper or correcting only errors related to skills students were studying at the time). The study found no significant differences among the four groups, concluding that neither frequent practice nor intensive marking will necessarily result in increased writing skill. Sutton and Allen (1964) studied 112 college freshmen divided randomly into six treatment groups. One group did no writing at all. Another wrote a theme a week which was evaluated by peers, while still another wrote one theme per week which was evaluated by professors. All students wrote six pre-test compositions and six post-test compositions. Each composition was evaluated by five raters using the Diederich scale. The mean composition scores for all sections declined significantly ($p < .01$).

Revision

Buxton (1958) studied frequency of writing and teacher comment in conjunction with revision. He used three groups of randomly assigned college students. A control group did no writing. The writing and revision group wrote one 500 word essay per week for sixteen weeks on assigned topics, each with intensive teacher evaluation and teacher supervised revision during a class period. The writing group wrote as many essays but were not required to write on an assigned topic. They received only three to four sentences of comment at the end of the paper and did no revision. Both the writing group and the writing/revision group made significant gains over the control group. All groups made gains from the pre-test to the post-test essays. The revision group's gain was significantly higher than that made by the other groups. However, the design of the study prevents our knowing whether to attribute the difference to revision, intensive marking, the requirement of particular topics, or some combination of these.

Beach (1979) posed a question about the effects of between-drafts evaluation on the revisions made by high school students. Using three groups of randomly assigned students, he asked one group to revise without intervening evaluation. A second group received evaluation from a teacher. The third group used a pre-designed form to evaluate their own writing. Rough and final drafts were mixed together and assigned to three judges for "degree of change" ratings and for quality ratings on various dimensions. The teacher evaluation group received significantly higher "degree of change" ratings than either of the other groups. However, they received higher quality evaluations only on the dimension of support, not on the dimensions of sequence, sentences, language, flavor, or focus. Further, there were no significant differences in quality ratings over the three sets of drafts for any of the groups.

Finally, a carefully designed study by Bridwell (1980) involved 100 high school seniors who were asked to write about a place which they knew well and to write so that another twelfth grader reading the essay would "be able to recognize the thing or place if he or she ever got the chance to see it for real" (p. 202). Students were first encouraged to collect "facts" about the place to bring to class for use while writing. Students had three days for the writing: one for the first drafts, one for revising the first draft, and a third for producing a final draft. In the process students averaged 61 revisions each. Their first and final drafts were submitted to raters trained in the use of the Diederich scale. The results reveal significantly higher scores for the second drafts than for the first ($p < .001$) on both general merit and mechanics.

Pre-writing Activities: Invention and Observation

A number of rhetoricians and teachers (e.g., Pike, 1964a and b, and Odell, 1974) have argued the necessity of helping students learn to deal with data as a prerequisite for writing. Although studies of the composing process (e.g., Emig, 1971; Pianko, 1979; Perl, 1979) neglect the problem of how writers deal with data before they write, it is intuitively obvious that some processes of screening, differentiating, integrating, and organizing must take place before writing begins. If not, the writing would appear as an undifferentiated mass—somewhat like overcooked rice left out on the table overnight. Though in many ways different from what is generally meant by invention, observational activities have a similar goal—to help students consider more carefully the data they write about (Hillocks, 1975). Odell (1974) strongly suggests that learning and practicing a heuristic results in writing which examines data more thoroughly. Hillocks (1979) indicates that the ninth and eleventh graders in his sample made significantly greater gains in specificity, organization, and support through observing and writing activities than through the traditional study of paragraph structure. Further, such gains are achievable in a relatively short period of time, ten to fifteen hours of classroom instruction.

Design

Instructional Variables

Nearly all the studies of teacher comment and revision share one feature in common: they ignore or preclude pre-writing instruction designed to prepare students for particular writing assignments. The studies of Gee, Buxton, and several others view instruction in composition as consisting of an assignment, the writing done by the student, and whatever happens after the fact of the student writing. They assume that the main effects on writing skill derive from an assignment plus the follow-up to the assignment—teacher comment or revision. That English teachers view assignment making as crucial to improving student writing is indicated by the persistence of such publications as *A Thousand Topics for Composition; Second Edition* (Sherer, 1980) and by the continued appearance of such articles as Throckmorton (1980) and its companion piece, "What's a surefire topic for non-sure-fire students?" (*English Journal*, 1980, 69(8): 62–69). Undoubtedly, the more interesting the topic, the better student response is likely to be. But sequences of high interest topics, with or without follow-up, have not yet been shown to bring about change in writing skill. This study examines the assignment assumption against previously tested observational activity.

Writing instruction for half the classes in this study, then, consisted of sets of observing and writing activities with the goal of increasing specificity, focus, and impact in a given piece. Each set of activities led to one of four interim composition assignments. The observing/writing activities, described in detail in Hillocks (1975), included the examination of sets of objects presumably belonging to one person and inferring personal qualities (pp. 7–8), examining various textures tactilely while wearing blindfolds (p. 9), examining and describing sea shells (pp. 9–10), listening to and describing sounds (pp. 10–11), doing physical exercise and describing bodily sensations (pp. 14–16), examining and describing pictures (pp. 16–18), pantomiming and describing brief scenarios (pp. 18–19), developing and acting out dialogues (pp. 19–21), and, finally, examining two model compositions for about one-half of one class period. All of these activities are designed to elicit high levels of student response concerning ideas for describing what has been observed, the listing of more and more precise details, judging the most effective details, and so forth, in small, student directed groups or in whole class teacher-led discussions. The instructional goal is to elicit responses to materials and activities in such a way that students respond to each other's comments with more ideas, questions, and evaluations and, in the process, become more and more aware of what the particular writing task involves and how others are likely to respond to their efforts. (See Hillocks, 1981, for the responses of college freshmen to this "environmental" mode of instruction.)

The control instructional condition consisted of the assignment of interim compositions plus motivational discussions preceding each. That is, prior to the writing, teachers led discussions helping students consider ideas they might use, particular details they might include, how they might focus their ideas, and so forth. Thus, the instructional control classes represent the widespread faith in the efficacy of assignments and follow-up, with the difference in this experiment, however, that all assignments and teacher comments were focused on increasing specificity, focus, and impact.

Teacher Comment Variables

Previous studies of the effects of teacher comment have examined certain dimensions of teacher comment including negative vs. positive, marginal vs. terminal, and extensive vs. intensive. They have not shown differences in the quality of writing. However, a comparison of the studies suggests an implicit aspect of teacher comment which all have in common: the comments are diffuse, ranging from substance, organization, and style to mechanics and punctuation. If teacher comments over a series of compositions focused on a particular aspect of writing, would they have greater effect? Beach (1979) attributes the higher quality ratings for "support" to the greater emphasis on support in the teacher comments. Experience suggests that concentrating comments on a particular aspect of writing might have a significant effect. Accordingly, this study examines focused comments. That is, all teacher comment, regardless of the instructional condition, focused on increasing the specificity, focus, and impact of the writing. All comments were positive and included suggestions for improvement.

Given the amount of time which teachers spend on writing comments, it seemed worthwhile to determine whether extended comments were more effective than brief comments. Brief comments were arbitrarily limited to ten words or fewer, while extended comments were to average well over ten words. A brief comment was to include a compliment and at least one suggestion for improvement. Extended comments were to include one or more compliments and very specific suggestions for improvement.

Revision Variables

Studies of revision have shown that students do make revisions from a first draft to a final draft and that the revisions improve the compositions in quality. However, an important pedagogical question remains unanswered; Does practice in revising increase writing skill? That is, does practice in revising increase the quality of subsequent first drafts? The present study addresses this question in conjunction with its questions about the effects of instruction and teacher comment. Students in half of the classes were asked to make revisions on each of the interim compositions.

Three teachers in two schools were enlisted to participate in this study, two from an upper middle class middle school in Chicago's North Shore area, one from a school in a blue collar community in northwest Indiana. Each of the teachers had four classes which participated in the study. In the Indiana school all four classes were eighth grade. In the North Shore school five classes were eighth grade, and three were seventh. This arrangement was necessitated by the difficulty of finding teachers with four classes at the same grade level. The one year difference in grade level was not considered to be significant.

Instructional sets were assigned randomly to the teachers' classes so that each teacher had one class with each of the following sets: observing and writing activities plus revision; observing and writing activities without revision; assignment plus revision: and assignment without revision. In addition, each class was divided randomly in half with one-half receiving brief comments and the other half receiving extended comments. This results in a $2 \times 2 \times 2$ design to test the following hypotheses:

1. The use of observing and writing activities without revision will result in statistically significant gains comparable to those achieved in earlier experiments (Hillocks, 1979).

2. Revision in conjunction with observational activity will result in greater gains than for observational activities alone or for revision alone.

3. The use of observational activity, revision, or the combination of the two will result in greater gains than instruction through assignment alone.

4. The effects of extended comments will be greater than those of brief comments.

Although interactions among the conditions were expected, no specific hypotheses were developed for interactions. All hypotheses were in the null form for statistical analysis.

Two pre-tests were administered, the first, five days and the second, one day prior to instruction. Two post-tests were also administered, the first on the day following the conclusion of instruction, the second four days later. The pre- and post-tests asked students to write in response to the following two assignments:

1. Write about a person, place, or idea that you feel strongly about. Be as specific as you can so that a person reading what you have written will feel as you do about it, will feel what you feel and see what you see.

2. Write about an experience that you feel strongly about. Be as specific. . . .

These topics are virtually the same as those used in Hillocks (1979).

The instructional period for each class was approximately four weeks. In the observation classes the time was taken up with observing and writing activities, motivational discussions for the interim compositions, and working on those compositions. Students in non-observational classes used the time for the study of literature or grammar, motivational discussions, and work on the interim assignments. Students in all classes were required to write on the following topics, after a discussion of possibilities which might be pursued:

A. Write about a room at home or some other place. Be as specific as you can so that someone reading your composition will see what you see and understand the character of the room.

B. Write a composition about a place. Give a physical description of the place, but focus on the sounds in that place. Be as specific as you can so that someone reading your composition will hear the sounds you hear or imagine or see the sights you see.

C. Write about one of the following experiences or some other like those that follow. Be as specific as you can to help your reader feel your experience. (All students were presented with a list of possible experiences including those on pp. 15–16 of *Observing and Writing.*)

D. Write a slice of life story about a confrontation between two or more people. Let your reader know what the people look like, how they act, what they say, where they are, and what happens. Be as specific as you can. (All students read and discussed two sample compositions by seventh and eighth graders before proceeding with this assignment.)

Analysis

Teachers saved all the interim compositions along with their comments for later examination. Teacher 1 from School A (northwest Indiana—blue collar) averaged just under 10 words per brief comment and slightly over 41 words per extended comment over the four interim compositions. Typical brief comments by Teacher 1 read as follows:

a. Interesting descriptions. Try to focus on one place next time.

b. Good dialogue. Could detail emotional feelings more.

Typical extended comments by Teacher 1 follow:

a. Good topic. You could include more about how you felt to build suspense. How did your body react to your fear? Did your heart race? How tense were you? Did you panic when you fell? How cold was it?

b. Good use of dialogue. You could also show the increasing nervousness as you waited for the bell. How did you feel inside? What were your friends doing? Focus should be on only one part of the incident.

Teacher 2 in school B wrote an average of nearly 14 words in brief comments and just over 38 words for extended comments. Typical brief comments from Teacher 2 read as follows:

a. Mary Ann—you list many activities here. Describe the sounds with comparisons.

b. Steve—you use some lively language. Watch word choice.

Typical extended comments from Teacher 2 read as follows:

a. Maury—you mention some telling details here. I would like to hear even more. What are the various sounds? What do they sound like? You use verbs well in this paper.

b. Matt—you write a couple of good metaphors here. Use active verbs as often as possible. *To be* verbs just don't accomplish much. With more development of sound, smell, and sight details, this could be excellent.

Teacher 2 preceded nearly every comment with the student's name and often wrote brief marginal comments, most of which were affirmations (good! yes!) of what the student had written. A few of the marginal comments were negative (cliché), and several were hortatory (add comparisons, avoid *there is*).

Teacher 3 also in school B averaged just over nine words for brief comments and about 22 words for extended comments. Both means include marginal comments similar to those written by Teacher 2, but which were primarily of the affirmative type. Typical brief comments for Teacher 3 follow:

a. Quite a good description, but try using more comparisons.

b. Some nice description here—good comparisons. Describe the coughing sound.

The following typify extended comments from Teacher 3:

a. A good start, but you do very little here with descriptive language. What about using some comparisons? Describe voices and facial expressions.

b. You do a pretty sound job of describing the sights, but what other sounds could you work with? What about the sound of skis as they glide over the snow?

The teachers were asked to record the time required to read the papers and write brief or extended comments on the four interim compositions for each of the four instructional sets. Teacher 1 in school A reports spending a total of 17 hours and 35 minutes marking the papers; Teacher 2 in school B reports 30 hours and 5 minutes; Teacher 3 reports 25 hours and 40 minutes. The differences in total time may be accounted for by two factors. Casual inspection reveals that school A students wrote considerably shorter compositions than did school B students. Further, Teachers 2 and 3 both marked mechanical errors in spelling and punctuation. Teacher 1 did not. Despite differences in total marking time, however, the proportion of time required for brief comments and for extended comments is remarkably similar from teacher to teacher. Teacher 1 spent 34.6% of the total on brief comments and 65.4% on extended; Teacher 2 spent 37.3% on brief and 62.7% on extended; Teacher 3 spent 34.7% on brief and 65.3% on extended comments. Providing extended comments required nearly twice as much time as did providing brief comments in each case.

The 1112 pre- and post-tests were coded in such a way that raters could not distinguish pre-tests from post-tests nor students from any given teacher's classes in any way. All identifying information other than the code number was removed from the compositions which were then mixed randomly together.

The five-point specificity scale described in Hillocks (1979) was used to rate the papers. Three raters, not privy to the experimental design, trained for approximately 17 hours, until they reached high levels of inter-rater reliability. Three rater reliability checks were conducted: one at the beginning of the rating process, one when raters had progressed about half way through the compositions, and one near the end. On each occasion, raters discussed and resolved their disagreements. Raters' initial judgments on each occasion were used to compute Pearson product moment correlations for each pair of raters as well as intraclass correlations for one rater and for all three raters using formulas developed by Ebel and reported by Guilford (1954). The resulting estimates of reliability, ranging from .80 to .98, are reported in Table 6–1.

Total pre-test scores for each student were computed by summing the scores assigned to the two pre-tests. Total post-test scores were derived in the same way. This provides a scale of 2 to 10 for examining changes in student writing. The IQ scores for students in the two schools were converted to standard scores and were used as covariates for analysis of covariance with the teacher and with instructional, revision, and comment conditions as independent variables.

Table 6–1 ESTIMATES OF RATER RELIABILITY COMPUTED BY THREE METHODS

Pearson Product Moment Correlation

Occasion	1	2	3
Rater A and B	.82	.95	.84
Rater A and C	.87	.88	.80
Rater B and C	.90	.93	.89
Ebel's Intraclass Correlations			
For one rater	.90	.94	.84
For three raters	.96	.98	.95

Results

Table 6–2 summarizes the true means, the mean gains, and the adjusted mean gains (in parentheses) for all instructional sets: pre-writing instruction/revision; pre-writing instruction/no revision; assignment/revision; and assignment/no revision. It also presents mean gains for students receiving long and short comments within each instructional set. Tests of t for correlated groups reveal that all instructional sets made statistically significant gains at p < .005 or p < .0005. As predicted, both of the pre-writing activity groups and the assignment/revision group outperformed the assignment/no revision group by fairly wide margins. In fact, the gain for the pre-writing activity/no revision group is twice that of the assignment/no revision group. A t-test for groups with pooled variance indicates that the difference between these gains is significant, p < .01 (t = 2.52). The differences between the gains of the other two instructional sets and the gain of the assignment/no revision group are not significant at .05.

Table 6–3 presents the results of an analysis of variance of gain scores using the classical experimental approach in which the covariate effect is estimated first, independent of everything else in the design. This analysis of gain scores by teacher, instructional condition (pre-writing activity or assignment), revision condition (yes or no), and comment condition (long or short) uses IQ as a single covariate. The analysis reveals a highly significant effect by teacher class sets (F = 18.584, p < .0005) which is difficult to interpret. The difference is between the teacher in the blue collar school and the two teachers in the upper-middle-class school. The mean IQ for blue collar students (96.9) is significantly lower than that for the upper-middle-class students (114.6, p < .001). The analysis of covariance controls for differences in IQ and suggests that other differences between the groups of students might well account for the smaller gains by the blue collar students. More importantly for this research, however, there were no significant interactions between teacher and

Table 6–2 THE EFFECTS OF INSTRUCTION, REVISION, AND TEACHER COMMENT ON STUDENT WRITING

	Pre-writing Activity and Revision	Pre-writing Activity No Revision	Assignment and Revision	Assignment No Revision
Pre-test Mean	4.453	4.319	4.687	4.938
SD	1.695	1.564	1.616	1.717
Post-test Mean	5.720	6.125	6.254	5.828
SD	1.997	2.245	2.018	2.157
Gain	1.267	1.806	1.567	.89
	(1.246)*	(1.824)*	(1.496)*	(.847)*
SD (Gain)	2.075	2.212	1.925	2.001
N	75	72	67	64
t	5.288	6.927	6.663	3.362
p <	.0005	.0005	.0005	.005
Mean Gains by Comment Type				
Short	1.08	1.69	1.64	1.12
N	39	36	34	33
Long	1.50	1.96	1.43	.55
N	36	36	33	31

Adjusted mean gains appear in parentheses.

any treatment, indicating that the treatments had similar relative effects for all teachers.

The analysis of covariance (Table 6–3) indicates two significant interactions, that between instruction and revision (p < .011) and that between instruction and comment (p < .009). The mean gain for students asked to revise (1.41) differs only minimally for the mean gain of those who did no revising (1.37). The difference, of course, is not significant. However, when revision is combined with assignment only, the mean gain is greater (1.567), though not so high as the mean gain for the pre-writing activity/no revision group (1.806). Strong gains for revision alone and for pre-writing activity alone suggest that taken together, the effects of the two techniques should be even greater. That, however, is not the case. The mean gain for the group incorporating both pre-writing and revision (1.267) is lower than that for either technique alone. Finally, the assignment only condition with no revision has the smallest mean gain (0.89), a gain which is considerably smaller than the others and significantly smaller than the mean gain for pre-writing activity

Table 6–3 ANALYSIS OF COVARIANCE: MEAN GAIN SCORES BY TEACHER, INSTRUCTION, REVISION, AND COMMENT

Source of Variation	Sum of Squares	DF	Mean Square	F	Significance of F
Covariate IQ	56.226	1	56.226	15.732	.0005
Main Effects					
Teacher	132.836	2	66.418	18.584	.0005
Instruction	9.341	1	9.341	2.614	.107
Revision	0.044	1	0.044	0.012	.912
Comment	2.034	1	2.034	0.569	.451
Two-way Interactions					
Teacher-Instruction	14.728	2	7.364	2.060	.130
Teacher-Revision	11.612	2	5.806	1.625	.199
Teacher-Comment	3.870	2	1.935	0.541	.583
Instruct.-Revision	23.327	1	23.327	6.527	.011
Instruct.-Comment	24.818	1	24.818	6.944	.009
Revision-Comment	0.108	1	0.108	0.030	.862
Three-way Interactions					
Teach.-Inst.-Revis.	2.722	2	1.361	0.381	.684
Teach.-Inst.-Comm.	8.931	2	4.465	1.249	.289
Teach.-Revis.-Comm.	0.049	2	0.024	0.007	.993
Inst.-Revis.-Comm.	0.005	1	0.005	0.001	.969
Four-way Interctions	0.751	2	0.376	0.105	.900
Explained	289.353	24	12.056	3.373	.0005
Residual	822.021	230	3.574		

with no revision (p < .01). Clearly then, the type of instruction coupled with the presence or absence of revision makes a difference. One possible explanation for the smaller than expected gain of the group which had both the pre-writing activity and revision will be broached in the discussion section of this paper.

The second significant interaction is that between the teacher comment condition and instruction (p < .009). The mean gain for all students receiving short comments is 1.39; for students receiving long comments the mean gain is also 1.39. By contrast, the mean gains for long and short comments by instructional condition differ sharply. They are presented in Table 6–4. A t-test for groups with pooled variance reveals that the mean gain for long comments with pre-writing activities (1.736) is significantly greater (p < .025) than the mean gain for students who received only the assignments and long comments (t = 2.03). The mean gain for students receiving long comments and pre-writing activities is also greater than the mean gains for both groups receiving short comments, but not significantly. These differences are reflected in the

Table 6–4 GAINS FOR LONG AND SHORT COMMENTS

	Pre-writing Activity	Assignment
Short		
Mean	1.333	1.463
SD	2.036	2.040
N	75	67
Long		
Mean	1.736	1.000
SD	2.264	1.911
N	72	64

distribution of mean gains for long and short comments by instructional sets as presented in Table 6–2. The mean gain for the group with long comments but assignment only and no revision (.55) is only half that for any other group and about one quarter that for the students with pre-writing instruction, no revision, and long comments. A Scheffé test indicates the latter difference to be significant at $p < .0127$.

Discussion

The gain achieved by the observation/no revision group is not surprising in the sense that similar gains have been achieved by similar methods in the past (Hillocks, 1979). But in light of other interventional studies of composition which often show minimal or no gain in a much longer period of time, the magnitude of the gain in this study and in the previous studies is certainly surprising. In this study the gain for the observation/no revision groups is 1.15 times their pre-test standard deviation in only four weeks.

Equally surprising, especially in view of earlier studies, is the gain achieved by the assignment and revision group, a gain which is .96 of the standard deviation of its pre-test score. As far as this researcher knows, this is the first study to indicate that practice in revising has an effect on writing skill—is responsible for better first drafts. But even the assignment/no revision group made a significant gain, though only about .52 times the size of the standard deviation of its pre-test score.

The changes in all these groups may be largely attributable to the fact that all aspects of instruction focused on particular goals. The observation activities, the four interim compositions, the teacher comments, and the student revisions all have the same emphasis: writing more specifically and with a more precise focus in order to convey an experience or set of perceptions to an audience more forcefully.

In contrast, the instruction in other studies of teacher comments, practice in revising, frequency of writing, et cetera, has appeared to be considerably more diffuse in its goals, aiming to improve all aspects of composition.

Unfortunately, this study has no control group with diffuse instruction or comment. One is tempted to speculate that a group with assignments, revision, and comments emphasizing a variety of writing skills would have made little or no gain in a comparable period of time.

The results of this research pose a curious problem. If assignment and teacher comment, revision, and pre-writing activities each have beneficial effects on student writing, then why should the use of all not result in the greatest gains? The observation/revision students received all three treatments. They engaged in the pre-writing activities, wrote the four interim papers and received teacher comments encouraging increased specificity, and revised at least part of each of the four papers. Although the gains for this group are not significantly lower than those for the observation/no revision group or those of the assignment/revision group, one might expect them to be higher. Discussion with the teachers has suggested one possible explanation. Students in the observation activity classes worked harder on the first drafts of the four interim papers, many of them producing two drafts unbidden, and in fact, produced better papers which they regarded as final drafts. The teachers involved explained that many of these students complained about having to revise *again*. The requirement of the research design that every student revise *each* of the interim papers may have been regarded as overly burdensome or even as punishment and, thus, have had a depressant effect. One wonders if older students would respond in the same way. It may be that a more selective policy on revision would result in the desired effects. Requesting revision only as necessary or requesting that students rework their choice of two different papers might prove more beneficial.

The results for teacher comment are interesting for a number of reasons. The overall mean gain for brief comment papers is the same as that for extensive comment papers. But when examined by instructional sets, the gain for extensive comment compositions is greater for groups with pre-writing observational activities, somewhat less for the assignment plus revision group, and considerably less for the assignment only group. The difference between the long comment mean in the observation/no revision group and the long comment mean in the assignment/no revision group was shown to be significant by the Scheffé procedure at $p < .0127$. Even though the differences within instructional sets are not statistically significant, the interaction across sets is significant. Longer comments with their increased number of specific suggestions may be more meaningful when they have been preceded by instruction which is related to their content. Indeed, when unaccompanied by related instruction, long comments with a series of suggestions may be interpreted as primarily pejorative or punitive and may discourage seventh and eighth graders. Whether or not extended comments of the same type would have the same effect on more mature students can only be determined by further research.

Most importantly, while the difference between the mean gain of the pre-writing activity/no revision group and that of the assignment/no revision group is .906, the difference between mean gains for the extended comment group and the short comment group is non-existent (less than .001). In fact, short comments appear to be about twice as effective as long comments for students with assignment only. Such contrasts indicate that if a choice must be made between providing extended comments and planning instructional activities, the decision should be for planning. For the three teachers in this study, extended comments required nearly twice as much time as the brief comments. Had teacher #3 in this study written extensive comments for all the interim compositions, we can assume that he would have spent a total of about 37.5 hours commenting on compositions over a four-week period (30 hrs. $\times$ .652 $\times$ 2). Had he written brief comments for all papers, however, he would have spent a total of about 22.38 hours marking papers, thus allowing himself an additional 15 hours for planning instruction.

This research has a number of implications for instruction and research. The following are among the most important. First, in combination with its predecessor (Hillocks, 1979), it indicates, contrary to what has become almost accepted dogma, that significant gains in writing skill are possible over short periods of time. Second, it demonstrates the utility of involving students in dealing with data, as part of the composing process but as a prelude to actual writing. Learning to deal with data in this sense involves far more than the usual pre-writing activity which is simply a warm-up for a particular assign-ment. Third, it suggests that practice in revising, when focused on particular goals or skills over several pieces of writing, can affect writing skills as dis-played in subsequent new pieces of writing, and not simply in subsequent revi-sions. Fourth, it suggests that teacher comment, when positive and focused on particular aspects of writing over a series of compositions, can be effective. Finally, in view of the number of studies which suggest that teacher comment has little or no effect on writing skill, the present research indicates the use-fulness of examining variables in combination rather than individually.

But if this study provides at least tentative answers to some questions, it raises many more. Are gains made in each instructional set retained over a long period of time? Are they retained at equal levels? What particular kinds of comment are most effective in increasing skill? Is there a combination of pre-writing activity, revising, and comment which can increase the effect size? Will pre-writing activities which involve students in data processing strategies other than simply observing have similar effects? For example, will examining data in order to generate and test generalizations increase organizational skill? Do focused teacher comments have greater effect than do diffuse comments, as the comparison of this study with other studies suggests? Experimental studies which pursue such questions may be able to provide important insight into instructional processes.

References

Bata, E. 1972. A Study of the Relative Effectiveness of Marking Techniques on Junior College Freshman English Composition. Unpublished doctoral dissertation, University of Maryland.

Beach, R. 1979. "The Effects of Between-Draft Teacher Evaluation Versus Student Self-Evaluation on High School Students' Revising of Rough Drafts." *Research in the Teaching of English* 13:111–19.

Bridwell, L. 1980. "Revising Strategies in Twelfth Grade Students' Transactional Writing." *Research in the Teaching of English* 14:197–222.

Burton, D. and L. Arnold. 1964. Effects of Frequency of Writing and Intensity of Teacher Evaluation Upon High School Students' Performance in Written Composition. Washington, D.C.: U.S. Office of Education, Cooperative Research Project #1523, (ED 003 281).

Buxton, E. 1958. An Experiment to Test the Effects of Writing Frequency and Guided Practice Upon Students' Skill in Written Expression. Unpublished doctoral dissertation, Stanford University.

Emig, J. 1971. *The Composing Processes of Twelfth Graders.* Urbana, IL: National Council of Teachers of English.

Gee, T. 1972. "Students' Responses to Teacher Comments." *Research in the Teaching of English* 6:212–21.

Guilford, J. 1954. *Psychometric Methods.* New York: McGraw-Hill.

Hausner, R. 1975. Interaction of Selected Student Personality Factors and Teachers' Comments in a Sequentially Developed Composition Curriculum. Unpublished doctoral dissertation. Fordham University.

Hillocks, G. 1981. "The Responses of College Freshmen to Three Modes of Instruction." *American Journal of Education* 89:373–95.

———. 1979. "The Effects of Observational Activities on Student Writing." *Research in the Teaching of English* 13:23–35.

———. 1975. *Observing and Writing.* Urbana, IL: ERIC/RLS.

McCabe, B. 1971. "The Composing Process: A Theory." In *The Dynamics of English Instruction* edited by G. Hillocks, B. McCabe, and J. McCampbell. New York: Random House.

Moffett, J. 1968. *Teaching the Universe of Discourse.* Boston: Houghton-Mifflin.

Odell, L. 1974. "Measuring the Effect of Instruction in Pre-Writing." *Research in the Teaching of English* 8:228–40.

"Our Readers Write: What's a Sure-Fire Topic for Non-Sure-Fire Students?" *English Journal* 69 (8):62–69.

Perl, S. 1979. "The Composing Processes of Unskilled Writers." *Research in the Teaching of English* 13:317–36.

Pianko, S. 1979. "A Description of the Composing Processes of College Freshman Writers." *Research in the Teaching of English* 13:5–22.

Pike, K. 1964a. "Beyond the Sentence." *College Composition and Communication* 15: 129–35.

———. 1964b. "A Linguistic Contribution to Composition." *College Composition and Communication* 15:82–88.

Sherer, T., ed. 1980. "A Thousand Topics for Composition (Fourth Edition)." *Illinois English Bulletin* 67(3):1–32.

Stevens, A. 1973. The Effects of Positive and Negative Evaluation on the Written Composition of Low Performing High School Students. Unpublished doctoral dissertation. Boston University.

Stiff, R. 1967. "The Effect Upon Student Composition of Particular Correction Techniques." *Research in the Teaching of English* 1:54–75.

Sutton, A. and E. Allen. 1964. *The Effect of Practice and Evaluation on Improvement in Written Composition.* Washington, D.C.: U.S. Office of Education, Cooperative Research Project #1993, (ED 001 274).

Taylor, W. and K. Hoedt. 1966. "The Effect of Praise Upon the Quality and Quantity of Creative Writing." *Journal of Educational Research* 60:80–83.

Throckmorton, H. 1980. "Do Your Writing Assignments Work?—Checklist for a Good Writing Assignment." *English Journal* 69 (8):56–59.

7

The Effect of Teacher Comments on the Writing of Four College Freshmen

Nina D. Ziv

English teachers have always been concerned with how to help their students to become better writers. While lectures and class discussions about good writing have their place in the composition classroom, one of the most direct methods of affecting students' writing performance is that of writing comments on their papers.

Research has shown that teachers have different priorities when they respond to student writing. Some studies indicate that teachers respond primarily to mechanics, grammar, usage, and vocabulary (Kline, 1973; Harris, 1977; Searle & Dillon, 1980). In contrast, Freeman (1978) found that teachers were more concerned with content and organization than with mechanical errors. Though the emphasis of their responses may vary, most teachers do comment on the finished products of student writing and consider these comments to be evaluations of their students' work. In such a model of teacher response, the teacher acts as a judge who grades students' papers and writes comments suggesting how the students can "fix up" their essays. When a teacher responds in this manner, he or she assumes that the students will learn what "good writing" is from the comments and will thereby improve in future papers.

Students who receive such comments on their papers may read them; however, they often do not write subsequent drafts in which they can act upon the comments, and thus the improvement desired by their teachers rarely occurs. Along with not being able to react to teacher comments immediately, students may not see a need to respond to these comments because they view them as *evaluations* of their work and not as the *responses* of an interested adult reader.

It is evident that teacher responses on the final products of student writing may not be reaching their goals in helping students to improve their writing. Indeed, Pianko (1979) wrote that if teachers are to effect a positive change in students' written products, they must change their focus from evaluating and correcting finished papers to helping students expand and elaborate on the stages of their composing processes. Researchers who have studied the various stages of the composing process (Emig, 1971; Stallard, 1974; Graves, 1975; Perl, 1978) have identified revision as a stage of the process which is of vital importance. Murray (1978) defined revision as what the writer does after a draft is completed in order to understand and communicate what has begun to appear on the written pages. The writer reads and develops what has been written and eventually after several drafts, develops a meaning which can be communicated to the reader.

Though revision is a major aspect of the writing process and one that students should engage in when writing their compositions, teachers frequently equate revision with what Murray (1978) called its external variety—that is, writers' efforts to communicate what they have found to a specific audience. In doing external revision, writers edit, proofread, and use the various conventions of form and language to put the finishing touches on their pieces of writing. Thus Beach (1976) found that if teachers evaluated any drafts, their comments usually concerned matters of form and language. In her work on the revision process, Sommers (1978) compared the writing of college freshmen with that of experienced adult writers and found that adult writers were concerned with revising the composition as a whole and had developed their own revision criteria, while student writers were more concerned with changes on the word or phrase level, and were using specific criteria they had learned from teachers or textbooks.

If teachers are to help their students to revise their papers on the conceptual and structural level as well as on the lexical and sentential levels, they need a model for commenting on student papers. Yet no such model has been established. One reason for this is that the few studies that have been done on the effects of teacher response during the writing process have yielded inconclusive results.

The purpose of this exploratory study was to explore the effects of teacher comments on successive drafts of student compositions in order to generate hypotheses concerning effective kinds of responses and thus begin to develop a model of teacher intervention. Such a model would include categories of teacher response which teachers could use to classify their comments. They could then correlate these comments with their students' actions on final drafts in order to see how students used particular kinds of comments to revise their papers.

The following questions were addressed in this study:

1. What is the effect of teacher comments on the conceptual and structural levels of a student's composition?

2. What is the effect of teacher comments on the lexical and sentential levels of a student's composition?

3. What is the effect of teacher comments on the overall quality of a student's composition?

Related Literature

The research on teacher response has been primarily concerned with determining the effects that different types of responses have on the overall quality of student writing and on student attitudes toward writing. Several researchers, for example, used experimental designs to compare the effects of comments which praised student writing with the effects of comments which criticized the writing (Taylor & Hoedt, 1996; Seidman, 1966; Clarke, 1969). These investigators found that one type of comment is no more effective than another in helping students to write better compositions. Other studies in which various methods of commenting were compared also failed to yield any conclusive evidence about the kinds of responses which would be most helpful for student writers (Bata, 1972; Wolter, 1975; Maranzo & Arthurs, 1977). The lack of significant conclusions in these studies may have been due to inadequate research designs. However, they may have also been the result of basing these designs on a model of teacher response in which comments only appeared on student papers that were already completed. Such feedback, not integrally built into the writing process, is of questionable value.

Yet studies on the effect of teacher responses during the writing process are rare. Buxton (1958) studied the writing development of two groups of college freshmen over the course of an entire year. One group received no grades on their papers and no comments except for a few general ones at the ends of their papers suggesting ways in which they might improve their future essays. When their papers were returned, these students were told to look at the comments and not to revise their papers in any way. A second experimental group received extensive marginal and interlinear comments, final comments suggesting ways they could improve their papers, and two grades reflecting their teachers' assessments of the content and "accuracy" of their papers. These students received their annotated papers and revised them during a class period while teachers went from student to student and helped them. Buxton reported significant differences between the revision and writing groups, leading him to conclude that college freshmen whose writing is criticized and who revise in light of this criticism can improve their writing more than students who receive a few general suggestions but do not revise. While Buxton's results appear to be significant, the comments were only part of the treatment variable, and thus it was impossible to know what their relative influence was on student writing improvement.

Kelley (1973) investigated the effects of two types of responses on student writing. In her study, one class of 28 twelfth-graders was randomly divided into two groups. One group received clarifying responses on the rough drafts of their essays, and the other group received directive responses. Kelley defined the clarifying response as "a question or series of questions designed to help the student evaluate the nature of his ideas and consider alternatives in relationship to the writing skills he is expected to demonstrate in his writing"

(p. 141) and the directive response as "a written comment which gives a specific direction to the student regarding improvement of the writing skills which
he is expected to demonstrate in his writing" (p. 141).

During the experiment, the classroom teacher wrote either clarifying or
directive comments on each student's papers concerning the ideas, wording,
flavor, and organization, and used a mechanics chart to indicate to the student
the frequency of mechanical errors—spelling and punctuation. After the
appropriate comments were written, the students revised their papers during
two class periods and then returned them to the teacher. Kelley found that
while neither type of response significantly influenced the amount of growth
in writing performance of students on between-draft revisions, there was a
strong indication that "the clarifying response may be more effective than the
directive response for expository essays" (1973, p. 116). Although Kelley's
conclusions indicate that one type of response may help students to improve
their writing more than another, her categories of commenting were very general and no attempt was made to ascertain how particular comments within
these categories affected specific aspects of student writing.

In addition to the Buxton and Kelley studies, some research has focused
on whether teacher corrections between drafts and subsequent revisions by
students have any effect on the elimination of mechanical errors in student
writing (Fellows, 1936; Arnold, 1962). King (1970) studied the effects of three
different types of comments on specific errors frequently made by students in
their writing and found that students understood teacher corrections less often
than comments which named the error or stated the rule that the student had
violated. King also began to divide the comments into well-defined categories
instead of the general categories of previous studies. However, like her prede-
cessors, she did not investigate how student writing performance is affected by
specific teacher responses.

Procedures

The foregoing survey of the literature on teacher intervention indicates that
further research needs to be done in order to find out how teachers can best
help their students during the writing process. Since experimental studies in
which researchers compared the general effects of different types of comments
yielded somewhat inconclusive results, I decided to use the case study method
to explore how four college freshmen perceived the specific comments I wrote
on their papers and how they used these comments in revising. The writers,
Linda, Mark, Vincent, and Joann, were four students enrolled in a regular section of the New York University Expository Writing Program. All entering
freshmen are required to take two semesters of Expository Writing and are
randomly assigned to a section of the course. Sections of the Writing Program
are limited to fifteen students and are taught by graduate students or faculty
members from NYU.

During the fall semester of the 1979–1980 academic year, I taught two regular sections of Expository Writing. At the beginning of the semester, I asked all my students to write an essay on a topic of their choice, and on the basis of these first papers, I selected two male and two female freshmen from one section who exhibited problems of organization, focus, and logic in their writing. After obtaining their consent to participate in the project, I met with each of them and interviewed them about their previous writing experience.

Students in the Writing Program attend writing classes for an hour and fifteen minutes twice a week. During a semester, they write and revise several expository essays on assigned topics, react and comment on other students' writing, and read and react to various published essays. Instructors also hold class discussions on revision strategies, style, and other writing problems that the students in a class might have. An important feature of the Program is the three-stage draft process that the students go through when writing their papers. The students in a section are divided into groups of four or five, and after they have written their first drafts, they bring in their papers with copies for all the students in their group. The students read their essays aloud, and their peers comment orally and then write their comments on the copies. After the peer group meetings, the students use the comments they have received to write a second draft outside of class. Finally, the students use the instructor's comments to write a final draft, which is typed and handed in for a grade.

During the semester in which the study was conducted, the research participants attended regularly scheduled classes and participated in classroom activities which included writing seven papers in a series of three drafts and completing one in-class assignment. While I did follow the course outline of the Expository Writing Program, I deviated from the general procedures by not giving students specific assignments. Instead, I used a variety of techniques to stimulate them to think about topics for their papers. Thus, the students kept journals and from time to lime I responded to their journal entries and suggested topics for their papers based on what they had written. Other sources of topics were writing inventories which the students filled out at the beginning of the semester, and prewriting sessions in which they discussed a variety of topics they were interested in developing. In addition to not assigning topics, I did not give grades on the final drafts of the papers. Rather, at the end of the semester, I asked the students to choose five of their final drafts and hand them in to me so that I could give each student one composite grade.

Collection of the Data

In order to assess how teacher comments were affecting student writing, I asked the research participants to react aloud and tape-record their reactions to the comments which appeared on the second drafts of their papers. Initially, I met individually with the participants in my office and returned the second drafts of their first papers to them. I then asked the participants to read their papers aloud and when they came to a comment I had made to record their reaction to it. Before a participant started to record, I demonstrated what I wanted him or her to do by reading a comment from the papers and giving my reaction to it. During each recording session, I remained in the room and did not interfere with the taping except to remind the participant to react to each comment aloud.

After the recording sessions were over, the participants took their second drafts home and revised their papers. They then typed final drafts and handed in all three drafts to me. The process described above was repeated five more times during the semester. However, for the remaining five papers, the participants reacted to my comments at home, and after revising their papers turned in all three drafts to me. At the end of the semester, the participants met individually with another instructor in the Expository Writing Program, who interviewed them about their writing experiences during the semester and their views on teacher intervention during the writing process.

Analysis of the Data

The data that I analyzed consisted of the comments I had made on the research participants' papers, their perceptions of my comments, and their actions in preparing the final drafts of their papers.

Teacher Comments

Since the categories in previous studies such as Kelley's were general in nature and not well-defined, I developed my own taxonomy of teacher comments by inductively sorting my comments into various categories. The major categories of this taxonomy are explicit cues, implicit cues, and teacher corrections. Explicit cues are those in which the teacher indicates to the student exactly how he or she might revise a paper or points out a specific error. Examples of explicit cues on the macro level are:

• *Conceptual level.* Substitution: Student writes a paper in which she discusses how she uses her imagination to cope with the monotony of riding the subway every day. One of her final lines is: "The faculty of the mind to conjure up adventures in order to deal with the monotony of routine is fascinating." Teacher comment intending that the student make a major conceptual change by changing the focus of the paper: *You could expand your essay with (1) as your central idea and use the subway as one example, Other monotonous chores may come to mind.* (1) refers to the sentence "The faculty of the mind. . . . "

• *Structural level.* Rearrangement: Student writes a paper about his composing processes and has a paragraph near the end of the paper about when he writes his essays. Teacher comment intending that the student rearrange the paragraphs; *You should put the last paragraph near the beginning where you set the scene for your composing processes.*

Examples of explicit cues on the micro level are:

• *Sentential level.* Deletion: Student writes the following sentence in a paper on the sensual nature of monsters: "He has so many different parts about him that could turn a female on." Teacher comment intending that the student delete a phrase: *The words "about him" are unnecessary in the sentence and make it sound awkward. In your rewrite, I suggest that you delete "about him" so that the sentence reads "He has so many different parts that could turn a female on."*

• *Lexical level.* Substitution: Student writes the following sentence in a paper on juvenile delinquency: "Juveniles are thirty percent of the population but they constitute almost 50% of the crimes in the United States." Teacher comment intending that the student substitute a word: *It does not make sense to say that juveniles constitute crimes. Try using "commit" or "are responsible for" and see what different meanings are conveyed when you substitute one of these words for the one you have written.*

• *Grammar:* Student writes the following sentence in a paper on the New York City blackout of 1977: "Finally, we drove out to Howard Beach, I spotted a church bazaar right before the toll booth to enter Rockaway." Teacher comment intending that the student change the punctuation: *This is a comma splice.*

• *Format conventions.* Spelling: Student writes the following sentence in a paper in which she compares life to a game of Monopoly: "The roll of the dice he controlls." Teacher comment intending that the student substitute the correct spelling of the word "controls": *Spelling.*

Implicit cues are those in which the teacher calls attention to a problem, suggests alternative directions for the student to pursue, or questions the student about what he or she has written. Examples of implicit cues on the macro level are:

• *Conceptual level.* Addition: Student writes a paper in which she compares life to a game of Monopoly. She does not give enough examples to make her analogies vivid to the reader. Teacher comment intending that the student elaborate on her ideas: *You apparently like to use analogies in your writing, which is a good technique. Somehow this paper is a little abstract. Perhaps some concrete examples for your generalizations would help.*

• *Structural level.* Substitution: Student writes a paper on the isolation people experience in New York City. Her concluding paragraph is about the suicide rate in this country. Teacher comment intending that she substitute another conclusion: *Do you think your conclusion follows logically from the ideas you discuss in the body of your paper?*

Examples of implicit cues on the micro level are:

• *Sentential level.* Deletion: Student writes the following sentence in a paper on the New York City blackout of 1977: "Most of the middle class citizens moved out of this area and moved to other places." Teacher comment intending that the student delete the phrase "and moved": *This is awkward.*

• *Lexical level.* Substitution: Student writes the following sentence in a paper on stereotypes: "Stereotypes not only enslave but reduce equality." Teacher comment intending that the student substitute another word for "reduce": *This word is inappropriate here.*

Actual teacher corrections, the third category, include the rearrangement, addition, and deletion of phrases and sentences, and the addition, deletion, and substitution of words in a paper.

Student Perceptions

I also categorize the perceptions of the research participants. Examples of these categories are:

• *Perceives teacher intention:* Teacher writes "Is this the right word?" next to "view" in the sentence "He'd view his apartment and punch the walls in frustration." Teacher's intention is for the student to substitute another word for "view." Student *perceives teacher intention:* "'View' is circled. 'Is this the right word?' I guess I could change that. Well, when you say he viewed his apartment, it sounded as if he's standing on top of a mountain looking down. It's not too clear, and I wasn't sure I was using the word in the right context."

• *Does not perceive teacher intention:* Teacher writes "Do you like the way this sounds?" next to the sentence "All that is seen is a uniform and according to preconceived notions, he is a lacky." Teacher intention is for the student to change the sentence into active voice by substituting "all people see" for "all that is seen" so that the sentence reads "All people see is a uniform, and according to preconceived notions, he is a lackey." Student *does not perceive teacher intention:* "You asked me do I like the way that sounds. Yeah, I like the way it sounds. Because I was talking about stereotypes and stereotypes are preconceived notions, and I thought that it sounded pretty good myself."

• *Explains own intention:* Teacher writes "What do you mean?" next to the word "impressionable" in the sentence. "In him you can see the young impressionable of today as he will appear tomorrow." Participant *explains own intention:* "You asked me what I meant by 'impressionable.' What I meant was that here was a young man, a young person, who really hasn't had too many experiences and that he's looking at the world all wide-eyed and bushy-tailed and eager and that being as young and naive and unknowing as he is, he is very, impressionable."

• *Suggests course of action:* Teacher writes "spelling" over the word "pandimonium" in the sentence "Now all out pandimonium broke out, people were raiding every store." Student *suggests course of action:* "You have that I spelled 'pandemonium' wrong. You didn't correct it so I'll go to the dictionary and see if I can look it up and correct the spelling."

Student Actions

In addition to categorizing teacher comments and student perceptions, I developed a taxonomy of actions taken by students on the final drafts of their compositions. The taxonomy includes categories on the macro and micro levels. Examples of student actions on the macro level are:

• *Conceptual level.* Addition: In the final draft of a paper on juvenile delinquency, the student discusses why juvenile offenders receive such light sentences, a new idea he had not written about in his previous drafts.

• *Structural level.* Deletion: In a paper on the crisis in Iran, the student writes a paragraph about the Pope's role as an intermediary between the United States and Iran. In the final draft, he deletes this paragraph from the text.

Examples of student actions on the micro level are:

• *Sentential level.* Addition: Student writes the following sentence in a paper on stereotypes: "Why do these invisible chains refuse to judge a man by the content of his character not the color of his skin?" In the final draft, the student adds the phrase "the people who enforce," so that the sentence reads: "Why do the people who enforce these invisible chains refuse to judge a man by the content of his character not the color of his skin?"

• *Lexical level.* Substitution: Student writes the following sentence in a paper on a "left-over hippie" from the '60s: "His life seemed to have ended in the last cycles of that era." In the final draft, the student substitutes "years" for "cycles" so that the new sentence reads: "His life seemed to have ended in the last years of that era."

Method of Analysis

Using these taxonomies, I coded each of the comments that I had written, the perceptions of the research participants, and their actions on their final drafts. When I coded my comments, I also wrote down the intention of each of them. For example:

COMMENT	PERCEPTION	ACTION
"This is a comma splice." Refers to "It was a warm July evening, my mother, father, and	"You have a comment that this is a comma splice." (Direct response— rereads comment)	Makes sentence into two sentences so that they read: "*It was a warm July evening. My mother, father and I*

I had finished dinner and were deciding what we could do for that nights entertainment."	"I'm not sure what a comma splice is . . . "	*had finished dinner and were deciding what we could do for that nights entertainment."*
(Explicit—sentence-phrase grammar Teacher intention—punctuation change)	(Direct response—does not perceive teacher intention) ". . . but I'll look it up in my little handbook."	(Sentence-phrase-grammer-punctuation change)
	(Direct response—suggests course of action)	

After coding the data, I correlated my comments on the second drafts of the research participants' papers with their actions on their final drafts and analyzed what changes, if any, had been made as a result of my comments. The participants' reactions were an important part of this analysis because they indicated whether the participants had understood the intentions of my comments and why they had made particular revisions.

On the macro level, I compared drafts to see whether as a result of my comments the research participants had made any structural changes in their paragraphs or in the text as a whole. Similarly, on the conceptual level, I compared drafts to see whether the participants had rearranged, deleted, or added ideas. On the micro level, I compared sentences and lexical items I had commented on in the second drafts with parallel sentences and lexical items in the final drafts in order to see what changes had been made. Another part of my analysis on the micro level concerned the corrections I had made on the research participants' papers. In order to analyze the effect of these comments, I compared the sentences and lexical items that I had corrected in the second drafts with the parallel sentences and lexical items in the final drafts. The majority of my corrections concerned grammar, spelling, and punctuation. I had also written explicit cues on the participants' papers pointing out errors in these areas, and thus was able to compare the research participants' responses and actions to teacher corrections and explicit cues on similar errors.

Using the results of my analysis of the effect of particular comments on individual papers, I charted the patterns of responses and actions of each participant to particular categories of comments and compared the responses and actions of all participants across the various categories of comments on both the macro and micro levels.

Discussion and Results

An analysis of the data on the structural and conceptual levels indicated that the research participants, who were inexperienced revisers, responded favorably to explicit cues in which I gave them specific suggestions about how they could strengthen or reorganize the ideas they had already formulated in their papers. For example, Vincent wrote a paper on the hostage crisis in Iran. One of his arguments concerned the Soviet Union's possible reaction to United States military intervention. I thought Vincent's argument was a weak one and suggested that he elaborate on it. Vincent added a paragraph about this issue and wrote a more convincing argument.

When students were still in the process of discovering what they were trying to say, explicit cues also helped them to make major conceptual revisions. For example, earlier (see p. 99) I gave examples from a paper written by Joann, in which she discussed how people cope with their daily ride on the dirty subways of New York by imagining more pleasant experiences. The paper was clearly written and well-organized, but, as noted previously, I thought she might be able to expand on her idea by writing about how people use their imaginations to cope with other monotonous chores. Thus, I suggested in my final comment:

> Joann—this is well-organized and I enjoyed it. You could expand your essay with 1 as your central idea and use the subway as one example. Other monotonous chores may come to mind.

The number 1 referred to one of the last lines in the paper, which read; "The faculty of the mind to conjure up adventures in order to deal with the monotony of routine is fascinating." Joann's response was:

> I see where it would be more interesting if I focused in on the mind fantasizing and brought about various situations in which one does that, like the various routines—the various circumstances which cause one to start daydreaming. I picked the New York subways because I guess that's where I daydream the most.

In her final draft, Joann began with the sentence I had suggested and turned the paper into a general discussion of how people cope with monotonous chores. Thus she wrote about the subway rider as well as the student listening to a boring lecture and the housewife trying to finish her housework.

Implicit cues, in which I questioned the participants about the ideas they had presented or suggested alternative directions for them to pursue, helped them to clarify their ideas or stimulated them to think about ways they could further develop the topics. Responding with these kinds of cues was also appropriate when the participants presented well-developed ideas or when I wanted to suggest alternative ideas for them to pursue in future papers. For example, one of Joann's papers, a character sketch of a "leftover hippie from '69," was clearly written and well-developed. My response was to suggest that she write another paper dealing with the general problem of leftover "flower children."

On the sentential level, my implicit cues were not helpful because the research participants frequently did not recognize what the problems were in the sentences I had commented on and/or didn't have the strategies needed to revise them. Thus in response to cues such as "Can you rephrase this?" and "Rewrite this sentence" they either deleted the sentences, made no revisions in them, or wrote revisions which were just as awkward as their original sentences or did not fit into the context of the paper. On the lexical level, only two of the research participants responded favorably to my implicit cues. The other two participants did not perceive the intentions of such cues. Thus, when I wrote "wrong word" next to "constitute" in the sentence "Juveniles are thirty percent of the population but they constitute almost 50% of the crimes in the United States," Vincent substituted "compose" for "constitute." Linda reacted to "Is this the right word?" by challenging my comment and making no revision at all in her final draft.

The data also indicated that while the research participants readily accepted my corrections, they did not always understand why I had made such changes. For example, in one paper Vincent wrote: "Remington is owned by Dupont, *who* is one of the wealthiest families in America and Standard Oil is owned by Rockefeller." I substituted "which" for "who" in the sentence and the writer commented:

> Okay, I have "Remington, who is owned by Dupont, who is one of the wealthiest." You changed the word "who" to "which is one of the wealthiest." Okay, I guess that's correct English. That's good. I appreciate that because, uh, I'm not sure when to use words like that.

Though in the final draft, Vincent made the substitution I had indicated, in his next paper he still did not know how to use relative pronouns. Thus he wrote, "I quote Wolfgang and Cohen which states exactly what I would like to say." In this case, I substituted "who" for "which" and crossed out the "s" in the word "states" so that the sentence read: "I quote Wolfgang and Cohen who state exactly what I would like to say." Vincent's response to my comment was: "Okay, yeah, it doesn't sound right so I'll fix that up"; in the final draft, he wrote the correct version of the sentence.

Linda wrote this sentence in one of her papers:

> Instead of that innocent and naive look, his face clearly shows his experiences: from that speculative, glassy look in his eyes; to his nose that has been knocked out of joint in youth; to those hard, unyeilding lips, with their cynical smirk and that condescending leer.

I changed the semi-colons to commas in the sentence, and Linda made the changes I had indicated in her final draft. In a later paper, she wrote:

> When one takes away the pride of a race by portraying it as second class citizens; when one race insults the dignity of another race by treating it in deed and manner as inferior; when one race displays blatant disregard of another by seeing it only through stereotypes; it not only takes equality but also freedom.

I again changed the semi-colons to commas, and Linda questioned me about it:

> Then I say "when one takes away the pride of a race by portraying it as second class citizens" and then I use a semi-colon, and then I say "when one race insults the dignity of another race by treating it in deed and manner as inferior" and I use a semi-colon, and "when one race displays blatant disregard of another by seeing it only through stereotypes" and I use a semicolon. All those times you made my semi-colons commas, and I'm not really sure why because I always thought that commas weren't right when a sentence was so long but you did it so I guess that I was wrong.

Linda's response and use of the semi-colon in this paper indicated that she had not learned anything about the use of semi-colons from my corrections on her previous paper. From these examples it is evident that teacher corrections alone are not helpful kinds of comments because students frequently revise their papers according to the corrections without understanding why they have been made.

Along with being ineffective in helping students to understand their errors, teacher corrections reinforced the participants'perceptions of the writing process and the teacher's role in the process. Indeed, two of the participants viewed revision as a matter of correcting errors and had always looked upon the teacher as someone who would show them how to "fix up" their papers. Because of the passive role they had played in the writing process, they preferred when I made the necessary corrections on their papers. Yet they and the other participants were capable of correcting their errors when I just wrote explicit cues on their papers, in which I pointed out errors and left it to them to make the revisions. For example, when I wrote "subject and verb do not agree" next to a sentence, the participants were able to correct this error. Likewise, when I wrote "sp" over a misspelled word, the participants corrected their mistakes.

Implications for Teaching

What emerge from the analysis of the data on both the macro and micro levels are continua of commenting along which a teacher might respond to her students' writing. Thus on the macro level, students who are inexperienced revisers will respond favorably to explicit cues which indicate to them how they may strengthen the ideas they have already presented in their papers. For example, teachers might write comments in which they suggest how student may rearrange paragraphs in a more logical order, elaborate on specific points in their papers, or add more examples to support generalizations they have made. If students are still in the process of discovering the topics for their papers, then explicit cues suggesting how they can make major conceptual changes can be helpful. When students become more experienced at revising, teachers may want to be less explicit in their comments and instead suggest alternative directions for them to pursue or question them about various aspects of the ideas they have presented in order to stimulate them to make conceptual changes.

On the lexical and sentential levels, explicit cues may also be effective in helping inexperienced revisers during the writing process. Thus if a word choice is inappropriate, a teacher might suggest a number of alternative words that the student can use in place of the original one. On the sentential level, a teacher might respond to an awkward sentence by suggesting a way of rewriting it. It is also important to note that while explicit cues telling students why sentences are awkward may be helpful, such students may also need to listen to their sentences aloud so that they can hear why a sentence is awkward and to learn some stylistic options for revising such sentences.

The research participants' responses and subsequent actions on their final drafts indicated that teacher corrections did not help them to understand their errors and that in fact they were capable of revising their papers if errors in punctuation, spelling, and grammar were pointed out to them. Therefore, teachers might refrain from correcting the grammar, punctuation, and spelling errors in student papers and instead name the errors so that the students can make the necessary changes themselves.

It is evident that inexperienced revisers need specific directions from their teachers about how to revise their papers. However, at some point when students are more experienced revisers, teachers might move along the continua on both the macro and micro levels and write more implicit cues. The continua of commenting, then, can be used as a guide for writing comments on student papers.

Yet, comments can only be helpful if teachers respond to student writing as part of an ongoing dialogue between themselves and their students. In order to create such a dialogue, teachers might begin by responding to student writing not as evaluators and judges but as interested adults would react to such writing. For example, in response to one of Mark's papers I commented that after reading the paper I wasn't sure of the point he was trying to make in it. Mark's response to my comment indicated that his perception of himself as a writer was a poor one. He said: "I really didn't know what I was doing and you sort of told me you didn't know what my main topic was." In trying to help a student such as Mark, teachers might comment in an encouraging and supportive manner instead of reinforcing the student's poor self-perception.

To further diffuse the student's perception that the teacher's role in the writing process is that of an evaluator, teachers might write comments on the final drafts of papers encouraging students to pursue further some of the ideas they have presented. For example, one way I responded to the paper on a "leftover hippie" was to suggest that Joann write another paper on the general problem of "leftover flower children." Though Joann chose not to pursue this idea, my comment indicated my interest in the idea she had presented, and encouraged her to think of me as a participant in a dialogue about her writing.

Another way teachers can help to create a dialogue with their students is for them to become more sensitive to the intentions of student writers. Indeed, as a result of my research, I became aware that I often did not perceive the intentions of the student's text but rather wrote comments reflecting my stylistic preferences. For example, when Vincent wrote "The budget crunch was felt by my school so they cut certain activities one of which was the track team," I commented "Rewrite the sentence" intending that he change the sentence into the active voice. In retrospect it was evident that Vincent's intention in the sentence was to emphasize the words "budget crunch," so the passive voice was appropriate there. Because of my stylistic preferences, however, I did not consider his intentions and thus asked him to rewrite his sentence.

Along with writing comments in a positive and empathic manner and becoming more sensitive to the intentions of student writers, teachers might try to find out whether their comments are having a favorable effect on their students. Using the taxonomies developed in this study, teachers can categorize their comments, correlate them with their students' actions on subsequent drafts, and then see what kinds of comments are being understood by their students. For example, if a teacher moves along the lexical continuum and writes a comment such as "Is this word appropriate here?" on several student papers, then she can correlate her comments with her students' actions on their final drafts and be able to see whether such comments are being understood.

When creating a dialogue with their students, teachers might follow the suggestions that I have made. Teachers should be aware, however, that many students have never written papers in a series of drafts and therefore may not be receptive to such an approach and to teacher comments during the writing process. Thus, Vincent said in his final interview that at first he had reacted negatively to the idea of a draft process because he had been used to writing a paper once and handing it in to the teacher for a grade. Since other students may have similar attitudes, teachers might discuss the value of revision and show their students samples of their own writing and revising processes.

Teaching students the value of revision may help them to change their perceptions of their roles in the writing process. At the beginning of my study, the participants rarely challenged my comments and preferred to play a passive role in the writing process. However, as a result of their experiences with teacher responses during the process, they began to change their attitudes and play a more active role. Thus, all of the participants went beyond the intentions of my comments on either the macro or micro levels in papers that they wrote in the latter part of the semester. Indeed, Joann's remarks during her final interview indicated that her attitude toward teacher comments had changed and that, in terms of her role in the writing process, she viewed herself as a participant in a dialogue between herself and her teacher:

> I guess the reason teacher comments never really influenced me before was because I got fairly good ones. You know, before it was always a mark or a statement. The teachers never went into any big descriptions about your writing. If you fulfilled the task, you know, it was okay. Suddenly this year, I see

it. I can question it. I can disagree with it. I can see, you know, the different aspects of it. That did make sense.

Suggestions for Further Research

While their reactions to my comments and their actions on final drafts did vary among the research participants, it was possible to generalize about the effect of my comments on all four students. It was evident that they responded favorably to my explicit comments on the conceptual and structural levels. It was also apparent that they did not respond well to my implicit comments on the lexical and sentential levels, and therefore might respond more favorably to explicit comments on these levels. Based on the results of my study, I have hypothesized:

1. Students who are inexperienced revisers will improve on the structural and conceptual levels if they receive explicit cues about how to revise their papers.

2. Students who are inexperienced revisers will improve on the lexical and sentential levels if they receive explicit cues about how to revise their papers on these levels.

Using an experimental design, these hypotheses could be tested on a larger population. The distinction I have made between two major types of comments, explicit and implicit, should enable a research to control closely the comments that are written on papers in such a study. In addition to testing my hypotheses, researchers might also use the dimensions of composition annotation suggested by King (1979) as a guide for studying the effect of other types of comments on student writing. For example, research might be done to investigate student actions in response to whether a comment is interlinear, marginal, at the beginning/end, or on a rating form.

Although the analysis in this study concerned the changes that occurred between the drafts that the research participants turned in to me and their final drafts, they actually wrote three drafts. They got an initial response to their work from their peers and then wrote a second draft, to which I responded. This progression of reactions was sometimes confusing to the participants because my responses often contradicted those of their peers. On the conceptual level, for example, I often pointed out the lack of focus in a paper and suggested a major conceptual change, in contrast to the peer group which had had a positive response to the idea that the participant had presented. Since the three-stage draft process in which both peers and teachers respond to student writing is an integral part of many composition classrooms, the problem of how these two sets of responses interact with each other might also be the subject of future research projects.

Most of the previous research that has been done in the area of teacher response to student writing has been concerned with how teachers evaluate the finished products of student writing. The model of teacher response which emerges from such research is one in which the teacher's role is that of an evaluator who comments on the strengths and weaknesses of her student's papers. When a teacher writes comments, the underlying assumption is that the students will respond to them and thus improve their writing performance. However, these implied dialogues rarely happen because students invariably look upon their teacher as a judge and, consequently, see themselves as participants in a "dialogue" in which they can do little but accept their teacher's criticisms. In this study I have suggested a different model of teacher response, in which teachers are no longer evaluators and students are no longer passive recipients of their teachers' judgments. Instead, teachers have an effect on the immediate products of student writing and through their supportive responses during the writing process, begin to establish an on-going dialogue in which both they and their students are active participants.

References

Arnold, L. V. 1962. Effects of Frequency of Writing and Intensity of Teacher Evaluation Upon Performance in Written Composition of Tenth Grade Students. Doctoral dissertation. Florida State University. Published in *Dissertation Abstracts International*, 1963, *24*, 1021A. (University Microfilms No. 63-6344).

Bata, E. J. 1972. A Study of the Relative Effectiveness of Marking Techniques on Junior College Freshmen English Composition. Doctoral dissertation. University of Maryland. Published in *Dissertation Abstracts International*, 1973, *34*, 62A (University Microfilms No. 73-17028).

Beach, R. 1976. "Self-Evaluation Strategies of Extensive Revisers and Non-Revisers." *College Composition and Communication* 27 (2):160–64.

Buxton, E. W. 1958. An Experiment to Test the Effects of Writing Frequency and Graded Practice Upon Students' Skills in Written Expression. Doctoral dissertation, Stanford University. Published in *Dissertation Abstracts International*, 1958, *19*, 709A. (University Microfilms No. 58-03596).

Clarke, G. A. 1969. Interpreting the Penciled Scrawl: A Problem in Teacher Theme Evaluation. Unpublished doctoral dissertation. University of Chicago. (ERIC Document Reproduction Service No. 039 241).

Emig, J. 1971. *The Composing Processes of Twelfth Graders*. Urbana, IL: National Council on Teachers of English.

Fellows, J. E. 1936. The Influence of Theme Reading and Theme Correction on Eliminating Technical Errors in Written Compositions of Ninth Grade Pupils. Unpublished doctoral dissertation. University of Iowa.

Freeman, S. 1978. The Evaluators of Student Writing. Research prepared at San Francisco State College, San Francisco. (ERIC Document Reproduction Service No. ED 150 079).

Graves, D. H. 1975. "An Examination of the Writing Processes of Seven Year Old Children." *Research in the Teaching of English* 9 (3):227–41.

Harris, W. H. 1977. "Teacher Response to Student Writing: A Study of the Response Patterns of High School English Teachers to Determine the Basis for Teacher Judgment of Student Writing." *Research in the Teaching of English* 11 (2): 175–85.

Kelley, M. E. 1973. Effects of Two Types of Teachers Responses to Essays Upon Twelfth Grade Students' Growth in Writing Performance. Doctoral dissertation. Michigan State University. Published in *Dissertation Abstracts International,* 1974, *34,* 5801A. (University Microfilms No. 74-6068).

King, J. A. 1979. Teachers' Comments on Students' Writing: A Conceptual Analysis and Empirical Study. Doctoral dissertation, Cornell University. Published in *Dissertation Abstracts International,* 1980, *40,* 4872-A. (University Microfilms No. 80-03942).

Kline, C. R., Jr. 1973. Instructors Signals to Their Students. Paper presented at a meeting of Conference on College Composition and Communication, New Orleans. (ERIC Document Reproduction Service No. 083 600).

Maranzo, R. J., and S. Arthurs. 1977. Teacher Comments on Student Essays: It Doesn't Matter What You Say. Study prepared at University of Colorado. (ERIC Document Reproduction Service No. 147 864).

Murray, D. M. 1978. "Internal Revision: A Process of Discovery." In *Research on Composing: Points of Departure* edited by C. R. Cooper and L. Odell. Urbana, IL: National Council of Teachers of English.

Perl, S. 1978. Five Writers Writing: The Composing Processes of Unskilled College Writers. Doctoral dissertation, New York University. Published in *Dissertation Abstracts International,* 1978, *39,* 4788A. (University Microfilms No. 78-24104).

Pianko, S. 1979. "A Description of the Composing Processes of College Freshmen Writers." *Research in the Teaching of English* 13 (1):5–22.

Searle, D., and D. Dillon. 1980. "The Message of Marking: Teacher Written Responses to Student Writing at Intermediate Grade Levels." *Research in the Teaching of English* 14 (3):233–42.

Seidman, E. 1966. Marking Students' Compositions; Implications for Achievement Motivation Theory. Doctoral dissertation, Stanford University. Published in *Dissertation Abstracts International,* 1967, *28,* 2605A. (University Microfilms NO. 67-17503).

Sommers, N. I. 1978. Revision in the Composing Process: A Case Study of College Freshmen and Experienced Adult Writers. Doctoral dissertation, Boston University. Published in *Dissertation Abstracts International,* 1979, *39,* 5374A. (University Microfilms No. 79-05022).

Stallard, C. K. 1974. "An Analysis of the Writing Behavior of Good Student Writers." *Research in the Teaching of English* 8:208–18.

Taylor, W. F., and K. C. Hoedt. 1996. "The Effect of Praise Upon the Quality of Creative Writing." *Journal of Educational Research* 60:80–83.

Wolter. D. R. 1975. The Effect of Feedback on Performance on a Creative Writing Task. Unpublished doctoral dissertation. University of Michigan. (ERIC Document Reproduction Service No. 120 801).

8

A Good Girl Writes Like a Good Girl

Written Response to Student Writing

Melanie Sperling
Sarah Warshauer Freedman

This chapter discusses one student's persistence in misunderstanding her teacher's written comments on her papers, even when these comments are accompanied by other response channels that serve, in part, to clarify the written comments. It presents the idea that student and teacher each bring to the written response episode a set of information, skills, and values that may or may not be shared between them, and it is the interplay of these three elements that feeds the student's reading and processing of teacher written comments and that leads to misunderstandings. This happened even for a high-achieving student in an otherwise successful classroom. An in-depth look at one student and the classroom context in which she learns to write, focusing on her grappling with her teacher's written comments, reveals the complexity of the teaching-learning process in the high school writing class.

In the writing classroom, as in any classroom, there are many opportunities for misunderstanding between teachers and students. The misunderstandings are particularly evident when teachers react to student work through written responses on student papers. If teachers march to vintage drummers, they call this activity "correcting," although the student is often not "corrected" as the

Authors' Note: Funding for this research was provided through a grant to S.W. Freedman by the National Institute of Education, Grant ENIE-083-0065, with supplementary funds provided by the Spencer Foundation. We wish to thank Colette Daiute for her clear and cogent written response to a draft of this chapter. We assume full responsibility for any misunderstanding of this response.

teacher expects. If the beat is newer, they are providing "feedback," although the feedback often falls short of its target.

The past ten to twenty years has seen a good deal of research on teacher written responses to student writing, fostered, in part, because written response has enjoyed the sanction of traditional pedagogy (e.g., CEEB, 1963) and has continued to be the dominant mode of response to student writing (Searle & Dillon, 1980). With increasing focus on the cognitive and linguistic processes of writing and composing, research has suggested improved written response practices, entailing the integration of written response into a protracted writing process where it has been shown to have merit: see, for example, Beach's (1979) study on the effectiveness of focused between-draft response on revision, Hillocks's (1982) look at the efficacy of written response that echoes other classroom activity, or Freedman's (1985; in press) studies of the integrated in-process response practices of successful teachers. Suggested improvements also reflect considerations such as Lees's (1979) for whether particular teacher comments place the burden of rewriting decisions—again, the assumption is made of a process orientation—on the student or on the teacher; Butler's (1980) concern that the "squiggles" that carry meaning for the teacher often carry none for the student; Sommers's (1982, p. 152) outcry over facile comments that can be "interchanged, rubber-stamped, from text to text"; or Hahn's (1981) discovery that students find comments to reflect their teachers' confused readings rather than their own confused writings and so discount the value of these comments. Through such studies we have gained valuable knowledge about the nature and effects of written response to student writing, enlightenment that would tend to lead to more considered use of this response mode, at least among better teachers, and toward its integration with other modes such as teacher-student conferences.

The Persistence of Student Misunderstandings

With all this, however, we have yet to uncover what often seems an uncanny *persistence* in students to misunderstand the written response they receive on their papers: Written comments are often misconstrued even when they are addressed to the most promising students in otherwise successful classrooms; they are misconstrued even when they are accompanied by teacher-student conferences, by peer response groups, as well as by whole class discussion focused on response. In other words, teacher written response is misunderstood even in classrooms that strongly reflect what we consider the best of current thought on the teaching of writing (Sperling, 1985). It would seem that, were we to uncover some of the elements not only of these misunderstandings but of the frequent understandings of teacher written response as well, finding their roots, as well as our perspective, in a larger learning context, we should have an opportunity to learn more about the forces that underlie the teaching and learning of writing. In this article we look in depth at one promising student's processing of teacher written comments in a response-rich classroom, considering the larger learning contexts that impinge on the student's interpretations.

Perspectives

We choose a case study to supplement past studies of teacher written response, which often tend to regard a given comment as a static product, disembodied from the cognitive or social forces operating within or between teacher and student. Yet these forces are key in the teaching-learning context. And context is a major consideration when we talk about what students do and do not understand. Work in learning and development by Vygotsky (1978) and others implies the aptness of looking at written responses and students' reactions to them as functions of the greater social and cognitive dynamic of the classroom.

According to Vygotsky, students learn and develop when *information, skills, and values* are negotiated socially. The cognitive consequences of social interaction are that what begins as social process—such as shared problem solving—is internalized and becomes part of the student's independent cognitive equipment. Vygotsky refers to this process as the internalization of socially rooted activities. Vygotsky's theories regarding this social dynamic of learning implicate as crucial to the student's assimilation of such adult problem-solving strategies the emerging *match* between teacher's and student's information, skills, and values.

The case study that we present here allows us to look at the information, skills, and values that teacher and student possess. While it would be an impossible task to unearth all conceivable information, skills, and values that an individual brings to any given task, our earlier work (Freedman, 1985; Greenleaf, 1985; Sperling, 1985) strongly suggests that these three factors are at least in part reflected in the teacher's and student's *definitions of the response situation*—that is, in their expressed sense of its purpose as well as in their apparent solutions to the writing problems addressed by the responses. These definitions, of course, cannot be "read into" the responses written on a student's papers or even into a student's revisions based on the responses. They must be garnered from the context in which the response is embedded, that is, from classroom talk and other activities surrounding teaching and learning and from the student's and teacher's perceptions of the activities. The teacher's definition, for example, emerges in part when the teacher tells his or her class, "I want you to look over what I've written on your paper, and I want to talk [to you] mainly about what you do not understand," implying that oral response is meant to supplement and thereby clarify the cognitive confusion that written response can create. The student's definition emerges in part in the research interview, such as when our case study student asserts that the teacher's oral response is solely an aid to deciphering his handwriting, an unnecessary event when a student is good at reading the handwriting of others, as she believes herself to be. Seen from the perspective of such contextual information, the interaction resulting from written response begins to reveal some of the complexity of the whole teaching-learning dynamic in the writing classroom.

In order to examine both the understanding and the misunderstanding surrounding written response on student writing, even among promising students in otherwise successful classrooms, we will present the case of Lisa, in Mr. Peterson's classroom, with an eye toward examining the information, skills, and values embedded in the learning context. Using one case-study student and teacher serves our purposes well, as we do not intend to generalize the idiosyncrasies of one or even several students or teachers to the greater population of students and teachers, but rather to focus in depth on an experience that theoretically should show something close to a "best case" view of written response. Any failings in communication in such a context should alert us to serious teaching and learning constraints. On the other hand, successes could point to where written response can be useful. The written response interactions in this case unfolded as part of a larger ethnographic study on the role of response in the acquisition of written language (Freedman, 1985, in press).[1]

Mr. Peterson, The Teacher[2]

During the seven weeks that we observed his ninth-grade English class, one overarching goal seemed to drive all of Mr. Peterson's teaching: He aimed to teach his students to think critically and creatively, both about their world and about the literature they read. Freedman (in press) offers a full account of how Mr. Peterson achieves his goals. Briefly, he used writing as one key way. He designed activities to help the students sharpen their powers of observation, to notice detail both in their everyday lives and in their reading, and he worked with them to develop sound judgments based on the detail they observed. He also pushed his students to look for the unusual, the interesting, the unexpected, the apparent contradictions—to think in novel and unique ways. Mr. Peterson introduced students to techniques for sharpening their thoughts as they worked to communicate them in writing. He stressed techniques to capture the reader's interest and imagination, to stretch the reader's experience, and to communicate sophisticated ideas—for example, using vivid and specific verbs, cutting out excess verbiage, practicing syntactic structures that allow contrast to be shown, and modulating the general and the specific.

Mr. Peterson's philosophy unified his curriculum; every one of his instructions, suggestions, assignments, and exercises served in the orchestration of student activity so that seemingly separate pieces of advice attached to discrete activities became part of a coherent blueprint for his students' growth as learners and as writers.

Lisa, The Student

Before the semester with Mr. Peterson began, our focal student, Lisa, had been identified to be high achieving: Her scores on a standardized test of basic skills ranked in the ninetieth percentile range; her grades the previous semester were all A's. As a student in Mr. Peterson's class, Lisa did all her assignments on time, sometimes even ahead of schedule, getting top grades on all her work. She interacted actively in groups and in the whole class, contributing much to classroom discussion and to peer group work. In her peer group, for example, Lisa was often the spokesperson, reading to the rest of the class her own or her peers' writing or volunteering answers to Mr. Peterson's questions. It was common for Mr. Peterson to assign individual writing tasks to be completed in small groups—each student in the group, say, creating sentences with particular characteristics such as vivid verbs or detail that he or she would share with group members, the group then choosing the best piece to read to the rest of the class. In Lisa's group, hers was often the piece read, and Lisa had no reservations about volunteering her own pieces when she felt they were the best from her group. When she read, she did so with a loud, clear voice, a voice that could be heard above others in her group when, on occasion, everyone in the group happened to be talking at the same time (see Freedman & Bennett, 1987, for more information about groups in Mr. Peterson's class). Also, it was often Lisa who reminded her classmates, or Mr. Peterson, of writing due dates or of reading assignments. Her behavior resulted in high visibility in class as a "good" student.

The Writing Assignment[3]

Mr. Peterson's students were to write a character study of a friend or acquaintance. To this end they first did practice writings and other prewriting activities related to the topic; then they wrote a series of drafts. During the writing process they participated in teacher-student conferences and peer response groups, and, in addition, Mr. Peterson responded to all writing with written comments. The character study assignment produced three major drafts of writing: (a) a rough draft of a short anecdote about the friend or acquaintance; (b) a final draft of the anecdote; and (c) a final draft of the fuller character sketch of the person, of which the anecdote served as part. From beginning prewriting to final draft due date, this writing assignment spanned five weeks. Lisa wrote about Sister Carolyn-Marie, her eighth grade teacher.

The Written Comments: Response Rounds

Mr. Peterson wrote comments on each draft of Lisa's character study. We have, as a result, many couplings of text and teacher comment with which Lisa interacts, either "understanding" or "misunderstanding"—couplings, that is, to which both Mr, Peterson and Lisa bring their own (shared or unshared) information, skills, and values. Text, comment, and reaction make up a unit, a kind of *round* of interaction, or *response round*, analogous to the oral turn-taking designation made by Garvey (1977), Following Garvey, a response round consists of a segment of student text, the teacher's written response, the student's reaction to that response, and, sometimes, the student's subsequent redrafting of the text. We begin our look at Lisa's interactions with Mr. Peterson's written comments by closely considering these response rounds.

Discovering Shared Information Between Teacher and Student

When we look at Lisa's understandings and misunderstandings, we do not have knowledge about all of the information, skills, and values shared by her and Mr. Peterson. Sometimes, for example, Mr. Peterson's comments seem to assume of Lisa past knowledge not made explicit in his classroom. In the ninth grade, for instance, many teachers might tacitly assume that students understand such concepts as "run-together sentence" or "sentence fragment"; have the skills to identify and solve these writing problems; and believe that run-together sentences or sentence fragments, in many contexts, denote "poor" writing because they betray ignorance of sentence boundaries, something readers in these contexts do not expect to encounter. We could not "observe" such unexpressed assumptions. Thus we can look only at what is *explicit* in the data and draw conclusions based on that.

For the larger ethnography, we generated a semantic network based on the teacher's and students' talk (Greenleaf, 1985; this compilation can be found in the Appendix). The network identified all the *information* about writing and the writing process that both teachers and students had explicitly expressed (for example, information on consistency of verb tense, or on descriptive detail, or even on "good writing") and suggested at least some of the explicitly stated beliefs held by both teachers and students regarding writing. These beliefs were referred to in the semantic analysis as the teacher's and students' notions of "ideal text" and "ideal writing process" (for a complete explanation of this analysis, see Greenleaf, 1985). Using the compilation of the semantic network analysis as a data check, we categorized Mr. Peterson's written comments on each draft of Lisa's writing according to whether or not he had been explicit in his classroom talk about the kind of problem or issues the comment referred to. That is, each comment does or does not have a referent in the classroom teaching. Accordingly, each comment is labeled either [+CLASSROOM REFERENCE] or [–CLASSROOM REFERENCE]. For example, on her final draft Lisa writes:

Cl, LI: SHE POSSESSED A DOMINATING PERSONALITY THAT COULD EASILY SHATTER ANY STERIOTYPE OF NUNS THAT HOLLYWOOD, WITH THE AID OF ITS SILVER SCREENS, MOLDED INTO OUR MINDS.

To this, Mr. Peterson suggests moving *HOLLYWOOD* to precede *STERIOTYPE* (he does not correct the spelling of "stereotype") and omitting the last prepositional phrase. The text with the teacher's comments resembles the following:

C1, P1:   SHE POSSESSED A DOMINATING PERSONALITY THAT

COULD EASILY SHATTER ANY STERIOTYPE OF NUNS

THAT (HOLLYWOOD) WITH THE AID OF ITS SILVER *You don't need this*

SCREENS, MOLDED INTO OUR MINDS.

We marked this change as having a referent in Mr. Peterson's talk (or [+CLASSROOM REFERENCE]), as the semantic analysis uncovered the fact that Mr. Peterson had often remarked in class that students should watch for "getting rid of excess words," the written comment reflecting, then, his ideal text, one with no excess words, and his ideal writing process, one that incorporates skills to edit out excesses.

On the other hand, some comments reflect no in-class referent observable to us. For example, also on her final draft, Lisa writes:

C2, L1: AGAIN SHE GAVE THE WHOLE CLASS A TEST, YET AGAIN SOME FAILED. THIS CAUSED HER SOME CONCERN, UNFORTUNATELY FOR OUR CLASS, CONCERN MADE SR. CAROLYN EDGY AND POSITIVELY MEAN.

To this, Mr. Peterson points out a run-together sentence:

C2, P1:   ... THIS CAUSED HER SOME CONCERN // UNFORTUNATELY

new sentence   FOR OUR CLASS, CONCERN MADE SR. CAROLYN EDGY ...

We marked this comment as having no classroom referent (or [−CLASSROOM REFERENCE]), as Mr. Peterson had not, according to the semantic analysis, referred in class to the grammatical problem of run-together sentences, there being no explicit indication, then, that run-together sentences violated some notion of ideal texts. While he may have been assuming past knowledge on Lisa's part, we could not mark a tacit assumption as a referent.

The reason for characterizing teacher written comments for having or not having a referent was simply to circumscribe, *based on what was observable*, the *information* that operated on the response rounds.

Discovering Demonstrated Student Skill

Even where the semantic network indicated that Mr. Peterson and Lisa shared information pertinent to Lisa's writing the various drafts of her character sketch assignment, Lisa could nonetheless fall short of demonstrating the skill to act on that information. We thus noted whether or not the parts of Lisa's text that Mr. Peterson commented on reflected a skillful execution of his notion of ideal text; these are labeled accordingly [+/−IDEAL TEXT].

For example, on the final character sketch, Lisa writes:

C3, L1: MY EIGHTH GRADE TEACHER, SISTER CAROLYN-
MARIE, HAD GREEN EYES AND SHORT, CURLY BROWN
HAIR WHICH SHE LOVED TO RUN HER FINGERS THROUGH.

To this Mr. Peterson comments:

C3, P1: GOOD.

For this passage, we noted that Lisa demonstrated skillful execution of writing
that Mr. Peterson valued; that is, the passage was [+IDEAL TEXT]. Of course,
it is impossible to know from the generalized comments of "good" exactly
what features of his ideal text Mr. Peterson was referring to; however, it is possible, based on information from the classroom context, to venture a possible
explanation. Because the assignment asked for a character description, and
because class discussion at this point in the semester focused a great deal on
generating specific descriptive detail in order to give a reader a vivid picture
of one's subject, it appears that Mr. Peterson's comment referred to Lisa's producing "specific and concrete" prose that "uses descriptions"—his expressed
ideal text.

On the other hand, some passages that Mr. Peterson marked did not reflect
execution of ideal text; these passages were thus [–IDEAL TEXT]. So, for
example, we noted that C1, P1, cited earlier for its observed in-class reference
to getting rid of excess words, also reflected a lack of student accomplishment
as Lisa did not execute this "ideal." The reason for characterizing Lisa's
marked passages for demonstrating or failing to demonstrate writing skill, was
simply to designate, *based on her written products,* the *skills* that operated on
the response rounds.

The Match Between Teacher and Student Understandings[4]

There were seven written response rounds for the rough draft of the anecdote.
Only one (14%) entailed a teacher written comment referring to information
that had not surfaced in the classroom during our seven-week observation; that
is, the comment was [–CLASSROOM REFERENCE] and depended on information potentially unshared by teacher and student. There were 15 written
response rounds for the final draft of the anecdote. Only 3 (20%) were
[–CLASSROOM REFERENCE]. There were 26 written response rounds in the
final character sketch. Only 7 (27%) were [–CLASSROOM REFERENCE].

Most comments, then, referred to information that had surfaced in class
during our seven-week observation, and thus to Mr. Peterson's expressed
notions of ideal text or ideal writing process, notions, that is, that the students
had been exposed to in class. Still, between 14% and 27% of his comments,
depending on the piece of writing in question, did not refer to information that

had surfaced in class, and we saw these as potentially knotty points where misunderstanding might be considerable. That is, these were places where Mr. Peterson relied on Lisa's sharing his information but where the information appeared not readily available to be shared, implying that Lisa had to process these comments potentially without sufficient information to "get it right."

In fact we have evidence that such ungrounded comments did pose unusual knots for Lisa, which she was not fully able to untie. And notably, our analysis showed that in *all* of Lisa's drafts where Mr. Peterson had written comments that we found to be without observable in-class referent (that is, for 100% of what we found to be [–CLASSROOM REFERENCE] comments), her revisions had in some way failed to demonstrate Mr. Peterson's ideal text. In other words, her composing process had somehow gone amiss, and these [–CLASSROOM REFERENCE] comments were potentially of little help to her as they had no anchor in his classroom.

Lisa, however, is an able student and makes telling attempts to unravel her unnamed writing problems. Let us look at Lisa's attempts to rewrite text on which Mr. Peterson had made one such [–CLASSROOM REFERENCE] comment. On the rough draft of the anecdote she writes:

Al, L1: ONE MINUTE SHE CAN HAVE A GRIN STRETCHING
FROM EAR TO EAR AND THEN THE VERY NEXT MINUTE . . .

Mr. Peterson underlines *STRETCHING FROM EAR TO EAR* and draws a line connecting her text to his marginal comment, which asks for "another way to say this." The text with his comments looks like this:

A1, P1:   ONE MINUTE SHE CAN HAVE A GRIN STRETCHING FROM EAR

TO EAR AND THEN THE VERY NEXT MINUTE . . . *another way to say this?*

We have no explicit evidence from class discussions or from conferences with Lisa of any particular problem that Mr. Peterson may have had in mind when he wrote his comment; we observed no expressed "ideal text" that he might have been referring to—that is, he never discussed cliches and how to avoid them. However, from our own background knowledge as well as from what ensued in the following draft, we might well assume that he wanted Lisa to eliminate the cliche, (grin) *STRETCHING FROM EAR TO EAR*. In this regard, two things are of note. First, as we indicated above, our semantic network revealed no lessons or discussion about cliches. Second, a close look at his written comment reveals that the line connecting his comment with Lisa's text points only at one word, *STRETCHING*. It is important to keep both these observations in mind when considering Lisa's rewrite of this line in the final draft of the anecdote:

B1, L1: ONE MINUTE SHE CAN BE GRINNING FROM EAR TO
EAR, THEN THE VERY NEXT MINUTE . . .

Lisa had eliminated the word *STRETCHING*, which Mr. Peterson's line had pointed at in the rough draft of the anecdote. However, this elimination has not solved the problem that Mr. Peterson was apparently referring to. For on the final draft of the anecdote Mr. Peterson responds by penning out *FROM EAR TO EAR*, still, presumably, attacking the problem of the cliche, a problem, it begins to appear, to which Lisa brings no ready background of her own and, as we know, no background from the context of Mr. Peterson's class. Lisa's revised text with Mr. Peterson's comment looks like this:

B1, P1:   ONE MINUTE SHE CAN BE GRINNING ~~FROM EAR TO EAR~~

           THEN THE VERY NEXT MINUTE . . .

On the next revision, the final character sketch, Lisa eliminates the cliche:

C1, L1: ONE MINUTE SHE COULD BE GRINNING, THEN THE
VERY NEXT MINUTE . . .

However, while on the surface Lisa gets rid of the problem, we have no evidence that she shares Mr. Peterson's information about cliches. We emphasize, though, that she shows herself to be a skillful follower of directions.

In contrast, there were many more response rounds for which Mr. Peterson's comments were [+CLASSROOM REFERENCE] rather than [−CLASSROOM REFERENCE]. These comments referred both to places where Lisa failed to execute a text in congruence with Mr. Peterson's ideal text and to places where Lisa's text was successful. In the rough draft of the anecdote, of the 6 [+CLASSROOM REFERENCE] written response rounds, 3 (50%) of Lisa's passages failed to execute ideal text (that is, they were [−IDEAL TEXT]); in the final draft of the anecdote, of the 12 [+CLASSROOM REFERENCE] written responses rounds, 5 (42%) of Lisa's passages failed to execute ideal text; in the final character sketch, of the 19 [+CLASSROOM REFERENCE] written response rounds, 10 (53%) of Lisa's passages failed to execute ideal text. In other words, about half the time Mr. Peterson's comments referred to Lisa's [−IDEAL TEXT]. But the other half of the time they referred to her [+IDEAL TEXT].

Lisa, not surprisingly, appears to have no trouble processing comments referring to [+IDEAL TEXT]. We have evidence that she readily interprets an abstract "good" or star drawn next to her text, and in subsequent drafts simply produces more of the same kind of successful prose. In the rough draft of the anecdote, for example, Lisa uses the verb *PERFORMED*, a "fancy" verb that elicits a star from Mr. Peterson. In the final draft of the anecdote she gives him *SNARL* and *SCREECHED*, which also get his stars. In the final character sketch she adds *NASTY SNARL, POUNCED*, and *SNAP*. These, too, are starred by Mr. Peterson. One sentence receives two stars:

C4, L1: EVENTUALLY EVERY [ONE] SQUEEKED BY, BUT THE PRICE SR. CAROLYN HAD TO PAY FOR A CLASS WHO UNDERSTOOD PUNCTUATION INSIDE AND OUT WAS A CLASS WHO WAS ALSO SICK AND TIRED OF PUNCTUATION.

In an interview, Lisa tells us that she was conscious of choosing *SQUEEKED*, and conscious that Mr. Peterson would like the word. Lisa also tells us that Mr. Peterson likes "phrases." When we probe her on this, she says, "Well . . . it's like idioms, or similes. Stuff like that. He likes those things. Or special words. You know. Big words. Whenever I write, I always have the thesaurus around. You know. For interesting words. I learned that in the eighth grade. I remember, our teacher said, when you get to high school, always use a thesaurus. So I just have. And it's helped." From our observations in class, we know, too, that students were given a great deal of group and class feedback on their use of vivid, "interesting" language, and were rewarded for it in various ways, such as in group games. The point here is that Lisa has developed the skills and strategies (using the thesaurus, for example) for producing vivid language, along with acquiring both in eighth grade and extensively in Mr. Peterson's class the information that vivid language is useful and important in writing. What it seems to take, at least in part, for Lisa to process readily Mr. Peterson's written comments, then, is redundancy across response modes that fosters her matching both his information and skills. However, a close look at other response rounds alerts us to what lies beyond matching the teacher's information and skills in Lisa's interactions with Mr. Peterson's written comments.

A Question of Values

We must remember that in this classroom rich in response, Lisa may draw on resources outside herself for processing written comments. That is, she may draw on her conference with Mr. Peterson, on her peers, or on other resources outside the classroom setting. In fact, Lisa does have conferences with Mr. Peterson more than once over drafts of this character study, clarifying information and discussing plans for revision. Yet in spite of her conferences with the teacher and in spite of opportunities to share her drafts with fellow students, Lisa persists in misunderstanding many of Mr. Peterson's written comments, which continue to provide stumbling blocks and confusion for her, as we shall see. We feel that more is at work here than a mismatch of teacher and student information and skill. Thus we probe for other forces that might influence her internal wrestling with these trouble spots, wrestling that could potentially result in shaping her cognitive model of successful writing process and successful written text. We find the following.

Lisa's Values: The Teacher Knows Best, So Do Whatever He Tells You

Interviews with Lisa reveal a closely held assumption that appears to drive much of her writing and that she brings to these written, and other oral, response rounds, specifically, that Mr. Peterson's comments reflect his wiser perspective on writing, and for this reason a student would do well to accept them—"always." In one interview, for example, when we comb through Mr. Peterson's written comments on her writing and focus on some text changes that he had made on her draft, she says that some students mind it when Mr. Peterson "changes their wording," but she doesn't because "Mr. Peterson has more experience and he probably knows what he's doing." She tells us that once, when her group wrote a collaborative piece, Mr. Peterson changed the wording and another student got "really upset." Says Lisa, "She was making too much fuss over it. Mr. Peterson came around and said, 'I wouldn't steer you wrong. I think this honestly sounds better.'" Lisa indicates that she approved of his stance. Lisa's recollection of the incident in class as well as her expressed feelings about Mr. Peterson's editing of her drafts, indicate the value she places not only on the teacher's point of view, but also on his right to impose it on hers.

Unlike many researchers, teachers, and fellow students, Lisa is ready and willing to approve of her text's being "appropriated" by the teacher. As she tells us, she has learned to write "under his [Mr. Peterson's] specifications, and stuff like that. Sometimes he wants you to put this first, and that last. You know. So you do that. Even if you don't think it's that effective. . . . Because when I write my own book, I can do it the other way. But I'm not writing my own book. So I'm writing for him actually."

Closely tied to the notion, then, of doing what the teacher tells you to do is another value: *You write to make the teacher happy.* In fact, we recall Lisa making quite public the value she puts on pleasing the teacher when, during one class discussion as Mr. Peterson searched for a successful rewrite to a paragraph that he was modeling, she raised her hand, waved it his way, and said, "Mr. Peterson, Mr. Peterson, can I read it [her rewrite]? I did it the way you wanted me to." Another assumption, then, that appears to drive Lisa's writing and that she brings to the written response rounds, is that one writes in ways that reveal how compliant one is to the demands/desires of the teacher-authority. Put succinctly, a good girl writes like a good girl. An interview that we had with Lisa at the close of the assignment sequence reveals her valuing of compliant behavior. She tells us that her writing has changed over the course of the semester because she has learned to "write for other people." When we ask her to explain what she means by that, she says, "They're going to grade it. They're going to read it. You know. You're doing it because they want you to. So it's for other people." This compliance carries her across teachers and semesters: "Every time I have a teacher, there's different things about what he wants you to do and what he doesn't want you to do. And you have to pick up new things each semester. Once you find out what they like, you just give them that specific detail. You know." As we saw earlier, Lisa knows that Mr. Peterson likes "little phrases and synonyms," so, she says, "I give him a lot of that in my paper. . . . He likes those things. He puts a lot of stars there" (referring to his written comments). The question is whether Mr. Peterson's value of vivid language is in fact in congruence with Lisa's for "giving him what he wants."

These values, though, give us a way to look at Lisa's interpretations of Mr. Peterson's written comments. And a comment such as "good writing," for Lisa, takes on meaning colored by these values, meaning that transcends giving a reader an aesthetically satisfying experience.

Mr. Peterson's Values: A Student's Ideal Is to Develop a Personal Voice

In an interview, Mr. Peterson tells us that he does not believe that simple compliance to his "wants" equals writing well. "Writing well," he says, "has to do with developing a personal voice." He says that ideally what the teacher "wants" is what any general reading audience wants—a well-developed writing style. This assumption is supported by the data on ideal text and ideal writing process that emerged from the semantic network analysis. In our interview, Mr. Peterson acknowledges that an attitude about pleasing the teacher is widespread among students—"It's part of going to school." Yet he feels that in order to learn really to write, students "have to work out some compromises to accomplish what's important to them." According to Mr. Peterson, when students learn to write, concerted attempts to be compliant with him may be at odds with what in fact will help them to develop as writers. Mere direction-following does not equal "interacting" with the teacher's information, skills, and values. This consideration alerts us to another, related value: *A student's ideal is to develop a personal sense of judgment about writing.*

In practice, then, whether or not Lisa's information and skills match the teacher's, Lisa brings values to the problem solving that Mr. Peterson does not share and that may feed Lisa's persistence in misprocessing some of his responses. Ironically, but not at all incidentally, the value Mr. Peterson places on students sometimes compromising his suggestions in favor of their own reasoned choices is never expressed in the classroom (that is, it is [–CLASSROOM REFERENCE]). We will illustrate this point with two response rounds that were seen as potentially vulnerable to Lisa's misinterpretation.

[+CLASSROOM REFERENCE] [–IDEAL TEXT]

A2, L1: MY EIGHTH GRADE TEACHER, SISTER CAROLYN MARIE, WAS THE MOODIEST PERSON I HAVE EVER KNOWN. ONE MINUTE SHE CAN HAVE A GRIN STRETCHING FROM EAR TO EAR . . .

Mr. Peterson circles *WAS* and *CAN* and draws a line form one to the other. In the margin he writes "tense." In addition, as we saw earlier, he underlines *STRETCHING FROM EAR TO EAR* and in the margin writes, "Another way to say this?" His comments on Lisa's text look like this:

A2, P1:   MY EIGHTH GRADE TEACHER, SISTER CAROLYN MARIE, (WAS)

          THE MOODIEST PERSON I HAVE EVER KNOWN. ONE MINUTE

tense   SHE (CAN HAVE A GRIN STRETCHING FROM EAR TO EAR . ?. *another way to say this?*

We ask Lisa about the circled words, accompanied by the word "tense." She has no trouble recognizing the marks as referring to her switching verb tenses. It is important to keep in mind a remark Lisa made earlier to us indicating that one of the things she tries to remember when she writes is tenses, because, as she says, she "jumps all over the place." It is also important that she tells us that Mr. Peterson has more experience than his students and "probably knows what he is doing." We see that Mr. Peterson's comments about verb tense touch upon three elements for Lisa: (a) information given in class about consistency of tenses; (b) Lisa's acknowledged lack of demonstrated skill with verb tense; (c) her valuing of a thorough and (probably) knowing authority whom she aims to please. Now, Lisa's writing does not immediately benefit from Mr. Peterson's comment about tense, for a tense shift occurs in the final draft of the anecdote, and Mr. Peterson marks it the same way as he had earlier. In her interview, Lisa says that for this second draft she "forgot" to change the verbs. Of note, though, is that while her skill with tense does not improve, she clearly does something about the verbs, as a comparison between the rough draft of the anecdote and the final draft of the anecdote reveals:

A2, L1: MY EIGHTH GRADE TEACHER, SISTER CAROLYN MARIE, WAS THE MOODIEST PERSON I HAVE EVER KNOWN. ONE MINUTE SHE CAN HAVE A GRIN STRETCHING FROM EAR TO EAR AND THEN THE VERY NEXT THAT GRIN CAN TURN INTO A NASTY SNARL.

B2, L1: MY EIGHTH GRADE TEACHER, SISTER CAROLYN MARIE, WAS THE MOODIEST PERSON I HAVE EVER BEEN ACQUAINTED WITH. ONE MINUTE SHE CAN BE GRINNING FROM EAR TO EAR, THEN THE VERY NEXT MINUTE, THAT GRIN CAN DIVERSIFY INTO A NASTY SNARL.

Lisa knows on one level that her verbs "jump all over the place." While she possesses the "right" information, she appears not to possess the skill to solve the problem. However, that she may indeed have the correct skill is indicated in the final character sketch, in which the tense problem is remedied:

C5, L1: ONE WEIRD THING ABOUT SR. CAROLYN WAS HOW
INTERCHANGEABLE HER MOODS WERE. ONE MINUTE SHE
COULD BE GRINNING, THEN THE VERY NEXT MINUTE,
THAT GRIN COULD FADE INTO A NASTY SNARL.

In the final draft of the anecdote (B2, above), her skills may be compromised
by the value she places on doing what Mr. Peterson and other teachers want.
That is, her changes of *KNOWN* to *BE ACQUAINTED WITH, HAVE A GRIN*
to *CAN BE GRINNING*, and *TURN* to *DIVERSIFY*, as well as the tense change
to present progressive instead of past, may, in part, also be a "direction-
following" response to Mr. Peterson's question, "Another way to say this?" her
remedy confounding the tense problem with the cliche problem that we discussed earlier. Unfortunately, the changes are not satisfactory, as on this draft
Mr. Peterson not only edits out *FROM EAR TO EAR*, but marks *DIVERSIFY*
as wrong too. Her lexical changes, her longer and fancier words, actually seem
to make things worse. However, she *is* "saying it another way" and she may
also be attempting to incorporate Mr. Peterson's ideal text that would demonstrate vivid verbs. Yet in trying to do what Mr. Peterson wants, Lisa seems not
to have sight of Mr. Peterson's underlying intents, which emerge in the classroom, for her to develop her own voice. Negotiating the solution to a writing
problem becomes complicated by this incongruity and Lisa's own judgment
appears to be lost. (See Sperling, 1985, for an account of the ways Lisa as well
as other students handle comments that require narrow as opposed to broad
interpretations—comments asking for changes in grammar or structure as
opposed to comments asking for changes in content, for example.)

[–CLASSROOM REFERENCE] [–IDEAL TEXT]

When the written response episode reveals no apparent shared information on top of no demonstrated student skill, a student's value system incon-
gruent with the teacher's can interfere even more dramatically with the student's internalizing the teacher's instruction. On the final character sketch, for
example, Lisa writes:

C6, L1: HAVING TO GUESS HER EVERY MOOD AND WHAT TO
SAY AROUND HER FROM TIME TO TIME GOT TIRSOME AND
TEDIOUS.

Mr. Peterson crosses out *HAVING* and writes in "We had," He crosses out
TIME and writes in "another, and this," so the commented text looks like the
following:

C6, P1:   HAVING TO GUESS HER EVERY MOOD AND WHAT TO
We had   another   —and this
           SAY AROUND HER FROM TIME TO TIME GOT TIRSOME
           AND TEDIOUS.

His changes yield, "We had to guess her every mood and what to say around her from time to another [sic] and this got tiresome . . ." (Mr. Peterson does not correct the spelling of "tiresome"). Also, Mr. Peterson's "this" Lisa reads as "thus." While a plausible interpretation because his handwriting is somewhat unclear, this reading renders a serious change in meaning and logic.

There is no reference in class to the ideal text that motivated Mr. Peterson's change, no reference, for example, to preferring direct human sentence subjects to long cumbersome phrases. Thus it appears that Lisa has no hook of information on which to hang her writing skills. However, she is eager to do what Mr. Peterson wants, and herein may lie her misunderstanding. When we ask Lisa what she thinks of this rewording—and to try to recall what she thought when she first saw it—Lisa is positive that Mr. Peterson has done the right thing. She tells us that Mr. Peterson's version sounds "more polished," more like a high school student writing than a middle school student, *especially*, incongruously, the "*thus*." Lisa accepts what he says, or seems to say, without question, uncritically. Because she is so willing, she fully engages with her interpretation of his rewording, sympathetic to what she erroneously perceives as Mr. Peterson's ideal text. Ironically, it is Lisa's penchant for good student behavior—paying attention to and accepting what the teacher says—that boggles the problem solving and eclipses her own judgment.

Conclusion

We have examined the written responses to the writing of one kind of student, a high achiever with a strong drive to be compliant. What we have found is that the written response round, that is, the interaction between responder and recipient through the medium of the written comment, invokes a complex problem-solving activity requiring strategies on the part of the student that incorporate not only information and skills that ideally match the teacher's, but, potentially, a host of values as well. These values are formed by a full social and school context that colors the very meaning of the problem solving.

While there are successful written response rounds between this teacher and student, the unsuccessful ones that emerge even under these desirable teaching conditions alert us to what may be unavoidable complexity in any teacher-student writing interaction: The student holds values that, even if well-intended, can be enough out of line with the teacher's as to interfere with the student's and the teacher's matching their definitions of writing problems and solutions.

By looking at Lisa's attempts to use Mr. Peterson's comments to solve her writing problems, and by considering the full range of equipment—the information, skills, and values—that she brings to the process, we learn something about Lisa—about her ability to judge both her writing and Mr. Peterson's feedback; about her dependency on the teacher as external authority; about her reluctance to take on authority herself. But beyond this, by closely observing an activity that we know to be rife with misunderstanding, we learn something about the dissonance between the skills and information of teacher and student and the complications to these brought by a dissonance of values.

With the researcher's lens, then, we can alert teachers to hidden constraints on their teaching, and perhaps demystify some of the persistence that students show in misconstruing teacher response. We hope that the kind of analysis we have done will help teachers to anticipate at least some student misunderstandings, which seem to reflect the context in which writing gets learned and taught. In their sleuth work, teachers need not work alone if they can find ways to get their students to talk about their values regarding writing in general and writing in school. The trick will be to convince certain students that pleasing the teacher may not be a magic formula for improving the way they write.

Appendix

Mr. Peterson's Class—A Model

Principles of Ideal Text
Anticipate reader reaction
    Be interesting (exciting, dramatic, spicy, involving)
        Use an interesting topic
        Use specific details and descriptions
            Contrive these, if necessary, from your imagination
            to liven up your writing and make it more fun to
            to read and write
        Use strong verbs, chosen carefully to suggest action and to
        convey more
        Get rid of excess words
            To eliminate repetition
            To get into your subject faster
    Be clear
        Use specific and concrete language
        Give specific examples
    Give descriptions that present a clear picture
    Make connections obvious
        Between paragraphs (ideas)
            Order them to create the best transitions

Within paragraphs

Write a strong topic sentence that gives
direction to the paragraph and connects the
sentences together

Give evidence to support the point made in the
topic sentence

Relate all sentences in the paragraph to the topic
sentence

Within sentences

Combine ideas when possible into one sentence
that makes the links and connections between
ideas, and which avoids sentences that are too
long and scattered

Do the assignment

Write a character sketch which the teacher will show you how to do

Figure out what the person's about

Analyze the person

Know the character well

Consider a range of possible subjects
Choose one that you already have a lot of
information about

Make observations

Take a close look at the person
Distinguish between observation and
judgement
Defer judgement—collect lots of examples
and descriptions instead

Interpret revealing behaviors

Think about what they say about the person
Make guesses based on your knowledge of the person

Discover and identify patterns in the persons's
behavior

Identify a quality or characteristic of the
person, a trait, from the specific
examples and evidence you have
Find traits which contrast with one
another

Describe and explain the person to make her/him
understandable to others

Use instances that demonstrate the character traits

Use stories that bring out the traits
Use anecdotes that catch the character of the
person and give examples of behavior traits
Use specific things the person says, quotes or

dialogues that reflect the personality of the
character
    Make these up or derive them from your
    feelings about the character, if necessary
Make language choices to catch reader interest and to
get an idea across
    Choose words carefully to:
        Label or describe ideas and traits
        Spice up your writing
        Simplify
        Avoid ordinary, average, or vague words
Follow the format provided by the teacher
    Begin with an opening sentence that engages reader
    interest
        Start with a picture
        Start with an action
        Start with a dramatic statement
        Start with a quote that catches the person's
        character or personality
    Make the first paragraph an introduction to the person
        Deal with his or her appearance as it relates to his
        or her personality and makes a comment on
        the way he or she chooses to portray her- or himself
            Describe clothing
            Describe looks
            Describe manner
            Describe movement
    Write three paragraphs in the middle that each deal
    with an aspect of the person
        Make connections between the ideas
            Use three separate but related qualities
            Link the traits by contrast
            Make links between qualities and examples
    Write a conclusion

Principles of Ideal Process
Make use of experience and imagination
    Make it up
    Imagine
    Improvize
    Stretch the truth
Steps in design
    Draft a paper

    Make language choices
    Include specific details
    Find an effective order
Hand it in to the teacher
Rewrite, revise, re-do
    Paying attention to teacher comments
    Trying to do better
Hand it in again
Jots and Tittles
    Appropriate length
    Conventions
        Of length
        Of spelling and punctuation
    Consistency
        Of tenses
        Of style
Get results
    Good grades
    A jump in writing ability

Independent Student Criteria

Good writing
    Is writing that sounds right
        Grammar
        Word choices
        Phrasing
        Paper organization
    Is whatever is rewarded by the teacher
        Plain, basic, straightforward
        Different from mine
        Harder to produce

Notes

1. For the 1985 study, our research team observed and recorded by means of field notes and audio- and videotapes, the daily activities in this ninth grade English classroom over a period of seven weeks. The research team recorded the teaching and learning of three complete assignment sequences during which students produced multiple drafts toward three essays. We collected extensive response data for one essay assignment for selected focal students who represented the range of academic achievement in their class. Data included all student papers with teacher responses written on them; video- and audiotaped records of all classroom activity; researchers' summary notes and comments on all activity; audiotaped interviews with the teacher;

and audiotaped interviews with the students. (See Freedman, 1985, in press, for a full account of student selection and data collection and reduction.)

2. The teacher was selected after an intensive search and screening for, among other things, offering a rich range of response, of which written response was one type, and offering a writing curriculum that covered the range of analytic writing tasks that high school students encountered as they are asked to produce academic papers (see Freedman, 1985, for a full account of teacher and classroom selection). Mr. Peterson produced written response on all drafts of his student's writing. Further, he accompanied this response with individual conferences because, as he said to us, "I've learned I can not assume students understand my clear and concise prose, so I no longer take chances. When I return a set of papers with my written comments I arrange a brief conference with each student, primarily to determine if he understands what I have written on his paper" (Freedman, 1985, Appendix 6, p. 14). We focus on Lisa (a code name) because, to do an in-depth case study, reflecting on information, skills, and values surrounding written response, we need to be able to draw on as much explicit data as we can, and Lisa, a high-achieving student, interacted most extensively with Mr. Peterson in the classroom as well as with us in our interviews.

3. Note: For our purposes here, examples are presented using the following conventions: The student draft is identified (A, first draft, anecdote; B, final draft, anecdote; C, final draft, character sketch); the round, in the order we present it, is given a number (e.g., "1"); the turn is identified as either Lisa's (L) or Mr. Peterson's (P); and, finally, the turn is given a number (e.g., "1"). Thus the first round that we look at from the final character sketch is identified as "C1"; Lisa's first turn is identified as "L1"; Mr. Peterson's first turn is identified as "P1." In all cases, we are faithful to the student's and teacher's texts.

4. During the seven weeks that we observed Mr. Peterson's classroom, the student wrote several descriptions and analyses of persons, either real or fictitious. Of the three major essay topics assigned during the time of our observations, we focus here on the first, for which we collected extensive data and for which Mr. Peterson gave a substantial amount of written response.

5. For a complete quantitative analysis of these data, see Sperling and Freedman (1986).

References

Beach, R. 1979. "The Effects of Between Draft Teacher Evaluation Versus Student Self Evaluation on High School Students' Revising of Rough Drafts." *Research in the Teaching of English* 13:111–19.

Bereiter, C., and M. Scardamalia. 1982. "From Conversation to Composition." In *Advances in Instructional Psychology (Vol. 2)* edited by R. Glaser. Hillsdale, NJ: Erlbaum.

Butler, J. 1980. "Remedial Writers: The Teacher's Job as Corrector of Papers." *College Composition and Communication* 31:270–77.

College Entrance Examination Board. 1963. *Freedom and Discipline in the Teaching of English.*

Freedman, S. 1985. *The Role of Response in the Acquisition of Written Language* (final report NIE-G-083-0065). Washington, DC: National Institute of Education.

————. in press. *Response to Student Writing: Teaching and Learning.* NCTE Research Monograph Series. Urbana, IL: National Council of Teachers of English.

Freedman, S. W., & Bennett, J. 1987. *Peer Groups at Work in Two Writing Classrooms* (final report to the Office of Educational Research and Improvement). Washington, DC: Center for the Study of Writing.

Garvey, C. 1977. "Contingent Queries." In *Interaction, Conversation, and the Development of Language* edited by M. Lewis and L. Rosenblum, New York: John Wiley.

Greenleaf, C. 1985. "Teacher and Student Models of Good Writing and Good Writing Process." In *The Role of Response in the Acquisition of Written Language* edited by Freedman, (final report NIE-G-083-0065). Washington, DC: National Institute of Education.

Greenleaf, C., and S. Freedman. 1986. *Preference Analysis of a Response Episode: Getting to the Cognitive Content of Classroom Interaction.* Paper presented to American Educational Research Association Conference, San Francisco.

Hahn, J. 1981. "Students' Reactions to Teachers' Written Comments." *National Writing Project Network Newsletter* 4:7–10.

Hillocks, G. 1982. "The Interaction of Instruction, Teacher Comment, and Revision in Teaching the Composing Process." *Research in the Teaching of English* 16: 261–78.

Lees, E. 1979. "Evaluating Student Writing." *College Composition and Communication* 30:370–74.

Mehan, H. 1979. *Learning Lessons: Social Organization in the Classroom.* Cambridge, MA: Harvard University Press.

Searle, D., and D. Dillon. 1980. "The Message of Marking: Teacher Written Responses to Student Writing at Intermediate Grade Levels." *Research in the Teaching of English* 14:233–42.

Sommers, N. 1982. "Responding to Student Writing." *College Composition and Communication* 33:148–56.

Sperling, M. 1985. "Written Response: Student Understandings and Oral Contexts." In *The Role of Response in the Acquisition of Written Language* edited by S. Freedman, (final report NIE-G-083-0065). Washington, DC: National Institute of Education.

Sperling, M., and S. Freedman. 1986. A Good Girl Writes Like a Good Girl; Written Responses to Student Writing. Paper presented at American Educational Research Association annual meeting, San Francisco.

Vygotsky, L. 1978. *Mind in Society.* Cambridge, MA: Harvard University Press.

About the Authors

Melanie Sperling is completing her doctoral work at the University of California, Berkeley, researching the high school teacher-student writing conference. She is editor of the *National Writing Project/Center for the Study of Writing Quarterly,* published at Berkeley's Graduate School of Education, and is coauthor of *The Active Writer,* a composition textbook for college freshman.

Sarah Warshauer Freedman is Associate Professor of Education at the University of California, Berkeley, and Director of the Center for the Study of Writing. She is the author of *The Acquisition of Written Language: Response and Revision.* In press is an NCTE research monograph, *Responses to Student Writing: Teaching and Learning.*

9

Teachers' Rhetorical Comments on Student Papers

Robert J. Connors
Andrea A. Lunsford

As far back as we can trace student papers, we can see the attempts of teachers to squeeze their reactions into a few pithy phrases, to roll all their strength and all their sweetness up into one ball for student delectation. Every teacher of composition has shared in this struggle to address students, and writing helpful comments is one of the skills most teachers wish to develop toward that end. Given that writing evaluative commentary is one of the great tasks we share, one might think it would have been one of the central areas of examination in composition studies.

Indeed, a number of thoughtful examinations of written teacher commentaries exist, most of them measuring empirically the comments of a relatively small teacher and student population. No studies we could find, however, have ever looked at large numbers of papers commented on by large numbers of teachers. We do not have, in other words, any large-scale knowledge of the ways that North American teachers and students tend to interact through written assessments. There are clear logistical reasons for this lack of large-scale studies; the gathering and analysis of a large data base are daunting tasks, and evaluating rhetorical (as opposed to formal) commentary is a challenge. But we had the data base gathered from previous research, and in the great tradition of fools rushing in where wise number-crunchers fear to tread, we thought we'd take a look at this question of teacher commentary.

As inveterate historical kibbitzers, we naturally started research by asking what sorts of comments teachers had made on student papers in the past. Have teacher comments become more or less prescriptive, longer or shorter, more positive or more negative? We headed for the stacks to try to find out. Rather to our amazement, we discovered that what we were proposing to look at—teachers' rhetorical comments on student papers—was a relatively recent phenomenon in general composition teaching.

The Historical Trail

Evidence of widespread acceptance of teachers acting as rhetorical audiences for their first-year students simply does not exist much farther back than the early 1950s.[1] Before that time, the most widely accepted idea was that teachers' jobs were to correct, perhaps edit, and then grade student papers. Now and then someone attacked this approach, but it seems to have held wide sway through the first half of this century. As Walter Barnes put it in 1912, writing students live

> in an absolute monarchy, in which they are the subjects, the teacher the king (more often, the queen), and the red-ink pen the royal scepter. . . . Theme correction is an unintelligent process. . . . In our efforts to train our children, we turn martinets and discipline the recruits into a company of stupid, stolid soldierkins—prompt to obey orders, it may be, but utterly devoid of initiative. (158–59)

The teacher who "pounces on the verbal mistake, who ferrets out the buried grammatical blunder, who scents from afar a colloquialism or a bit of slang" (159) seemed to Barnes a weak writing teacher, but by far the most common kind.

The idea that the teacher's most important job was to rate rather than to respond rhetorically to themes seems to have been well-nigh universal from the 1880s onward, perhaps as a result of the much-cried-up "illiteracy crisis" of the 1880s and 1890s. Those who have examined older college themes preserved in archives at Harvard and Baylor have noted that teacher "comments" overwhelmingly comprised formal and mechanical corrections (for example, see Copeland and Rideout). College programs, in fact, very early came up with "correction cards," editing sheets, and symbol systems that were meant to allow teachers numerically to assess students' adherence to conventional rules, and it seemed reasonable to extrapolate that approach to issues of content, organization, and style. Thus were born during the first decade of this century, the various "rating scales" that represented the first systematic attempt we know of to deal with the issue of rhetorical effectiveness in student writing.

This is not the place for a complete history of the rise of rating scales, the various purposes they covered, the arguments they engendered, or the epistemological assumptions that fostered their development. Suffice it to say that between 1900 and 1925 a number of scales were proposed for rating composition. It's probably fair to say that these scales evolved from the rising status of scientific method and statistics and from writing teachers' uncomfortable awareness of exactly how "subjective" their grading of papers was (James). Teachers wished for a defensible rating instrument, and, beginning with the Hillegas Scale in 1912, educational theorists proposed to give them one. Many developments and variations of Hillegas's scale followed: the Thorndike Extension, the Trabue Scale, the Hudelson Scale, the Harvard-Newton Scale, the Breed-Frostic and Willing Scales, and others (Hudelson 164–67).

We don't want to suggest that these composition scales were entirely devoted to formal and mechanical ratings; their interest for us, in fact, lies primarily in their attempts to evolve an early holistic-style set of standards by which the more qualitative elements of composition could be "reliably" judged. This pedagogically interesting attempt found a supporter in no less than Sterling Leonard, much of whose early work in composition involved his attempt to build more rhetorical awareness into rating scales he felt were too much weighted toward formal aspects (Leonard 760–61). Interest in the perfect rating scale, however, eventually waned, doubtless because rating rhetorical elements was simply too complex and multi-layered a task for any scale. As two scale-using researchers admitted in 1917, after having been through a complex study using a variant of the Harvard-Newton Scale, "This study raises more questions than it answers. In fact, it cannot be said to have settled any question satisfactorily" (Brown and Hagerty 527).

The fact that rating scales usually served as instruments for administrative judgment rather than for student improvement also led to their gradual abandonment by many teachers. Fred Newton Scott, with his customary sagacity, identified this problem early on, noting in 1913 that "whenever a piece of scientific machinery is allowed to take the place of teaching—which is in essence but an attempt to reveal to the pupil the unifying principle of life—the result will be to artificialize the course of instruction" (4). Scott drew a strong distinction between a system which grades a composition for administrative purposes and that which evaluates it as a stage in the pupil's progress. Hillegas's Scale clearly served the former purpose, and thus Scott ended his discussion of it with this Parthian shot:

> I leave this problem with you, then, with the seemingly paradoxical conclusion that we ought in every way to encourage Professor Thorndike and Dr. Hillegas in their attempts to provide us with a scale for the measurement of English compositions, but that when the scale is ready, we had better refrain from using it. If this sounds like the famous recipe for a salad which closes with the words "throw the entire mixture out the window," you will not, I am sure, if you have followed me thus far, be under any misapprehension as to my meaning. (5)

The liberal wing of the profession (including most of Scott's PhD students) followed this line, and the controversy over rating scales lasted for better than a dozen years.

By the mid-1920s, the excitement over rating scales died down as teachers began discussing the most effective ways of "criticizing a theme" outside of the question of grading it. Various kinds of advice were advanced: raise the standards as the course advances; don't be too severe; always include a bit of praise; don't point out every error.[2] All good advice, but the attitude of these authors toward the job of the teacher was almost universally in support of critical/ judgmental rather than editorial/interventionist relations with students. "Correction" of papers was always uppermost, even to "liberal" teachers and writers. James Bowman, whose "The Marking of English Themes" of 1920 provides a sensible discussion of teacher marking, devotes only one short paragraph to the whole issue of teacher comments: "The comments are of far greater importance than the mark which is given the theme. These should be stern and yet kindly. While they should overlook no error, they should, in addition, be constructive and optimistic. It is necessary, above all, for the teacher to enter intimately and sympathetically into the problems of the student" (242–43). No one would argue with these ideas, but, even if well-intentioned, they are immensely general. Against that one paragraph, the rest of the article discussed correction of errors and assignment of grades.

This ratio held sway in most quarters. Oh, there were the forward-looking articles that always surprise first-time readers of old volumes of the *English Journal*—like Allan Gilbert's "What Shall We Do with Freshman Themes?" which proposes a socially-constructed and process-oriented regimen of peer review and group conferencing.[3] But for every Gilbert or Leonard or Scott or Gertrude Buck there were ten Hilda Jane Holleys, for whom "Interest and originality" was but one of ten areas rated (and third from the bottom of her chart, too, way after "Grammar" and "Vocabulary") and Louise Griswolds, proposing to reread each graded theme and change the grade to F if every formal error had not been corrected.

Such formal-error correction characterized teacher response through the twenties, thirties, and early forties, and the centrality of the correction approach was not widely questioned until the advent of the communications movement during the late forties. Then, the concept of teachers best serving students by "correcting" their papers, like many other accepted traditions in writing pedagogy, began to come under sustained fire from a new generation of writing teachers.[4] Jeffrey Fleece in 1951 made what seemed to many a novel suggestion: that teachers actually consider themselves as students' real audiences and respond to their essays accordingly. Since "purpose" was the watchword of the communications movement, said Fleece, why not stop pretending that the teacher was not the only final and actual audience for students, and make use of that audience relationship? On papers with a real purpose, said Fleece, "the teacher should react to the content in some way, to guarantee the student's continued confidence in his interest" (273).

Fleece's view hardly seems radical today, but at the time it was received as a startling suggestion about the relations that students and teachers in writing might have. Even students were unused to having what they *said* in papers taken seriously. In an essay called "Conversing in the Margins," Harold Collins reported in 1954 that:

> When I return the themes, hands go up over pained faces, and injured innocence makes itself heard.
>
> "Aren't you supposed to stick to the grammar and punctuation and that sort of thing and not bother about what we say, the—er—content of our themes?"

"I had only one error in spelling and three in punctuation. What do you mark on?" (He means, "Why didn't I get an A or a B?")

"Do we have to agree with you? That doesn't seem. . . ."

I must justify my extensive commentary, explain why I have seen fit to stray from such textbook concerns as diction, spelling, punctuation, sentence structure, and organization. With some warmth, I protest that I am not a theme-reading machine, a new marvel of electronics grading for grammar. Though it may be hard to credit, I am a real human being, and so I am naturally interested in what my students say in their themes . . . (465)

Between 1900 and 1940, the concept that most students could have anything to "say" in their writing that would *really* interest the teacher was hardly imagined except by a few rare teachers.[5]

By the middle fifties, however, educators were more and more expected to try to address their students' essays as "real" audiences and to write long personal comments. "It requires extra time and care on the teacher's part," admitted Delmer Rodabaugh. "Perhaps it is not strictly his job to go to so much trouble, but trouble turns to pleasure when he begins to get results" (37). Rodabaugh admitted that what he proposed was not new, but was "a deliberate and persistent attempt to extend what we all do." This new effort, based on the idea that students should get full-scale rhetorical comments both in margins and at the end of papers, was very much in place by the end of the 1950s, and new teachers after that time who gave no rhetorical advice along with their formal corrections did their work with certain guilt.

But what, exactly, did that work really come to? The attitudes that first appeared during the heyday of the communications movement still control much of what is presumed today about written teacher responses to student writing. Since the 1950s the field of composition studies has waxed, and its attitude toward teacher response to student writing has remained marked by the essential assumption that the teacher must and should engage the student in rhetorical dialogue. Around this assumption lies a large literature, which began to burgeon in the middle 1960s, hit a peak in the early 1980s, and has recently come up for discussion again in an excellent collection of essays edited by Chris Anson.[6]

We won't review this literature here, since so many people in the Anson collection have already done that better than we could. But we did notice, as we looked through the many thoughtful essays about teacher response, how few of them have studied the subject in numerical depth. Many discussions about response are inspiring, but most are either prescriptive, idealistic, or theoretical. Now and then a discouraging word has been heard—Albert Kitzhaber's flinty assessment of how few Dartmouth teachers actually wrote any comments on papers in the early 1960s, Cy Knoblauch and Lil Brannon's glum assertion in 1981 that no kind of written comment from teachers did much good or harm or had much attention paid to it, or Nancy Sommers's study of 35 teachers responding at Oklahoma and NYU, which concluded that "the news from the classroom is not good," that teachers were not responding to students in ways that would help them engage with issues, purposes, or goals (154). But most of the rest of the college-level literature is largely exploratory. No really large-scale study of the sorts of comments teachers were actually making on student papers existed, at least none that we knew of. We thought we'd give it a try.

The Sample and the Methodology

In 1986, we had collected 21,000 teacher-marked student essays for a national study of patterns of formal error. After identifying a randomized, stratified sample of 3,000 papers, we asked 50 analyzers to find examples of the top twenty error patterns in the writing of contemporary college students. The results of that study were published in 1988 as "Frequency of Formal Errors in Current College Writing."[7] As we sat through the long day of analysis and talked afterwards about what we'd seen that was interesting, everyone agreed that the whole issue of the ways in which the teachers responded to the student writing was something we ought to study. Not, of course, the ways in which teachers marked up the formal and mechanical errors, which nearly always tended to be done using either handbook numbers or the standard set of mysterious phatic grunts: "awk," "ww," "comma," etc. No, what we wanted to try to look at was a sometimes vague entity that we called "global comments" by the teachers. What were teachers saying in response to the *content* of the paper, or to the specifically *rhetorical* aspects of its organization, sentence structure, etc.? What kinds of teacher-student relationships did the comments reflect?

We had a data base that we could use. Back in 1985, when we had been soliciting papers from teachers nationally, we had specifically asked that we be sent only papers that had been marked by teachers; some of the papers had very minimal markings, but each one had been evaluated in some way, had passed under the eye and been judged by the pen of a teacher. Our original request letter asked only for student papers "to which teachers have responded with interlinear, marginal, or terminal comments." The Methodology Police would probably bust us for the way the sample was gathered; the 300 teachers who sent us papers were a self-selected group who responded to an initial mailing (offering books from the St. Martin's Press trade list in exchange for commented papers) that went to over 8,000 teachers. We can't be sure why these folks were the ones who came forward, but even though the paper sample itself is randomized and nationally stratified by region, size and type of college, and so on, the teachers themselves were self-selected. Though it would be more satisfying to be able to say we had papers from 3,000 teachers who were chosen randomly from some giant national bingo drum, getting such a sample is simply beyond us. As it stands, we have a larger sample, and a better national distribution, than any previous study. Nothing, as one of our students once wrote, is extremely perfect.[8]

Okay, the data base was in hand. Now, as before, we faced the question of what instrument we would use to try to understand what we might find in the 3,000-paper sample.

We figured that we might as well work as inductively as we could, so we again selected 300 random papers, 150 for Andrea and 150 for Bob. We then looked carefully at these 300 papers, trying to note any important patterns we could see of teacher response to global rhetorical issues. Each of us came up with a list, and then we compared lists. We found that we had both noted some responses based on individual comments and some that were based in the *forms* and *genres* of teacher comments. We melded our lists and came up with a checklist form that we hoped would capture a substantial number of the different kinds of global comments our readers might see.

With lots of help from Eric Walborn, Heather Graves, and Carrie Leverenz in the Ohio State graduate program, one Saturday morning in May 1991 we assembled a group of 26 experienced writing teachers and eager readers. Lured by the prospect of a promised twelve feet of high-quality submarine sandwiches, these champions of the proletariat plunged into a learning curve and then into large stacks of papers, looking only at the teacher comments on each paper, and searching for a number of specific elements to record.[9]

We were specifically interested in what we called "global comments" by teachers, general evaluative comments found at the end or the beginning of papers. Such comments may be quite long or as short as a single word, or they may take the form of marginal or interlinear comments in the body of the paper which are rhetorically oriented and not related to formal or mechanical problems. Global comments by teachers are meant to address global issues in students' writing: issues of rhetoric, structure, general success, longitudinal writing development, mastery of conventional generic knowledge, and other large-scale issues.

In other words, we asked our readers to ignore any comments on the level of formal error, grammar, punctuation, spelling, syntax, etc., unless those comments were couched in a specifically rhetorical way, i.e., "Your audience will think harshly of you if they see lots of comma splices." What we wanted to try to get at were the ways in which teachers judge the rhetorical effectiveness of their students' writing, and the sorts of teacher-student relationships reflected in the comments that teachers give. The following table summarizes what we found.

NUMERICAL RESULTS: GLOBAL COMMENTARY RESEARCH

Total number of papers examined: 3,000

	# of 3,000	Percentage
Number of papers with global or rhetorical comments	2,297	77% of all Ps
Papers without global or rhetorical comments	703	23%
Number of papers graded	2,241	75%

Number of papers with initial or terminal comments	1,934	64%
Number of initial comments	318	16% of Ps with I or T comments
Number of terminal comments	1,616	84% of Ps with I or T comments

Purpose of comments:

To give feedback on draft in process	242	11% of Ps with I or T comments
To justify grades	1,355	59%

Global comments in general

Comments that are all essentially positive	172	9% of Ps with I or T comments
Comments that are all essentially negative	451	23%
Comments that begin positively and then go to negative	808	42%
Comments that begin negatively and then go to positive	217	11%
Comments that lead with rhetorical issues	692	36%
Comments that lead with mechanical issues	357	18%
Very short comments—fewer than 10 words	460	24%
Very long comments—more than 100 words	101	5%
Comments focused exclusively on rhetorical issues	472	24%
Comments focused exclusively on formal/mechanical issues	435	22%
Comments that argue with content points made in paper	478	24%
Comments that indicate use of mechanical criteria as gate criteria ("The comma splices force me to give this an F despite. . . .")	150	8%
Comments that give general reader response ("like/ dislike")	322	17%

Comments evaluating specific rhetorical elements:

Supporting evidence, examples, details	1,296	56% of all Ps with comments
Organization	643	28%

Purpose	240	11%
Response to assignment	246	11%
Audience	137	6%
Overall progress, beyond commentary on paper	176	8%
Comments that deal with specific formal elements:		
Sentence structure	767	33% of all Ps with comments
Paragraph structure	417	18%
Documentation	154	7%
Quotations	142	6%
Source materials	133	6%
Paper format	372	16%

Grades and Patterns of Commentary

We looked at 3,000 papers. Of that number, 2,297 (77%) contained global comments. We had asked in our letter only for teacher-marked student papers, not for specifically "global" comments, so this percentage seems heartening. In fact, the 77% of teachers who took the time and effort to write even minimal global comments on student papers seem to us rather to diminish the claim sometimes heard that teachers do nothing with student papers except bleed upon errors. Of our sample, more than three-quarters dealt in some way with larger issues of rhetorical effectiveness.

The number of papers bearing some sort of grade was 2,241, or 75% of the total. These grades did not, we hasten to say, always appear on papers with global comments; in fact, our readers noted with some amazement how many of the graded papers contained no other form of commentary on them. The overwhelming impression our readers were left with was that grades were implicitly—or often explicitly—overwhelming impediments both for teachers and for students. If papers had no other markings, they had grades or evaluative symbols.[10]

The grades themselves took an extraordinary variety of forms, ranging from standard letter grades, with pluses and minuses; to standard 100-point number grades; to cryptic systems of numbers, fractions, decimals; and finally to symbolic systems of different kinds, including varieties of stars, moons, checks, check-pluses and -minuses. We had meant to attempt an average of these grades, but the different systems they used and the different contexts out of which they came made such an attempt seem silly; we had no idea how to average notations such as ***, 94/130, 3.1, +, F+, and ☺. So we desisted.

Of the 3,000 papers, 1,934 (64%) had identifiable terminal or initial comments on them. Such comments, appearing at the end or the beginning of a paper, serve as the teacher's most general and usually final comment on the work of the paper as a whole, and so we paid very close attention to them. Of the two styles, the terminal comments were by far the most common. We found that only 318 papers (16% of all the papers with overview-style comments), placed that general overview at the beginning of the paper; the other 84% of teachers using these comments placed them at the end of the paper, usually along with the grade. There are probably simple reasons for this phenomenon. Terminal comments, especially those with grades to justify, are written on the last page of the essay, seeming to result from the reading process more naturally. They flow when the teacher's memory is freshest, at the point when she has just stopped reading. Their being buried in a later page allows them to be more private and even secret, unlike initial comments, which announce the teacher's judgment to the world in public fashion. But some teachers seem to prefer initial overall comments, perhaps because they hope to engage the student in thinking about central issues *before* looking at the rest of the commentary.

As we looked over the patterns of general commentary our readers found, we were reminded of how much rhetorical *forms* can tell us about the purposes and attitudes of those using them. Every intellectual field might be said to have its announced public values and its secret soul. Most composition teachers know what the field *says* is important—our public "tropes," so to speak. We talk and write often of purpose, of audience, of organization, of proof, of process and invention and revision and so on. These words fill our journals, our professional books, our conferences, and especially our textbooks. But do we really follow through? Do comments on papers show us acting on these public tropes, giving them more than lip service? Or do we have more genuine and less overt agendas? That was one of our major questions as we looked at these longer comments. As we examined the longer comments, we began to find patterns, and we came more and more to see our findings as a sort of exploration of the tropics of teacher commentary. Teachers, we found, tend to return to well-understood topoi as well as to familiar terms, phrases, and locutions as they make their judgments on student writing. These topoi and tropes of commentary have several origins: they are public and private, conscious and habitual, social and individualistic. They are powerful tacit genres, and we were particularly interested in how these patterns of commentary reflected the beliefs of the field of composition studies.

Initial and terminal comments in particular have, we discovered, certain patterns and genres that they tend to fall into. The rarest of these tropes is the comment consisting of nothing except praise and positive evaluation. Of the papers with global comments, only 9% exhibited this pattern of totally positive commentary. These figures correlate with Daiker's Miami of Ohio study and illustrate how American teachers tend to be trained in finding and isolating problems in writing (104). Rarely can teachers keep themselves to completely positive commentary. As our readers noted, these positive comments tended to be the shortest of all the global comments found, as well as the friendliest. They were nearly all found next to A-level grades, and the teachers seem commonly to have felt that such good grades needed little explanation or commentary. Interestingly, our readers mentioned that completely positive global comments were the most personal comments, and were even commonly signed with the teacher's initials—a phenomenon not noted in mixed or negative global comments. "Very well done," "Your usual careful job," and "Superb!" were all examples of this pattern, which by its rarity and the sometimes surprising intensity of the praises rendered probably indicates how starved teachers feel for work they can wholeheartedly praise.

The next most common pattern we found consisted of comments that began by critiquing some aspect of the student's writing—very often a formal or mechanical aspect—and then moved into a positive commentary on the effective aspects of the papers. We called this *admonitio*, and it was still rather rare, with only 11% of the comments falling into the class.

More than twice as common was the comment consisting of nothing except negative judgments. Of our commented papers, 23% fell into this category, and they usually accompanied the worst grades. These completely critical comments ranged from savagely indignant to sadly resigned, but all gave the message that the teacher was seriously disappointed with this effort and was not equal to the task of finding anything about the paper to like. On a paper about the writer's feelings after being called to an accident scene where a sixteen-year-old girl had died, the comment was, "Learn to use subordination. You might have given us more on the drunken driver and your subsequent thoughts about him. You are still making comma splices! You must eliminate this error once and for all. Is it because you aren't able to recognize an independent clause?" George Hillocks, reviewing studies relating to teacher comments in his *Research on Written Composition*, found that although negative comments did not have any definitive effect on the quality of students' writing, they did strongly affect students' attitudes toward writing (160–68).

The most common trope in global comments proved to be the comment that began positively, with some praise of some element of a paper, and then turned negative toward the end. "Jodie—You describe much of Rodriguez's dilemma well. I'd like to see some of your own ideas expanded—they deserve more attention! And be careful of those apostrophes!" A full 42% of all terminal and initial comments—almost half—fell into this category. The reasons for its popularity probably derive from the by-now traditional wisdom about always trying to find something to praise in each student's work. Seeing that many teachers do conscientiously try to find at least one good point to comment on in a paper was heartening.[11]

In terms of the order of presentation of materials in the terminal and initial comments, the most common order was *global/local*, leading with rhetorical comments, followed up by comments on mechanical or formal issues.

Twice as many comments—36%—began with rhetorical comments as with formal comments, and this order ties in with the positive-negative duality; the single most common kind of comment we found consisted of a positive rhetorical comment followed by complaints and suggestions of different sorts, often concerning mechanical elements in the paper. "Paul, you've organized the paragraphs here well to support your thesis, but your sentences are all still short and simple, and you really need to check the comma rules."

The lengths of terminal and initial comments ranged widely. The longest comment we found was over 250 words long, but long comments were far less common than short. The average comment length throughout the run of papers was around 31 words, but this is not a very meaningful figure. Very short comments—fewer than ten words—were much more common than longer comments. A full 24% of all global comments had ten words or fewer; of these, many were a very few words, or one word—"Organization" or "No thesis" or "Handwriting—learn to type!" or "Tense!" Conversely, only 5% of comments exceeded 100 words. The portrait of teacher-student interchange painted by these numbers is one in which overworked teachers dash down a few words which very often tell students little about how or why their papers succeed or fail. The rarity of longer comments seemed to our readers to indicate not so much that teachers had nothing to say as that they had little time or energy to say it and little faith that what they had to say would be heard.

We found that only 22% of the longer comments were concerned exclusively with formal issues, indicating that 78% of all the longer global comments made by teachers took cognizance of rhetorical issues in the paper. (This number corresponds to the very small number of papers whose comments indicated that formal or mechanical criteria had been used as "gate criteria," without success in which a passing grade was impossible. Only 8% of the comments indicated uses of such gates as "The comma splices force me to give this paper an F despite. . . .") Some comments (24%) were focused exclusively on rhetorical issues and never went into any detail about mechanics, but the most common tropes of teacher comment took *both* rhetorical and mechanical elements of the paper into consideration. In general, teachers seem determined to respond to what their students are saying as well as how they say it, which is interesting news to those critics of contemporary teaching who claim that writing teachers are obsessed only with errors (and which substantiates what we found in our previous study of formal errors).

Tropes Within Commentary

One section of our tally sheets was devoted to recording numbers for how often teachers commented on some of the more common rhetorical elements that are a staple of freshman textbooks and teaching. What we found was instructive, and somewhat surprising. From the comments counted by our readers—and here we counted all global comments, not just terminal and initial comments—

teachers comment in large numbers only on two general areas: supporting details and overall paper organization. A full 56% of *all* papers with global comments contained comments on the effectiveness—or more commonly, the lack—of supporting details, evidence, or examples. The next most commonly discussed rhetorical element, at 28%, was overall paper organization, especially issues of introductory sections and issues of conclusion and ending, and thematic coherence.

Since most textbooks, and many teachers, put considerable stress on the two large issues of purpose and audience, we might expect that teacher comments would similarly emphasize these issues. We were surprised, then, to find that very few teacher comments discussed them. Only 11% of the papers we examined had comments that could, even with liberal interpretation, be considered to be about purpose in the essay. Even rarer were comments about the writer's approach toward audience, with only 6% of papers mentioning anything about audience considerations such as tone or voice. According to our readers, the impression left by reading most teacher comments was that the audience for the writing was clearly the teacher, only the teacher, and nothing but the teacher, and thus most comments on audience outside of those parameters seemed redundant.

We also found that 11% of the papers contained comments concerned with how successfully the paper responded to the assignment. Many of these papers were clearly written either to formal assignments ("comparison/contrast paper," "narrative essay," "research paper," etc.) or to full content-based assignments ("Give a synopsis of the Orwell essay followed by your own examples of doublespeak," etc.). Many of these papers did not contain comments specifically directed toward the assignment in spite of their clear nature as assignment-driven, but very often when the writer chose an incorrect genre or failed to take some specific instruction into proper consideration, the teacher would call it out as a serious failure. "This really is not a process analysis at all," complains one teacher about an essay called "What Are Friends For?" "You haven't given instructions to follow in performing or achieving something," The paper, which seemed acceptable to our readers except for failing to meet these generic expectations, received a D+.

Finally, we asked our readers to look at comments that went beyond the paper at hand to relate this piece of work to other work the teacher had seen the student accomplish. "Jennifer, I've enjoyed having you in class, and we've really seen some improvement. Good luck! I hope that next quarter you find more people that you fit in with." Here, again, we found that such commentary was thin on the ground; only 8% of the papers displayed any comments that dealt with the writer's work as a developing system. The other 92% dealt only with the individual work at hand, making no comments on progress or development. Various reasons may account for this lack of longitudinal commentary. Our most immediate hypothesis is that teachers simply have too many students and too many papers to have time to look for the "big picture" of any one student's development.

While this research was meant to deal with global or rhetorical comments rather than mechanical elements in student writing, we couldn't separate those two factors absolutely. The formal and the mechanical are always rhetorical as well, and we wanted to try to look at the ways in which teachers commented on the rhetorical effectiveness of formal decisions student writers had made. Here we found that the most widely noted formal feature was sentence structure, with 33% of the commented papers mentioning it. (These were not merely syntactic or grammatical complaints or corrections, but longer comments on the effectiveness of sentences.) Paragraph structure was also mentioned in 18% of the commented papers, which was a bit of a surprise, since textbooks bear down so hard on paragraphs as organic units. General paper format—margins, spacing, neatness, cover sheets, etc.—elicited response on 16% of the commented papers.[12]

Finally, we examined the terminal and initial comments for their purpose. It was not always possible to divide comment into clear categories, of course, but we wanted to see what we could tell about the writing processes encouraged in the classrooms of the teachers whose comments we had. We found that the majority of the comments at the beginning or end of the papers served one purpose: to justify and explain final grades. Over 59% of the initial and terminal comments were grade justifications, "autopsies" representing a full stop rather than any medial stage in the writing process. In contrast, only 11% of the papers with such comments exhibited commentary clearly meant to advise the student about the paper as an ongoing project. It's probable that our process of paper-gathering specifically solicited papers at the final stage of the writing process, papers which had already been revised and which had been submitted for final grading. Nevertheless, this study suggests that consistent and widespread use of multiple drafts and revisions may hold more in theory than it does in practice.

Reader Impressions

We worked on recording numerical information for about five hours, at which point we broke to munch subs and talk about what we'd seen in the teacher comments on the papers and about our impressions. These impressionistic responses are, of course, just that—and therefore are not generalizable. We nevertheless found them fascinating, because they emerged immediately from the people who read through all those 3,000 papers. Because numbers tell only one story, we want to include our readers' voices here.

The primary emotion that they felt as they read through these teacher comments, our readers told us, was a sort of chagrin: these papers and comments revealed to them a world of teaching writing that was harder and sadder than they wanted it to be—a world very different from the theoretical world of composition studies most readers hoped to inhabit. It was a world, many said, whose most obvious nature was seen in the exhaustion on the parts of the teachers marking these papers. Many of the more disturbing aspects of the teacher-student interaction revealed by these comments could be traced to overwork. A teacher with too many students, too many papers to grade, can pay only small attention to each one, and small attention indeed is what many of these papers got. A quarter of them had no personal comments at all, a third of them had no real rhetorical responses, and only 5% of them had lengthy, engaged comments of more than 100 words.

Just as students invent the university every time they write, teachers invent not only a student writer but a responder every time they comment. One characteristic of the responder that many teachers construct, our readers said, was its nature as a general and objective judge. Many of the comments seemed to speak to the student from empyrean heights, delivering judgments in an apparently disinterested way. Very few teachers, for instance, allowed themselves the subjective stance implicit in telling students simply whether they liked or disliked a piece of writing. This kind of reader-response stance was found in 17% of the global comments; the other 83% of comments pronounced on the paper in a distanced tone, like reified personifications of Perelman's Universal Audience, "You've structured the paper well in the block format," "You have a suitable opening paragraph with thesis statement," or "There are some lapses in style that need attention" were much more common than comments like "Don't get discouraged. Good writing takes years."

Similarly, teachers seemed unwilling to engage powerfully with content-based student assertions or to pass anything except "professional" judgments on the student writing they were examining. Only 24% of the comments made any move toward arguing or refuting any content points made in the paper, and many of these "refutations" were actually formal comments on weak argumentative strategies. In some way, then, teachers seem conditioned *not* to engage with student writing in personal or polemical ways. What we found, in short, was that most teachers in this sample give evidence of reading student papers in ways antithetical to the reading strategies currently being explored by many critical theorists.[13] (It's our guess that even the most devoted reader-response critics, by the way, tend to produce similar disinterested commentary on student papers.) For whatever reasons, our readers found evidence to support the contention of Robert Schwegler that "professional practices and assumptions have encouraged composition instructors to suppress value-laden responses to student writing and ignore the political dimensions of their reading and teaching practices" (205). Schwegler's conclusion that "the language of marginal and summative commentary . . . is predominantly formalist and implicitly authoritarian" is one our study clearly supports (222).

The authoritarian attitude came through most clearly in the insensitivity our readers felt some of the teacher comments evinced. They sensed, they said, not only exhaustion but a kind of disappointment on the parts of many teachers, and, as a result, patience was often in short supply. "Do over, and pick one subject for development. This is just silly." "Throw away!" "You apparently do not understand thing one about what a research paper is." At times the harshness, which might be justified in particular contexts, even segued into a downright punitive state of mind; one teacher wrote at the end of a paper, "Brian, this is much too short, as I'm sure you know. You've not fulfilled the requirements of the course. Besides receiving an F for the paper, I'm lowering another grade 20 points. You should have consulted with me," Another teacher wrote:

> I refuse to read this research paper. You have not done adequate research, you have not narrowed the topic as directed, you have not followed the format described, *and you have not been directed by my comments during the research assignment.* (emphasis added)

Here is disappointment brimming over into accusation and acrimony.

Some teachers were disturbed when students seemed not to have a grasp of materials that teachers expected them to have mastered. This disappointment, our readers said, seemed to stem from a disjunction between what teachers thought they taught and what they then evaluated. "Ken, you know better than to create comma splices at this point in the semester!" wrote a teacher in rueful disappointment, but Ken obviously did not. In assuming that Ken purposefully had "created" some comma splices after no doubt being taught that such creations were to be avoided, the teacher showed a dissociation between *her* knowledge as she assumed it was disseminated into the class and *Ken's grasp* of some fairly complex and experience-based conventions.

Our readers also told us that the large number of short, careless, exhausted, or insensitive comments really made them notice and appreciate comments that reflected commitment to students and to learning. They noted lengthy comments from teachers who seemed really to care, not only about students' writing, but also about the students themselves:

> Elly—this is not a good essay, but you'd have to be superhuman to write a good essay on this topic, given how important and immediate it is for you. I *feel* for your situation—I know what it is like to feel like a different person in a different place, and however much people tell you it is possible to change anywhere, it surely is MUCH harder in some places than others. (Run away to NYC!) Unfortunately, my job is not to encourage you to run away, but to write a good essay. Let's make it a short but specific one: tell me *one* incident that will show how you used to put yourself down, and *one* incident during your visit to NYC that shows how you didn't put yourself down or were even proud of yourself.

Some might complain that this teacher is being too directive, telling the student exactly how to revise, but after looking at many papers with no evidence that a revision option had ever existed and no evidence that the teacher cared much for the student or her situation, this kind of comment really captured our readers' attention.

Another trait our readers admired was the skill of careful marginal comments. Teachers who use marginal comments and a revision option were praised by our readers for their thoroughness and the care they took in calling all sorts of rhetorical elements—not just very large-scale ones—to students' attention. One teacher particularly won raves from the readers; his marginal questions were dense—questions like "When did she do this?" and "You didn't know how to steer?" were interspersed with shorter notes like "Paragraph?"— and the whole was followed up with a half-page typed response to the paper, giving comments and suggestions for the next draft. At the same time we admired this teacher's work and care, however, we also wondered, as one reader put it, "When does this guy ever sleep?"

It was also good to discover teachers experimenting with different systems to help students revise. Although, as we suggested, many teachers seemed to see revision as merely the editing out of formal errors, other teachers clearly encouraged revision for content issues. One teacher had even invented a "contract" form for revision, which was a sort of written proposal of the changes the student would make in a draft, and a promise from the teacher—signed and dated—of what grade would be given the paper if the changes were successfully carried out.

Many of the teachers commenting in our study did seem to use the concept of teaching the writing process in their responses to students, but all too often the process reflected a rigid stage model. Some students were asked to attach their outlines or invention materials to the draft handed in, leading to comments like "This is terrible prewriting!" Our readers saw few attempts to discuss any recursive model of writing, and although prewriting was sometimes mentioned, revision had very little place in the comments we read. With only 11% of the papers showing any evidence of a revision policy (and we deliberately asked our readers to use the most liberal definition of "draft in process" possible, even to the extent of defining a graded paper as a draft if it gave evidence of being the final draft of a previous series), and many of the "revisions" suggested being the editing and correction of errors, the practices mirrored by these comments are still governed by the older form of "one-shot writing."

Although we had not meant to look at formal or mechanical comments, our readers told us that it had been impossible for them to ignore the editing and corrections they saw. There was, they said, a pervasive tendency to isolate problems and errors individually and "correct" them, without any corresponding attempt to analyze error patterns in any larger way, as is recommended by Mina Shaughnessy and the entire tradition that follows her. The "job" that teachers felt they were supposed to do was, it seemed, overwhelmingly a job of looking at papers rather than students; our readers found very little readerly response and very little response to content. Most teachers, if our sample is representative, continue to feel that a major task is to "correct" and edit papers, primarily for formal errors but also for deviation from algorithmic and often rigid "rhetorical" rules as well. The editing was often heavy-handed and primarily apodictic, concerned more with ridding the paper of problems than with helping the student learn how to avoid them in the future.

In spite of what we know about how grading works against our goals, our readers saw evidence everywhere that much teacher commentary was grade-driven. A large number of teachers used some form of dittoed or xeroxed "grading sheet" clipped or stapled to the student's essay. These sheets, which varied in format, were sometimes obviously departmental in origin, but a number of them were individual. They were great boons to grading, because teachers could circle a few words or phrases, rate several different dements in the paper independently and easily, and go on to the next paper with hardly any personal commentary on the paper. These rating sheets also allowed teachers to pass hierarchical judgments on rhetorical matters; one teacher used an editing sheet that gave checks and points for the quality of the prewriting. Our readers discerned a relationship between use of these grading sheets and lower grades on papers, which they ascribed to the atomistic division of the paper such sheets encourage and the teacher's resulting difficulty in seeing the piece of writing holistically or with much affect. Some teachers had a set of "penalty points" criteria which produced an automatic F if a certain number of types of error was found. "I stopped here," wrote one teacher in the middle of a research paper. "You've already messed this up to the point of failure."

One notable subset of these rating sheets were the "correction sheets," sometimes found in labeled "correction folders." Correction sheets were not merely reactive, but prophylactic as well. Some contained written instructions demanding that students examine their teacher-marked paper, then list the error symbol, the error name, the rule that the error had broken, and the rewritten sentence in which the error originally had appeared. This technique, which appeared in a number of papers, did not always use a separate sheet; very often, students were asked to rewrite elements with formal errors as part of the *post-grading* work on the paper. In one case, in fact, we found a teacher who, after each error marking, placed a row of numbers—1, 2, 3, 4, 5—on succeeding lines in the margin. The student's task, as far as we can reconstruct it, was to identify the error and then write the correct word or phrase out five times in the margin so as to really "get it through her head."

But even those teachers not using grading sheets often gave few reasons why they approved of or condemned some aspect of a paper. The judgments expressed in writing by teachers often seemed to come out of some privately held set of ideals about what good writing should look like, norms that students may have been taught but were certainly expected to know. One of our readers called this tacit assumption the problem of "writer-based teacher response," and it was as pervasive among our teachers as writer-based prose is among students.

The reactions of our readers made us realize anew how difficult the situations of many teachers remain today. Behind the abstractions we push about as counters in our scholarly game, there exist real persons facing real and sometimes grim circumstances. We have a long road ahead of us if we are to make real and useful so much of what we confidently discuss in our journals and our conference talks. So the news we bring back from the Tropics of Commentary is both good and bad. The good news is that teachers are genuinely involved in trying to help their students with rhetorical issues in their writing. Counter to the popular image of the writing teacher as error-obsessed and concerned only with mechanical issues, the teachers whose work we looked at clearly cared about how their students were planning and ordering writing. The classical canons invoked in more than three-quarters of the papers we examined were invention and arrangement, not merely style. Similarly, more comments were made on the traditional rhetorical issues of supporting details/examples and general organization than were made on smaller-scale issues. Very few comments were entirely negative, and very few showed use of formal and mechanical standards as completely dominating standards of content. Grading standards have softened up a little in the last 70 years, but not as much as many people may have thought.

The bad news is that many teachers seem still to be facing classroom situations, loads, and levels of training that keep them from communicating their rhetorical evaluations effectively. Even given the nature of our sample, there was not much reflection in these papers of revision options, or of contemporary views of the composing process. The teachers whose comments we studied seem often to have been trained to judge student writing by rhetorical formulae that are almost as restricting as mechanical formulae. The emphasis still seems to be on finding and pointing out problems and deficits in the individual paper, not on envisioning patterns in student writing habits or prompts that could go beyond such analysis. As D. Gordon Rohman put it as long ago as 1965, merely pointing out errors or praising good rhetorical choices is based on a fundamental misconception, the idea that:

> if we train students how to recognize an example of good prose ("the rhetoric of the finished word"), we have given them a basis on which to build their own writing abilities. All we have done, in fact, is to give them standards to judge the goodness or badness of their finished effort. *We haven't really taught them how to make that effort.* (106)

For reasons of overwork, or incomplete training, or curricular demand, many of the teachers whose comments we looked at are still not going beyond giving students standards by which to judge finished writing.

It may be, in addition, that to some degree teachers perceive that their comments *don't count*—that students ignore them, that the discursive system at work in institutional grading won't allow for any communication *not* algorithmic and grade-based. As our readers, with their admirable idealism, told us, many of the comments they saw seemed to be part of a web of institutional constraints that made teacherly "voice" in commentary a rare thing. If we're accurate in this perception, it is the entire industry and institution of rank ordering, hyper-competition, and grading that is culpable, and teachers are as much victims of it as students.

Janet Auten's recent claim that we need a rhetorical context for every disruption we make in a student text is certainly compelling, and her suggestions that teachers become aware of their separate roles as readers, coaches, and editors are helpful (11–12). What we would like to see are future studies that would build such awareness by describing *in detail* the topography we have only sketched in here, perhaps in "thick descriptions" of teacher-responders at work, in their full context. Ethnographies of response would certainly provide a starting point for analyses of instructional constraints, for the ideologies of teacher response, and for the ethos of this particular teacher-student interaction. But in addition to knowing more about the complex act of response, we have to work at seeing that what we know *now* is enacted in writing programs. We need to start putting into programmatic practice what we've learned about effective teacher commentary from scholars like Nancy Sommers, Lil Brannon, and Chris Anson. Doing so might best begin, for each of us, at home—by cataloguing and studying our own tropics of commentary. By determining those genres and tropes of response we tend to privilege, perhaps we can begin to learn how our students "read" these teacherly tropes, which seem so obvious and helpful to us but may not be so easily deciphered by those still striving to enter the community we take for granted.

Notes

1. During the nineteenth century, of course, when most writing courses were taught at the sophomore level and above, teachers at the better colleges often engaged with their students' essays at some length in commentary. This practice of serious and lengthy engagement died out quickly, however, after the first freshman writing courses began to evolve with their drastic overwork and underprepared students. By 1900 the practice of engagement with the content of student essays was the rate exception to the rule.

2. Those who thought this piece of advice was relatively new will be surprised to learn that it can be dated with certainty back to 1921, and we have no doubt that, traced truly, it predates Quintilian. Each generation seems to feel that truly humanistic pedagogy began only a decade or two ago. See Bowman, 249–53, Hewitt, 85–87, and Daiker, 105.

3. Gilbert, writing in 1922, is a startlingly "modern" voice who often sounds a lot like David Bartholomae or Ann Berthoff. Listen:

> The course in freshman rhetoric—without plenty of reading—is an attempt to make bricks of straw only. . . . The teacher of Freshman English must deserve his right to stand on the same level as any other teacher of Freshmen, and must deal with big things, ideas, and books that hit the intelligence of the students. This does more to improve slovenly sentences, than does constant worrying of details. The mint, anise, and cumin must be tithed, but the teacher of Freshmen who gives himself to trivial things and neglects the weightier matters of good literature does not make his course a power for literacy. (400)

Gilbert goes on to recommend literature as a springboard for students' own choices of what to write, then suggests that students read their papers before the class because to do so "gives the writer an audience," after which comes group criticism, then personal conferences with the teacher, then group conferences. Sadly, Gilbert was a rather lonely voice in his time.

4. For more information on the importance of this generation to composition pedagogy, see the "Introduction" to *Selected Essays of Edward P.J. Corbett.*

5. Fred Newton Scott had been encouraging teachers to read their students' essays rhetorically, of course, but although we admire Scott today, his influence (and that of his students) was not enough to change composition pedagogy in general.

6. For an overview of the work done during the seventies and early eighties, see Griffin. For good discussions of contemporary ideas and attitudes, see the essays in Anson, several of which have very complete bibliographies.

7. Those who want to know the details about how the 3,000 randomized and stratified papers were selected for this study are referred to the long footnotes in our 1988 study. These papers are not the same ones, but they were pulled from the pile of 21,000 using exactly the same methodology.

8. One of our *CCC* referees made the irrefutable point that the self-selected nature of our sample meant that this study could make no claim of reflecting all of the possible kinds of student-teacher interaction:

> For instance, if I had received the request to send in a set of papers, and the set I had currently at hand were papers I mark in preparation for personal conferences, to discuss how the paper should be revised for a further draft, then indeed I would become one of the 7,700 who declined, simply because my commenting on that type of draft is extremely minimal. . . . I wouldn't send the set in because I am sure the researchers would be able to make little out of it, and yet the very kind of conferencing and push toward revision and treatment of writing as an act in progress and not as a completed copy is the kind of teacher commentary that the authors complain they found little of in the "database."

This observation is very accurate, and it is a prime reason why we make no attempt to claim that our sample represents all teachers, or to derive percentages about teachers using revision, etc. What we wanted to try to analyze here was specifically *written* commentary, the rhetorical interaction that goes between teachers and students via the traditional marginal and terminal commentary. We make no claims at all about the various other sorts of student-teacher interaction possible; indeed, there is no way we can know any more than what is suggested by the papers we studied. Nonetheless, we can't agree with Lil Brannon's assessment, given at a panel on this research at the 1992 CCCC, that "we do not learn very much from this kind of study." For many teachers and students, written commentary remains the primary interchange they have, and understanding it better cannot be unimportant.

9. The ratings of our 26 readers were not checked for traditional kinds of inter-rater reliability either by us or by repeated ratings. Because of the "slippery" nature of rhetorical possibility, such tight controls were simply not realistic. We counted on the number of readers and their level of expertise to give our study the only kind of reliability we

thought practical. We have little doubt that 26 other readers looking at 3,000 other papers would come up with slightly different numbers, but we would be surprised if those numbers led to substantially different inferences.

10. As our readers looked at these papers, they had the impression that the grading curve on them was lower than their own, and while we could not, as we said, complete a serious statistical analysis of the grades because we had no context for many of them, a very rough analysis of the first 350 pure-letter grades on our sheets turned up the following, which, for the sake of interest, we contrast with similar information gleaned from Bowman (248) on grades at the University of Missouri in 1920:

	1915–1920	1980–1985
A-range grades	4%	9%
B-range grades	21%	39%
C-range grades	52%	37%
D-range grades	16%	12%
F grades	7%	3%

Sue Carter Simmons's research with Barrett Wendell's gradebook provides an interesting corroboration of those early figures. His English A grades at Harvard between 1887 and 1890 were in these ranges: A–4%, B–16%, C–46%, D–30%, and F–4% (178–79). Our findings are very speculative, and concentrating only on the pure letter grades clearly skews the results in this rough comparison, but certainly we see some grade inflation, especially at the B-range level. At many schools today, grade inflation has turned the old "gentleman's C" into the "partier's B," thus putting a crack in the classic bell curve, but these numbers do not seem to us to be completely out of line with grading expectations from our own teaching.

11. Of course, these sorts of comments can easily become mechanically formulaic, as was early recognized. For a funny (and early) view of these and other rhetorical commentary formulae, see Eble.

12. In this same section of the study we also asked our readers to look for comments aimed at uses of quotations, use of source materials, and use of documentation and citation forms; all three of these elements elicited comments from between 6% and 7% of all commented papers. The conclusion we draw from these numbers is simply that between 6% and 7% of the papers examined were generic "research papers," and could thus be expected to contain quotations, sources, and cites, all of which are likely to be commented on by teachers. Quotations were seldom found outside of research papers and literary analyses; students, it seems, rarely use sources or citations unless pushed to do so by specific assignments.

13. This whole question of how teachers engage as readers of student writing has tantalizing implications about men's and women's ways of knowing and about gendered response and teacher-student interaction. In this study, we did not build in any systematic ways of identifying the gender of either teachers or students. Given our data base, it could have been done, but it would have made what we did do immensely more complex. That piece of research remains in the future, but we do hope to take it up.

References

Anson, Chris M., ed. 1989. *Writing and Response: Theory, Practice, and Research.* Urbana, IL: NCTE.

Auten, Janet Gebhart. 1991. "A Rhetoric of Teacher Commentary: The Complexity of Response to Student Writing." *Focuses* 4:3–18.

Barnes, Walter. 1913. "The Reign of Red Ink." *English Journal* 2 (March):158–65.

Bowman, James C. 1920. "The Marking of English Themes." *English Journal* 9 (May): 245–54.

Brannon, Lil. 1992. "Response." Conference on College Composition and Communication. Cincinnati, March 20, 1992.

Brown, Marion D., and M. E. Hagerty. 1917. "The Measurement of Improvement in English Composition." *English Journal* 6 (October):515–27.

Collins, Harold R. 1954. "Conversing in the Margins." *College English* 15 (May):465–66.

Connors, Robert J., and Andrea A. Lunsford. 1988. "Frequency of Formal Errors in Current College Writing, or, Ma and Pa Kettle Do Research." *College Composition and Communication* 39 (December):395–409.

Copeland, Charles T., and H. M. Rideout. 1901. *Freshman English and Theme Correcting at Harvard College.* New York: Silver-Burdett.

Corbett, Edward P. J. 1989. *Selected Essays of Edward P. J. Corbett.* Edited by Robert J. Connors. Dallas: Southern Methodist UP.

Daiker, Donald A. "Learning to Praise." Anson 103–13.

Eble, Kenneth E. 1957. "Everyman's Handbook of Final Comments on Freshman Themes." *College English* 19 (December):126–27.

Fleece, Jeffrey. 1952. "Teacher as Audience." *College English* 13 (February): 272–75.

Gilbert, Allan H. 1922. "What Shall We Do with Freshman Themes?" *English Journal* 11 (Sepember):392–403.

Griffin, C. W. 1982. "Theory of Responding to Student Writing: The State of the Art." *College Composition and Communication* 33 (October):296–301.

Griswold, Louise. 1929. "Getting Results from Theme-Correction." *English Journal* 18 (March):245–47.

Hewitt, Charles C. 1921. "Criticism—Getting It Over." *English Journal* 10 (February): 85–88.

Hillocks, George Jr. 1986. *Research on Written Composition: New Directions for Teaching.* Urbana, IL: NCRE.

Holley, Hilda. 1924. "Correcting and Grading Themes." *English Journal* 13 (January): 29–34.

Hudelson, Earl. 1923. "The Development and Comparative Values of Composition Scales." *English Journal* 12 (March):163–68.

James, H. W. 1926. "A National Survey of the Grading of College Freshman Composition." *English Journal* 12 (October):579–87.

Kitzhaber, Albert R. 1963. *Themes, Theories, and Therapy: The Teaching of Writing in College*. New York: McGraw-Hill.

Knoblauch, C. H., and Lil Brannon. 1981. "Teacher Commentary on Student Writing: The State of the Art." *Freshman English News* 10 (Fall):1–4.

Leonard, Sterling A. 1925. "Building a Scale of Purely Composition Quality." *English Journal* 14 (December):760–75.

Phelps, Louise W. "Images of Student Writing: The Deep Structure of Teacher Response." Anson 37–67.

Rodabaugh, Delmer. 1954. "Assigning and Commenting on Themes." *College English* 16 (October):33–37.

Rohman, D. Gordon. 1965. "Pre-Writing: The Stage of Discovery in the Writing Process." *College Composition and Communication* 16 (May):106–12.

Schwegler, Robert. 1991. "The Politics of Reading Student Papers." *The Politics of Writing Instruction: Postsecondary*. Ed. Richard Bullock and John Trimbur: 203–26. Portsmouth, NH: Boynton/Cook.

Simmons, Sue Carter. 1991. A Critique of the Stereotypes of Current-Traditional Rhetoric: Invention and Writing Instruction at Harvard, 1875–1900. Dissertation, University of Texas at Austin.

Sommers, Nancy I. 1982. "Responding to Student Writing." *College Composition and Communication* 33 (May):148–56.

Scott, Fred Newton. 1913. "Our Problems." *English Journal* 2 (January):1–10.

About the Authors

Robert J. Connors is an associate professor of English at the University of New Hampshire. He is the author of a number of articles on rhetorical history and theory and received the Richard Braddock Award from CCCC in 1982.

Andrea Lunsford is professor of English and Vice-Chair for Rhetoric and Composition at The Ohio State University. She has published numerous articles and books and was co-winner with Lisa Ede of the Richard Braddock Award in 1985. With Lisa Ede, Bob and Andrea co-edited *Essays on Classical Rhetoric and Modern Discourse*, which in 1985 received the Mina P. Shaughnessy Award from the MLA. They are co-authors of the *St. Martin's Handbook*. 2nd edition.

10

Twelve Readers Reading

A Survey of Contemporary Teachers' Commenting Strategies

Ronald F. Lunsford
Richard Straub

How do well-informed teachers of writing make written responses to their students' writing? What might we learn by looking at their ways of responding? These were the questions that led the late Rick Straub and me to undertake the project that would eventually take shape as *Twelve Readers Reading: Responding to College Student Writing.* Somehow we were able to enlist (the metaphor seems appropriate) a dozen teacher-scholars to read and respond to a sampling of essays and display their own best responding styles. Nine of them were from large state institutions; two were from private schools; one was from a community college. The recruits: Chris Anson, Peter Elbow, Anne Gere, Glynda Hull, the late Richard Larson, Ben McClelland, Frank O'Hare, Jane Peterson, the late Donald Stewart, Patricia Stock, Tilly Warnock, and Edward White. We asked these teachers to respond to a sampling of student essays that we thought representative of the kinds of writing produced in first-year college-writing courses. The sampling was made up of rough final drafts and included expressive, referential, and argumentative writing.

   In addition to the texts themselves, we provided the teachers with background information about the writing situation (much of it hypothetical), to help them contextualize the essays and lead them as a group to look at each of the texts in some common light. We typically included an assignment for the writing as well as information about the stage of drafting, the point in the course at which the paper was written, the focus of instruction, and the previous writing assignments. For half of the writings, we presented, in addition, a brief profile of the student writer. Figure 10–1 shows a sample context sheet with background information about the writer of one of the papers in our study.

WRITING 12
ROUGH DRAFT: "STREET GANGS: ONE POINT OF VIEW"

BACKGROUND

This informative paper is the third paper of the course, the third time students have taken an assignment through several drafts with in-draft commentary. The class has been studying the principles of informative writing and paying special attention to the use of examples. Students have already completed invention activities and a first rough draft toward this paper, neither of which you have made written responses to. They will take the assignment through two more drafts.

Rusty is the kind of student who comes into writing classes apprehensive and expecting not to do well, largely because, as he wrote in his journal at the beginning of the course, his "grammar and structure are not too good." He keeps to himself in class, and he has not talked with you after class or in conference about his writing or his performance in the class, even though your written responses on his first two papers indicated that you expected more from him—in substance and correctness—in his future papers. Now he hands in this paper.

THE ASSIGNMENT

For your third paper, I'd like you to write about a hobby or activity in which you regularly engage and in which you have some level of authority or proficiency. In an informative essay of 600-900 words, inform or advise a general audience (say, the members of this class) about an aspect of this hobby or activity. As you write, try to say as best you can what precisely you mean, in a way that perhaps will spark your readers' interest in the subject.

In our work on this paper, we will pay special attention to the use, as distinct from the mere *citation*, of examples to examine and illustrate a point. As you write, keep this objective in mind.

We will take this paper through four drafts. The first is an exploratory draft, a place where you should try to get some words and ideas produced and begin to get them into some general shape. It may well be sketchy and rough. Do what you can to make it a place where you think through and discover what you want to say. You need not concern yourself with being neat and orderly—this is not a draft for readers, but for you as a writer at work. The second and third drafts are working drafts, places where you begin to do more careful shaping and crafting, and perhaps some more discovering and producing, some more experimenting. The fourth is a "final draft"—not in the sense that it is complete and forever done with, but in the sense that you can "finally" let it go now that your writing is ready for readers.

Figure 10–1 Context Sheet for Writing 12.

We sent fifteen cases to these teachers and asked them to respond to twelve. We encouraged them to make the kinds of comments they would make if they were to receive these essays under the circumstances we defined. We also invited them to modify the context as they wished, noting any changes they made. Since the writings were not from their own classrooms and the situations would require a good deal of (re)constructing, we decided to have them look at their responses not as samples of real-life exchanges but as models of their ways of responding, perhaps as examples they would use in training teachers. While the artificial circumstances must have influenced these teachers' readings, we came to believe that their responses are probably not

Writing 12
Rusty S.
Second Rough Draft

Street Gangs: One Point of View

I'm writing this paper on street gangs because I was once part of one, and I feel that this gives me some authority to write a legitimate opinion.

I never asked or set out to join a gang, it just happened by association. I knew some guys who were members of the Cripps and by hanging around them I was sort of "taken in" by the gang and generally thought to be a part of them by everyone else.

This is interesting. Somehow I always thought joining a gang involved initiation and so forth.

Unlike some members I tried to maintain a low profile. I didn't provoke fights or do destructive things on purpose, but we had a strong bond. If one person was in trouble, no matter who or what kind it was, everyone was there regardless.* *(see my comments at the end)*

This sticking together almost always occured in a physical sense. If one of our guys were to be beaten up, the rest of us would take a revenge of some sort, whether it be by beating someone up or vandalizing someones property, we always got even. That was a basic rule, nobody could "be one up on us", we always had to get even.*

Except for this one occasion, I can't really remember us actually going out and starting trouble for no "reason". We were at the pool, and what we did was single out one person at a time.* Once we had a target, one of us would go up to that certain someone and "sucker punch" him and before he could retaliate the rest of the gang would break it up.

Oh, my - were you ever the one to do the punching?

Figure 10–2a Sample Comments to Writing 12.

substantially different from the kinds of responses they routinely make on writing in their own classrooms—or from the kinds of responses they would make on these essays if they were to receive them from their own students. To illustrate the kinds of commentary we received from these teachers, here are two sample responses we received on "Street Gangs: One Point of View," the first sample in the conventional combination form of marginal comments and a summative end note, by Glynda Hull (Figure 10–2a); the second in the form of a separate letter to the student writer, by Frank O'Hare (Figure 10–2b).

Being a member had its ups and downs. The worst part was being
paranoid about something happening to you. It wasn't a frightening
feeling, but more like a burden. You knew something, somehow,
somewhere would eventually happen, either to you or the gang. Many
times I paid the price for being part of the Cripps with black eyes or
broken noses. I even had my windshield busted once. ✳

This is a great way to describe the paranoid feeling.

The good side was the family type atmosphere between us, we were
more than friends, almost like cousins or even brothers. That sense
of support that I got from being part of that gang was unmeasurable.
Walking down the halls of school and having everyone know that your in
this gang was great, almost like an "ego-trip". For it did make some
of the guys cocky. This overall feeling is hard to explain, it deals
a lot with acceptance and friendship. I guess these two things were
what kept me in the gang so long. I liked the feeling of being part
of something that (where I come from) is almost like a status symbol.
My parents called this insecurity, this may be, but more importantly
it gave me a purpose and an identity.

This is interesting too. I don't think most people recognize the family-like attraction of being in a gang.

I admire the way you're able to acknowledge your parents view but go on to give your own.

During the time I spent in the gang, we were more a "party" gang.
We got into trouble and fights, but not with other gangs. Gangs at
the time were more friendly and were only gangs by name. I mean
everyone knew each other and it was only the name of the gang and
their symbols that separated us.

Our symbols were one, a blue and red hankerchief worn around the
right ankle, a diamond stud earring in the left ear and most important
the thin white cane each member had. This was in relation with our
name: "THE CRIPPS". *This is interesting — is it common for gangs to choose names and symbols that could be associated with disability or weakness?*

Figure 10–2a *continued*

Although no two samples could fully represent the ways the twelve teachers in the study respond to student writing, these are like the other responders'
comments in several important respects. The readers in our study respond in
full and often highly elaborate statements, not in symbols, abbreviations,
shorthand, or technical language. They spend most of their time commenting
on matters of content, organization, and purpose, and give only moderate
attention to the outward and obvious features of writing: mechanics, word
choice, sentence structure, and style. Beyond the conventional forms of

I left the gang last year because it started getting to violent, especially the growing conflicts between gangs. Many gang fights started to break out in the streets, schools and school related events.✱ I just couldn't handle this, somebody could get really hurt or killed. I also felt I didn't need the ego boost anymore. I felt I could be my own person, with my own traits and characteristics. To sum it up, I grew up.

Rusty— you have the makings of a very interesting paper here. Here are two suggestions for your next draft:

(1) I want you to add some extended examples — not just one sentence or two, but whole paragraphs. I've marked several places you could make some additions with an asterisk (✱). On the first page, for example, you might tell specifically about a time when someone got in trouble and everyone was there. Give details: what time, when, what situation, where. These long examples should be used to illustrate and provide evidence for points you're making.

(2) After you've added the examples, get some scissors and tape, and cut your paper up — one paragraph per strip of paper. Experiment with putting these paragraphs in different orders. Which ones seem like beginning material? Which ones come next? And 3 so on! If there isn't any order that seems better than another, then try to imagine what you would need to do to your paper to connect up the paragraphs. Then tape your draft together again.

Figure 10–2a *continued*

teacher response—criticism, commands, and corrections—they make regular use of praise, advice, reader responses, and all manner of questions. These are not the kind of responses that Nancy Sommers (1982) criticized in "Responding to Student Writing" as vague, contradictory, unhelpful, and mean-spirited. They are sharp, elaborate, engaged, considerate, and constructive.

Rusty, I get the feeling that you are still thinking through your experiences with the gang and that you haven't yet decided the significance of this experience.

In the first paragraph, you seem hesitant about your right to write about this subject. Of course, your opinion about this subject is of value. Your opinion will be not only legitimate but authoritative.

This hesitancy has, I think, caused you to neglect focusing on your purpose in this paper. It would probably be useful for you to sketch quickly an informal outline of your draft. What major points do you want to establish?

Why did you talk about keeping a low profile?

You seem to be combining the bonding issue with "starting trouble."

You claim that your gang didn't look for trouble, and yet the fifth paragraph discusses the only time you did.

Paragraph six needs specifics. What incident or incidents led you to use the terms "paranoia" and "burden"? You suffered black eyes and broken noses and yet weren't afraid. Please explain.

Paragraph seven does a good job of establishing your sense of identity.

Paragraph eight is confused and confusing. Are you saying that gang rivalries weren't as nasty as they appear to be? If so, the point is interesting and well worth explaining to your readers.

Paragraph nine: what point are you establishing here?

This subject is well worth writing about, but you must decide what your major points will be.

Two comments about code:
1. The level of your vocabulary is just a little too informal.

2. I have marked six places where you failed to recognize sentence boundaries. Please examine these examples and see if you can rewrite them correctly. Please come in for a conference and we'll discuss this problem. All six are, in reality, examples of just one problem.

Figure 10–2b Sample Comments to Writing 12.

These comments are designed (in Sommers' words) "to engage students with the issues they are considering and help them clarify their purposes and reasons in writing their specific text" (155). From another perspective, they seem to follow Knoblauch and Brannon's (1981) advice that teacher comments should look to offer students the incentive to engage in their writing and continue their work as writers.

In order to sort through and give some order to these teachers' methods of response, we devised a detailed rubric for analyzing their individual comments from two perspectives. The first, "focus," identifies *what* a comment refers to in the writing—for instance, whether the comment mainly addresses the writer's wording, organization, or ideas. The second perspective allows us to examine *how* the comment is framed. It directs our attention to the shape of the comment, or what we call its "mode." The mode of commentary characterizes the image a teacher creates for herself and the degree of control she exerts, through that comment, over the student's writing.

We examine the focus and mode of each teacher comment—in effect, each new statement the teacher makes to the student, whether it appears in isolation or as part of a cluster of comments, whether it is placed in the margins or in a separate note.[1] We classify each comment, placing it in one of seven categories under "focus" and in one of ten categories under "mode." The following table outlines our rubric for analyzing teacher comments:

Table 10–1 FOCUS/MODE RUBRIC

Focus	Mode
Global	Corrective
Ideas	Negative-Evaluative
Development	Qualified Evaluative
Global Structure	Imperative
	Advisory
Local	Praise
Local Structure	Indirect Request
Wording	Problem-Posing
Correctness	Heuristic
	Reflective Statements
Extra-textual	

The Focuses of Commentary

The "focus" of a comment describes *what* a comment refers to, whether it is a formal feature in the student's text or a feature of some larger context of the writing. We identified six formal categories of response—three dealing with global matters (ideas, development, global structure) and three dealing with local matters (local structure, wording, correctness). We identified one additional category for comments that treat issues beyond the immediate text; for example, comments about voice, audience, the assignment, and the student's composing processes. In cases where the focus of a comment is not readily

---

1. A comment is defined as any response with the same focus and mode. If two sentences maintain one focus and mode, they are considered as one comment. But any time the focus or the mode changes, one comment ends, and another begins.

apparent, the choice of whether a comment is placed in one category or another is determined by the language of the teacher's comment—not by what the comment seems to refer to in the student's text.

Ideas

Idea comments deal with matters of content at or beyond the level of the sentence: the thoughts, assertions, arguments, lines of thought, and reasoning of the writing.

- An insightful observation.
- Should all activities that are dangerous be made illegal: drinking, car racing, hang gliding?

Development

Comments that ask for additional support, definitions, elaboration, or explanation of the writer's ideas—namely, of statements that are already present in the text—are labeled as development. The requested information requires additional sentences, not just additional words or phrases (a matter of specificity, which is included under "Wording").

- What happened? Tell us more.
- Evidence? Examples? Can you provide a definition?

Comments that acknowledge or compliment the writer's detail, examples, definitions, or support are considered as ideas, not as development, since the material is already present in the writing, not being requested.

Global Structure

Comments that are concerned with the organization of large units of discourse are labeled as global structure. This category includes comments about the overall arrangement of the essay, the relation of materials within different paragraphs, and the order of paragraphs. It also includes comments about introductions and conclusions, about the main point or points of the writing, and about the unity, coherence, and emphasis of the work as a whole.

- Does this paragraph belong with your discussion of membership?
- You seem to get off track here.
- I'd recommend that you focus on your favorite season, fall.

Local Structure

Local structure comments deal with the structure within a sentence, between consecutive sentences, or within a paragraph. Typically these comments are concerned with the arrangement of sentences (or parts of sentences); the clarity, directness, coherence, and emphasis of sentences; or the connection between sentences.

- Try to rework these sentences to avoid the repetition.
- I'd consider cutting the last phrase so you can end on a strong note.

Wording

Comments about wording deal with the writer's word choice within a sentence, including effective naming within sentences and problems with clarity, economy, or appropriateness.

- Right word?
- Another neat image.

Wording comments may ask the student to get more specific with the wording or phrasing within a sentence.

- Try to get more precise here.
- Which songs?

Corrections/Conventions

Comments that deal with errors in grammar, mechanics, punctuation, and spelling—matters that are conventionally viewed in terms of right and wrong, correct and incorrect—fall under the category of corrections or conventions.

- Subject-verb agreement error.
- Comma splice: should be period or semicolon.

Also included are comments that deal with formal conventions, such as paragraphing, citation and documentation, titles, and manuscript format.

- Start a new paragraph here.
- Captivating title.

Extra-Textual Comments

Extra-textual comments refer to concerns beyond the formal text—for instance, about the audience, the writer's intentions or purpose, the voice of the writing, the topic, the writing assignment, the student's writing activities, and the student's experience.

- Who is your audience?
- You've chosen a good topic for yourself.

- How do you come across here?
- This paper is a real improvement on your previous draft.

Also included are comments that address the essay as a whole and the student's general work on the writing.

- This is a very moving and effective piece of writing.
- You've done some promising work here.

The Modes of Commentary

In analyzing "mode," we are analyzing the typical ways teachers give shape to their responses and the different degrees of control these types of comments imply. Our analysis is based on two complementary assumptions. First, the form of a comment strongly influences how the comment functions and what it comes to mean. Second, the form of a comment is not enough: any analysis of how comments function must also consider content and voice. We also assume, as will become apparent when we look at the modes in full sets of responses, that the meaning and control implied by any given comment may very well be influenced by the surrounding comments.

Our analysis of modes goes beyond a simple labeling of the outward, grammatical form—that is, whether comments are presented as statements, commands, or questions. As Knoblauch and Brannon (1981) rightly note, the "superficial form" of a comment is an unreliable way to distinguish among different types of teacher responses. Some statements are more controlling than other statements, some questions are more controlling than other questions, and some questions are more controlling than some statements. But the surface forms of teachers' comments do tell us something. Consider the following two comments, for instance:

- Move this paragraph to the start of your paper.
- You might want to move this paragraph to the start of your paper.

It might well be argued that these two sentences perform the same speech act—that is, request that the paragraph be moved. But that is not to say that the two are synonymous. There is a definite change in meaning—and in the relationship between teacher and student—when the sentence changes from an imperative to a declarative statement. Although the power relations that conventionally adhere between teachers and students might suggest that a student receiving the second "request" will likely comply with that request, we think the different ways the comments are framed can make a difference in the way they are interpreted. The form of a comment does make a difference in meaning.

At the same time, we believe that it is not enough to analyze the form of teacher comments. If we are to capture the different ways teachers shape their comments and, through them, enact various relationships with their students, we must also take into consideration the voice and the content of their comments, since changes in the substance of a comment may make a critical difference in its meaning and in its implicit control, as in the following case:

- You might move this definition to the start of your paper.
- You must move this definition to the start of your paper.

In analyzing the modes of teachers' comments, then, we look to describe the different ways that teachers bring together the voice, content, and form of their comments and, in doing so, establish different relationships with students. Different modes implicitly create different images and roles for the teacher, establish different roles and tasks for students, and enact different degrees of teacher control over student writing. While some modes tend to exert firm control over the student's writing (corrective, evaluative, and imperative comments), other modes tend to exert moderate control (qualified evaluations, advisory comments, praise, closed questions), and others only modest control (open questions, reflective statements). The detailed classification should help us make fine discriminations about what teachers attempt to do in their comments—the relationships they establish and the tasks they set forth—and help us to describe teachers' responding styles more fully and consistently.

Correction

In the corrective mode, the teacher actually makes a change in the text.

Negative Evaluation

In a negative evaluation, the teacher makes what is presented as an objective criticism about the writing.

- Vague description.
- Poor sentence structure.

Qualified Negative Evaluation

In a qualified negative evaluation, the teacher presents a negative evaluation of the text, but qualifies it in some way or draws attention to its subjective nature.

- I have trouble seeing your main point.
- This is a bit too technical for me.

Imperative

In the imperative mode, the teacher requests a change in the text or some action by the student, usually by means of a command.

- Add more details.
- Put the conclusion in a separate paragraph.

Advice

The teacher recommends or suggests a change in the text in the advisory mode, offering advice that leaves a measure of choice to the student.

- You might add some detail here.
- I'd try to state this more directly.
- What about starting with this point?
- Try stating that point in a sentence or two.

Praise

When using praise, the teacher makes a positive judgment about the writing, whether it is presented objectively or acknowledges the subjectivity of the responder.

- A vivid image.
- This is an interesting way to start the paper.

Indirect Request

With indirect request, the teacher uses a question that begins with "Can you" (or "Could you") to prompt the student to engage in some activity of revision.

- Can you give an example?
- Could you develop this argument?

Problem-Posing Questions

The teacher uses a question to identify a problem in the text or some issue that needs to be considered. Problem-posing comments take one of two forms, depending on how much room they leave the student to decide whether a change is to be made.

In *closed problem-posing questions*, the teacher strongly implies that something is wrong with the text and insinuates in the wording of the comment itself the teacher's answer to the question. In doing so, the teacher limits the realm of possible responses from the student. In a way, these comments are imperatives or evaluations cast in the form of questions. They often contain a negative or an intensifier.

- Can't this be said of fall in any northern city?
- Is this paragraph really necessary?
- Isn't one example enough?

In *open problem-posing questions*, the teacher calls attention to some issue or potential problem in the writing, yet leaves it to the student to figure out what, if anything, needs to be done. The teacher implies that something might need to be changed and prompts the student to consider the matter:

- Is this your main point?
- What will some readers like about this quality, and other readers dislike?

Characteristically, closed problem-posing questions are phrased in a way that draws attention to the teacher and places him in the role of a critic or troubleshooter; open problem-posing questions are phrased in a way that draws attention to the student and casts him in the role of critic.

Heuristic Questions

The teacher asks the student to add to or think further about the content of the writing. There are two types of heuristic commentary, one which presents "closed" questions, the other which presents "open" questions.

In *closed heuristic comments*, the teacher uses a question to guide the student to add specific information to the text, information that is usually readily available from his experience:

- What beach?
- How old were you?

In *open heuristic questions*, the teacher invites or challenges the student to consider his ideas further. These comments are always concerned with the content of the writing, specifically, with turning the student back into his statements and thoughts:

- How is fall in Syracuse different from fall in other northern cities?
- In what ways has your illness changed your outlook and behavior?

These questions are "open" in the sense that they do not request specific information but instead allow the student the freedom and responsibility to think about the subject on his own.

Reflective Statements

This is a catchall category for explanatory, instructional, hortatorical, interpretive, reader-response, and other comments that are not evaluative, directive, or advisory. They usually present the teacher's reflections on the writing, either as an instructor or as an individual reader.

In *explanatory* comments, the teacher explains or elaborates on an earlier comment:

[*I'd consider adding an example.*] It would solidify your point.

In *instructional* comments, the teacher explains some concept or informs the student about outside knowledge or material that is related to the writing:

A comma splice occurs when two main clauses are connected with a comma.

In *hortatorical* comments, the teacher encourages or exhorts the student to adopt some attitude or take some action:

I bet you can come up with a lot of descriptive details about this.

In *interpretive* comments, the teacher describes what the text says or interprets its meaning or significance. The teacher "plays back" the writer's words and ideas but does not offer a judgment or reaction:

Here is your second argument.

In *reader-experience* comments, the teacher illustrates how she processes particular passages of the student's writing, by giving a moment-by-moment reading of the words on the page:

I'm wondering if you'll pick up on this point again later.

In *reader remarks*, the teacher presents her own thoughts and associations— not about the writing itself—but about the writer's subject or something the writer has said:

I love winter too.

In *reader reactions*, the teacher presents her reading or interpretation of the text and, as she does so, insinuates some evaluation, positive or negative, about the writing:

I don't disagree with your *position*, but somehow I find myself fighting with you as I read.

The detailed analyses of focus, contexts, and modes of teacher comments were meant to define these teachers' commenting strategies, capture the sometimes subtle distinctions in their ways of responding, and make possible comparisons among their various responding styles. We felt such a fine-tuned instrument was necessary to capture the strategies these teachers use in responding to student writing.

Though we were not ignorant of the importance of context in the making of meaning and not unaware of the limits of the clinical nature of the study, we believed there was something important to get at in the ways these teachers framed their comments—and constructed themselves—on the page. Recognizing the limitations of our admittedly restrictive hypothetical contexts, we were content nevertheless to learn what we could about the ways these teachers envisioned the act of responding to student writing. We envisioned the study as a place to begin from. We hoped to establish a basis and method for future studies that might investigate real teachers' interactions with real students in actual classroom settings, in all their immediacy, messiness, and complexity.

Analysis and Results

We trained two graduate students to assist in analyzing our data: 2,529 comments found in a modified sampling—five rough drafts and five final drafts—of the original fifteen essays in the study. In separate readings, the analysts labeled these comments with an interrater reliability of 0.85. The following tables provide a breakdown of the 2,529 individual comments these teachers made on the final sampling of papers, across a total of 113 sets of responses.

As a group, these teachers devote a large majority of their comments to the overall content, shape, and purpose of the writing. Fifty-five percent of their comments are given to content and organization. Another 24 percent look at the writing in terms of the larger contexts that inform it—for example, the audience, the assignment, the students' writing processes, and the work of the class. Only 21 percent focus on areas that are the dominant concern of traditional writing instruction and traditional response: sentence structure, wording, and error. These teachers read student texts at the level of meaning, and they look to lead students to expect more of themselves and their writing than merely making it clear, concise, coherent, and correct. They employ a range of modes and make frequent use, across the board, of moderate and nondirective modes of commentary. Only 16 percent of their comments are presented in the three modes that are the staple of traditional teacher commentary and that tend to be the most direct and controlling: corrections, criticisms, and commands. Twelve percent are presented as praise. The rest (72 percent) are framed as qualified evaluations, advice, questions, and, perhaps most notably, various

Table 10–2 ANALYSIS OF THE TWELVE READERS' FOCUSES ON SAMPLE

	Number	Percentage
Ideas	736	29
Development	351	14
Global Structure	313	12
Local Structure	107	4
Wording	275	11
Correctness	144	6
Extra-Textual	603	24
TOTAL	2,529	100

**Table 10–3 ANALYSIS OF THE TWELVE READERS'
MODES ON THE SAMPLE**

	Number	Percentage
Corrections	94	4
Negative evaluations	189	7
Qualified negative evaluations	101	4
Imperatives	143	5
Advice	243	9
Praise	294	12
Indirect requests	43	2
Closed problem-posing questions	175	7
Closed heuristic questions	99	4
Open problem-posing questions	171	7
Open heuristic questions	130	5
Interpretive comments	201	8
Explanatory comments	319	13
Reader-response comments	200	8
Other	127	5
TOTAL	2,529	100

forms of nondirective statements. Their comments, as a result, show fairly dra-matically a general tendency to avoid the kind of highly judgmental, highly directive commentary that might lead them, as Sommers (1982) puts it, to "appropriate" student writing and to usurp control from student writers.

The following analysis describes, in discrete sections, various responding strategies these teachers put into practice, in an effort to capture their overall tendencies as a group and, in doing so, define a broad set of contemporary principles of teacher response. After that analysis, we examine the ways these strategies are brought together holistically to create distinct responding styles, in an effort to dramatize the range of styles these teachers employ and suggest the ways different response styles may be constructed for different teachers, different students, and different writing and classroom situations.

Number, Length, Scope, and Specificity of Comments

These twelve composition specialists write a substantial number of comments: an average of twenty-two per paper. However, the average number for individual readers varies widely—from a low of twelve comments per paper (Hull and

Warnock) to a high of 35 (Stock and Stewart). (Anson actually makes thirty-seven comments per paper, but he is in a category by himself, since he tape-records his responses to students.) The number of comments seems to be a function of how the comments are laid out. The six teachers who write marginal comments and a note at the end of the student's text make an average of sixteen comments per paper. The six teachers who make few, if any, comments on the text and instead write a separate letter to the student (including Anson's taped remarks) make an average of twenty-eight comments. The genre of marginal comments seems to allow (and even demand) a certain brevity: there's only so much space in the margins, and teachers have tended over the years to say as much as they can in the fewest words, in the tightest spaces. Teachers who write letters to the student end up writing more comments because they cannot rely on specific passages from the student's text to provide context; they have to provide that context by paraphrasing particular ideas and highlighting certain issues in the essay. The format may also encourage them to do more in the way of illustrating and explaining their responses: the letter, even more than the traditional end note, is a piece of writing in its own right, and in it teachers will more likely be drawn to explain and illustrate their points.

Whether the teachers write their comments in the margins, in a brief end note, or in a separate letter to the student, they rarely attempt to cover a range of concerns. Instead, they typically limit their scope to what they consider the two or three key issues in the writing. Faced, for instance, with the task of responding to "Street Gangs," a rough draft that is still unfocused and only sketchily developed in parts, the teachers usually look to help the student develop, consider the focus of the writing, and shape the material more purposefully on the next draft. They hold off on dealing much, if at all, with the writer's wording, sentence structure, and errors. Only three readers—Stewart, Larson, and Anson—usually address more than an average of three issues per paper.

Notably, these teachers write the same number of comments on rough drafts and final drafts. They also write no fewer comments on good papers than on poor or immature papers. And they are not reluctant to write a lot of comments on highly personal, revealing writing. They write an average of twenty-seven comments apiece on "Leukemia," a paper in which the student recounts his own treatment for this cancer, and twenty-eight comments apiece on "Tribute," an essay about the alcohol-related death of the writer's father. In fact, these writing teachers write the most comments on papers that have an abundance of ideas and seem full of potential for revision: "Street Gangs," "The Four Seasons," and the two personal essays just mentioned, "Tribute" and "Leukemia." They made fewer comments than average on drafts that were short and lean of thought and engagement: a generic essay about working as a waitress, a ten-sentence draft on the seatbelt law, and a response essay that makes strong claims but is radically underdeveloped.

Most of the teachers' comments are written out in full statements, and many of them are elaborated. As a group, they average fourteen words per comment. The comments are almost always clear and specific. Roughly half of the comments are also text specific, tying the response directly back to words from the student's text. The following examples illustrate these teachers' penchant for writing comments that will communicate their views effectively to their student readers:

- Did you wear the symbols and carry the cane in school?
- If danger is the issue, how do you respond to the idea that cars are dangerous?
- When you begin to recount specific experiences they tend to take over. Instead of explaining fishing you move into a narrative of one event. This is particularly true beginning in the middle of page 2 with the section that begins, "After fishing the lillypads that morning . . ."

The teachers do not rely on technical language, yet they do not shy away from employing it when it seems necessary. In fact, their comments suggest that one important function of commentary is to connect the concepts of the class—the evolving vocabulary of the course—to the student's writing:

- How do these ideas relate to your purpose as stated in the last sentence of paragraph 1?
- Again, we need details to know what you mean.
- Good idea to return to opening metaphor to give a sense of closure.
- I struggle to find a focus, to find what you really want me to know about the Cripps and your membership in it.

At times, their comments are presented in terse, elliptical phrases: "oral tone," "tense," "refers to?" "proof?" On isolated occasions, they carry a hint of sarcasm. But, in the vast majority of cases they are reader- and student-friendly. The responders often go out of their way to avoid jargon and speak to students in simple, casual terms. In his response to "The John Cougar Concert," McClelland notes the strengths in the article and then says; "As a reader, I can vicariously experience just about everything there—except, that is, for the music. I'm having trouble hearing the main event. Cougar's music. And since you are my ears, I'm counting on you to define and evaluate it for me." In responding to Nancy's penchant for summary writing (in "What If Drugs Were Legal?"), Peterson writes, "I think you've fallen into the interesting detail trap here." At one point in her response to David's writing, "The Four Seasons," Hull, instead of labeling his writing as "cliched," writes: "You use a lot of phrases that are often used in conjunction with the seasons." These strategies are part of a larger effort to make their comments understandable to students and encourage them to make use of the comments in their subsequent writing.

The Focus of Teacher Comments

The comments of these twelve teachers were aimed at the meaning and purpose of writing, not its outward formal properties. Forty-three percent of their comments focus on ideas and development.

- Good observation.
- Your paper might be clearer if you state, point by point, your opponent's view as clearly and objectively as you can.
- If you didn't start trouble, how come all the black eyes and broken noses?
- What else can you say in favor of your position?
- Why is this weather not meant for you?

Another 12 percent focus on organization:

- This is an effective beginning for me—dramatic and poignant.
- Does this belong with your discussion of membership?
- Experiment with putting the drafts in different orders.

An additional 24 percent deal with matters beyond the text, focusing on the rhetorical context, the classroom context, various genre conventions, the composing process, the student's experiences, and the writing as a whole. A total of 79 percent of their comments, then, are concerned with the content, organization, and contexts of student writing. Only 15 percent draw attention to wording and sentence structure, and only 6 percent to correctness (i.e., mechanics, usage, punctuation, and spelling).

Since we did not count corrections that were made by crossing out items in the text or by using editing symbols (it has to be composed of words for us to consider it a "response"), the number of comments on correctness may be a bit misleading. But even considering the markings they make on the students' texts, these teachers do not give a great deal of attention to error. This is not to say that they are unconcerned about editing. In papers with serious errors, most of the teachers acknowledge the problems and call on the student to attend to them in revision. Nine out of the twelve readers address these issues on the essay with the most errors—"Leukemia"—even though it dealt with one of the most sensitive topics in our study. As a rule, however, the twelve teachers do not dwell on matters of style and correctness.

When they do deal with these local problems, they cite the problem briefly, perhaps point to a few examples, and then explain how the problem can be fixed, or suggest that the student work on the problem on her own; in other cases, they invite the student to a conference in which the problem can be discussed, as the following comments do in various ways:

- This sign ($) means you are using a comma to connect sentences. Review the handbook, chap 4, on this. We will talk about it at our next conference.

- Two comments about code: The level of your vocabulary is just a little too informal. I have marked six places where you failed to recognize sentence boundaries. Please examine these examples and see if you can rewrite them correctly. Please come in and we'll discuss the problem. All six are, in reality, examples of just one problem.

- You must also do a much better job of editing the paper. There are some problems with syntax and pronoun references, as well as common garden variety errors in punctuation and spelling. If you don't understand the marks on your paper, see me and I'll explain them to you.

In these ways, the teachers call attention to concerns they have about editing and error, but manage to keep the emphasis on the overall shape and content of the writing. Even the readers most interested in local concerns—White, Stewart, and Larson—give only one-third of their comments to correctness and style, and the rest to matters of content and development. Several teachers devote almost all of their comments to global matters: Elbow, 89 percent; O'Hare, 93 percent; and McClelland, 97 percent. It seems clear that the twelve teachers reject the view that composition instruction should concentrate on matters of form. Instead, they seem to agree with James Moffett that writing is, in essence "someone saying something to someone else."

Even though we can say that, in general, these teachers attend mostly to global issues, there is a noticeable difference between their comments to early and late drafts of essays. Consider, for example, the twelve teachers' comments on the two "roughest" rough drafts, "Against the Seat Belt Law" and "What If Drugs Were Legal?" and the two most nearly-finished drafts from the sampling, "A Broken Man," and "The John Cougar Concert." In the case of the rough drafts, 67 percent of the teachers' comments concern content and organization and only 8 percent treat local matters; in contrast, only 41 percent of the comments made on the later drafts concern content and organization, and a substantial 30 percent of the comments concern matters of correctness, wording, and sentence structure. The teachers seem to feel that the writers of these latter drafts are at a place where they can benefit from attention to local matters.

The Orientation of Teacher Comments

The twelve readers routinely read and evaluate student writing in terms of the larger contexts that inform it. Their comments are made in the context of rhetorical situation, the stage of drafting and revision, and the circumstances of the individual student writer. Fully one-fourth of their comments focus on contextual matters, and many more present other, formal concerns in the light of these broader contexts. The following sections examine the contexts that figured most prominently in these teachers' comments.

Audience   The extra-textual concern these teachers most frequently cite is audience; here are some typical examples.

- What do you want your reader to draw from all this?
- What is your overall purpose and who is your audience?
- You need more detail, and you also need more focus—to select and shape info so readers can easily understand what you're saying.
- As a reader, I want to experience vicariously the primary sensations of the activity.

The twelve readers view the writing in terms of its effects on readers in 92 of the 113 sets of comments in the sampling. Many of the teachers offer abundant commentary about audience and look to impress upon students that the teacher is not the only or the principal audience for their writing. To be sure, not all these teachers view "the reader" in the same sense. O'Hare and Stewart typically call attention to some general readership ("the reader," "your audience") or some specific target audience (e.g., "readers *of Field and Stream*," "parents of teenage children," or "the members of the class"). Elbow, Stock, and McClelland often present their own reactions as individual readers:

- I need some kind of help here, not sure what. (Elbow)
- You hooked my interest immediately. (Stock)
- If you had not told me that winter was your favorite season, I would not have guessed it. (Stock)
- My pleasure was measurably diminished because your depiction lacked precise, sensory details. Thus, rather than experiencing the actual scene of your hometown, I caught only dim glimpses into an overgeneralized world. (McClelland)

Assignment   These teachers also regularly view the student text in relation to the assignment and to the genre constraints of different types of writing:

- You have certainly "sparked my interest," as the assignment called for. You were supposed to tell readers why this subject was important to you.
- In academic writing, the trick is to express your opinion with authority—but to make sure your argument is more than just your opinion.
- As you revise this draft try to concentrate on explaining bass fishing rather than telling the story of one fishing trip. You can certainly draw on your own experiences to illustrate points you make, but try to prevent the narrative from taking over.

Not all teachers treat this issue in the same way. Some, like Larson, Stewart, and McClelland, insist that the writing meet the parameters set out in the assignment.

- The paper remains essentially a report of the concert and your personal responses. The assignment, however, asked for an "evaluation" based upon criteria and supported by reasons. To some extent you've given criteria (the emotional "roller coaster") and other standards (the audience's responses), but you do less with these bases for judgment than the assignment meant to elicit. (Larson)

- Now, what must you do to make succeeding drafts of this paper better? First, you're going to have to focus on the assignment. This is not a personal experience essay. Too much of your paper is given over to your love of fishing for bass in Orlando and an account of one day's fishing on Lake Ivenhoe. While your personal experience can certainly be incorporated into this kind of paper, it's not what the editor of *Field and Stream* wants. (Stewart)

- I compose this version of a neighborhood scene in early spring not for you to copy, but to give you an example of the "sense of place" that this assignment calls on a writer to depict for readers. (McClelland)

Others, like Elbow, Stock, Anson, and Warnock, seem more interested in having students develop their own sense of the topic and decide in which direction to take it. They allow students greater leeway in following the specific requirements of the assignment and look to lead the student to investigate the effects of different genres.

- What's interesting to me, also, is that such details (his hair, your running out of breath) make it more like a story and less like a standard review. Where it was mostly, "what he did," it's become a bit more, "what it was like for me going to the concert." (Elbow)

- The essay ends too soon for me, Steve. I wanted some way to know that I had heard it all. With an editorial suggestion at the end of the essay, I offer one direction you may want to go. So I think this is an OK start, and I'm not so much worried about whether it fits the assignment perfectly (which was to write about something that you've got some special knowledge of) as how *you* can define and shape it. This seems to be pretty opinion based, and so you might turn it into a sort of editorial essay, something you might read in an opinion section of the newspaper. If that feels right, go with it. (Anson)

- I hope you will continue to work with this. Have you shown it to family members? Can you imagine writing this for strangers who might benefit from your experiences? What would you like to do with this now? (Warnock)

Just how much teachers stick to the assignment seems to depend, among other things, on whether they view the teaching of writing more in terms of product or process—that is, whether they look to help student writers develop their abilities by working to produce better, complete texts or by simply working on practical problems of composition through repeated work with drafting and revision. Teachers like White, Larson, and Stewart have a clear concern for the written product. They concentrate on how the text itself can be improved and define "improvement" squarely in terms of what the writer is able to accomplish in the final draft. Others, like Elbow, Anson, Stock, and Hull, are willing at times to downplay the final written product in order to encourage the student to practice certain writing processes or, through trial and error, come to develop their confidence and authority as writers. Those who teach more to the written product tend to keep a close eye on the assignment. Those who put more emphasis on helping students engage in the writing process for its own sake put less emphasis on assignment.

Stage in Drafting   The twelve readers were presented with papers at various stages of drafting: early, middle, and final. In early drafts, they tended to focus more extensively on large conceptual and rhetorical matters and, in later drafts, to be more selective in their commentary. The more developed the writing in front of them, the more likely they were to expand the scope of their comments. Nevertheless, the teachers also seemed intent on continuing substantive work on "final" drafts when they felt the writer still had not adequately worked through the writing. We must take care in what we say about their approach to revision because of limitations in our study. Though several cases in the study provided a series of drafts, most of the cases presented only a single draft, independent from earlier drafts or revisions based on earlier comments. So it was probably difficult for these teachers to gauge a student's work from one draft to another, and it was difficult for us, in turn, to compare the responses these teachers give at various stages in the drafting process. If their practice on the sampling is indicative of what they might do in actual situations (in situations that would allow them to look at revised drafts in light of both the previous draft and comments they made on this previous draft), they may well use very similar responding strategies on different stages of drafting, with the exception of the previously mentioned alterations of the focus and scope of their comments.

Student's Experience   As a whole, these teachers view a student's writing as an extension of that student's experience. They look *through* the text to the individual student behind the writing, imagining the writing in connection with the writer's own ideas, experiences, and perspectives and, more important, with the student's work as a writer. This is most often the case for Elbow, Hull, Gere, Anson, and Stock, but it is also true of others.

Use of the Student's Own Experience and Views

- Your revision should keep the good organization and concept, but show careful attention to making the memories *yours*, by detail, rather than just anyone's. (White)

- What, finally, is *your* point of view about gangs? (Gere)
- Part of the problem, for me anyway, stems from two things—a tendency to exaggerate without providing specific, realistic details, and a tendency to interpret the phenomenon you're describing very subjectively, so that *your* impressions, *your* sensations and feelings are at the center of the piece. (Anson)
- To be sure, it is a tough problem: How to communicate one's special understandings. After all, you haven't invented the language, you have inherited it. All you have in language is what you have been given. I find, however, that you can take the given and give it an original turn ("soft-scrunching of that magical white carpet underneath your feet"), and as I read your essays, I hope for that from you. (Stock)

Voice, Engagement, and Authority

- What I like is your voice and presence and the sense of immediacy through lots of detail. (Elbow)
- Good—you're an expert on these lakes and can write about them to bass fishers who have just moved into the Orlando area. (Peterson)
- This paper reflects your energy and your enthusiasm for fishing—qualities I don't want to see you lose in revising to produce your next draft. (Larson)
- You have considerable knowledge of the topic. (Stewart)
- You take more chances, you wade into deeper water. Serious problems, but again more energy and presence. You're acting like a real writer here. (Elbow)

The Student's Earlier Work in the Class

- You and I know from some of your past writing (and from flashes of promise in this text) that you are capable of composing very effective essays. (McClelland)
- By not revising the Disney paper you've left that timid fake voice from the beginning of the semester when you were scared to speak out on paper. Playing it safe. . . . With your skills now, you can go back and actually be there a bit and give us something real about that evening. (Elbow)

The Modes of Teacher Comments

Across the board, these teachers use significantly more nondirective modes than directive ones. Only 16 percent of their comments are framed in the most directive modes—corrections, criticisms, and commands:

- The teacher changes "*unmeasurable*" to "*very important to me.*"
- You don't provide any arguments for your position. All you offer are assertions.

- The same problems show up in your descriptions of other seasons.
- Focus this paragraph on this argument and develop your case.

For the most part, when they present evaluations of the writing or direct the student to make certain changes, they present their comments in moderate forms—as qualified evaluations and advice. Thirteen percent of their comments are framed in these more moderate forms:

- You might explain a bit more carefully what this program is.
- I would encourage you to think about how much you want of yourself and your experiences.
- You've got to be careful, I think, about doing too much, or some readers may think the piece sounds trite or overblown.
- If it was "almost" or nearly but not quite like an ego trip, I'd like to know specifically in what ways it was and in what ways it wasn't.

Fully 71 percent of their comments are framed in nondirective modes: as praise, questions, and various sorts of reflective statements. Time and again, the readers make it a point to identify strengths in student writing. As a group, they write 12 percent of their comments as praise:

- Good detail.
- This is a great way to describe the paranoid feeling.
- This last sentence is really interesting.
- Your description of Orlando's lakes and of Lake Ivanho in particular gives me a real feeling for the place and for fishing there because you include so many concrete examples and details.
- One thing that works well is the balance of short and long sentences, and also the variety of structures here.

Just how much praise they offer, however, varies widely from teacher to teacher. Four teachers—Elbow, O'Hare, Peterson, and Gere—write between 18 and 23 percent of their comments in the form of praise. Larson and McClelland write only 4 percent. Although a number of composition theorists have routinely called on teachers to find more opportunities to praise student writing, these teachers do not shy away from comments that help students see ways of improving their writing. They do so in a variety of modes. Twenty-five percent of the teachers' comments take the form of questions. Half of those are closed questions, which indirectly lead the student to add readily available information or to view the writing in a particular way. The other half are open questions that invite the student to think further about her ideas or lead her to consider the shape of the writing:

- What connections do you see among issues of membership, identity, and growing up?

- Are the winters as bad as those in Buffalo, with all that snow?
- What incident or incidents led you to use the terms "paranoia" and "burden"?
- Should you focus on that lake exclusively or talk about Central Florida in general?
- You say at the end of your paper that you've told only the good things about the seasons. Why might this be pleasant to some readers but offensive to others?

The teachers' use of questions varies widely. Anson and Elbow present only around 10 percent of their comments as questions; Gere and Warnock, on the other hand, present over 40 percent of their comments as questions. Teachers who use a lot of closed questions, like Peterson and Larson, still direct the student's work with revision but moderate their control by using questions instead of criticisms and commands. Teachers who use a lot of open questions—for instance, Gere, Warnock, Hull, and O'Hare—allow students to retain greater control over their writing even as they leave their response more open-ended and challenge students to think about their writing more fully on their own.

Perhaps the most interesting finding in the study deals with the kinds of comments the teachers make *beyond* these more familiar modes. A surprisingly large number (34 percent) of these teachers' comments are given to declarative statements that do not correct, criticize, or praise. These comments summarize, describe, or interpret the student's writing. At other times their comments present a lesson, explain some principle, explain another comment, or offer an example. Still other comments urge the student on, provide a reader's (not so much a critic's or a teacher's) response. Here are some examples:

- First, you say that the law is a violation of a person's freedom, (interpretive)
- One reason that you belonged was the sense of fraternity ("acceptance and friendship") (interpretive)
- [*I suggest that you offer your reader more details.*] For example, on page 1, you might provide a phrase defining and/or describing sink holes for those of us who don't know what they are. I'm talking about a phrase like the one you have written on page 2, to define what you mean by "hidden underwater structures." (explanatory)
- Sometimes it's useful to make a concession to an opponent, but it must be qualified or limited to some specific point that does not detract from your main objection to the opponent's position. (instructive)
- I had a similar experience at fifteen when my father died. (reader-response)

- [I must say, I liked the fact that you chose auburn as a color because Auburn the city is so close to Syracuse.] I actually stopped to think if that might be why Auburn has the name it does. (reader-response)
- I stumbled as I read your first two sentences. (reader-response)
- I am really looking forward to reading your next draft of "Street Gangs." (hortatorical)

These nonevaluative statements talk with the student without directly evaluating the writing or leading her to take on any revision. They have the effect of tempering the control a teacher exerts over the student by providing feedback and help instead of handing down judgments and making demands. They make response a two-way street between student and teacher, writer and reader. The abundance of these comments shows just how much commentary a teacher can provide without taking on the role of critic, editor, gatekeeper, judge, or even coach, questioning reader, or guide.

As we noted earlier, there are some changes in these teachers' modes from rough drafts to final drafts. On final drafts, there are fewer directive comments (corrections, criticisms, and commands), and there is more praise, for obvious reasons. There are also fewer imperative and advisory modes on final drafts, probably because the teachers have assumed the more evaluative posture that is frequently taken on in final drafts. It must be noted, however, that these teachers routinely view even final drafts as writing that is open for revision, whether students are going to be allowed or encouraged to actually hand in a rewrite or not. For these teachers, writing comments is not simply an act of review and evaluation; it is not simply a chance to get the writing further along; it is an opportunity to help students see how their writing is being read by a reader and lead them to continue work on their writing. Response for them is not only a prompt for revision; it is an act of teaching, a mode of instruction.

Response Styles and Control in Teacher Commentary

Although a major goal of *Twelve Readers* was to determine the ways in which our enlisted teachers responded as a group, we were not content to leave it at that. We also wanted to examine some of the more obvious differences among these teachers' responding styles. That led us to characterizing the responding style of each of these teachers. In order to do so, we posed the following questions as we examined their responses to our sampling. What kind of relationships do these teachers establish with student writers through their comments? How much do they direct students to make certain changes or pursue certain paths of revision? How much do they allow students to make their own choices in producing a piece of writing? Control is determined to a large extent by the modes of commentary teachers employ—how much they employ strong directive modes like corrections, criticisms, and commands, how much they use less directive modes like qualified evaluations and advice, and how much they use open questions and reflective statements. But it is also a function of the number and scope of the comments, the length and specificity of the comments, and the predominant focus of the comments.[2]

The more comments teachers make, the more direction they are likely to provide and the more control they are likely to assume. To be more precise, the more comments a teacher makes and, in doing so, the more areas of writing he or she covers, the more controlling the responses. Stewart's comments are more controlling than McClelland's, to a large extent because he writes more comments per paper than McClelland and consistently covers more territory in his responses. Yet, paradoxically, the more specific and detailed one's individual comments, the more direction and help they offer.

As a teacher's comments become shorter and more cryptic, students have to search more and more carefully for exactly what the teacher is saying; in such situations, students are being told what is not working or what they should revise, but they may not fully understand what is wrong and what they might do in revision. We see the reverse effect of longer comments in Donald Stewart's responses. Stewart's commentary is less directive than one might at first think because he offers detailed explanations and examples of how the student may take up his ideas for revision. Similarly, O'Hare's commentary is made less, not more, directive when he adds questions to help the student better understand the concerns he has in mind and help the writer think through them. Anson's commentary is more directive than Hull's, although they both offer a lot of advice, largely because he writes three times as many comments as she. At the same time, however, his commentary is more helpful because he explores various options for revision and illustrates how his advice may be taken up. The strength of Hull's style lies in the way she pinpoints one or two issues for students to address and then shows them, through questions and advice, how to take up these issues on their own. The number of comments itself, then, is only a broad indicator of control. We have to consider whether the comments are presented in order to cover more areas of writing or to help the student understand and act on the teacher's primary responses.

There are several interesting connections between the focus of commentary and control. In one sense, it would seem that the more a teacher focuses on local issues of style and correctness, the more controlling his comments will likely be. White, Larson, O'Hare, and McClelland all make appreciable use of criticism and advice. But White's and Larson's styles might seem more directive because they focus so many of their comments (37 percent and 32 percent)

---

2. It is also, of course, a question of the teacher's actual classroom demeanor and persona and the ways the teacher has interacted with students in general and with the individual student in particular. But these classroom-based factors are beyond the scope of this study, which is limited to matters of teacher response and teacher–student interactions as they are implied in and constructed from the comments the teacher makes on the page.

on sentence-level concerns. O'Hare and McClelland together give only 9 percent of their comments to the same areas. The more a teacher looks at the surface features of writing, the more likely he will dictate specific changes and the more controlling his commentary will be. Alternately, the more a teacher focuses on the larger contexts of writing, the less controlling his response style will be, since he will be viewing the issue from a broader perspective.

There is another way to look at this issue, however. Students may well perceive comments about organization and the development of ideas that are already on the page as less troublesome and less controlling than comments about their ideas themselves. Concerns about organization and development are conventionally given over to the teacher's authority, since they deal with *how* the ideas are presented. Students are less likely to give control of their ideas over to teachers, since they assume that they have the right to determine what they think and say in their writing—at least in their writing for composition classes. (As they put it, "You're not grading us on our opinions, are you? This is a *writing* course.") The more a comment appears to work against the writer's ideas, the more controlling it may seem to be. In fact, these may well be the most controlling comments that a teacher can make: ones that tell students their ideas don't work or that come across as telling them what they should say. A student may find Larson's and McClelland's comments less controlling than those of a teacher who concentrates on sentence style and error, but she may also find them pretty controlling when they seem to determine what she can say. Hull's commentary is less controlling insofar as she leaves the specific content up to the students. When she does have some concern about their content, she usually raises it as a question or urges them to consider what they have said in terms of different audiences and discourse communities. Still, it should be noted that comments about the writer's content can only be so controlling because the material of the writing must finally come from the students themselves (at least when they are writing on topics from their own experience and on topics that they choose); teachers must somehow defer to the students' invention. It should also be said that the inverse of directing students to look at the content of their writing—in effect, allowing them to say whatever they want and never questioning their ideas—is a much more troublesome approach to take.

These other influences notwithstanding, the control of a teacher's response is seen most readily in, and decided most fully by, the relative explicitness and elaboration of his or her comments and the modes chosen for those comments. White's comments are more controlling than Peterson's and Gere's largely because he frequently writes abbreviated comments and presents almost half of his comments in straight directive modes, whereas Peterson and Gere frequently employ qualified evaluations, advice, and questions. Larson's commentary is more controlling than Anson's, though they both use a lot of advice, because Larson employs many terse comments and a high percentage of evaluative comments and closed questions, while Anson offers detailed explanations, examples, and alternatives. Anson's commentary, in turn, is more controlling than Elbow's because Anson makes abundant use of advice and qualified evaluations while Elbow relies mostly on playing back his reading of the student's text in reader responses.

Concluding Remarks

Ultimately, the control of a teacher's comments is best viewed not as a certain kind of control or even as a single point on a range of styles, but as a band of oscillating points on a continuum, an EKG that is sensitive to a complex of factors. Descriptions of a teacher's control look to index the extent to which a teacher overtly imposes his or her own vision for the writing on students. All teacher response is, by the very nature of teacher–student power relations, to some extent controlling. Response styles that exert less control over the student's writing are not necessarily better than, or preferable to, styles that exert greater control, or vise versa.

Control is best seen as a result of several key factors: the teacher's persona, the teacher's teaching style, the writer, and the situation in which a piece of writing is being composed. Different combinations of these factors call for different degrees of control. To see the advantages of directive commentary, all we have to do is to see it not simply as a way of *directing* students down a certain path of our choosing but as a way of *giving direction* or *offering help* to students. To see the disadvantages of nondirective commentary, all we have to do is consider what it does not typically offer students: specific strategies for dealing with revision, in a direct way. Response styles become problematic when teachers go to the extremes: when they barrage the student with short, terse comments on mostly local matters, in the most directive modes, according to their own unswerving agendas, making their commentary not just directive but *authoritarian*; and when they make so few comments (and those that they do make are so general) that their commentary becomes *detached*, offering the student little by way of help or direction.

These twelve teachers adopt a range of response styles that assume various degrees of control over student writing, but they all fall somewhere in the broad middle of the spectrum of teacher responses:

Authoritarian—Authoritative—Interactive—Nondirective—Detached

Teacher-Centered———————Student-Centered

As a group these teachers reject styles of commentary that are overly directive and controlling, that take control out of the hands of the writer and impose the teachers' values and views—their "ideal texts"—on student writing. And they engage themselves in their responses more than enough to avoid leaving their commentary detached. Even the most directive teachers in the group go to some length to put a check on the control they exert over student writing and revision. And even those whose response styles are nondirective employ comments that somehow lead the student to see the text in certain ways and engage her in certain strategies of revision. As a group, the twelve teachers share a wide range of strategies and through their comments look to lead students back into their texts, develop their views of writing, and give them the practice they think they will need to help them become better writers.

The study we undertook in *Twelve Readers* suggests the rich repertoire of strategies and styles that teachers have at their disposal as they look to reflect on their own methods and goals for commenting on student writing, develop their own response styles, and learn to use their commentary strategically, according to their purposes and goals, for different students in various rhetorical situations, in various instructional settings.

References

Knoblauch, C. H., and L. Brannon. 1981. "Teacher Commentary on Student Writing: The State of the Art." *Freshman English News* 10:1–4.

Sommers, N. 1982. "Responding to Student Writing." *College Composition and Communication* 33 (2):148–56.

Straub, Richard, and Ronald Lunsford. 1995. *Twelve Readers Reading: Responding to College Student Writing.* Cresskill, NJ: Hampton Press.

11

Listening to Students

Contextualizing Response to Student Writing

Peggy O'Neill
Jane Mathison Fife

Writing teachers devote much time and energy responding to student writing. Teachers also spend a lot of time analyzing their response practices in professional forums such as journals and conferences. However, we found through our experience designing and preparing a project about teacher response practices that students are an important—but often overlooked—source of information in analyzing and understanding response. Much research on response has focused on teachers' written comments to a student text, without emphasizing the student readings of these comments and the context informing those readings (Sommers; Brannon and Knoblauch; Connors and Lunsford; Straub and Lunsford; Sperling). In the quest to understand and improve response practices, compositionists need to listen to the primary audience of those comments, their students. Student voices can teach us about response in the writing classroom and about potential directions for future research, but these voices are often missing from the response literature.

Listening to the student voices in an exploratory study we conducted led us to rethink our delineation of what constituted "response." Instead of seeing the response situation as consisting of a student's written drafts and a teacher's written responses to these drafts at various stages, we came to see that a complex interaction of pedagogical, textual, and personal contexts had the potential for engaging students in an authentic, constructive conversation with teachers about their writing. Our account is not a conventional report of research findings, but rather draws on our research to suggest what we can learn from these student voices about how they see response and what broader contexts of the response situation can be significant to them as they learn to write and talk about their writing with more confidence.

Peggy O'Neill is an assistant professor of writing at Georgia Southern University where she teaches writing and writing pedagogy courses. Her research interests include writing assessment theory and practice. Jane Mathison Fife is an assistant professor of English at East Central University in Ada, Oklahoma. She has taught first-year writing, persuasive writing, advanced composition, technical communication, and composing theories.

Specifically, we argue that we need to expand our conception of the response situation to encompass all the interchanges about evaluation—valuing of writing and writers—that go on in writing classes. We suggest two ways of complicating how the response situation is constructed in research about teacher commentary: 1) acknowledge the multiple and intersecting factors that influence student interpretations (perceptions) of how teachers respond to their writing, and 2) look beyond teacher written comments, broadening the focus to include other important contributions to the response context such as classroom communications, student reflections, and students' perceptions.

Listening to Students

Although much of the composition research on response examines teachers' comments as isolated artifacts, some studies have examined students' interpretations of teachers' comments to determine what comments students find most helpful (Fuller; Jenkins; Ziv; Hayes and Daiker; Auten, "How"; Auten, "A Rhetoric"; E. Smith; Straub, "Students' Reactions"). David Fuller, Ruth Jenkins, and Ernest Smith investigate how students in their classes react to teachers' comments, situating these comments within the contexts of teachers' goals for their commentary. Some of these studies, however, use a survey format to ask students about their reactions to comments (Auten, "How"), even using sample comments that were not in response to papers the students had actually written (Straub, "Students' Reactions"). All of these attempts to take student perspective into account limit their focus to teacher-written comments, not attempting to define the response situation of the classroom more broadly and contextually. Richard Straub even concedes that "the particular context has an effect on how students view teacher response," acknowledging that in "the full context of the classroom, the directive comments of one teacher may not be comparable to the directive comments of another teacher" (113). Student perspectives may have been included in the data gathering of some studies, such as in Sommers' and Sperling's work, but the written remarks are the main focus of the analysis. Studies that do envision the response situation as larger than teacher-written comments usually focus only on one aspect of response such as student-teacher conferences (Newkirk, "First"; Newkirk, "Writing"; Patthey-Chavez and Ferris) or peer group conferences (Auten, "How"; Nystrand and Brandt; Walvoord) without addressing their interconnections. While Sarah Freedman does look at multiple modes for response in writing classrooms, other researchers have not extended her work to explore the inter-connections between these different modes of response. Although Melanie Sperling and Sarah Freedman demonstrate how complex the response situation is in "A Good Girl Writes Like a Good Girl," composition researchers have not followed that up with contextualized studies focusing on the college writing classroom.

Our initial study examined two instructors of first-year college composition, Anna and Sharon,[1] as they moved from a traditional grading system in which individual papers were graded throughout the semester to a portfolio system that involved reading and responding to student drafts but grading the portfolio only at the end of the semester. The data collected included three sets of interviews with a total of ten students, copies of the students' written texts, the teachers' responses over two semesters, interviews with the teachers, and think-aloud protocols of the teachers reading and responding to drafts and portfolios.[2] While we initially viewed the students' responses to questions about teacher commentary as additional data for contextualizing the teachers comments, their responses made us question our original approach, which was to conduct a textual analysis of the comments similar to studies by Connors and Lunsford, Straub and Lunsford, or S. Smith. The student interviews also made us realize that discrepancies existed between teacher/researcher perceptions and student perceptions.

As part of our study, we asked students to discuss the written comments they received from their teachers. We initially conceived of these interviews as background information because we planned to focus our analysis on the written comments of the teachers—as most of the published research does—as they switched from using a traditional grading system to portfolios. In designing the questions we asked students, we assumed that students would construct both their perceptions of the comments and the teacher-responder from the teachers' written comments. The answers we got in interviews, however, soon made us aware of the multiplicity of factors that contribute to students' perceptions of teachers' comments. For example, when asked about the tone of his teacher's comments, one student answered in terms of the teacher, not the written comments: "Friendly. Like she's in the class with you instead of a teacher. She's more like a friend than a teacher." When asked again specifically about the tone of his teacher's written comments, he answered a bit differently: "Pretty to the point. Constructive criticism. Which was good. You don't want somebody telling you everything was good when it's not. So it was helpful." During an interview primarily about written response, this student's first impulse to answer about how his teacher came across in person made us aware that as researchers our assumptions about the primacy of written comments in students' construction of the teacher-as-responder was questionable. Many other factors we had not considered in the planning and implementation of our study seemed to be significant to the students' understanding of teachers' comments: personal interactions with the teacher, a teacher's face-to-face demeanor, and students' comparisons of the teacher and her comments with past teachers and comments.[3] As we continued to examine the student interview transcripts, the teachers' responses, and the scholarship on response, we came to question an assumption that underlies much of the existing research. Straub verbalizes this often tacit assumption: "In fact, it is arguable that, during the time the student reads a set of comments, the image of the teacher that comes off the page becomes the teacher for that student and has an immediate impact on how those comments come to mean" ("Concept of Control" 235).

While Straub's assertion may be right about the immediate impact of the written text on student interpretation of comments, our study suggests that a significant influence in the interpretation of the teacher as commentor is context and that students' reading of comments are also strongly influenced by context. Using categories such as "facilitative" and "directive," or more detailed schema such as Connors and Lunsford's, didn't address the complex and often messy nature of the interactions between teachers and students. Furthermore, as researchers coding the comments of our peers, teachers with whom we shared offices and fellow graduate teaching assistants with whom we took classes, we felt that the coding misrepresented or distorted the teachers' comments. For example, many of the comments, such as the ones below, could be coded as directive although our experiential knowledge and interview data indicated that Sharon and Anna were not directive teachers:

- "Develop this paragraph some more—Did your family buy the Escort? Do you like Ford's technology but not their business?"
- "Try to think of even more concrete detail—a specific goal you scored, what happened when you'd go out after games . . . "
- "Put this in lower-case letters."
- "Again, give me an example or examples."

For us, coding many of the comments depended on how we interpreted them and the context in which they occurred. Other commenting practices, as illustrated in this end comment written by Sharon on a draft in progress, seemed to complicate matters even more:

> I really like this and can tell that you have a lot invested here. I would go back through and fill it out some more—I marked places where I was confused, but you can really play around and try to pick some suggestive details to make it clearer and give it more impact. Look at George Wolff's "Symbiosis" again (or just look at if you haven't already) and notice how racist he is with all of his details and such—they tell a story that is bigger than the immediate one which you could do as well. . . . Let me know what you think.

This lengthy end comment (only partially quoted) contextualizes the marginal notes that appear directive (e.g., "How do the rest of them act?" or "This statement seems contradictory") and seems to let the student know that he is free to address the teacher's concerns in his own way. However, Sharon explicitly sends the writer back to a text and makes specific suggestions on how to use it, but then she ends with an invitation to the student to respond to her comments. Did the student really see the questions and suggestions as questions and suggestions, or did he feel they were directions for him to follow in his revisions? Did he see the last comment as a genuine invitation or an empty gesture? Did he think his grade on his portfolio would be affected if he didn't follow the suggestions? We weren't sure, and textual analysis of the comments couldn't answer our questions. Furthermore, parsing an end comment such as this one into discrete categories, as in Connors and Lunsford's schema, doesn't capture the effect of it as a whole. Because the coding and interview analysis occurred after the data collection ended, we were not able to directly question students about specific teacher comments such as the one above; however, we were able to re-think our approach and our analysis of the data we did collect.

Based on our qualitative study, we identified three key ways that students interpret their teacher's written response to their writing:

1.   Comments are read in the context of previous teachers' comments.

2.   Comments are read through the student's perception of the teacher's ethos.

3.   Comments are interpreted as just one facet of a broader framework for response that the teacher sets up in the class.

Other factors, such as race, gender, age, and class (to name just some of them) may also contribute to a student's response to the teacher's comments and the teacher-responder, although investigation of these factors was beyond our scope. We realize that the strategies we identify are not necessarily as discrete as we present them here, but in creating this taxonomy we hope to highlight the subtle, atextual influences that shape the context through which students read their teachers' comments.

Comments Read in the Context of Previous Teachers' Comments

Many students judged their teacher's comments in comparison with the commenting habits of their previous teachers. To describe how her teacher's comments were directed to content rather than surface features, Lori, one of Anna's students, said:

> I never really had teachers that commented about the content of a paper. They just commented about parentheses, question marks, you need a comma here. She commented more about how we did on the paper, what we wrote about. . . . In the past, I was like, why write if they're just going to say I did this wrong and I did this wrong and I did this wrong.

Students were often impressed by comments on content because it suggested that the teacher really read the paper. Steve made a similar comparison explaining that his high school teachers "would just write 'good' at the top of the paper but nothing specific. It shows that she actually reads certain parts of it. It's not that she just scans it or something." Roger's response about his teacher Sharon was a common one:

> If she didn't care, she wouldn't say what she says. . . . Any teacher who's going to read all your papers. . . . My papers got scanned in high school. Because, you know, all those papers. And the comments weren't real thorough. If they catch a grammatical error, they circle it. But she makes comments in reference to the whole paper, not just a section.

Here a comparison with previous comments he had received led this student to construct his teacher as a caring responder because of the thoroughness and scope of her comments. All of the students interviewed interpreted the specific comments and response to the content as positive in light of their previous experiences. Even if the comparisons weren't positive (and just about all of the students we interviewed made a favorable comparison), the students still seemed to use their previous experience with teacher response as they interpreted immediate comments.[4]

Comments Read Through a Perception of the Teacher's Ethos

While their judgment of the teacher's commenting style in relation to their experiences in previous classes was a significant part of students' construction of the teacher-responder, their judgment of comments in terms of the teacher's classroom ethos seemed more significant to their overall constructions. As mentioned above, when asked about the tone of their teachers' comments, students often responded with their perception of the tone or attitude the teacher conveyed in the classroom but with further prompting made distinctions about the tone of written comments. Lori's remarks about Anna included, "She's a lot more down-to-earth. She's not like on the teaching level up here. She tries to be a lot closer to you to tell you how to get into it more." Lori's interpretation of the teacher's attitude toward her students seems to shape Lori's perception of her written comments, as in the following statement: "She doesn't want to scare anybody off by saying you didn't do this, you didn't do this, you didn't do this. She tries to put confidence into you that you're a good writer and that you have some writing ability in there somewhere." Rob used this anecdote to explain his perception that his teacher, Anna, put extra effort into teaching instead of approaching it as "just a job":

> One example would be when we were writing our first paper and she wrote one also and brought it in to read it. I think when she did that the whole class said, "She's okay. She's all right. She's really just trying to help us, trying to teach us something. Give her a break and try to learn."

Amanda, a student of Sharon's, draws similar conclusions about how her teacher projected a caring attitude in the classroom: "The way she came across to the whole class, she wasn't real authoritative like 'I'm the teacher, I say what's going to go.' She would talk to us and see what we wanted." Lori made a similar point about Anna: "In class she's a teacher but she tries to talk on your level, not like some big queen teacher . . . " Ultimately, it was this projection of a caring attitude in the classroom and in personal interactions with students that seemed to be an important influence in how they approached the written comments and ultimately how they understood them, as Roger demonstrates:

> She wants us to do good. . . . She doesn't want to give anybody bad grades. She wants us to do really good. If she has to sound like rude on the paper—sometimes there's nothing you can do. You have to tell us what you think. But if she thinks it's going to help us, that's fine. But if she thought it wasn't going to do any good and was just hurtful, she wouldn't do it.

Roger's perception of Sharon is corroborated by Curtis: "She was all for us. She would come in and be enthusiastic about everything. She was our age so we kind of just bonded with her, and she's there for us."

Although these students perceived their teachers as more on their own level, they still acknowledged the teachers as expert readers and writing authorities. As Steve explained, he privileged Anna's comments over peers' not just because she was the grader but because she is more experienced: "We haven't read as many papers and aren't as good at critiquing other papers." Shonda expressed a similar point of view: "If I want to use her comments and suggestions then I can do that. . . . I feel like I trust in her comments that she's telling me the right thing so I'll consider, I'll use them. I think that her comments are very valid and she got the point." Shonda sees response as an exchange in which she has an active role: she considers the comments and follows the suggestions that she sees as "valid." Similarly for Curtis, Sharon's comments are negotiable and should fit with the goals he has for his papers. For the most part, he tries to follow her suggestions because "If that's what she wants to see, then it's what I need to write about." But he adds that he sees her advice as improving his writing: "After I write the paper, I see how it's a lot better than it was." However, Curtis also feels justified in disagreeing with her when he thinks she has misunderstood his purpose; he says. "I've probably overruled her like maybe two suggestions out of maybe twenty-five. So that's just because maybe she didn't understand where I was coming from, and I just maybe changed a word or two." Because of the influence of the teacher's ethos on student interpretation of comments, students read critical comments as helpful, as Amanda articulates: "In some ways it [Sharon's response] makes me feel better about my writing because I don't feel like a complete failure, and she is honest about it and tells why it may not be good or why it is good."

Our interviews with these students illustrate the significant influence a teacher's ethos can have on the students' interpretation of written comments, suggesting that research on response that focuses exclusively on the teacher's written comments paints an incomplete picture about how students read the comments and how they perceive the teacher-responder.

Comments as Just One Facet of a Broader Framework for Response

Students read the comments they received as part of the larger classroom context. In the interviews, students articulated differences in how they read responses from their teachers, and how teachers commented, based on the design of the class. For example, during the first semester, both teachers commented on drafts-in-progress and then commented and graded a final draft before students moved on to a new writing assignment. In reflecting on the commenting practices in this system, students explained that they read comments on drafts in terms of how to get a good grade on the final draft. Roger, for example, remarked about the written response he received on drafts that some things Sharon wanted him to do he "didn't think were valid . . . but if it were something big I would change because I knew if she didn't like it I wouldn't get a very good grade on the paper." On final drafts, Roger didn't pay attention to comments but "just looked at the grade." Other students expressed similar understanding and use of the comments. Steve, for instance, explained that once he received a grade on a paper he put it "in a corner never to be seen again." Lori felt that the context of the class influenced not only her reading of the comments but the way Anna responded to the papers: "I think last semester . . . we were getting individual grades on [papers] so she didn't really stop and say, 'Well, I wonder what she was thinking right here' . . . she wasn't as specific." All students agreed that when the teachers switched to portfolios, they wrote more comments and more specific comments. In fact, most students saw that the move to portfolios changed the teachers' commenting practices to some extent, as well as students' interpretation of the comments.

During the second semester, both teachers used portfolios yet had very different approaches to the structure of the class. However, students from each class described many routine opportunities to communicate with their teachers about their writing and the response they received. These interactions—which included a spontaneous conversation between student and teacher, a quick question to the teacher during class, a conference outside of class, or even a written response to the teacher's comments—supplemented the teachers' written comments and made important contributions to the students' readings of the comments. The structure of the classes contributed to the students' perception of the access they had to their teacher and opportunities for talking about the teacher's comments.

Sharon structured her class as a writing workshop. She gave students descriptions of four kinds of assignments that they needed to include in their final portfolios and encouraged students to develop papers on their own in addition to these four required texts. Each week, Sharon scheduled one class meeting as a workshop session where students met in groups to discuss each others' work. While there were no due dates for drafts of papers, she encouraged students to give drafts to her as often as they wanted for her to respond in writing. Students reacted to this relaxed structure positively for the most part, remarking on how they perceived it to have influenced Sharon's commenting.

One student explained that because not everyone turned drafts in at the same time, Sharon "was able to maybe spend more time on a draft because she might not get everybody's on the same day so she might have more time to read yours." Another of Sharon's students, Roger, summed up the connection between the response and class activity: "What we do in class is just reinforcing what she writes on papers." Sharon's students also repeatedly explained that if they did have a problem or question about her written response, they could talk to her about it whether in class or during a conference out of class. Remarks such as Curtis' were common: "As soon as she hands [a draft] back, and I read it, I'd tell her about what I was thinking."

Anna's portfolio class was structured differently, with set due dates for each of the five assignments. She hoped that using portfolios would allow students to benefit from what they learned about writing over the whole semester before being graded. She also expected to improve students' self-evaluation skills by requiring reflective memos for each draft as well as a detailed portfolio cover letter. In this introductory letter, students would explain their choices for revised, polished work (two out of the five assigned papers) in terms of the course, goals, which included development of the students' awareness of conventions of academic texts and the rhetorical expectations of academic audiences. Lori explained that she liked the portfolio system because "if you are writing a paper and having a lot of trouble with it you can turn it in and get her comments back and then revise it"; so, Lori could "learn from [her] mistakes" and make choices about revisions. Steve also saw a connection between the portfolio system and the way he used Anna's comments:

> [I]nstead of writing a paper and getting a grade on it and tossing it in the corner never to be seen again, now we've been looking at these papers throughout the whole semester. Now we can pull the older ones out and look over them, look it over again and maybe actually learn like 'Hey, I forgot about that that she wrote down there.' And maybe I'll put those to use on this paper. And so we need to pull them out throughout the semester, keep them in mind.

Anna's students, like Sharon's, talked to her about the written comments they received noting that they felt "comfortable" in conferencing with her. Shonda explained, "She is there for help, but you are writing it yourself. And if you think something is wrong, you can go to her and say 'I don't think this is right. Can you look at it?'" They also saw the class, and the teacher, as interested in their development as writers: "I think she [Anna] wants us to get a lot of our own goals out of this class. . . . I think she wants us to focus on what we're learning and our goals." As one student explained, the reflective memos and cover letters were a place where they could explain themselves:

> I think [reflective memos are] good because, I mean, a lot of times. I messed up on something . . . . And we could just write down any kind of problems, and that helps me because I always have a lot of problems. If you think some-

thing is kind of icky in your paper, you didn't know if you should have done it
or not, you can ask her about it and she'll write back and say, "It's OK. Keep it."

Anna, like Sharon, provided low-risk opportunities for students to discuss their
writing—both product and process—as well as their written comments. The
students' reading and interpretation of the response situation proved complex
since they read the written response as part of the entire classroom context
including their previous experiences, the teacher's ethos, and the class structure. Textual features such as wording, phrasing, and structuring may also be
important factors, according to the students' responses, but they were not necessarily the most important.

Learning from Students

By listening to the students in our study, we realized that a primary focus on the
written text in teacher response research is inadequate in explaining how the students—the intended audience for those comments—read them because written
comments function within a larger contextual framework. The comments also
help create the context and students' understanding of it, especially when students' classroom experiences and written comments are mutually reinforcing.
Students are not, after all, distant, objective researchers trying to code comments
but rather writers and readers who come to the written comments with experience
and knowledge. Research on teacher response has focused on the comments as
textual artifacts at the expense of context even in more recently published work
(Straub, "Concept of Control," "Students' Reactions," "Teacher Response";
Straub and Lunsford; S. Smith). Examining only a teacher's response ignores a
student's contribution to the exchange and provides a limited understanding of the
role of response in a writer's development and writing pedagogy.

In addition to tacitly supporting a response dynamic in which teacher commentary is the primary text, many of the studies on teacher commentary operate
with the implicit understanding that a "true" meaning of the comments exists
divorced from a social context. The irony of this stance towards comments is that
we have abandoned this position in terms of other texts—literary texts or
student-generated essays. As the Introduction to *Encountering Student Texts*
explains: "Before teachers can evaluate or respond to student writing, though,
they must interpret it, and the ways they interpret it are shaped by a multitude of
assumptions and values—about language, about student writing, about their students, and about their roles as readers" (Lawson et al. viii). We need to extend
this analysis of the reading of student texts by their teachers to the reading of
teacher comments by their students. In other words, by extending the notion of
reading espoused here (which is informed by such theorists as Kenneth Burke,
Stanley Fish, Wolfgang Iser, and Barbara Herrnstein Smith), reading written
responses to student writing is just as complex and contextual as reading other
texts. As teachers, then, we need to attend to not only what we write in response

to student writing but also to the context in which we write it. Choosing the appropriate phrases and words is only part of the response situation; we need to be aware of how the context in which students read those comments—including pedagogical practices and classroom climate—inform the students' readings of our written responses. As teachers, we need to create opportunities for students to respond, to engage in real conversations, not just metaphorical ones, about their writing and our teaching. Portfolios, cover letters, reflective memos, and "talk backs" (Yancey) are just some of the ways that teachers have begun to reconceptualize response patterns and provide ways for students to participate more fully in the response round. Interviews with our students suggest that these practices are effective for students to develop as writers, but our exploratory study does not address many of the questions and issues surrounding these practices. Research is still needed that attempts to elicit student perspectives on multiple aspects of response in the writing classroom, research that looks at the interconnections of written and verbal feedback about student writing, and research that envisions the response situation as a complex, two-way conversation between students and teachers that incorporates speaking and writing.

Just as teachers have begun to reconceptualize response practices, researchers need to reconceptualize their definitions of response, questions about response practices, and methods of inquiry. Some questions have already been addressed: Are the comments facilitative or directive? Are they positive or negative? Are rhetorical issues addressed? Are mechanical and grammatical issues addressed? However, others need to be explored as well: How do the comments function in the classroom? How do the students read the comments? How do students respond to the comments? What factors (e.g. race, class, age, learning disabilities) influence teachers' responses and students' readings of them? To address questions such as these, researchers need to look at more than the textual comments: classroom observations, discourse analysis of spoken texts, and text-based interviews are some of the methods that can enhance our textual analysis. Composition researchers need to give more attention to classroom contexts, teacher ethos, and students' previous experiences, as well as other factors, to develop a more complex understanding of effective response methods and how comments function within the larger context of the writing classroom. As researchers and teachers, we need to listen to our students and learn from them; this kind of approach to response research can complicate and complement the extensive textual work on teacher response practices that already exists.

Notes

1. Names of all participants have been changed to pseudonyms.

2. Student interviews were conducted during the second semester. The first interviews occurred during the fourth or fifth week, the second interviews during the eleventh or twelfth weeks, and the final interviews after the students received their grades. Although we both were equally involved in the data analysis and drafting, we played different

roles during the data collection: one of us was one of the teachers while the other conducted the student interviews, teacher protocols, and teacher interviews.

3. Although we identified these factors from the student interviews, we were not able to examine them more closely in practice through observations because the patterns did not emerge until after the data had been collected for the semester. Furthermore, the research design that had been approved by the university's human subjects committee did not include observations of classrooms or student-teacher interactions. Because of the original focus of the study, we did not conduct text-based interviews during which students responded to individual comments on their papers. We did, however, examine the teachers' comments on the papers. The comments for the most part corroborated students' perceptions that the teachers were positive, encouraging, and focused on their success. Our point, however, is not to demonstrate that the students misread the comments or that the teachers' comments contradicted their classroom ethos or philosophy, but rather we want to demonstrate that the texts have meaning for the students as part of a rich, dynamic situation that has not been considered in much composition research.

4. Because the initial focus of the study was on the teachers and their practices, not the students and their responses, we interviewed and collected papers from students who had the teachers for both semesters of first-year composition; however, students were not required to stay with the same instructor for both courses and most didn't given the size of the program and the difficulties in scheduling. Most of the students in our study, however, did make the effort to take the same teacher both semesters. Although the student sample can be considered biased—the students began the project with a positive attitude towards the teachers—the point we make is that the students' perceptions of the teachers as people come into play when they read the teachers' comments.

References

Auten, Janet Gebhart. 1991. "A Rhetoric of Teacher Commentary: The Complexity of Response to Student Writing." *Focuses* 4:3–18.

———. 1992. "How Students Read Us: Audience Awareness and Teacher Commentary on Writing." *Writing Instructor* 11.2:83–94

Brannon, Lil, and C.H. Knoblauch. 1982. "On Students' Rights to Their Own Texts: A Model of Teacher Response." *College Composition and Communication* 33:157–66.

Connors, Robert J., and Andrea Lunsford. 1993. "Teachers' Rhetorical Comments on Student Papers." *College Composition and Communication* 44:200–23.

Freedman, Sarah W. 1987. *Response to Student Writing*. Urbana, IL: NCTE.

Fuller, David. 1987. "Teacher Commentary that Communicates: Practicing What We Preach." *Journal of Teaching Writing* 6:307–17.

Hayes, Mary F., and Donald Daiker. 1984. "Using Protocol Analysis in Evaluating Responses to Student Writing." *Freshman English News* 13.2:1–4.

Jenkins, Ruth. 1987. "Responding to Student Writing: Written Dialogues on Writing and Revision." *Writing Instructor* 6.2:82–86.

Lawson, Bruce, Susan Sterr Ryan, and W. Ross Winterowd, eds. 1989. Introduction. *Encountering Student Texts: Interpretive Issues in Reading Student Writing*, vii–xvii. Urbana, IL: NCTE.

Newkirk, Thomas. 1989. "The First Five Minutes: Setting the Agenda in the Writing Conference." In *Writing Response: Theory, Practice, and Research,* edited by Chris Anson, 317–31. Urbana, IL: NCTE.

_____. 1995. "The Writing Conference as Performance." *Research in the Teaching of English* 29.2:193–215.

Nystrand, Martin, and Deborah Brandt. 1989. "Response to Writing as a Context for Learning to Write." In *Writing Response: Theory, Practice, and Research,* edited by Chris Anson, 209–30. Urbana, IL: NCTE.

Patthey-Chavez, G. G., and Dana R. Ferris. 1997. "Writing Conferences and the Weaving of Multi-Voiced Texts in College Composition." *Research in the Teaching of English* 31.1:51–90.

Smith, Ernest. 1989. "'It Doesn't Bother Me, But Sometimes It's Discouraging': Students Respond to Teachers' Written Responses." *Journal of Teaching Writing* 8: 253–65.

Smith, Summer. 1997. "The Genre of the End Comment: Conventions in Teacher Responses to Student Writing." *College Composition and Communication* 48: 249–68.

Sommers, Nancy, 1982. "Responding to Student Writing." *College Composition and Communication* 32:148–56.

Sperling, Melanie. 1994. "Constructing the Perspective of Teacher-as-Reader: A Framework for Studying Response to Student Writing." *Research in the Teaching of English* 28:175–203.

Sperling, Melanie, and Sarah W. Freedman. 1987. "A Good Girl Writes Like a Good Girl: Written Response and Clues to the Teaching/Learning Process." *Written Communication* 4:343–69.

Straub, Richard. 1996. "The Concept of Control in Teacher Response: Defining the Varieties of 'Directive and Facilitative' Commentary." *College Composition and Communication* 47.2:223–51.

——. 1997. "Students' Reactions to Teacher Comments: An Exploratory Study." *Research in the Teaching of English* 31.1:91–119.

——. 1996. "Teacher Response as Conversation: More Than Casual Talk, an Exploration." *Rhetoric Review* 14:374–98.

Straub, Richard, and Ronald F. Lunsford. 1995. *Twelve Readers Reading: Responding to College Student Writing.* Cresskill, NJ: Hampton.

Walvoord, Barbara E. Fassler. 1986. "Student Response Groups: Training for Autonomy." *Writing Instructor* 6.1:39–47.

Yancey, Kathleen Blake. 1998. *Reflection in the Writing Classroom.* Logan: Utah State University Press.

Ziv, Nina D. 1984. "The Effect of Teacher Comments on the Writing of Four College Freshmen." In *New Directions in Composition Research,* edited by Richard Beach and Lillian Bridwell, 362–80. New York: Guilford.

12

Marking the Paper

Lou LaBrant

And you take hold of a handle by one hand or the other by the better or worse hand and you never know maybe till long afterward
which was the better hand.

—THE PEOPLE, YES, Carl Sandburg[1]

The papers have been collected; they are yours to mark. What do you need to
know, to consider, to do? Here is perhaps the most difficult test of teaching
skill; for what you write on the student's paper should have more than one
result. Will your comments lead him to write again, or to fear writing? Will
they stimulate a desire to write better, or merely a fear of making errors? Will
you be opening an exchange of understanding, or will you and the student
communicate less and less from now on? What happens when the paper is
returned, carrying your addition to the ideas expressed? How do you mark this
paper?

It may be stated categorically that any good clerk can be taught to check
usage, count errors, and produce a grade as valid as grades usually are; yet to
many teachers marking means merely "correcting" and grading. Such an attitude is based on a most limited idea of what writing is about. Our student will
need increased skill with structure, usage, and such forms as paragraphing,
punctuation, placement of material on the page, neatness, and spelling; he will
need to grow in ability to organize material, to use rhetorical devices. Unless,
however, he wants to write, uses writing for significant purposes, and
approaches writing with honesty and a sense of responsibility for what he says,
it is hard to see why it matters whether or not his skill is increased. We have
far too long wasted time and energy on polishing unimportant, meaningless,

1. Copyright, 1936, by Harcourt, Brace and Company, Inc. Reprinted by permission of the publisher.

irresponsible writing. Marking the paper will encourage or discourage the acceptance of responsibility. The question thus recurs: What is the teacher to do with this paper which his student has handed to him?

First Requirement: Thoughtful Reading

The first step is to read the paper. This statement is not intended to be flippant. Reading means giving thought to what is being said, seeing the paper as a whole, reacting in terms of whatever has been done. If humanly possible, the reading should be done first without marking unless the teacher can automatically make check marks as he reads for ideas. (Experienced teachers can usually do this; beginning teachers usually need two readings, one for ideas, and one for usage, punctuation, and structure.) Reading should lead to some understanding of what prompted the paper, what limited it, what its strengths and weaknesses are, what it really says. After this reading the teacher is ready for comment. Certain issues have prime importance.

Criticism of Ideas

Obviously the first requirement is that the student be encouraged to continue to express his ideas. Unless there are to be more papers, little learning will ensue. This may not mean more writing on the same theme, but the present paper is a step toward the next. Especially during the early weeks of the term, the teacher must put forth unusual effort to encourage and suggest further communication. What does this mean in practice? Certainly not to write baldly, "Continue" or "Do another." Nor to praise insincerely what is not desirable. Students are quick to sense this superficial attempt to stimulate writing. The most important stimulus is to comment directly on the experiences put forth, even though these may be relatively unimportant and feeble. If the student writes about a current political issue, comment is easy; but the humble paper telling about a day in camp is another matter, more difficult because little is really revealed. Like a good conversationalist, the teacher must pick up where the other left off. If the paper tells a story, there may be a point at which the teacher can write "Amusing"; "Reminds me of a drive my family once had along a dangerous stream"; "Many feel as you do"; "This suggests another story you may want to write some day"; or "Do the other boys and girls know why you came home?" Whatever the comment, it should suggest respect for what the student has written, expectation of further writing, and interest in the account. It should be mentioned at this point that a writer is more influenced by attention than praise. There is a subtle compliment even in disagreement: the writer is a person to be considered, else his ideas would not matter to anyone. Such a comment as "This part seems to me beside the point" implies clearly that the rest of the paper does have point or purpose or value.

Sometimes a little device like the following is useful. A teacher who found that his students were unusually fearful of teacher comment mentioned the first day that as he read papers he had a habit of underscoring in red any sentence or phrase which seemed to him unusually interesting or effective. (He used black for corrections.) Thus red marks, so often associated with failure, became quickly recognized evidences of the opposite. Needless to say, the teacher managed to find some spot for using the red line on most of the papers. The device permitted him to take advantage of even one or two well chosen words.

Often, particularly when the first papers are weak and uninteresting, the teacher will be hard put to see in many of them anything worth a comment. There is the temptation to fall back on such remarks as "Good," "Interesting," or other empty praise; these remarks are to be avoided. They are to be avoided in the first place because they imply that the teacher's praise is of great importance. Good writing should not be done to *please* a teacher; good writing is an exchange of opinion, experience, emotion. It is essential to make clear to the student that the successful paper stimulates reaction in other people. This is a reason for having a paper by each student read in class early in the term. Often the teacher will write as much as the student. He will comment on an event by telling a little story of his own; he will ask questions, suggesting thereby a second paper; he will explain why some passage is not clear; he will ask for meanings. If this takes a great deal of time during the first weeks, it should be remembered that this is the season of the year when the teacher is most free for such work and that time spent then will be much more than repaid later in the year. As early as possible, responsibility for carrying on writing should be shifted to the shoulders of the students themselves. The teacher should not long have to motivate writing for most of the class.

Skillful comments will not only encourage further writing from the student but will lead to more significant topics. Let us say that the student, in perhaps the tenth grade, writes about picnics, hikes, or other rather trivial events, merely recounting the when, where, and obvious circumstances. A suggestion such as one of the following may be helpful: "Evidently you saw many things which you do not mention." "Are you a collector? Do you select your specimens?" "This picnic, *as you describe it*, seems like a thousand others. What happened that made you remember it? Was it something about the food, building the fire, or the friends you had with you? I don't think we understand." "Your story about the family trip leads me to think you and your parents enjoy doing things together, but I may be wrong. Could you let the rest of us know something about this?" "You mention liking to watch crowds in the station, but no two crowds are alike. What did you see? Weren't the people close enough to you that you could tell them apart? Surely you didn't just see them as a mass." "This event suggests that you were lonesome. When I am lonely I always feel sorry for myself and have a tendency to think about all the wrongs I've ever experienced."

The foregoing are very commonplace comments, but if you will examine them you will see that they are designed to dig a little deeper into the experience of the writer. Once faced with a real paper you will think of significant comments if you are really interested in the student and his writing.

Criticism of Writing

As the writing progresses, the comments will go into the character of the writing itself. Even young children in the junior high school often use words which have no clear meaning, and need to be brought to an understanding of how important it is that a person should know what he is writing about. "Labor," wrote a young high school student, evidently putting down what he had heard some adult say, "needs to be controlled." The teacher's comment was simply: "What do you mean by *labor?* Do you refer to all of the people who work, people like your father, who is employed in an office? Do you mean teachers? Farmers? I am also not sure what you mean by 'controlled.' Do you mean that workers should be managed the way soldiers are managed? Could you make all of this clear?" The student finally recognized that he was using words without knowing what they meant. He wrote that this was so, and began to limit his pronouncements to simpler statements. Another student wrote about Jews. The teacher's note asked whether he meant people who had some ancestor who believed in the Jewish religion, or whether he meant people who themselves had a certain religious belief. The question sent the young writer to a series of discoveries. "Every kind of school work deserves rewards," wrote a ninth grade girl. She then drew the conclusion that students who make good grades should wear the felt letters usually awarded to athletes. The teacher called her attention to "award" and the need for explaining the word which she was using in two senses in the same discussion. As a result the girl spent considerable time exploring the nature of awards and rewards, with the result that her whole understanding—not to mention her paper—was greatly improved.

The illustrations just given are probably sufficient to show that, through comments, the teacher leads the student to explore new areas of experience and also to develop the areas already entered. Marking papers becomes in this way stimulating to both student and teacher. Nor need the markings be deadly in their seriousness. Amusing comments on inconsistencies, on implications, or on parallel experiences suggested by the account can make the reading of criticism pleasant. The total effect should, in most cases, be constructive. There are times, however, when it may be good medicine to suggest, "If I were you, I would throw this away and write something new."

Criticism of Form and Structure

Doubtless by this time some teacher is impatient to hear mention of "corrections." What do we do to errors in sentence structure, usage, spelling, and punctuation? Errors are, of course, not to be disregarded. Structure controls meaning, and until it is clear and suited to the writer's purpose there can be no clear communication. Punctuation is likewise a means toward clarity, but should not be considered until the basic pattern of the sentence is established. Punctuation, approved usage, conventional spelling, attractive placement on the page, and paragraphing are conventions, designed to make reading simpler and more pleasant.

Criticism of Meaning and Structure

If one or more sentences are confused, a first step in marking is to draw a line along the margin and write "Sentence Structure" (or "SS"), "Confused," "Meaning?" or any other expression which suggests that the writer has not said what he seems to be trying to say. Sometimes the problem is merely one of punctuation. Students should learn to recognize some abbreviation (possibly "P") as indicating this. Little is gained if the teacher indicates the correct point. The student has seen plenty of correct forms. He needs now to struggle for the form which clarifies his own thought. Sometimes sentences will be run together, with no punctuation or perhaps a comma where a period should be used. A line under such a section with a marginal note may be effective. Write, for example, "This is run together. It does not make sense to me." Any child beyond the second grade knows that a declarative sentence should end with a period. *Finding where his sentence ends* is the difficulty. The student needs to struggle for the form which clarifies his own thought. This he will do if he is given two kinds of help: first, respect for his own piece; and second, time for the rewriting.

Usually even the more difficult structure problems are cleared up when the ideas are discussed with the student. The writer can clarify the sentence because *he knows what is intended.* Dangling clauses or phrases can be properly related as the one who has something to tell attempts to clarify his meaning in terms of a situation, real or imaginary, which is clear in his mind. It happens, of course, that sometimes there is no clear thought. Until the idea is clear, there can be no good writing.

It may be worth while here to recount an experience which throws some light on the important problem of the fragment, the uncompleted sentence. Almost every course of study and almost every composition book or workbook contains exercises designed to teach students to complete incomplete expressions. It seems strange that the idea has not occurred to teachers that the incomplete expression is evidence of a vague or confused experience and that it is unlikely to occur when the student is writing about something of major importance to him. Some years ago the writer of this book was attempting a study of sentence structure, and for that purpose needed the rapid natural writing of a thousand students. These ranged from early fourth through the twelfth grade. Since it seemed desirable to get rapid writing, separated in so far as possible from classroom controls, the following method was used.

Most of the pupils were told that there had been considerable discussion concerning a longer school term—ten or eleven or more months instead of nine. They were asked what they thought of the idea and requested to write down their opinions hurriedly, since the questioner had only a short time. Eagerly the children wrote. They used pencils, yellow paper, and had no time for revision. When the resulting papers (averaging more than 150 words each) were studied, it was discovered that, although 20,000 clauses were written, there were only three fragments. This does not mean that there were no errors in punctuation and that such a sentence as "If you do this I will quit" was never cut in two by a period. But the full basic structure was there; only three from the thousands of sentences were unfinished. Why? The apparent answer is that the children had something important to say and, consequently, did not fail to finish statements they began. A youngster who thinks, as most of these did, that nine months of school is certainly a long stretch does not omit the main clause in writing "If you do this, *I will quit.*" Subsequent experience with teaching in a program where the writing was based largely on the child's own experience confirms the conclusion that if writing is clearly purposeful, if the writer knows what he has to say, the problem of the fragment error simply does not exist. There will, of course, be fragments deliberately used, but not omissions which leave the reader wondering.

The teacher should never forget that good structure is a reflection of the relationships in the mind of writer or speaker. A dependent clause should be used only when ideas call for one. There has been much false teaching that complex sentences should be introduced to provide variety of style. Style should *always* be subservient to truth: until one knows the relation between two statements he would do well to leave them as simple, independent units. Frequently, too, relationships seen by an adult are not recognized by the young writer. A teacher should consequently use great caution about suggesting changes which involve subordination.

Pronoun Reference

Junior high school students use many pronouns, and are beginning to have a difficulty which we all experience. Making some forty-odd words stand for all the nouns in the language is never easy. (One of the common errors found on the papers of graduate students is the pronoun without a clear antecedent.) The most direct correction is probably to underscore the faulty pronoun and write "Who?" in the margin. Sometimes instead the teacher chooses a reference he knows is wrong and writes "John?" being reasonably sure that John is not the one referred to. The purpose in any event is to call the attention of the writer to his lack of clarity and to point up the issue. This is usually more effective than sending him to a handbook for a rule about pronouns. "I cannot tell whether you mean John or Peter" is more easily understood than "There is a rule concerning pronoun reference to the effect that . . ."

Spelling

The very bad speller is usually (some psychologists say *always*) a psychological problem. Frequently he is the child who has gained attention through bad spelling. Overanxious parents or teachers have made him so self-conscious that he cannot spell words he would otherwise handle easily. These severe cases should be given into the hands of a good psychologist where possible; but in no such case should the teacher emphasize the spelling. Often the simple method of ignoring spelling, and persuading parents to do so too for a three or four month period, will produce enormous gains. Bad spelling can be, and often is, an attention-getting device. "My mother spends hours helping me" is a warning to the teacher to avoid a similar method of rewarding the student for errors.

The reader should remember that the junior or the senior high school student has a vocabulary running into many thousands of words. Often overemphasis on spelling prevents his using most of those he knows. It is wise to accept as normal a considerable number of misspelled words, making the correction as easy as possible and taking for granted the obvious fact that ability to speak and to understand words runs far ahead of ability to spell them. There is no evidence that students are spelling less well today than students used to do; there is much evidence that students are trying to spell thousands of words which schools formerly never called for. Establish with the student the habit of putting into correct form all those papers which he thinks worth keeping and finishing. But do not be surprised and do not appear horrified if the young writer makes many spelling errors on his first drafts.

Adapting Criticism to the Individual

It should be evident to any thoughtful person that receiving criticism of one's writing can be a most discouraging experience. There is in every class the student whose paper is messy in appearance, or whose structure or spelling or usage is very poor. This is the student who dreads writing papers, and is unhappy the day they are returned. Frequently he is the least capable. He envies the "good" paper, the high mark of the student across the aisle. The situation seems very unfair to him. There sits the complacent owner of the perfect paper, faced with no corrections; here he sits, confused, unskilled with language, faced with twenty errors. Obviously he has before him more work than the capable student, and obviously also he is not likely to learn much as he struggles with twenty bad spots in his paper. He would do well if he really understood and corrected four. This is just what he should be allowed to do. It is poor teaching to demand what the teacher knows cannot be done. Corrections, suggestions for revision, and criticisms of content should be given in proportion to the ability of the student to use them. They are means to improvement, not penalties for being dull or inexperienced or incompetent. Therefore, as the teacher indicates errors in usage, he will keep in mind the writer and his abilities. This may mean overlooking all but the most glaring errors; it may mean more help for the weak student; it may also, as will be indicated later, mean an adjustment in requirements for rewriting.

Teachers sometimes say that all students should be treated alike. If an error is marked for one, it should be for another. The world "alike" can apply to many relations. Treating all with like care may mean very different handling of two papers. No one would argue that treating all children "alike" meant dressing them all in suits of the same size. If the marks on papers are limited to errors, the procedure invites comparison. If, however, suggestions are understood as means to ends, if there are copious notes dealing with the communication as such, the teacher is free to mark in terms of the potential learning of the student.

Rewriting the Papers

Revision is the next step. Probably not all papers need rewriting, but many do. A time for this work should be set aside in the regular class periods. This permits conferences, time for approving corrected or revised papers, and help in working out difficult problems. If instead of attempting to rearrange the student's sentence, or to check each misplaced or undesirable form, the teacher has indicated difficulty by such terms as "Confusion," "Lack of punctuation," "Word order," or "Awkward," if there are passages underscored, with the words "Not clear" in the margin, the problem of making better statements will be thrown back on the writer. His first step may be to talk over with the teacher or a classmate what it was he meant to say. If the whole paper calls for more effort than the student seems able to give, one paragraph or page may be selected and only this section cleaned up. Spelling may be corrected without rewriting an entire page. If the teacher's corrections have been made in pencil there is a possibility that simple corrections may be made, the comments erased, and the paper approved for filing.

For the more competent student there are questions of better organization, suggestions for sections which may be sharpened, perhaps a chance to write an added paper. There is no need that everyone in the class should produce an identical number of papers any more than there is need that everyone should write papers of identical length. We make absurd demands for quantity, much as though a hostess were to assign to each guest the length of time he might talk. Some students write freely, and yet are not the best writers. Some write short, compact statements, characteristic of their general behavior. The most prolific writers in our century are not necessarily our greatest.

Giving a Grade

Discussion of marking papers has not dealt with grades, those inadequate measures which we teachers have so firmly established to our own undoing. Early in the term it is well to discuss grades if they are to be given and, in any event, to set up with the students values to be considered. Some of these may be the neatness and correct form of papers, or the punctuality of the student in writing and revising work. Other values, more difficult to appraise, may be clarity, interest, effectiveness, depth, sincerity, or variety of the papers. All of these being considered, what is the degree of improvement? Comparing the student's attempts in September to his work in January or June, do we see some gain? Has he, perhaps, attempted to write verse or short stories, whereas he once wrote merely descriptions or narratives of personal doings? Does he rewrite more intelligently now than at first? Whatever the values set, the year's folders, with the faulty originals and the neat, approved final drafts, all can come out for inspection during the last week of the semester or the year. There will be some thin folders, some unrevised efforts, probably some obvious gains. In conference between student and teacher, a mark can be decided. No one should believe that this grade is absolute, perfect, or altogether just. But it makes more sense than the arbitrary grade, based on tests, number of errors, and the length of the paper. It goes without saying that there is something more intelligent to be done in evaluation than using a letter or a figure. Many schools have substituted reports which really tell both student and parent about what has been going on at school. It is a strange commentary on communication skills in many schools that teachers—the teacher of composition included—can find nothing more coherent to say about a young student and his exploration of ideas than "B" or "A" or perhaps "D."

There is no magic formula for marking papers: the teacher must take the writing of a growing youngster who is attempting what is perhaps the hardest thing a human being can do (to organize his own thinking and record that on paper)—the teacher must consider this writing, and along with it the writer, and make in an imperfect way the most helpful comments he can devise. Marking papers thus becomes a severe test of the teacher's own power of communication. Here is no mechanical process; rather, here is a test of the competence of the teacher of English to demonstrate the skill he teaches.

13

Some Semantic Implications of Theme Correction

William J. Dusel

Of all the sweeping indictments which have been made by the critics of American public education the charge most difficult to ignore is that "most high school graduates are unable to spell correctly, punctuate conventionally, compose grammatical sentences, and develop unified paragraphs—in short, to write passable prose." The community in which local high school English teachers have not been accused directly or indirectly of slighting the second "R" is rare. Several kinds of answers to such charges have been offered: the lower caliber of student; the increased number of pupils and responsibilities assigned to the English teacher; the irresponsibility of charges based on the naive assumption that there can be a single standard of "correctness." Such answers are sufficient to acquit the English teacher of charges of incompetence, but they fail to remove the cause of dissatisfaction—undeniable and unnecessary weakness in the writing of high school graduates. A fourth kind of answer is essential, one that admits the need for improvement in the teaching of writing and then recommends desirable changes.

In an attempt to formulate such an answer, the California Council of English Associations recently sponsored a statewide study of the teaching of writing in California secondary schools. More than 400 experienced teachers, representing 150 different communities throughout the state, contributed their ideas on the way writing should be taught, described the working conditions under which they must teach it, and sent in examples of their marking and grading techniques. The great body of opinions, reports, and samples of work which were collected for analysis has given the California Council unusual perspective in identifying the problems which confront teachers of writing in California secondary schools. It has also made clear some of the directions in which improvement lies. That the sampling was of more than local significance is indicated by the fact that the teachers who participated in the study had received their professional training in thirty different states and the Dominion of Canada.

In re-examining the job of teaching composition, it was helpful, first, to review four basic questions to which every teacher of writing must find some answer. The answers which are offered here constitute the best thinking of the experienced English teachers participating in the Council study and include the relevant findings of educational psychologists.

How do pupils learn to write? Learning to write effective English prose, like learning any other skill, starts with motive, is given direction by purposes and goals, proceeds through imitation and innovation, and matures through practice. Ordinarily the pupil's discovery that writing is a form of self-expression and a means of informing, entertaining, and influencing others provides a strong intrinsic motive. The countless daily opportunities for practical written communication in and out of the classroom supply a variety of immediate purposes. The rich linguistic environment created by radio, television, motion pictures, newspapers, and good books provides a wide assortment of models of effective communication on all levels of usage. Curriculum requirements in most states, calling for an hour of English instruction to be given daily, from elementary grades up through the junior year of high school, provide time for continual practice in writing.

Without presuming to specify the exact amount of practice needed to develop proficiency in writing, the teachers and nationally recognized authorities on the teaching of English who participated in the California Council study advise daily, or at least weekly, exercises in careful, purposeful writing. They recommend, as an overall, rule-of-thumb average, 250 words of composition per week for each pupil (varying from 150 words per week average for freshmen to 350 words per week for seniors, with modifications according to special needs and abilities). They feel, however, that the value of all such practice is determined by how effectively it is motivated and supervised.

Why do teachers mark their pupils' written work? Marking is such a traditional way of supervising composition work that teachers rarely feel the need to justify it. They mark because their own compositions were always marked, or because their colleagues, administrators, pupils, and pupils' parents expect it. If pressed for a justification of the procedure, most teachers would probably say that they mark papers in order to teach pupils how to write better. Yet a critical examination of their marking practices would raise some puzzling questions of motive. Are those teachers who are so careful to point out every conceivable weakness in a pupil's composition really marking to teach? Or are they intent on establishing their superiority, their self-importance, or their professional competence (as proof-readers)? Are those whose comments crackle with sarcasm and caustic reproach really trying to teach? Or are they marking to wound and punish? Few human motives are simple; undoubtedly teachers are not conscious of why they write what they write on hundreds of papers each week. But certainly the basic motive prompting English teachers to mark pupils' compositions *should* be to facilitate learning.

What should teachers try to communicate through the marking of papers? If marking is a form of instruction, it should communicate the kinds of information which the learner needs in order to improve. To strengthen the pupil's motive or interest in writing, teachers should mark to show their respect for the writer as a human being with dignity, with important ideas, feelings, purposes, and potentialities. This they may be able to do best by expressing their interest in the writer's unique view of the world and their desire to understand it. In order to encourage the writer to formulate more challenging purposes and goals, they should help him to relate immediate successes in the classroom and community to future goals of greater consequence. In order to help the writer to derive the most value from his practice, they should direct his attention toward desirable procedures and away from undesirable ones; and they should keep him informed of his progress. Clearly, effective marking is more than a mechanical recording of one's reactions in the margins of pupils' compositions. It should be highly selective, revealing only those reader-reactions which will be helpful to the writer at his present level of maturity and accomplishment. All other reactions are best expressed at faculty meetings.

Is marking necessary? Some pupils, especially those whose linguistic environment offers exemplary models of effective speaking and writing and whose powers of analysis are exceptional, will develop proficiency in language without much help from teachers. But most pupils are dependent on guidance and supervision—to arouse and maintain interest, to focus attention on what to do and what not to do, and to inform of progress. Is this best done by marking and grading compositions? Over ninety percent of the English teachers in the California study believe it is. One very effective method of instruction does not require the marking of papers—the private conference with each pupil on his compositions. The typical English teacher, however, with five or six daily classes of thirty or more pupils, cannot offer very much of this kind of service. Instead he must read his daily accumulation of papers after school hours when pupils are not around; and he must depend on brief written comments to communicate his reactions and suggestions.

Pitfalls in Marking

When these assumptions of experienced English teachers are used as criteria in appraising the conventional writing program, two serious weaknesses are evident. One is a widespread failure to require sufficient amounts of supervised practice in writing. English teachers are convinced of the value of frequent practice; they do not discontinue it willingly. But they report that every set of 250-word compositions received from 150 pupils (the mode pupil-load indicated by the California Council study) adds an extra twenty or more hours of correcting, grading, recording, and rechecking to the regular work week. And almost all of such work must be done in the evenings and on week ends. Because these teachers have all the responsibilities of teachers of other subjects (preparing daily lessons, making out and grading examinations, handling extra-curricular activities) *plus* the reading and marking of a steady stream of written compositions from their pupils, few feel that they can, or should, require the optimum amount of writing practice. The excessive pupil-load which discourages teachers from teaching writing as they believe it should be taught can be adjusted only through enlightened administrative leadership and community support, and need be discussed here no further.

The second weakness in the writing program, however, is within the power of the English teacher to eliminate. It is a widespread inefficiency in methods of correcting and evaluating pupils' writing. A detailed comparative study of the marking practices of 400 experienced English teachers has revealed the inadequacy of the conventional abstract symbols and monosyllables as forms of communication. It has also inspired new respect for psychologically sound and semantically efficient ways of marking compositions.

Consider first the communicative powers of the most common form of mark to appear on the compositions—the letter or number grade. How clearly does it communicate? Regardless of how carefully the teacher attempts to prevent misunderstanding by making clear in advance *his* meaning of the conventional letter symbols, there will remain one significant difference between the meanings which the teacher ordinarily intends an "A" or a "D" to convey and the meanings which pupils receive. This difference lies in the emotional charge which the symbol carries. The teacher places the mark calmly and objectively on the paper as an indication of rank in the class or as a description of performance; the pupil reads an emotional meaning into the symbol—possibly interpreting it as a sign of the teacher's liking him or his mind (adolescents are whole people). Consequently, the "A" elates; the "F" frightens, angers, or depresses. With each pupil these stock symbols have been accumulating connotations from year to year, teacher to teacher, and will call forth the strangely tenacious overtones of feeling every time they are used.

The slower children may understandably be upset by having to accept daily notice, in the form of low grades, of their inferiority or unattractiveness. It is quite possible that poor grades, year after year, on the English compositions of such children are responsible for much of the general disinterest in English as a course and in writing as a form of self-expression; the untalented become discouraged and quit trying.

Another questionable marking practice is the use of certain judgment words as comments. To an English teacher, an "awkward" sentence is a failure to write English, to express an idea clearly and efficiently. He may, conscientiously and unemotionally, wish to bring to the young writer's attention this inept construction; so he writes "awkward" (or simply "awk" or "K") in the margin. Consider the possible meaning of that word to a young person. It may be precisely the same as if it were offered in criticism of his dancing. That is, it suggests a ridiculous exhibition of failure and may produce the same humiliation. The words "clumsy," "weak," "confused," "disorganized," and "incoherent" are similar terms commonly employed in apparent ignorance of their painful connotations to the insecure adolescent. Consciously or subconsciously the pupil seeks to avoid those situations which undermine his self-respect or which remind him of his immaturity. He should not be made to fear to express himself in his native language. Such comments, then, fail in two ways: they fail to communicate the technical point of criticism in an impersonal way; and they fail to tell the writer what he should do to improve.

The style of the teacher's handwriting also may mislead the pupil. One need not believe in the claims of graphologists to admit that strong emotion is often indicated by the vigor and violence of pen strokes or by the size and heaviness of the letters. The larger the letters, the louder we imagine the voice to be. And who likes to be shouted at? Even if the words are nothing more than "NO!" or "WHAT?" or "COMMA BLUNDER!" Perhaps the teacher *intends* to communicate emotion. Then the question arises, which emotion? If the insecure writer reads impatience, irritability, or anger into the markings, he will respond with resentment; and such a response is not conducive to learning.

One more failure in communication is apparent from the California study. Any teacher of writing knows that proportion is an effective rhetorical means of securing emphasis: the most important point usually deserves the most lengthy and complete treatment; the least important point may be dismissed in a few words. People talk most about the things that they are most interested in. A conscientious teacher, wishing to help a pupil become more effective in his writing, and realizing that errors in spelling, punctuation, sentence structure, and diction weaken an otherwise interesting and sensible essay, decides to help him eliminate his mistakes. In the process of marking, this teacher fairly covers each page with comments on mechanical weaknesses. Consider what this kind of criticism may mean to the pupil. Though he may not yet follow the principle of proportion in his own writing, he will certainly respond to it in his reading. "The only thing that's important in writing," he will interpret the teacher's marking to mean, "is to spell correctly, punctuate properly, and construct grammatical sentences. *You* don't!"

Many teachers attempt to remind the pupil of the value of content by adding such postscripts to their criticism as "interesting" or "good ideas" or by giving a separate grade for the "cargo" of the composition. But one such indication of the teacher's interest in the soundness, originality, and clarity of thought can hardly counterbalance the forty-nine reminders of the importance of mechanics.

In still another way teachers forget the effect of proportion in marking papers, and consequently fail to communicate. Teachers of writing apparently enjoy passively and find fault actively. There can be no other explanation for the fact that almost every mark on almost every paper which was contributed to the survey was a response to a weakness. When teachers fail to express their satisfaction and appreciation along with their grievances, they give their pupil a distorted picture of their total reactions to his work. The obvious inference he draws is something like "The teacher thinks I'm hopeless. He finds something wrong with every sentence I write. What's the use? I wonder what's on television."

Even more unfortunate than the small number of young people who are visibly upset by such marking practices is the greater number who may be secretly disheartened and confused in values by the ambiguities of conventional symbols and the disproportionate emphasis on mechanics and mistakes. And it is likely that such discouragement begins in the elementary grades.

Suggestions for Marking

One fact established by the Council survey helps explain why English teachers mark papers as they do: it takes three times as long to analyze a theme for ideas and organization and signs of improvement, and to comment on these, as to check it for mechanics alone. Until teachers are given a lighter pupil-load and are provided with daily marking periods as part of their assigned schedule, they cannot be expected to read carefully and mark effectively the recommended amounts of writing practice. Meanwhile, conscientious teachers will give each pupil as much practice in purposeful writing as their teaching load permits them to supervise. The following suggestions may be helpful to those who wish to make more cleanly communicative whatever marking they can find time to do.

Show appreciation of successful writing. An excellent paper which is returned to a pupil practically untouched may not seem as successful to the writer as the teacher intends it to seem. The pupil has no way of knowing whether unmarked parts of his writing have been read or not. There is real need to develop as many symbols of appreciation and enjoyment as of dissatisfaction.

The words of praise—"good," "excellent," even "wonderful!"—are useful, but being adjectives of judgment rather than of description, they rarely indicate the point of excellence. They should be followed by the appropriate substantives, so that the writer knows both what was good about his writing and also what made it good. With that additional information he may be better able to repeat the success in his next composition.

Writing the word "yes" occasionally in the margin is an excellent way of letting the writer know that the reader is nodding his head in agreement or understanding. For variety the teacher might comment with "I agree" or "true" or even "You're so right."

One of the most effective, but most time-consuming, forms of appreciative response is the teacher's amplification of the pupil's idea. Such a sign of respect and acceptance may assure the writer of the genuine interest of the teacher more effectively than can any letter grade, including the "A+."

Emphasize the importance of purpose and idea in written composition. Teachers who sincerely believe that the ideas which the pupil wishes to communicate are more important than the mechanics of expression can make their values known by the way they mark. If faulty mechanics must be pointed out, teachers can show how the error distorts or clouds the meaning. If a modifier is misplaced, they can indicate the ludicrous meaning conveyed and ask if that was the one intended. If the antecedent of a pronoun is missing or indeterminable, they can use the comment attributed to the late Harold Ross: "Who he?" Such a question focuses the writer's attention on meaning; whereas conventional symbols like "ref" or "faulty antecedent" seem to criticize on technical grounds that only English teachers consider important.

In general, rather than name errors, teachers might do better to ask questions—questions which the pupil, through inexperience or negligence, raises in the mind of a friendly reader who wants to understand.

Some teachers try to achieve a desired balance between comments on ideas and concern for mechanics by reacting to the former in the left margin, to the latter on the right of each page. This technique makes startlingly graphic the average teacher's tendency to neglect content as he marks.

One of the most promising methods of marking to emphasize idea involves the limiting of comments on pupils' compositions to interested responses to ideas only. Errors of mechanics, diction, and sentence structure are noted on separate record cards kept by the teacher. To process a pupil's composition, the teacher reads it through twice. The first time he looks only for the kinds of errors which he and the class have decided are taboo at that grade level. Each error observed is recorded as a tally mark in the appropriate column of the pupil's record card. Words misspelled are listed at the bottom of the card. In the second reading (the most time-consuming one) the teacher considers the ideas which the writer is attempting to express, and comments in the margin on these ideas and on the progress shown by the writer—a completely positive kind of criticism. After checking the writing of his pupils in this way for several weeks, the teacher will be able to see, from the frequency distribution of tally marks, the kinds of remedial instruction and drill needed by each pupil. He then can either assign sections of a workbook for individual study or discuss in general class session the difficulties common to all. Keeping such a complete record of the errors of each pupil enables the teacher to bring to the writer's attention only as many points as should be considered at one time, without losing the opportunity to refer eventually to the rest of the weaknesses.

After the pupils have studied and drilled on their special problems, they are given their tally cards and their folder of compositions and are asked to find and correct all the kinds of errors they have been studying. In this way each pupil proof-reads material of his own creation; and because he has been prepared to view his past writing in a new, more critical light, he can appreciate the value of his remedial work and see the progress he has made.

This procedure, because it separates the fault-finding from the free exchange of ideas which should characterize the English class, seems promising. The pupil's composition—an unselfconscious effort to communicate an important idea to a respected person—is returned in something of the same spirit in which it is offered, with comments on the significance, the implications, the uniqueness or universality of the writer's thoughts. Repair work is undertaken whenever the writer has been convinced, by the growing satisfaction he receives from being understood and appreciated, that accurate writing is worth the trouble.

Indicate faults in such a way as to facilitate learning. Many teachers mark compositions apparently on the assumption that a person who has his mistakes pointed out to him will thereby be made anxious to correct those mistakes. Others assume that a grade will serve as an incentive to further effort. While still others must imagine that their own corrections of a pupil's mistakes will prepare him to write correctly next time. Teachers who are familiar with the laws of learning, with the importance of motive and emotion and activity and insight, will be perfectly aware of the unreliability of these three forms of marking as guides or spurs to learning.

A pupil's errors must, of course, be brought to his attention. But finding fault with a young person without losing his friendship, or more important, without killing his interest in writing, is work too delicate and difficult to entrust to crude, wildly connotative symbols—marks that say more than the teacher intends. The eternal problem of the teacher of writing is how to remove the sting of correction, how to lessen the chagrin of the adolescent who has revealed his ignorance. The teacher can never be certain of the writer's ability to take criticism of anything as personal as his language, his thoughts, actually his personality.

Getting pupils to judge their own work on clearly defined standards which have been accepted by the group enables the teacher to identify beforehand many of those who are likely to be upset by unfavorable criticism. Pupils who are unrealistic in appraising their work need counsel, if they are to be kept teachable, before the teacher grades them.

Offering the non-committal word "interesting" in response to some adolescent's untenable but firm conviction is the kind of respectful response that keeps lines of communication open for later, more complete and enlightened discussion.

Teachers should usually refrain from putting a low grade on a student's composition if they expect that the grade may have a depressing effect on him. He is more in need of knowing how to improve his work than of being reminded that he has failed. An "F" is concrete, immutable. It's in the records and, what's worse, in the pupil's mind. It will not be washed away by kind words and helpful comments. The pupil may not even be able to hear, or at least really understand, subsequent explanations and suggestions. Teachers of English might well consider paraphrasing the safety rule of the rifle range ("Never point a gun at anything you do not intend to kill") to read "Never put the mark of failure on the work of any person you do not intend to hurt." In day-to-day evaluation, the absence of a grade is safer communication than a mark of failure. This is not to say that there must be no judging of failure; but only that in evaluation short of the final reckoning, no worthy purpose is served with most pupils by branding their unsuccessful efforts with a scarlet "F."

Teachers who wish to help *all* their pupils to become better writers and who have some clear ideas on how to teach writing will try to mark so as to be understood perfectly. They will acquire a strong distrust of letter grades and monosyllabic comments, remembering the unpredictable power of many of these traditional symbols to mislead or upset the young person. They will depend more on carefully phrased sentences, directed to the individual writer. And some day, when lightened teaching loads permit, they will teach writing even more effectively through teacher-pupil conferences.

Those teachers who interpret all this concern for the feelings of learners as molly-coddling may feel that such care as has been suggested to keep interest in writing alive is ridiculous. They may recount the shocks they themselves have withstood from their own teachers who never hesitated to call a spade a spade: "And it made a man of me!" they will conclude. The ability of the strong to survive rough treatment, however, does not justify inefficient teaching. The loss is with the weak—those who lose heart and quit trying, those who decide prematurely that college is not for them, the majority who leave school unable to write a clear, grammatical, spirited friendly letter. Mass education in a democracy must strengthen the weak, not eliminate them. And the average pupil requires careful handling, at least until he has found his own reasons for wanting to learn to write.

About the Author

William J. Dusel is Supervisor of Student Teaching in English at the San Jose State College.

14

In Praise of Praise[*]

Paul B. Diederich

Teachers who insist on marking every error in every student composition should ask themselves whether such an all-out attack really
works. Paul Diederich believes it does not, and in this essay he suggests an approach to annotating papers which is selective, positive,
and humane.

The average English paper corrected by the average English teacher looks as
though it had been trampled on with cleated boots and has about the same
effect on the student. I realize that some good-hearted teachers believe that this
savagery is necessary, just as "practical schoolmen" a hundred years ago knew
for certain that the only way to teach a boy Latin was to whip him.

I believe that many English teachers have a false theory about how to get
rid of those pesky little errors that disfigure most student writing. They seem
to think that drowning them in red ink will do away with them.

The only trouble with this approach is that it doesn't seem to work. The
results of a recent series of grammar and usage tests given each level of college preparatory students in one of the oldest public high schools on the
Eastern seaboard indicated that errors were being eliminated at the rate of
about 2 percent a year. Chances are these errors would probably have declined
at about this rate if English teachers had ignored them.

I am strongly tempted to believe, although I have no way of proving it,
that all this outpouring of red ink not only does no good but positive harm. Its
most common effect is to make the majority of students hate and fear writing.
So far as they can see, they have never done anything on paper that anybody

[*]Paul B. Diederich, "In Praise of Praise," *NEA Journal*, LII (September 1963), 58–59. Used by
permission of Paul B. Diederich and *NEA Journal,* Mildred S. Fenner, Editor.

thought was good. No matter how hard they try, every paper they hand in gets slapped down for something or other.

The art of the teacher—at its best—is the reinforcement of good things. I am reminded of an experience from my own college days. I had one of the original "theme-a-day" courses at Harvard, taught at that time by Professor Hurlbut. So far as I can remember, he practically never said anything bad about our papers. About two or three times in an average paper we did something that was worthy of praise. We usually knew it, and his comment invariably indicated that he knew it, too. The space between these high points in our papers was filled with the usual student bilge, which he never honored with a comment. Whenever he said nothing, we knew that the verdict was "undistinguished" but that he was too much of a gentleman to say so.

About all Professor Hurlbut ever did in class was to read papers that he regarded as unusually good, without telling us who had written them. We sat there gasping, wishing that we had written them ourselves. He seldom stopped to say what was good about these papers. We either knew it, or his voice told us. In rare cases he might ask, "Now what was particularly good about that?"

I cannot remember a single instance in which he ever asked what was bad about a paper. For him to express dispraise was as rare as for him to lose his temper—which was almost inconceivable.

I believe that a student knows when he has handed in something above his usual standard and that he waits hungrily for a brief comment in the margin to show him that the teacher is aware of it, too. To my mind, these are the only comments that ever do any student any good.

Up to this point, I must have given readers the impression that there is no place whatever for brutality in the treatment of student writing. Actually, there is a place for it, when it is used in the following way: Duplicate and pass out to your class one student paper on each assignment. Use an anonymous paper from a different class, so that the students who criticize it may be sure that the writer will not be present to have his feelings hurt.

Have the students study this paper as homework, grade it, and mark it up with every sort of criticism and suggestion for improvement. Next day in class, let them argue over their grades and suggestions.

During this session everything bad that can be said about a paper ought to be said, and you may count on the students to say it. You may even have to defend the paper against an unjustified attack.

Since these sessions are an exercise in criticism, I think the sample papers should be of all kinds: good, bad, and indifferent. Some teachers balk at this idea, holding that students should never see an example of admittedly poor writing lest it corrupt them. I answer them by pointing out that the way students write is the result of hearing the language used imperfectly sixteen hours a day, every day of their lives. One more instance of imperfect language, recognized as such, and followed up by devastating criticism, is not going to corrupt them more than they have been corrupted already.

I believe that student papers should be dealt with something like this:

Find in each paper at least one thing, and preferably two or three things, that the student has done well, or better than before. Then, if you must, find one thing, and preferably not more than one thing, that he should try to improve in his next paper. Whenever possible make this a suggestion, not a prescription.

Learning one new thing per paper is certainly more than most students learn at present. As for the other ninety-nine errors that disfigure the paper and disgrace the school, simply ignore them. If you mark them all, or even half of them, the student learns nothing; he only advances one step further toward a settled conviction that he can't write and there is no use trying.

If you pursue my suggested policy, a few parents may bring student themes to school, point angrily to errors they recognize, and ask why they

One day, I descended the stairs in my longest skirt, knee high socks, loafers, and my red, bulky turtle-neck sweater. My paternal grandmother was sitting primly on our pink flowered chair, sipping a cup of tea. As I walked into the room, I thought she was going to spit the tea all over the wall. *Shattering contrast!*

Lovely choice of details

"Beverly!" she screamed to my mother. "Beverly, you must do something about this child. Why, the way she dresses is obscene! Just look at the length of her skirt."

well-chosen word. In character.

Her face was red and purple-striped, and since I had never seen her in such a rage, I became rather frightened.

Splendid! Sounds just like her.

"Why, when I was a girl, if I had worn that outfit, people would have suspected that I was of questionable morals. Why don't you buy that girl some high-button shoes and black stockings?"

My mother tried to calm her by saying, "Now, now, mother, that is the fashion of the times, you know."

"Pshaw!" answered my grandmother and tottered grandly out of the room. *Some would say that one cannot totter grandly; but I think grandma could. Like Charles De Gaulle.* I think the trouble with families is that they are not up with the times, but I have no time to prove it. It takes me too long to button up those high-button shoes.

A snapper of an ending! Very effective to leave it like this — without putting in the intervening steps.

You make grandma come to life. A few bold strokes, and everything in character.

PB Diederich A!

were overlooked. You can easily work out of this jam by indicating a few of the flaws that the parent has overlooked, telling him that no student could possibly learn that much about writing from a single paper, and pointing out that you have carefully selected one weakness for the student to try to eliminate in his next paper.

If a student concentrates on one error at a time, progress is possible; if he tries to overcome all of his weaknesses at once, he will only be overwhelmed. I do not know where the scientific truth lies, but I have more faith in the value of a few appreciative comments than in any amount or kind of correction.

15

Two Types of Grading[*]

Kentucky English Bulletin

The first of these methods of theme grading—that of identifying and correcting mechanical errors—is valuable but is inadequate alone. It is the second method—the combination of marginal notations and terminal comments—that the compilers of this booklet advocate as a method which is both practicable and effective. In the first set of corrections the grader has conscientiously marked every error in spelling, punctuation, and grammar that he could find. When the student gets his theme back, however, he may feel quite discouraged, for the clipped abbreviations and symbols, the machine-like, impersonal tone has told him only that he has done poorly. The second grader, on the other hand, has read the composition carefully enough to discover the writer's purpose and plan and to appraise his successes as well as his failures. Furthermore, he has taken the time to formulate comments designed to help the author understand his faults and to correct them. As with the first correction, the student's errors have been marked, the grade is still a D, but there is a significant difference in the tone of the two sets of corrections. In short, there is no escaping the fact that the most important thing about the grading of papers is not the grade which a student receives, or even the marginal notations, but instead the critical comments, the constructive suggestions, and the encouraging words which the teacher writes on the paper when he places a grade on it or which he says to the student later in conference.

---

[*]The main value of the essay samples in the *Kentucky English Bulletin*, a publication of the Kentucky Association of Teachers of English, is the detailed analysis of two types of grading used for the same theme. In the first type, too much attention is given to mechanics; the second deals more with the writer's purpose and the tone of the comments is one of encouragement. Two other themes in this section have the added attraction of being graded by large numbers of evaluators who are in surprising agreement. From *Principles and Standards in Composition, Kentucky English Bulletin*, 6, 1 (Fall 1956), 318–23, 331–33, 337–39. Used by permission of W. S. Ward, Editor.

Too many errors. There are others which I could have marked.

you fail to stick to your subject

Grading to Identify and Correct Mechanical Errors

I Have Learned That the Swiftest Traveler Is He That Goes Afoot

P   Most people today would say that traveling afoot is not a good way to travel. Perhaps for them that is right but if they only realized it, they have to depend upon someone else if they travel in any other manner.

agr.   Traveling afoot a person can start when they please and stop when they please. You may find an interesting place and decide to stay for a while, being

awk.   afoot and no one else to worry about, getting a job perhaps to have a little income while in this place. When you have settled your curosity you can move on with out any interfereance from anyone.

Being afoot you will probably travel very slowly, therefore getting more

Inc. *sent.*   enjoyment out of the scenery. A large town, beautiful rugged mountains, cool stream and waterfalls, or anything that has any artistic beauty in it. Each or any of those may keep you fascinated for several days or week if you are alone on foot, whereas if you were with someone traveling otherwise you might not even stop to admire their beauty for even one day.

Ref. *Ref.* *agr.*   Someone may tell you that you can travel with them on a trip, but it may be ten years before they decide to make the trip. Also with someone else there is always split decisions on where places to go, when to go, how to go, and many other

awk.   situations that one person has to face but just has himself to convince on how he is to go about the trip. He can always change his mind without herting anyone else's feeling's also if he is alone and afoot.

The greatest reason for traveling afoot being the fastest method of

P   travel is: You do not have to wait on any man, It does not require the

P   assistance of any mechanical object, generally the man who travels afoot can start any day and not having to worry about what he has left behind.

Be more careful with your proofreading.

The Returning of Themes

Theme Revision: When a student has his paper returned to him, he should be required to revise it so that he may receive full value from his writing experience. This revision may vary all the way from minor corrections on a superior paper to a complete rewriting of a paper that is poor in organization or that fails to give meaning to generalizations through the use of concrete particulars.

Your paper contains all sorts of errors, but I see in it much promise also. Let's have a conference soon!

Do you really prove that traveling afoot is anything to? has anything to do with speed? is What thesis statement have you really developed?

D

Grading to
Teach Writing
and Thinking

I Have Learned That the Swiftest Traveler Is He That Goes Afoot

What is the normal punct. of a compound sent.?

Most people today would say that traveling afoot is not a good way to travel. Perhaps for them that is right but if they only realized it, they have to depend upon someone else if they travel in any other manner.

Re-read your theme and see how often you shift back and forth between 3rd and 2nd person.

Traveling afoot a (person) can start when they please and stop when they please. (You) may find an interesting place and decide to stay for a while, being afoot and no one else to worry about, getting a job perhaps to have a little income while in this place. When you have settled your *sp.* curosity you can move on with out any *sp* interfereance from anyone.

Commas follow introd. elements containing verbs

Tense

Being afoot you will probably travel very slowly, therefore getting more *you have four subjects but where is their verb?* enjoyment out of the scenery. (A large town,) (beautiful rugged mountains,) (cool stream and waterfalls) (or anything that has any artistic beauty) in it. Each or any of these may keep you fascinated for several days or week, if you are alone on foot, whereas if you were with someone traveling otherwise you might not even stop to admire their beauty for even one day.

Someone may tell you that you can travel with them on a trip, but it may be ten years before they decide to make the trip. Also with someone else there is always split decisions on, places to go, when to go, how to go, and many other situations that one person has to face but just has himself to convince on how he is to go about the trip. He can always change his mind *sp* *Did you proofread?* without herting anyone else's feeling(s) also if he is alone and afoot.

The greatest reason for traveling afoot being the fastest method of travel

Do you know what a comma fault is?

is: You do not have to wait on any man, It does not require the assistance of any mechanical object, generally the man who travels afoot can start any day and not having to worry about what he has left behind.

1. *Your paper is based on a good idea and has a recognizable organization. Par. 1 states your over-all purpose; pars. 2, 3, 4 develop three reasons to support par. 1; par 5 is a recapitulation of 2, 3, 4. See if you can restate the topic sentence in each par. more clearly so as to make the steps in your progress more unmistakable.*

2. *See if you can find examples of faulty agreement in sent. 1 of par. 2, and sent. 2 of par. 4.*

3. *Sent. 2 of par. 1 and sent. 2 of par. 4 are so garbled that the reader must reread and finally guess at their full meaning and purpose. See if you can improve them.*

Conferences: Conferences are designed to help individual students with their personal writing problems as distinct from the general difficulties which many in the class share and which therefore should be taken up in class. With some students much of the time will be given over to mechanics, but it is important that the teacher reveal his concern with what the student is trying to say. It is important that the student come to value his teacher as a sympathetic, if critical, reader who expects themes to be individual and interesting. Otherwise the student is likely to think of his conferences as help sessions on punctuation and his themes as routine sets of grammatical sequences properly punctuated. This is not to say that a teacher will have spent his conference time unwisely if much of it is devoted to mechanics, but ordinarily he will have done better if he shows the student how he failed to limit his subject, define his terms, arrange his materials well, or develop an idea convincingly; how honest exposition is the fair consideration of evidence, not the defence of biased opinion; and so on.

It should be understood, of course, that conferences are not for weak students only. The superior student and the average student as well should receive profit: the latter can be shown how his C paper lacks something; the former can be stimulated by having his instructor explore the implications of his papers, suggest thought-provoking topics for future writing, recommend books that he might find interesting; and so on. If a superior student leaves a conference with the feeling that he has done nothing more than have a little chat, or if the conference fails to get beyond grammar and mechanics, the instructor has probably been at fault. The well-planned conference does orally what the combination of marginal and terminal comment described above does in writing. It seeks to relate the student's weaknesses and strengths to the overall intention of his theme and thus to foster in him a greater insight into his writing problems.

Conclusion

In some schools—both high school and college—the procedures set forth in the preceding pages are likely to be regarded as above immediate attainment. The fact remains, however, that though the objectives may seem somewhat ideal to many, they have already been achieved in many schools and can be achieved with relative ease by many others; and they must be achieved by all if our graduates are to be able to express themselves with reasonable clarity and correctness. As has been pointed out already, any student or any school will be better off for having striven toward these objectives.

The number of compositions which a student writes during a year need not be great, but the teaching that goes into each one needs to be thorough. This does not mean, of course, that there can be no written assignments except under the near-ideal conditions just described. There should be. Short impromptu themes, an essay type of examination, any sort of writing that gives practice will also give fluency and confidence and thus is greatly to be desired. But beyond these kinds of writing must be the kind that is done under conditions approximating those described in the foregoing pages.

Themes, Analyses, and Comments

Notes on Grades and Analyses to Follow

A paper is no more graded in a vacuum than it is written in a vacuum. Hence grades and comments occasionally reflect the fact that a particular error is especially obnoxious to one teacher and hence draws a sharp penalty, whereas to another teacher, less offended by the defect in question, the merits of the same theme may seem rather impressive. It is probably impossible, therefore, to set forth—and even more difficult to apply objectively—criteria and standards that will enable all who read to agree immediately on the grade which a theme should receive.

Despite individual differences and the inevitable necessity for subjective judgments, however, the grades and comments of those who have participated in the preparation of this booklet are notable for their agreement. With hardly an exception there is either a concentration on one grade or else a near-equal division between two contiguous grades. It is worthy of comment also that the evaluations by high school and college teachers coincide to a remarkable degree. There seem to be slightly higher standards among the college teachers, but the rise between high school and college is probably about the same as for each grade in high school.

The reader is reminded also that he is to assume that the themes were written by students just as they were graduating from high school or just as they were entering college, and that the grades were given and the comments prepared with such students in mind.

Finally, the letter system of grading (A, B, C, D, E), though widely used in Kentucky schools, may be translated for those not familiar with it as follows: A, superior; B, good; C, average; D, poor but passing; E, failing.

Theme 5	Grade Distribution
Rated A	A = 27
	B = 14
	C = 15
	D = 0
	E = 0

SPRING

Spring is a combination of many things. It is the brightness of the sun as it floods the world with its indispensable light. It is the moon rising like a huge red ball which later changes to yellow and pours its soft light over the quiet earth. It is sudden showers and strong winds, fleecy clouds and blue skies. Spring is melted snow and ice and swollen streams which cause devastating floods. Spring is the reappearance of familiar birds—the modest little wrens, the brilliant cardinals, the cheerful robins, the quiet blue birds, and the ostentatious blue jays. It is also the industrious "measuring worm" methodically and patiently measuring the slender new blades of grass or perhaps the dead, dry stalks of one of last year's weeds. Spring is a turtle coming out of the mud to sun himself on the bank of a pond; it is a chorus of frogs in the evening. It is the chattering squirrel as it noisily eats its diminishing supply of nuts and completes its meal by robbing a tree of the soft, new leaf buds. Spring is the redbud and dogwood trees displaying their brilliant colors; but even before these, it is the golden blossoms of the forsythia bushes. It is the dandelion-dotted lawns or the grass-dotted dandelion patches. Spring is little boys eagerly digging for fishing worms and going wading in forbidden creeks. It is the old farmer plodding along resolutely behind his plow and strong white horses. It is the young couple strolling hand-in-hand along the road side. Spring is the eager sun bathers, each one trying to get a darker tan than the others. Spring is jumping rope, shooting marbles, and playing softball games. Spring is a feeling—the joy of living, seeing, and learning. The combination of all of these things, and many more, makes up Spring as we know it.

Comment

In Spring the aim is to suggest the emotional quality of a season by an enumeration of carefully chosen and arranged details. All of the details are concerned with the notion of renewed vitality and thus prepare the reader to accept the concluding generalization that Spring is a feeling—"the joy of living, seeing, and learning." The paper's excellence is further accounted for by the emphasis put on arrangement, an emphasis which appears on the sentence level in the consistently used device of parallelism, in the grouping of sentences with related details, and in the over-all inductive framework. Within the framework there is a time-honored progression (used, for example, in the opening lines of the *Canterbury Tales*) beginning with weather phenomena, going on to the behavior of wildlife, and concluding with human activities. The technique verges on the poetic, particularly in sentences 2–5, where the controlling image of water, though not directly mentioned until sentence 4, is anticipated in the earlier sentences by the sun which "*floods* the world" and the moon which "*pours* its soft light" on the earth.

There is room for improvement here, though not a great deal. The last sentence does little more than repeat the first, and both sentences seem external to the real development, which reaches its conclusion in the next to last sentence. The writer might consider omitting them altogether. Would paragraph indentations be helpful to mark the sentence groupings? Undoubtedly, as the theme now stands. However, at least as good a device would be to regularize the use of the subjects "Spring" and "It," so that "Spring" would occur only in the opening sentence of each group and "It" in the remaining sentences. Perhaps, too, a case can be made for moving sentences 10 and 11 (on trees and flowers) to a place following the opening "weather" section (sentences 2–5) as giving a more "natural" progression: weather, vegetable life, animal life, human life.

Finally, it might be remarked that theme topics such as this often lead to unfortunate results. That is to say, a less skillful writer may fail to exercise restraint and hence may attempt a pseudo-poetic, inflated style that is very objectionable to a mature reader. Even the present writer (in her use of cliches like "modest wrens," "cheerful robins," and "chattering squirrels") comes dangerously close to this fault at times.

Theme 8	Grade Distribution
Rated A	A = 32
	B = 12
	C = 3
	D = 0
	E = 0

I WAS SCARED

It all began one morning in early October, 1950. Tired men, dirty and short tempered, climbed aboard the convoy trucks they had loaded during the previous night. The convoy rolled at eight o'clock; everyone, including myself, felt better because it was our first time to relax in three days.

The morning, like most October days, was cool and refreshing, and most of us slept, at least until the sun rose high enough to make it miserably hot and impossible to relax. As we passed through the ravaged and bombed out cities, I had mixed feelings toward the people we saw there, a feeling of pity and a feeling of hate.

Soon we left the little villages behind and began climbing into the mountains where signs of human life are not seen for long intervals of time. Everything was quiet except for the rumble of heavy trucks and a lonely GI singing, "Carry Me Back to Old Virginia."

Even in Chosen the mountains are pretty this time of year with the leaves turning all colors and falling to the earth, blanketing it with beauty that cannot be described, only felt deep inside.

Yes, everything was quiet and peaceful until up ahead came the chatter of machine guns and the occasional crack of a Garand. I began to feel a little nervous and scared, no not scared, at least not yet. You see, it was my first experience with war. Our truck was the last in a long line, and as we were descending into a small valley, the brakes became hot and began to freeze. We knew we would have to break convoy. There was a bombed out bridge at the base of the hill; we had to go around it and through a small creek: here is where it all began and nearly ended. When the truck reached the creek, the brakes were so hot we could not climb out of the embankment. The rear guard came by and asked if we needed assistance, which we declined because the only thing to do was wait for the brakes to cool.

The rest of the convoy went on, and we waited there, expecting to catch them later. There were five of us. While we were waiting, the chatter of guns could still be heard in the far off mountains—cleaning up, they called it, and that should explain itself since the front lines had moved on farther north.

A guy starts thinking when he is in a spot like that, and I was doing my share of it. A buddy just handed me a cigarette, when all hell broke loose. Bullets riddled the cab of our truck, and the chatter of machine gun fire roared in our ears. We hit the dirt or, I should say, hit the mud of the creek bed. Yes, I was scared. There we were, five guys alone in a small creek facing a Red machine gun and an unknown number of men. Yes, I was scared, plenty damned scared, and even worse than that, I knew of nothing to relieve the situation; but I wasn't alone.

We all said a silent prayer and thanked God that our little friends were such lousy shots. I often wondered how a greenhorn would feel with his first taste of war: then I knew. Only a few seconds had passed, yet it seemed like a life-time. Then, as suddenly as it began, the firing stopped. I could still hear the chattering of those guns and splattering of lead. It pounded in my head as though they were still firing. One of the guys yelled something; at first it didn't register, and then I looked up the road we had just come over; that column of dust was the loveliest thing I had ever seen.

The Convoy had been only a few minutes behind us. Their lead jeep, with a machine gun mounted in its cab, came roaring down the hill spitting out death. By this time the Reds had disappeared.

We had been initiated into the ranks of those who knew what it meant to be afraid. There was no shame because of our fear; we had discovered a new meaning for the word and silently agreed to respect it in its own right.

Comment

I Was Scared has what appears to be one of the simplest of all plans of organization, that of natural time order. This order alone, however, is not enough to guarantee an effective story or incident, for problems of selection and arrangement arise within any kind of general framework. The writer has solved these problems with considerable success by selecting details which chart not only the progress of the convoy but also the shifting moods of the men involved. Thus the movement is from the feeling of relaxation engendered by the quiet and beauty of the October morning as the convoy moves into the foothills, to the nervous tension aroused by the distant rifle fire and the trouble with the brakes of the truck during the descent into the valley, then to the paralyzing fear when the attack occurs in the creek bed, and finally when the second convoy brings relief, to the sober realization of the new meaning for the word "fear." The style ably supports the aim—which is to tell the truth simply and vividly without the varnish of false heroics; it abounds with sharply phrased details like "the occasional crack of a Garand," "the splattering of lead," and with the idioms of natural speech—"you see," "cleaning up, they called it," "a guy starts thinking," "plenty damned scared." It is clear that this writer is unusually mature: he knows how to grasp his own experiences and give them significant shape.

The faults are faults of detail only. The writer should be asked whether anything is gained by making the very specific reference to the *time* of the incident in the first sentence and withholding the *place* till paragraph 4. His attention should be called also to the way the tenses of the second sentences of paragraphs 7 and 8 (past instead of past perfect) work against the basic time order of the events he is relating. He should clear up such small matters as the incorrectly used reflexive ("including *myself*") in sentence 3 of paragraph 1; the cliche "spitting out death" in paragraph 9; and the needless comma before the song title in paragraph 3. Lastly, he should understand the reader's bewilderment to learn at the start of paragraph 9 that "The convoy had been only a few minutes behind us." Since only one convoy, the writer's own, has so far been mentioned, more explanation is needed at this point. Preparation for the rescuing convoy might be made in the first paragraph without destroying suspense, simply by revising the third sentence to "Our convoy, the first of two, rolled at eight o'clock. . . ."

16

Learning to Write by Writing

James Moffett

Most of what I have had to say so far has concerned curriculum. In this chapter my concern is method, in particular the sort of method most appropriate for the notion of curriculum that has been expounded.

What is the main way in which human beings learn to do things with their minds and bodies? Let's not think first about learning to write—we'll get to that soon enough. Let's think about learning to walk, ride a bicycle, play a piano, throw a ball. Practice? Coaching by other people? Yes, but why does practice work? How do we become more adept merely by trying again and again? And what does a good coach do that helps our trials get nearer and nearer the mark? The answer, I believe, is feedback and response.

Feedback

Feedback is any information a learner receives as a result of his trial. This information usually comes from his own perception of what he has done: the bicycle falls over, the notes are rushed, the ball goes over the head of the receiver, and so on. The learner heeds this information and adjusts his next trial accordingly, and often unconsciously. But suppose the learner cannot perceive what he is doing—does not, for example, hear that the notes are rushed—or perceives that he has fallen short of his goal but does not know what adjustment to make in his action. This is where the coach comes in. He is someone who observes the learner's actions and the results, and points out what the learner cannot see for himself. He is a human source of feedback who supplements the feedback from inanimate things.

Except for slight alterations, the text of this chapter was delivered as a lecture on April 7, 1967, at the Yale Conference on English and printed in the *Papers of the Yale Conference on English,* copyright © 1967 by the Office of Teacher Training, Yale University. Reprinted by permission of Edward Gordon, Director of the Conference.

But, you may say, learning to write is different from learning to ride a bicycle or even learning to play the piano, which are, after all, physical activities. Writers manipulate symbols, not objects. And they are acting on the minds of other people, not on matter. Yes, indeed. But these differences do not make learning to write an exception to the general process of learning through feedback. Rather, they indicate that in learning to use language the only kind of feedback available to us is human response.

Let's take first the case of learning to talk, which is a social activity and the base for writing. The effects of what we do cannot be known to us unless out listener responds. He may do so in a number of ways—by carrying out our directions, answering our questions, laughing, looking bored or horrified, asking for more details, arguing, and so on. Every listener becomes a kind of coach. But of course a conversation, once launched, becomes a two-way interaction in which each party is both learner and source of feedback.

Through their research in the early stages of language acquisition, Roger Brown and Ursula Bellugi have been able to identify two clear interactions that take place between mother and child.[1] One is the child's efforts to reproduce in his own condensed form the sentence he hears his mother utter. The other is the mother's efforts to expand and correct the child's telegraphic and therefore ambiguous sentences. Each time the mother fills out his sentence, the child learns a little more about syntax and inflections, and when the child responds to her expansion of his utterance, she learns whether her interpretation of his words was correct or not. Linguists never cease to marvel at how children learn, before they enter school, and without any explanations or teaching of rules, how to generate novel and well-formed sentences according to a paradigm or model they have unconsciously inferred for themselves. In fact, many of the mistakes children make—like *bringed* for *brought*—are errors of overgeneralization. This ability to infer a generality from many particular instances of a thing, which also accounts for some children's learning to read and spell even without phonics training, is of course itself a critical part of human learning. The learner's abstractive apparatus reduces a corpus of information, such as other people's sentences, to a usable rule. It is a data-processing gift that enables us to learn *something*, but not how to *do* something.

To learn to talk, the child must put his data into action and find out what happens. Thus he learns his irregular verbs when he says, "I bringed my cup," and some adult replies, "Well, I'm glad you brought it," Throughout school, imitation of others' speech, as heard and read, remains a major way of learning language forms, but conversational response is the chief means the child has for making progress in speech production itself. Later, after the syntax and inflections have become pretty well fixed, the responses the learner gets to what he says are not expansions but expatiations. That is, his listener reacts to

---

1. Reported in "Three Processes in the Child's Acquisition of Syntax," *Language and Learning*, Janet Emig, James Fleming, and Helen Popps, eds. (New York: Harcourt, Brace, and World, 1966).

his ideas and his tone, picks up his remarks and does something further with them, so that together they create some continuity of subject.

Learning to use language, then, requires the particular feedback of human response, because it is to other people that we direct speech. The fact that one writes by oneself does not at all diminish the need for response, since one writes for others. Even when one purports to be writing for oneself—for pure self-expression, if there is such a thing—one cannot escape the ultimately social implications inherent in any use of language. As George Herbert Mead argued so well, even in our unuttered thoughts, we speak as though to another because we have long since incorporated the otherness of the social world to which language is irrevocably tied. Furthermore, we have all had the experience of looking back on something we have written earlier and of responding much as another person might do. Thus, once beyond the moment of writing, the writer himself becomes "other," and can feed back helpfully to himself.

But no feedback of whatever sort can help the learner if his will is not behind his actions, for will is the motor that drives the whole process. Without it, we ignore the results of what we have done and make no effort to adjust our actions so as to home in on the target. The desire to get certain effects on an audience is what motivates the use of speech. This is what rhetoric is all about. So the first reason why one might fail to learn is not caring, lack of motivation to scan the results and transfer that experience to the next trial. The other principal cause of failure is, on the other hand, a lack of response in the audience. One cares, one makes an effort, and no one reacts. For me, the character Jerry, in Albec's *The Zoo Story* epitomizes the desperation of one who cannot get a response. To get some effect on the unresponsive Peter, he runs through the whole rhetorical gamut—chitchat, anecdotes, questions, shocking revelations, quarreling, until finally he resorts to tickling, pushing, and fighting. It is Jerry who says, "We *must* know the consequences of our actions." And sarcastically: "Don't react, Peter, just listen."

Speaking from his experience with autistic children who had withdrawn and given up, Bruno Bettelheim has touched on the importance of both initiation and response. From the very first, he says, an infant should be given the chance to communicate his needs, not have them anticipated, and be responded to when he is communicating the need, not fed according to some other timing.

> It is for this reason that time-clock feedings are so potentially destructive, not merely because they mechanize the feeding, but because they rob the infant of the conviction that it was his own wail that resulted in filling his stomach when his own hunger timed it. By the same token, if his earliest signals, his cry or his smile, bring no results, that discourages him from trying to refine his efforts at communicating his needs. In time he loses the impulse to develop those mental and emotional structures through which we deal with the environment. He is discouraged from forming a personality.

But those are infants, not adolescents, and we teach our students to write, we don't feed them. Bettelheim continues:

> Even among adults the joke that fails to amuse, the loving gesture that goes unanswered, is a most painful experience. And if we consistently, and from an early age, fail to get the appropriate response to our expression of emotions, we stop communicating and eventually lose interest in the world.

"But," we say, "I praise my students, I give them an encouraging response."

> But this is not all. If the child's hungry cry met with only deep sympathy and not also with food, the results would be as bad as if there had been no emotional response. . . . should his smile, inviting to play, be met with a tender smile from the parent but lead to no playing, then, too, he loses interest in both his environment and the wish to communicate feeling.[2]

Smiling, gushing, or patting the back are not to the point. A response must be real and pertinent to the action, not a standard, "professional" reaction. Any unvarying response, positive or not, teaches us nothing about the effects of what we have done.

If, as I believe, writing is learned in the same basic way other activities are learned—by doing and by heeding what happens—then it is possible to describe ideal teaching practices in this way and compare them with some current practices. Ideally, a student would write because he was intent on saying something for real reasons of his own and because he wanted to get certain effects on a definite audience. He would write only authentic kinds of discourse such as exist outside of school. A maximum amount of feedback would be provided him in the form of audience response. That is, his writing would be read and discussed by this audience, who would also be the coaches. This response would be candid and specific. Adjustments in language, form, and content would come as the writer's response to his audience's response. Thus instruction would always be individual, relevant, and timely. These are precisely the virtues of feedback learning that account for its great success.

Clearly, the *quality* of feedback is the key. Who is this audience to be, and how can it provide a response informed enough to coach in all the necessary ways? How is it possible for every member of a class of thirty to get an adequate amount of response? Classmates are a natural audience. Young people are most interested in writing for their peers. Many teachers besides myself have discovered that students write much better when they write for each other. Although adolescents are quite capable of writing on occasion for a larger and more remote audience and should be allowed to do so, it is difficult except in unusual situations to arrange for this response to be relayed back to

---

2. These quotations are from "Where Self Begins," *The New York Times Magazine*, February 17, 1966. The article itself was drawn from *The Empty Fortress*, by Bruno Bettelheim (New York: Free Press of Glencoe, Inc., 1967).

the writers. For the teacher to act as audience is a very intricate matter fraught with hazards that need special attention.

First, although younger children often want to write to a "significant adult," on whom they are willing to be frankly dependent, adolescents almost always find the teacher entirely *too* significant. He is at once parental substitute, civic authority, and the wielder of marks. Any one of these roles would be potent enough to distort the writer-audience relationship; all together, they cause the student to misuse the feedback in ways that severely limit his learning to write. He may, for example, write what he thinks the teacher wants, or what he thinks the teacher doesn't want. Or he writes briefly and grudgingly, withholding the better part of himself. He throws the teacher a bone to pacify him, knowing full well that his theme does not at all represent what he can do. This is of course not universally true, and students may react in irrelevant and symbolic ways to each other as well as to the teacher. But in general, classmates are a more effective audience.

The issue I want to make clear, in any case, is that the significance of the responder influences the writer enormously. This is in the nature of rhetoric itself. But if the real intent of the writing is extraneous to the writing—on a completely different plane, as when a student turns in a bland bit of trivia to show his indifference to adult demands—then the effect is actually to dissociate writing from real intent and to pervert the rhetorical process into a weird irony. Much depends of course on the manner of the teacher, and, curiously enough, if the teacher shifts authority to the peer group, which is where it lies anyway for adolescents, and takes on an indirect role, then his feedback carries a greater weight.

But, it may be argued, students are not informed and experienced enough about writing to coach each other. Won't their feedback often be misleading? How does the teacher give them the benefit of his knowledge and judgement? Let's look a moment at just what students can and cannot do for each other. Part of what they can do is a matter of numbers; multiple responses to a piece of writing make feedback more impersonal and easier to heed. Group reactions establish a consensus about some objective aspects of the writing and identify, through disagreement, those aspects that involve individual value judgments. It is much easier for peers than for the teacher to be candid and thus to give an authentic response, because the teacher, usually aware of his special significance, is afraid of wounding his students. A student responds and comments to a peer more in his own terms, whereas the teacher is more likely to focus too soon on technique. A student, moreover, may write off the comments of a teacher by saying to himself, "Adults just can't understand," or "English teachers are nit-pickers anyway," but when his fellow human beings misread him, he has to accommodate the feedback. By habitually responding and coaching, students get insights about their own writing. They become much more involved both in writing and in reading what others have written.

Many of the comments that teachers write on themes can be made by practically any other person than the author and don't require a specialist. The failure to allow for the needs of the audience, for example, is responsible for many difficulties indicated by marginal comments like, "misleading punctuation," "unclear", "doesn't follow", "so what's your point?", "why didn't you say this before?", and so on. Irrelevance, unnecessary repetition, confusing organization, omitted leads and transitions, anticlimactic endings, are among the many things that anyone might point out. Again, numbers make it very likely that such things will not only be mentioned if they are problems, but that the idiosyncrasy of readers will be cancelled out. Probably the majority of communication problems are caused by egocentricity, the writer's assumption that the reader thinks and feels as he does, has had the same experience, and hears in his head, when he is reading, the same voice the writer does when he is writing. It is not so much knowledge as awareness that he needs.

What help can a teacher give that peers cannot? Quite a lot, but the only time he makes a unique contribution to the problem of egocentricity is when the students all share a point of view, value judgement, or line of thought that they take for granted, in which case one may question whether the teacher can or should try to shake their position, which is probably a factor of their stage of growth. Imposing taste, standards, and attitudes that are foreign to them is futile and only teaches them how to become sycophants. But there is value in the teacher's expressing his point of view so they at least know that theirs is not universal.

Where the teacher can be most help, however, is in clarifying problems after students have encountered or raised them. Adolescents—or, as I have discovered from experimenting, even fourth-graders—can spot writing problems very well, but often they do not have enough understanding of the cause of a problem to know how to solve it. This insufficient understanding more than anything else causes them to pick at each other's papers in a faultfinding spirit or to make shallow suggestions for change. A student reader may complain, for example, that a certain paper is monotonous in places and suggest that some repeated words be eliminated. But the real reason for the monotony, and for the repeating of the words, is that there are too many simple sentences, some of which should be joined. The teacher projects the paper with the comment about monotony and leads a problem-solving discussion. This is where the teacher's knowledge, say, of a generative grammar comes in—not as technical information for the students but as an aid to the teacher. Embedding some of the sentences in others involves, as well as transformations, the issue of subordination and emphasis, so that the problem of monotony can now be seen as also a lack of focus.

The teacher, in other words, helps students to interpret their initially vague responses and to translate them into the technical features of the paper that gave rise to them. Notice the direction of the process—the emotional reaction first, then the translation into technique. This amounts to sharpening response while keeping it paramount, and will help reading as well as writing. While helping to solve specific writing problems, the teacher is at the same time dispelling the negativism of comments and creating a climate of informed collaboration in which feedback is welcomed.

The role of the teacher, then, is to teach the students to teach each other. This also makes possible a lot more writing and a lot more response to the writing than a teacher could otherwise sponsor. He creates cross-teaching by setting up two kinds of group processes—one that he leads with the whole class, and a smaller one that runs itself. It is in the first kind, which I just illustrated, that the judgment and knowledge of the teacher are put into play. Periodically, the teacher projects papers for class discussion, without presenting them as good or bad examples and without trying to grind some academic ax. No detailed preparation is needed. He picks papers embodying issues he thinks concern students and need clarifying, getting his cues by circulating among the small groups, where he learns which problems are not getting informed feedback. He asks for responses to the projected paper and plays these responses by alert questioning designed to help students relate their reactions to specific features of the paper before them. If they indicate problems, he asks them to suggest changes the author might make. In these class discussions the teacher establishes tone and a method of giving and using feedback that is carried off into the small groups.

The procedure I recommend is to break the class into groups of four or five and to direct the students to exchange papers within their group, read them, write comments on them, and discuss them. This would be a customary procedure, run autonomously but constantly reinforced by the model of class discussion the teacher continues to lead. It can be of help *during* the writing process, before the final draft. The small size of the group, the reciprocity, tend to make the comments responsible and helpful. The teacher makes it clear that all reactions of any sort are of value—from strong emotions to proof-reading. A writer should know when he has succeeded in something; honest praise is very important. Descriptive remarks are very helpful—of what the paper seems to be or do, and of the effects it had on the reader. All these responses can be compared by talking over together the comments on each paper. Later in this discussion, the author says what he meant to do, and suggestions for bringing the paper more in line with his intentions are made if needed. The teacher sits in on the groups in rotation, acting as consultant and joining the discussion without necessarily having read the papers.

After the sessions, the papers may be revised. The more use to which they are put, the better. In fact, the small groups would most of the time act as editorial boards to prepare papers for some purpose. Themes should be printed up, exchanged with other groups just for reading, performed, and many other things. Eventually they go into folders kept for each student and when the teacher has to evaluate student work for the benefit of administration, he makes a general assessment of the writing to date. No grades are given on individual papers.

The teacher of course may respond individually to any paper at any time during a discussion or during a conference. Whether he writes comments on the paper himself depends on several things. Do his students still need an adult to validate and give importance to their work? In his commentary helping or hindering? Is it necessary? If a student does not want a certain paper read by anyone but the teacher (which happens less often in small groups, where trust is stronger), the teacher honors the request and serves as reader and commentator himself. For some assignments the teacher may feel that his comments are especially relevant, for others not. In any case, if student cross-commentary occurs during the writing process and is at all effective, the amount of commentary the teacher needs to make should be small, as indeed it should be anyway. Mainly, the teacher has to know the effects of *his* action, how students are taking his feedback. First-person comments are best and will set an example for student cross-commentary. A teacher should react as an audience, supplementing the peer audience, Above all, a piece of writing should not go to a dead-letter office. Both the non-response or the irrelevant response persuade the learner that nothing is to be gained from *that* line of endeavor, and the impulse to write withers.

Trial and Error

I would like now to go back to aspects of the action-response model of learning other than the quality of the feedback. These have only been implied so far. Plunging into an act, then heeding the results, is a process of trial and error. That is the first implication. Now, trial and error sounds to many people like a haphazard, time-consuming business, a random behavior of children, animals, and others who don't know any better. (Of course, by "random" we usually mean that we the observers are ignorant of the reasons for the behavior.) Trial and error is by definition never aimless, but without help the individual alone may not think of all the kinds of trials that are possible, or may not always see how to learn the most from his errors. And if it is a social activity he is learning, like writing, then human interaction is in any case indispensable. So we have teachers to propose meaningful trials (assignments) in a meaningful order, and to arrange for a feedback that insures the maximum exploitation of error.

The second implication is that the teacher does not try to prevent the learner from making errors. He does not preteach the problems and solutions (and of course by "errors" I mean failures of vision, judgment, and technique, not mere mechanics). The learner simply plunges into the assignment, uses all his resources, makes errors where he must, and heeds the feedback. In this action–response learning, errors are valuable; they are the essential learning instrument. They are not despised or penalized. Inevitably, the child who is afraid to make mistakes is a retarded learner, no matter what the activity in question.

In contrast to the exploitation of error is the avoidance of error. The latter works like this: the good and bad ways of carrying out the assignment are arrayed in advance, are pre-taught, then the learner does the assignment, attempting to keep the good and bad ways in mind as he works. Next, the teacher evaluates the work according to the criteria that were laid out before the assignment was done. Even if a system of rewards and punishments is not invoked, the learner feels that errors are enemies, not friends. I think any learning psychologist would agree that avoiding error is an inferior learning strategy to capitalizing on error. The difference is between looking over your shoulder and looking where you are going. Nobody who intends to learn to do something wants to make mistakes. In that sense, avoidance of error is assumed in the motivation itself. But if he is allowed to make mistakes with no other penalty than the failure to achieve his goal, then he knows why they are to be avoided and wants to find out how to correct them. Errors take on a different meaning, they define what is good. Otherwise the learner engages with the authority and not with the intrinsic issues. It is consequences, not injunctions, that teach. We all know that, don't we?

But doesn't this process lead to more failures? A learner needs very much to feel successful, to score. If he learns everything the hard way, doesn't he get discouraged by his mistakes? For one thing, trial-and-error makes for more success in the long run because it is accurate, specific, individual, and timely. For another, if the teacher in some way sequences the trials so that learning is transferred from one to the next, the student writer accumulates a more effective guiding experience than if one tried to guide him by preteaching. And feedback of the sort I am advocating—because it is plentiful and informed— does not just leave a feeling of failure, of having "learned the hard way," in the sense of coming out a loser. When response is real and personal, it does not leave us empty, even if our efforts missed their mark.

The procedure, moreover, of getting feedback *during* the writing instead of only *afterwards* allows the learner to incorporate it into his final product (as, incidentally, adults do when we are writing professional articles). I recommend also a lot of chain-reaction assignments, such that one paper is adapted into another. This amounts to a lot of rewriting, not mere tidying up but taking a whole new tack under the influence of suggestions from other students. It is with the isolated, sink-or-swim assignment that the student goes for broke. Finally, the error-avoiding approach has hardly given students a feeling of confidence and success; since it is the predominant method of teaching writing, it seems fair to attribute to it a lot of the wariness and sense of failure so widespread among student writers today.

The Case Against Textbooks

The third implication of action–response learning follows from the last one about the futility of preteaching writing problems. If we learn to write best by doing it and by heeding the feedback, then of what use is the presentation of materials to the learner? Don't presentations violate the trial-and-error process? Don't they inevitably entail preteaching and error-avoidance? My answer is yes.

If I reject all prepared materials for writing, it is not that I am failing to discriminate among them. I know that they come in all sizes, shapes, and philosophies. It is not the quality but the fact of these materials that I am speaking to.

The assumption I infer from textbooks is that the output of writing must be preceded and accompanied by pedagogical input. Now, there are indeed some kinds of input that are prerequisites to writing—namely, conversation and reading—but these are very different from the presentations of textbooks. Let's look at the sorts of materials that are used to teach writing.

This material may be classified into six overlapping sorts, all of which might appear in any one unit or chapter. The first sort consists of advice, exhortation, and injunction. It is the how-to-do-it part, the cookbook material. Here are some fabricated but typical samples. "Make sure you allow for your audience." "Catch the reader's interest in the first sentence." "Make sure your punctuation guides the reader instead of misleading him." "Connect your ideas with linking words that make transitions." "Write a brief outline of the points you want to make, then write a paragraph about each point." "For the sake of a varied style, it is advisable to begin some sentences with a main clause and others with subordinate clauses or phrases." "A vivid metaphor will often convey an idea more forcefully than a lengthy, abstract explanation." "Build up your descriptions from details that make your readers see." "A good narrative has a focus or point to it that is not obscured by irrelevant details (remember what we learned about focus in the last unit?)."

What is wrong with practical pointers and helpful hints? As I have suggested, preteaching the problems of writing causes students to adopt the strategy of error-avoidance, the teacher's intention clearly being to keep them from making mistakes. The learner is put in the situation of trying to understand and keep in mind all this advice when he should be thinking about the needs of the subject. The textbook writer is in the position of having to predict the mistakes that some mythical average student might make. The result is that, in true bureaucratic fashion, the text generates a secondary set of problems beyond those that an individual learner might truly have to deal with in the assignment itself. That is, he has to figure out first of all what the advice means at a time when it can't mean very much. Often he makes mistakes because he misconstrues the advice. In trying to stick to what he was told, he is in fact working on two tasks at once—the fulfillment of the advice and the fulfillment of the assignment.

Since not all learners are prone to the same mistakes, some of the pointers are a waste of time for the individual personally; he would not have erred in those particular ways. The exhortations and injunctions often inhibit thought. But most critically of all, they prevent both the learner and his responders from knowing what he would have done without this preteaching. It is essential to find this out. The learner has to know his own mind, what it natively produces, so that he can see what he personally needs to correct for. Students who fulfill the advice well have passed the test in following directions but have missed the chance to learn the most important thing of all—what their blind spots are.

After all, allowing for the audience, catching interest in the first sentence or paragraph, guiding the reader with punctuation, making transitions, varying the style, using metaphors, giving narrative a point—these are common-sense things. What interests me is why a student fails to do these things in the first place. The fact is, I believe, that writing mistakes are not made in ignorance of common-sense requirements; they are made for other reasons that advice cannot prevent. Usually, the student *thinks* he has made a logical transition or a narrative point, which means, again, he is deceived by his egocentricity. What he needs is not rules but awareness. Or if he omits stylistic variation, metaphor, and detail, he does so for a variety of reasons the teacher has to understand before he can be of use. Scanty reading background, an undeveloped eye or ear, a lingering immaturity about not elaborating are learning problems that exhortation cannot solve. Particular instances of failing to do what one thinks one is doing, and of failing to use the full resources of language, should be brought to light, the consequences revealed, the reasons explored, the need for remedies felt, and the possibilities of solution discovered. Unsolicited advice is unheeded advice, and, like time-clock feeding, imposes the breast before there is hunger.

A second class of material found in textbooks is expository. Here we have the definitions and explanations of rhetoric, grammar, logic, and semantics. In other words, information about language and how it is used. Part of the game played here is, to borrow the title of a Henry Read poem, the naming of parts. The assumption seems to be the primitive one that naming things is mastering them. It goes with the attempt to convert internal processes into an external subject. By pedagogical sleight of hand, an output activity is transformed into something to be read about. The various ways of constructing sentences, paragraphs, and compositions are logically classified and arrayed. The student can then be put to work on writing as if it were any other substantive content: he can memorize the nomenclature and classifications, answer questions on them, take tests, and on some fitting occasion, "apply" this knowledge.

The explanations tell him what it is he is doing when he strings utterances—not he, of course, but some capitalized He, for this is the realm of general description and theory. The material may be up to date—the new linguistics and the new rhetoric—but the method couldn't be older: "There are three kinds of sentences: simple, complex, and compound." "Articles, demonstratives, and genitives make up the regular determiners." "An inductive paragraph goes from particulars to the main statement, and a deductive paragraph begins with the main statement and descends to particulars." "Ideas may be presented in any of several patterns: they may be repeated, contrasted, piled up in a series, balanced symmetrically, and so on." The elements of fiction are plot, character, setting, and theme." "People use the same words, but don't mean the same things by them."

Such generalities, like advice, induce in the students a strategy of avoiding errors, of trying to do what the book says instead of doing justice to the subject. Whereas advice tells you what you *should* do with language, exposition tells you what people *do* do; it codifies the regularities of practice. The message is essentially the same: apply these rules and you will be all right. Good teaching, rather, helps the individual see what he in particular is doing with language and, by means of this awareness, see what he in particular might be doing. There is no evidence that preteaching general facts and theories about how people use language will help a student learn to write.

Since the most natural assumption should be that one learns to write by writing, the burden of proof is on those who advocate an indirect method, by which I mean presenting codifications about rhetoric and composition in the hope that students will apply them. Today there are many good theories of rhetoric and composition. Teachers should study these, for, like grammatical formulations, they may help the teachers understand what their students are doing or not doing in their writing. But to teach such formulations, through either exposition or exercises, would hinder more than help.

A third class of materials comprising textbooks is exercises. Sometimes the student is asked to read some dummy sentences and paragraphs and to do something with them. For example: "Underline the one of the following words that best describes the tone of the sentence below." "Rewrite the sentence that appears below so that one of the ideas is subordinated to the other." "Change the order of the sentences in the following paragraph so that the main point and the secondary points are better presented." "Read this paragraph and underline the one of the sentences following it that would serve as the best topic sentence." "Make a single sentence out of the following." Or the student may be asked to make up sentences or paragraphs of his own: "Write a sentence describing some object or action, using modifier clusters as in the examples." "Write a descriptive paragraph following a space order (or a time order)."

Exercises are obviously part and parcel of the preteaching approach characterized by advice and exposition. A point raised and explained in the text is simply cast into the form of directions so that the student will apply the point directly. The philosophy here is a curious blend of hard-headed logical analysis and folklorish softheadedness. That is, the teaching of "basics" is construed in this way. Basics are components, particles—words, sentences, and paragraphs. The learner should manipulate each of these writing units separately in a situation controlling for one problem at a time. He works his way from little particle to big particle until he arrives at whole compositions resembling those done in the outside world. The single-unit, single-problem focus derives from linguistic and rhetorical analysis done in universities, not from perceptions about learning.

The folklorish part is represented in the old saw about having to crawl before you can walk. But crawling is an authentic form of locomotion in its own right, not merely a component or sub-skill of walking. For the learner, basics are not the small-focus technical things but broad things like meaning and motivation, purpose and point, which are precisely what are missing from exercises. An exercise, by my definition, is any piece of writing practiced only in schools—that is, an assignment that stipulates arbitrary limits that leave the writer with no real relationships between him and a subject and an audience. I would not ask a student to write anything other than an authentic discourse, because the learning process proceeds from intent and content down to the contemplation of technical points, not the other way.

First of all, when it is the stipulation of the text or the teacher and not the natural limit of an utterance, a sentence or a paragraph is too small a focus for learning. How can you teach style, rhetoric, logic, and organization in a unit stripped of those authentic relationships to subject and audience that *govern* the decisions about word choice, sentence structure, paragraph structure, and total continuity? Judgment and decision-making are the heart of composition. With exercises the learner has no basis for choosing one word or sentence structure over another, and rhetoric becomes an irony once again. It is a crime to make students think that words, sentences, paragraphs, are "building blocks" like bricks that have independent existence and can be learned and manipulated separately pending the occasion when something is to be constructed out of them.

And when students make up a sentence or paragraph demonstrating such and such kind of structure, they are not learning what the teacher thinks they are: they are learning that there is such a thing as writing sentences and paragraphs for their own sake, that discourse need not be motivated or directed at anyone, that it is good to write even if you have nothing to say and no one to say it to just so long as what you put down illustrates a linguistic codification. The psychological phenomenon involved here—called "learning sets" by H. E. Harlow, and "deutero-learning" by Gregory Bateson[3]—is that when someone learns a certain content, he also *learns that way of learning.* This second kind of learning tends to be hidden because it is not under focus, and yet for that very reason may be the more lasting. The student learns how to do exercises, and this learning is of a higher order, ironically, than the learning of the different sentence or paragraph structures contained in the exercises. Thus in an a-rhetorical learning situation, he learns to discourse a-rhetorically!

When decomposition precedes composition, many such unintended and harmful side-effects occur that seem to go on unnoticed because we are fastened on the logic of the subject instead of the psychologic of the learner. Scientists have long been aware that when you isolate out a component for focused observation, you are changing it. Live tissue under a microscope is not live tissue in the body. A sentence or paragraph stripped of its organic context, raised several powers, and presented in the special context of analysis and

---

3. See pp. 215 and 216 of *Communication: The Social Matrix of Psychiatry*, by Jurgen Ruesch and Gregory Bateson (New York: W. W. Norton & Company, Inc., 1951).

advice represents serious tampering with the compositional process, the consequences of which are not well recognized.

Second, a student doing a paragraph exercise, say, knows the problem concerns paragraph structure, whereas in authentic discourse the real problem always is this, that *we don't know what it is we don't know.* A student may do all of the exercises correctly and still write very badly because he is used to having problems plucked out of the subjective morass and served to him externally on a platter, and has consequently developed little in the way of awareness and judgment. For example, he *can't* decide how to break into paragraphs because he must write only one paragraph.

Third, students adopt a strategy for beating the game of exercises: they take a simplistic approach, avoid thinking subtly or complexly, and say only what can lend itself readily to the purpose of the exercise. To make the paragraph come out right, they write things they know are stupid and boring.

Fourth, the poetic justice in this strategy is that the exercises themselves ignore the motivational and learning needs of the student. The result is just the opposite intended: the learner dissociates the technical issues in the exercise from honest discourse. The learner becomes alienated, not only by this but by the hidden message of exercises, which says, "We are not interested in what you have to say; we just want a certain form." His defense is to do the exercise by the book in an ironically obedient fashion to show them for just what they are. You bore me and I'll bore you. This dissociation in the minds of students between school stuff and writing for real is one of the deep and widespread symptoms that has made English teaching ripe for reform.

The last three kinds of materials are not bad in themselves but suffer from being embedded in the paraphernalia I have been polemicizing about. For this reason I will deal with them briefly. The first is the presentation of samples of good writing to serve as models. As I have said, learning to write entails a lot of reading, but when passages from the old pros are surrounded by rhetorical analysis and pesky questions about how Saroyan got his effects, a disservice is done to both reading and writing. How would you as an adolescent react to a message such as this: "See how Steinbeck uses details; now you go do that too." And there is no evidence that analyzing how some famous writer admirably dispatched a problem will help a student recognize and solve his writing problems. From my own experience and that of teachers I have researched with, I would say, rather, that models don't help writing and merely intimidate some students by implying a kind of competition in which they are bound to lose. The assumption is still that advance diagnosis and prescription facilitate learning. The same reading selections could be helpful, however, if merely interwoven with the writing assignments as part of the regular reading program but without trying to score points from them. Learners, like the professional writers themselves, incorporate anyway the structures of what they read; what they need is more time to read and write authentically. The service publishers could do is to put out more straight anthologies of whole reading selections grouped according to the various kinds of writing but un-surrounded by questions and analysis. The student should write in the forms he reads while he is reading them. There can be a lot of discussion of these selections, but the points of departure for discussion should be student response to the reading.

Another kind of textbook material—writing stimulants—is closely related to models because sometimes these prompters are also reading selections. Or they may merely be the text writer's own prose as he tried to set up ideas or talk up topics, two intentions that are better realized in class conversation. Sometimes the stimulants are photographs—possibly a good idea, but the pictures are always too small in the textbook. Whatever the kind of stimulant, the wiser course is to let it arise out of the daily drama of the student's life in and out of school, including his regular reading. In this way the stimulants are automatically geared to what the students know and care about. To present stimulants in a book is to run an unnecessary risk of irrelevance and canned writing.

At last we come to the assignment directions themselves. They, of course, are justified, but for them who needs a book? Even the windiest text writer could not get a textbook out of assignment directions alone. It is better anyway for the teacher to give the assignment because he can adapt it to his particular class—cast it in a way that they will understand, relate it to their other work, and so on.

Let me summarize now my concerns about presenting materials to students as a way to teach writing. They install in the classroom a mistaken and unwarranted method of learning. They take time, money, and energy that should be spent on authentic writing, reading, and speaking. They get between the teacher and his students, making it difficult for the teacher to understand what they need, and to play a role that would give them the full benefit of group process. They add secondary problems of their own making. They sometimes promote actual mislearning. They kill spontaneity and the sense of adventure for both teacher and students. They make writing appear strange and technical so that students dissociate it from familiar language behavior that should support it. Their dullness and arbitrariness alienate students from writing. Because they predict and pre-package, they are bound to be inappropriate for some school populations, partly irrelevant to individual students, and ill-timed for all.

I believe the teacher should be given a lot of help for the very difficult job of teaching writing. A lot of what is in textbooks should be in books for teachers, and is in fact partly there to educate them, not the students. The real problem, as I think many educators would admit, is that too many teachers cannot do without textbooks because they were never taught in schools of education to teach without them. Textbooks constitute a kind of inservice training in teaching method and in linguistic and rhetorical analysis that they never received before. Thus the trial-and-error approach would be considered too difficult for most teachers; they wouldn't have the background, perception, and agility to make it work. The extreme of this belief is that teacher-proof materials are necessary to compensate for teacher inadequacy. If this is so, then let's be frank and solve the problem by renovating teacher training and by publishing more books for teachers on the job, not by putting materials in the hands of students. If it is acknowledged that textbooks do not exist because they embody the best learning process but because teachers are dependent on them, then we would expect them to dwindle away as the education of teachers improves. But I don't see that texts are a mere stop-gap measure. There is every indication that they will become more powerful, not less. The investments of everyone are too great. I don't mean just the publishers, who are merely supplying a demand; I mean that we are all caught in a self-perpetuating cycle that revolves among education schools, classrooms, school administrations, and publishers. The teaching of writing will not improve until the cycle is broken. It is not up to the publishers to break it; they will put out whatever teachers call for. Although a number of teachers do teach writing without texts, it is too much to expect a revolution to start in classrooms without a lot of change in school administration and schools of education, which is where the cycle can be broken.

If I have strayed here into essentially noneducational considerations, it is because I believe the only justification for textbooks in writing is an essentially noneducational one. My main purpose has been to propose that writing be taught naturalistically, by writing, and that the only texts be the student productions themselves. I regret that I have had to speak so long against something, but it is not enough to propose; a way must be cleared. I see tremendous evidence against the preteaching approach, embodied in textbooks, and no evidence for it. The great advances in language theory, on the one hand, and in programming techniques on the other, are unfortunately reinforcing that approach. The prospect that frightens me is that we educators are learning to do better and better some things that should not be done at all. We are rapidly perfecting error. Which is to say that I think we should heed better the feedback we get about the consequences of our own teaching actions.

17

The Art of Writing Evaluative Comments on Student Themes

D. G. Kehl

"Let there be no horse manure between teachers of English." So reflects Jacob Horner, teacher of prescriptive grammar at Wicomico State Teacher's College, in John Barth's novel *The End of the Road* (Avon, 1968), just before Horner attempts to seduce a Wicomico High School English teacher. This sagacious reflection seems particularly applicable to the subject of theme evaluation.

But let there be no manure between composition teachers and their students, we might add. While it is generally agreed that much of what students write for teachers is *awful*—not in the older sense of "awe-inspiring" but in the modern sense of the term—it is less generally acknowledged, but equally as true, that much of what teachers write—or fail to write—in evaluation of student writing is *offal*.

As theme graders, perhaps there is in each of us a great deal of Leo Duffy, erstwhile teacher of composition at Cascadia College in Bernard Malamud's novel *A New Life* (Dell, 1963):

> He graded papers, accumulated in a pile on his desk all term long, in one mad week at the end of each semester, staying up nights with the assistance of pills; then returning hundreds of themes and quizzes in ferocious batches a day or so before the d.o. [departmental objective exam], having deprived his students of the benefit of learning from previous papers what errors to avoid on later ones. . . . He threw away, ungraded and unrecorded, more than one set of themes, because his dachshund, which had been trained to react on paper, wet on them. He apparently did his grading on the floor.

For composition teachers motivated less by doggery and more by doggedness, the lessons here are abundant: Don't grade themes on the floor; return themes promptly; and, above all, don't despair even when it appears that student writing has in fact gone to the dogs or when even young dogs cannot seem to learn new rhetorical "tricks." To deprive students "of the benefit of learning from previous papers what errors to avoid on later ones"—whether from the teacher's failure to return papers promptly or from his failure to write helpful comments—is to indulge in what Malamud's protagonist later calls "a great irrelevancy." Effective composition teaching, in short, consists essentially of training *students* to "react" on paper and then reacting ourselves to their reactions.

Many teachers, while they recognize the importance of training students to react in lucid, forceful prose, have apparently not recognized the importance of *their* reacting to student writing in equally lucid, forceful prose. "What has to be done," Jacques Barzun writes in *Teacher in America* (Doubleday, 1954), "is to dramatize the relation between writer and reader." Barzun says further: "The teacher of writing must vividly express his annoyance at being bored, baffled, and outraged by bad writing, until the writers recognize that he, being a reader under compulsion, has a claim on their best efforts. To put it another way, their writing is a social gesture, not just make-believe, and he must dramatize his response."[1] If, as Robert Frost wrote over forty years ago, "everything written is as good as it is dramatic," much student-directed teacher writing must not be very good. Only when the composition teacher reacts both extensively and intensively to student writing does he dramatize the relation between reader and writer.

These two major aims then—to help students recognize their writing weaknesses and avoid them on future papers and to dramatize the writer-reader relationship—provide the *raison dêtre* of teacher comments. The composition teacher must be, and he must teach his students to be, both a reactor and a redactor. The intent is to react to and assist in redacting a student's writing often enough and fully enough that he will become sufficiently conscious not only of his ideas and purposes but also of his audience and the techniques by which he can effectively communicate.

The reasons—or in some cases the alibis—for not writing adequate comments are familiar because most of us have used them at one time or another. There is, for example, the matter of time required to write any kind of beneficial comment. But if we do not have time for dramatizing our response to student writing, both by written comments and by individual conferences, what *do* we have time *for*? This, it would seem, is the essence of the composition teacher's job. For that matter, it seems to be the task of *every* teacher, for, as Aldous Huxley said: "Most of our mistakes are fundamentally grammatical. We create our own difficulties by employing an inadequate language to describe facts. Thus, to take one example, we are constantly giving the same name to more than one thing, and more than one name to the same thing. The results, when we come to argue, are deplorable. For we are using a language which does not adequately describe the things about which we are arguing" (Books for Libraries Press, 1927). The teacher-student dialog over these fundamental

1. In a letter to me, March 14, 1969.

"grammatical" mistakes seems to be an essential part of the whole educative process. Indeed universities would do well to prize the quantity and quality of a teacher's evaluative writing directed to students as much as they prize—and rightly so—his scholarly writing directed to colleagues. Both forms of writing, it would seem, are indispensable to effective teaching.

Another demur often heard is that the "writer's cramp and eyestrain" do not really pay off anyway. Lois V. Arnold, in her essay "Writer's Cramp and Eyestrain—Are They Paying Off?" (*English Journal*, January 1964), concludes that "intensive evaluation is seemingly no more effective than moderate evaluation in improving the quality of written composition." But Earl W. Buxton has concluded that college freshmen whose themes are thoroughly and intensively marked improve their writing more than those whose themes receive only scattered general remarks.[2] Of course, what we need to know in both cases is the nature of the comments written, for without this information the conclusions are of little value. It seems valid to conclude that the practice of commenting on student themes has often been faulted because the wrong kinds of comments have too often been written. Each teacher must experiment until he finds the most effective evaluative-instructive techniques. If he finds, however, that his comments are not effective, he should examine the nature of his comments rather than merely ceasing to write them.

Still another expostulation against the writing of comments is the popular, current notion that pointed comments will cause traumatic reactions in the students. In most cases this is sheer nonsense; in cases where comments do have ill effects, the fault seems to lie in the *nature* of the comments, not in the fact that comments are written. Although the blunt comments may "administer a shock at first," writes Jacques Barzun, "they are also flattering. 'Somebody cares about what I want to say.' The teacher is no longer a paid detective hunting stray commas." Young people say they *want* us to "tell it like it is"; the real difficulties arise when we tell it like it isn't or when we don't tell it at all.

Assuming, then, that evaluative comments are needed and that the writing of these comments is an art, a skill that can be learned, let us turn to the nature of the comments written.

Is it not ironical that so many comments written on student themes are weak and ineffective for many of the same reasons that the student themes themselves are weak and ineffective? Lewis Mumford's recent advice to composition teachers is pertinent: "Practice what you preach; and if it doesn't work, revise your preaching."[3] Or, we might add, revise your *practice*. All too many of our comments violate the very standards of judgment applied to student writing—for

2. "An Experiment to Test the Effects of Writing Frequency and Guided Practice Upon Students' Skill in Written Expression" (unpublished doctoral dissertation). (Palo Alto: Stanford University, 1958).
3. In a letter to me, June 24, 1969.

example, those mentioned by William J. Dusel in his article, "How Should Writing Be Judged?" (*English Journal*, May 1957): order, perception, appropriateness of style, concreteness of style.

Meaningful, beneficial comments must not be too general, too truncated. Simply to write "awk" once or twice in the margin and assign a "C-" is not doing the job. How likely is it that the student will know about the razor-billed auk or even the great auk, that species of arctic bird which dives and swims, using its wings as paddles but which is a poor flier and clumsy on the land? Or even if he does know, how is it going to improve his writing? Such a hieroglyphic is about as beneficial as that which appeared, along with a plump, red "D," on one student's paper. Eagerly searching the pages for some explanatory comment, the student found what looked like "frog" and concluded that he had received the "D" because his theme jumped around too much. Does such a crypto-comment, no less fragmentized than the student's "incomplete sentence," communicate any more successfully? Students deserve to be told what their weaknesses are and helped to improve them, or on subsequent themes they will continue to practice their errors.

Such comments as "Not bad except when you try to get funny"; or "Not adequate development for what presumably the topic of the essay is"; or "This theme just won't wash" are too general and nebulous to be beneficial. Teachers who make them should either stop preaching to students about specificity and clarity or revise their own practice. We purport to teach students *expository* writing, but our own writing to students is often less than expository, explaining nothing and exposing little except our gross inconsistency.

Summary comments are frequently disorganized, discursive, desultory. For example:

> Your essay doesn't have enough transitional devices. [How *many are* *"enough?"*] Paragraphing doesn't seem to follow any plan. [Which specific paragraphs? What plan?] Poor paragraph development. [Which paragraphs? How can they be developed?] Connect your ideas. [Isn't this what you said above? How can it best be done?] Do something about mechanics. [This is like saying, "Go get educated," or "Stop being illiterate."] Your theme is all disconnected. [Physician, heal thyself!]

Another weakness of student writing often shared by pedagogical comments is lack of perceptive focus. Often a theme is weak for one or two *major* reasons which, if corrected, would hide a multitude of sins. Simply to write "poor organization" is inadequate if the problem lies in failure to formulate a lucid, focused thesis commitment. To write "weak coherence" is of little help if the theme has no sense of structure. To write "bad paragraph" accomplishes little unless the student is made to understand why it is "bad," for example, through the Christensen rhetorical analysis of paragraphs. The precise, perceptive teacher must sense what the student is trying to say and point out not only *where* but also *how* his writing fails.

Only when we stop implying by our comments that our students should do as we *say* rather than as we *do* will our comments be really effective. As Professor Carlton Wells has expressed it, "marginal and terminal comments, however brief, should always be legible, precise, and well expressed" (*English Journal*, November 1966). Similarly, Richard Larson has advised: "See that your comment is thoughtfully, precisely, and tightly written. It may act as a model of writing for the student (it is, after all, a sample of your writing); even if it isn't a model of excellence, it ought not to be an illustration of what you have been trying to make your students avoid" (*College Composition and Communication*, October 1966).

Still another major fault of comments written on themes is related to a recently popular subject: voice.[4] Admittedly, the concept of voice is important in student writing, but why have we heard nothing at all about the *teacher's* voice, especially in his comments on student papers? According to Duhler and Zarin, awareness of one's voice involves three things: "a knowledge of one's material, an awareness of the manner in which that material should be presented, and a sense of the effect of that presentation on a specific audience."[5] Summary comments are ordinarily ineffective for one or all of these reasons. The first two—imperception and imprecision—we have already discussed briefly. The third—insensitivity—is equally as important.

Sometimes, if there is a voice at all in pedagogical comments, it is only the negative, carping voice of Professor Buncombe: "You've split two infinitives, faulted a comma, fragmented a sentence, dangled two modifiers and squinted a third. I've knocked a letter grade off for the misspelled word. Next time it'll he two letter grades." Or it is the mechanical nonvoice of the computer: "P. 17d.g., awk, sp. 25G, dev. 28.1, awk-awk, C-13, F, 666." Or, it is the perpetually caustic voice of Mr. Momus: "Simple-minded! Not an intelligent sentence in the whole essay. You are without a doubt totally ineducable. Are you bothered by the realization that you have the solution to the generation gap in 300-words-or-less?" Or, conversely, it is the perpetually effusive, indiscriminatory voice of Mr. Smilax: "Excellent! Bravo! Good ideas, good structure, good logic, good mechanics. Keep up the good work—and watch out, Johney Updike!" Or it is the jargonizing voice of Dr. Syntax who, with due apologies to William Combe, searches today not for the picturesque but for the verbal arabesque: "Your tagmemic matrices are not emically definable units. There is trouble too at the morpheme level of the grammatical hierarchy." Or it is the activistic voice of Relevance: "Am I seeing the true you here? See me. I'll help you in your search for self. You're uptight. Too much concern with *how* you put it; let go and let it flow. Not gutsy enough. Expand your mind and

---

4. See, for example, Taylor Stoehr's article "Tone and Voice," *College English* (November 1968) 150–61.
5. Walter Dubler and Eve Zarin, "The Concept of Voice," *Writing College English* (New York: Holt, Rinehart, & Winston, 1967), pp. 3–11.

the style will come. Strive for more relevance." There are, of course, other voices, such as the *voix celeste,* condescending to thunder in hieratic tones from the ethereal regions; or the *sotto voce* so feeble that it cannot be heard.

Above all, the voice must be human. Behind every piece of writing *is* a human being. And every comment about student writing should communicate, in a distinctively human voice, a sincere respect for the writer as a person and a sincere interest in his improvement as a writer. Too often dehumanized voices wake them—and they drown.

The human being behind the voice, being human, establishes the atmosphere for composition urged by poet William Stafford: "A student's writing should be welcomed and responded to—not necessarily praised greatly, and certainly not attacked for inadequacy:—just as we talk best when in congenial company, so we write best when met with response and easy adjustment to whatever it is we find ourselves led to express."[6] In a word, the teacher's voice should react and interact rather than merely counteract. Comments should be both constructive and instructive, both exact and exacting, both extensive and intensive. This is not to say, of course, that one need comment on everything or attempt to make the paper look as if it has hemorrhaged. The intent should not be to mark up but to remark on; we should be less constrictive and more constructive; we should be preoccupied less with the student's weaknesses than with his potential strengths.

To be truly beneficial, the summary comment (in preference to the so-called "terminal" comment, which connotes an incurable disease) should accomplish four things. It should *appraise*, evaluate, the degree of effectiveness of the whole and its parts. It should *analyze* both the major strengths and weaknesses of the essay. It should, in lucid, succinct prose, *apprise* the student of his major problems. And finally it should *advise* him as specifically as possible how he can realize the potential of his writing in his revision of the essay and in future writing. Each of these four steps involves an implicit question which the teacher must answer. To appraise beneficially, he answers the question: Does the paper have a clear sense of purpose and does it effectively accomplish its purpose? That is, does it *communicate*? To analyze, he answers the question: Wherein does the paper succeed and wherein does it fail—and why? To appraise, he answers the question: What are the *major* weaknesses and how can I best make the writer aware of them? To advise, he answers the question: What does the writer need to know and do in order to realize his potential both in this paper and in future ones?

To achieve these ends, the teacher would do well first to read the entire theme for its general effectiveness, looking for major problems and a point of focus, a "handle" for a comment. Sandburg wrote in *The People, Yes*:

6. In a letter to me, March 27, 1969.

You take hold of a handle by one hand or the other by the better or worse hand
and you never know maybe till long afterward which was the better hand.[7]

One such "handle" or point of focus for getting at the writing problems is
the Christensen method of rhetorical analysis, which can be used in marginal
and summary comments to generate sentences and paragraphs of greater tex-
tural depth. With practice, the teacher, instead of simply writing "poor paragraph," can analyze a representative paragraph, labelling the levels of generality, and thereby illustrate specifically why the paragraph is weak and how it
can be improved. This focus on levels of generality can be used to generate not
only sentences, paragraphs, and, by extension, the entire essay, but also language. For example, application of the principles of Korzybski's Abstraction
Ladder can generate more specific, more concrete diction. The student theme
"The Wall," weak primarily because of its lack of specificity, invites this kind
of focused comment.

"The Wall"

The "generation gap" exists as a wall, only because the children of today will
not listen. They will not attempt to communicate with their parents; and,
therefore, they have built this "wall" separating themselves from their parents.

Today, children are constantly "downgrading" their parents, because, to
them, their parents take too long to get accustomed to the new ideas and
philosophies of the world. Children can't seem to understand that, to their
parents, all the ideas and philosophies of today are changes, whereas, to the
children, they are their ways of life; not changes, and changes take time to
get accustomed to.

Children often forget that their parents were once children, also. This
can be easily visualized since children only see their parents as adults.
Children often feel their parents never experienced a child's world—from
infancy through adolescense—so, as a result, they feel that their "growing-
up" is a totally strange experience to their parents.

It is true that today's children are being brought up in a different environment and way of life from that of the one their parents' were brought up in; but,
too, children must realize that their parents were brought up in a totally new
environment and way of life from that of their parents. Communication difficulties were obviously experienced by the children's parents and differences of
opinion were most likely expressed and discussed, so the children's problems
are not all so new. Children should realize this fact and think about it.

The whole trick to parent-child communication is to listen and learn. No
harm has ever been done by this. Children still have the freedom to either
chew up what they hear, and spit it out, or chew it up and store it. The children will be surprised to find that what their parents have been through, and

---

7. Carl Sandburg, *The People, Yes*. Reprinted by permission of Harcourt Brace Jovanovich, Inc.

what they've learned is common to what the children are experiencing now. Parents, they'll [children] find, are not "another breed of animal"; but the same breed as themselves, only a little older and a lot wiser.

A little listening and trying will prove to be a rewarding experience. Soon that brick wall, preventing communication, will crumble, and be recognized as a child-made disaster.

A summary comment using the Christensen focus might be as follows:

Your essay, although it has some potential in its attention to child-parent misunderstanding, frustrates far more than it communicates; it raises its own "wall" between writer and reader by failing to be specific and concrete. You tend to make a generalization and then, without clarifying and exemplifying, go on to another generalization. Most of your sentences, as you will note from my rhetorical analysis, remain on the 1 and 2 levels. Often, instead of moving to a lower level, you repeat the material, adding little or nothing more specific. E.g., in paragraph 3 you repeat the same idea in different, but still general, abstract terms.

Rewrite the paper, adding subordinate sequences to make the texture denser. Organize carefully, making sure you know what you intend to do in each paragraph; then formulate valid "top" sentences expressing the controlling idea of each paragraph.

Your opening paragraph could be written as follows. (Note the subordinate and coordinate levels of generality.)

[1]The generation gap exists because parents and children often fail to communicate with each other. [2]Effective communication is an art that must be cultivated. [3]It is a two-way process requiring mutual effort. [4]It requires, above all, mutual respect and understanding. [4]It requires also that each party listen to and learn from the other. [4]And it requires an attempt to find common ground and break down existing barriers.

Move such abstractions as "children of today," "all the ideas and philosophies of today," "communication differences," "different environment," and "ways of life" to lower, more specific levels. For example:

"New ideas"
anti-establishment
doing your own thing
physical appearance
grooming
long hair

Another "handle" or point of focus is that of "voice." Often the major weaknesses of a theme can be traced to the failure of the student to express a "true voice." According to the editors of *The Personal Voice* (Lippincott, 1964), voice in good writing is "the liberated yet controlled expression of a human being deeply committed to what he is saying. A true voice appears, if at all, when the writer ceases to evade or merely toy with his ideas. . . ." At the core of most bad writing is expression that is unliberated (giving the impression that it has been groaned up), uncontrolled, uncommitted, evasive, and insincere. Eudora Welty has said: "The trouble with bad student writing is the trouble with all bad writing. It is not serious and it does not tell the truth." And according to Donald Hall, "concentration upon honesty is the only way to exclude the sounds of the bad style that assaults us all." It ought to be pointed out, however, that frequently this lack of commitment and sincerity can be traced to the nature of the assignment. A good writing assignment, as Hans Guth has pointed out, "must do justice to three requirements: It should be meaningful, realistic, and specific"—three qualities which are often missing both in our assignments and in our comments. The student theme "The Wall" is weak to a large degree because no "true voice" is expressed; an uncommitted pseudo-voice evades and merely toys with ideas. If the writer can be made aware of his pseudo-voice and helped to express a "true" one, many of his problems will disappear. A summary comment focusing on voice might be as follows:

> Your theme reads as if it has been ground out mechanically; no clear sense of voice is conveyed. This is a very rough draft; read it aloud and concentrate on the "voice." You may wish to salvage a key idea—failure to listen—and begin again.
>
> I get the impression that what voice does come through may be a pseudo-voice. Do you *really* believe that any "gap" that may exist is caused solely and entirely by "children"—or do you assume this pseudo-voice because you feel it is what your reader will approve?
>
> Secondly, your voice is evasive, failing to exemplify and develop the key ideas. This failure to develop with specific, concrete examples from your own experience suggests a lack of commitment to what you say, a superficiality of treatment, and an aloofness from your reader.
>
> Furthermore, the pseudo-voice moves in circles rather than in a clear, linear sequence. For example, note the question-begging in sentence 2, paragraph 1 and the verbosity, especially of paragraphs 2, 3, and 4. Revise the paper, working on expressing a clear, true human voice.

A third effective "handle" applies Robert Gorrell's concept of thesis commitment and response. Most weaknesses in an essay can be directly related to the thesis commitment—either in the failure of the student to formulate a specific, tenable commitment or in his failure to follow through and support the commitment.[8] The following summary comment written in evaluation of "The Wall" illustrates this focus.

---

8. See James L. Green's "A Method for Writing Comments on Student Themes," *English Journal* (February 1968) 215–20.

Your paper is weak primarily for two reasons. You commit yourself to a restrictive, untenable assertion—the "wall" exists only because children will not listen. Obviously, this is not the sole reason. Don't you suppose adults might be partly responsible as well? Secondly, you don't keep your commitment to the reader. You don't follow through and show specifically what this failure to listen entails. "Children of today" would seem to commit you to discussion of contrast between today's generation and the parent generation. Do you suppose children in some cases "will not listen" because nothing of note is being said? Don't you suppose some children *do* listen and attempt to communicate? You need specific examples to support your commitment.

Even individual sentences do not follow logically from preceding ones. E.g., sentence 1, paragraph 1 speaks of failure to listen; sentence 2, rather than elucidating or following through on this idea, talks about the failure to communicate and, in itself, begs the question.

Your paper suggests other ideas not included in the thesis commitment, none of which is adequately developed. For example: Children will not communicate (sent. 2, par. 1); children down-grade their parents because they misunderstand them (par. 2–4); children should listen and learn (par. 5–6).

Rewrite the theme, formulating a lucid, tenable thesis commitment and then following through on it. For example, this might be a tenable thesis commitment: A generation gap exists because some parents and children often misunderstand each other and fail to listen to each other.

The writing of evaluative-instructive comments is an art to be learned only by practice and by application of the distinctively human attributes urged for composition teachers by poet Howard Nemerov: "Patience, good humor, kindness, and uncompromising vigor."[9]

As an art involved in teaching an art, student-directed teacher writing must be doubly concerned with technique. Francis Christensen concludes his seminal article, "A Generative Rhetoric of the Paragraph," as follows; "The teacher who believes, as I do, that the only freedom in any art comes from the mastery of technique, may find here the means both to kindle and restrain" *(College Composition and Communication,* October 1965). The effective summary comment, the purpose of which is not only to evaluate but also to teach, will both restrain and kindle. To restrain—to indicate restrictive limits of effectiveness and ineffectiveness—is not enough; the comment must also kindle, a word which suggests, etymologically, two metaphors: to "set a fire under" and to "give birth to" or generate. The truly beneficial comment ignites rather than extinguishes; it engenders rather than stifles. It carries out Browning's curt injunction: "Do the thing shall breed the thought," Generating, breeding thought is the composition teacher's "thing" to do, and he must "do his thing."

---

9. In a letter to me, March 25, 1969. Nemerov adds, as further advice to the composition teacher: "It might be wise to stress at the very start that our civilization lives on words to an unprecedented extent, so that anyone at all may find himself 'a writer'."

Thus, commenting effectively, he functions at once both as impregnator and as midwife, assisting in drawing forth the shrieking, ill-formed infant thought and then in cleaning up the puling brat.

The effective comment, necessarily both reasoned and reasonable, consists, above all, of a reaction to and suggested redaction of student writing. "There is no true rhetoric," wrote Richard Weaver, "without dialectic." The relationship between teacher-reader and student-writer must be corresponsive. And teacher-reader response—questioning, challenging, restraining, kindling—is ultimately successful only to the extent that the student becomes his *own* critic, carrying on the dialog within himself before, during, and after writing. When this happens, the evaluative comment has become what it should be—a veritable heuristic.

18

The Teacherless Writing Class

Peter Elbow

I have been speaking till now as though writing were a transaction entirely with yourself. It *is* a transaction with yourself—lonely and frustrating—and I have wanted, in fact, to increase that transaction: help you do *more* business with yourself. But writing is also a transaction with other people. Writing is not just getting things down on paper, it is getting things inside someone else's head. If you wish to improve your writing you must also learn to do more business with other people. That is the goal of the teacherless writing class.

Imagine you are blind and deaf. You want to speak better. But you are in perpetual darkness and silence. You send out words as best you can but no words come back. You get a few clues about your speaking: perhaps you asked for something and didn't get it; or you got the wrong thing. You know you did something wrong. What you aren't getting is the main thing that helps people speak better: direct feedback to your speech—a directly perceived sense of how different people react to the sounds you make.

This is an image of what it is like when you try to improve your writing all by yourself. You simply don't know what your words make happen in readers. Perhaps you are even taking a writing course and a teacher tells you what he thinks the weak and strong points were and suggests things you should try for. But you usually get little sense of what the words actually did to him—how he *perceived* and *experienced* them. Besides, he's only one person and not very typical of other readers either. Writing is a string you send out to connect yourself with other consciousnesses, but usually you never have the opportunity to feel anything at the other end. How can you tell whether you've got a fish if the line always feels slack?

The teacherless writing class tries to remedy this situation. It tries to take you out of darkness and silence. It is a class of seven to twelve people. It meets at least once a week. Everyone reads everyone else's writing. Everyone tries to give each writer a sense of how his words were experienced. The goal is for the writer to come as close as possible to being able to see and experience his own words *through* seven or more people. That's all.

To improve your writing you don't need advice about what changes to make; you don't need theories of what is good and bad writing. You need movies of people's minds while they read your words. But you need this for a sustained period of time—at least two or three months. And you need to get the experience of not just a couple of people but of at least six or seven. And you need to keep getting it from the *same* people so that they get better at transmitting their experience and you get better at hearing them. And you must write something *every* week. Even if you are very busy, even if you have nothing to write about, and even if you are very blocked, you must write something and try to experience it through their eyes. Of course it may not be good; you may not be satisfied with it. But if you only learn how people perceive and experience words you are satisfied with, you are missing a crucial area of learning. You often learn the most from reactions to words that you loathe. Do you want to learn how to write or protect your feelings?

In the following pages I try to help you set up and use a teacherless writing class. If you are ever confused, remember that everything is designed to serve only one utterly simple goal: the writer should learn how his words were *actually* experienced by these particular readers.

Setting Up the Class

You Need a Committed Group of People

For a successful class you need the same people writing and taking part every week. People need time to get better at giving reactions and hearing them. Learning to make use of a teacherless class is a struggle. It's too easy to avoid the struggle by letting the class peter out. People have to know the others will be there.

The best solution is to have a few trial classes for people to explore the class. Keep having trial classes and bringing in more people until you finally get at least seven people who will make an explicit commitment for the next ten weeks. Don't start the real class till you have those seven. And make sure everyone has explicitly stated his commitment. It's only ten weeks, but that period is crucial.

You may want to restrict the class to the committed, or else invite in others who are not sure they can come consistently. Two warnings, though: avoid more than twelve in one class; and avoid having people there who haven't put in a piece of writing themselves.

What Kind of People?

There are obvious advantages to having friends, colleagues, or people who have a lot in common. If all are working on the same kind of writing, this helps everyone understand each other better.

But I always stick up for the advantages of diversity: different kinds of people working on different kinds of writing. It can make some strain. But the feedback is better. The poet needs the experience of the businessman reading his poem just as the businessman needs the experience of the poet reading his committee report. If each thinks the other's writing has no meaning or no value this is an advantage rather than a disadvantage. Each needs to experience what it was like for the other to find the writing worthless, and where the other sees glimmers. A poet needs the experiences of other poets, but if that's all he gets the range of reactions is crucially restricted: poets are liable to react too exclusively in terms of the tradition—how it follows some poems and departs from others. Whenever people work in only one genre, they gradually become blind to certain excrescences.

What to Write?

The main thing is that it doesn't matter so long as you write something. Treat the rigid requirement as a blessing. Since you must crank out something every week, expect some of it to be terrible. You can't improve your writing unless you put out words differently from the way you put them out now, and find out how these new kinds of writing are experienced. You can't try out new ways of generating words unless many of them feel embarrassing, terrible, or frightening. But you will be surprised in two ways. Some passages you hate you'll discover to be good. And some of the reactions which most improve your writing are brought on by terrible writing—writing you wouldn't have shown to someone if you'd had more time to rewrite.

Use whatever procedure you think best for deciding what to write. Write the same kind of thing over and over again—even the same piece over and over again if you wish. Or try out wildly different things. There is no best or right way. If you have the desire to write, there is probably some particular kind of writing you dream of doing. Do it. Or if there's something different you feel you should work on first, follow your own advice.

If you continually have trouble thinking of something to write, you should probably begin to suspect that some part of you is trying to undermine your efforts at writing. But don't spend so much time psyching yourself out that you don't get writing done.

If you are stuck for things to write, here are some suggestions.

Ten-minute writing exercises are probably the best way out of this problem.

Put words on paper in order to make something observable happen. This gives you a down-to-earth, concrete way of deciding whether the words worked. For example, write a letter asking for a refund on something; a letter to be published in a newspaper; something funny enough to make someone actually laugh out loud; a letter that will get someone to go out on a date with you; a journal entry that actually takes you out of one mood and puts you in another. Try to stop thinking about whether the writing is good or bad, right or wrong: ask whether it *worked* or *didn't work*.

Hand in writing you need for some other purpose, such as for a course or a job. Use it in class first so you can improve it on the basis of reactions. (Watch out here that they concentrate on telling you how they experienced it and not try to tell you how to fix it. You can decide later how to fix it if they'll give you their perceptions.)

Describe a person, place, or incident that means a lot to you.

Describe such a person, place, or incident but from an unfamiliar angle: for example, describe the place as though you were blind and could only know it through your other senses; describe the person as though you had only met him once or as though it were he describing himself; describe the incident as though it had never happened and you were only imagining it.

Describe something while you are in a definite mood. Or pretend to be in that mood describing it. Or write in a particular mood. Don't mention the mood in the writing and get readers to tell you what mood comes through.

Write something in the voice of someone you know. Don't so much try to think about his voice or the way he speaks or writes: just try to be *in* his head and speak onto the paper. Don't tell readers who it is. Get them to describe the speaker they hear.

Write a conversation or a dialogue between two or three people. Again, try to write from within the voices and get the readers to tell you about the voices they hear.

Write about a character or object in a story, movie, or photograph.

Write an important letter. The classic one is a letter of blame to your own parents. Or a letter of appreciation.

Define something that is important to you but difficult to define. Suggestions: how is it different from things that are similar; what is it a subset or subdivision of; what are subsets or subdivisions of it.

Tell a belief or conviction of yours in such a way as to make the reader believe that you really do believe it. (This is what is involved in applying to a draft board for conscientious objector status.) This is not the same as trying to make *him* believe it.

Describe a belief or develop an argument in order to convince someone who disagrees. Keep in mind that this is often impossible.

Write a poem. Suggestions: find one you like and rewrite it, translate it, or write one just like it; write the poem as it would be if it were about a different topic or expressing a different feeling; write another poem this poet would write; write the poem this poet would write if he were you; write the words or lyrics that go with a piece of music; write a love poem.

Should You Hand Out Copies or Read Your Writing Out Loud?

There are advantages both ways. Giving out copies saves class time: silent reading is quicker, you can stop and think, go back, read more carefully, and if it is a long piece of writing, people can take it home with them and read it there. This procedure may be more possible than you think. Many photocopying processes are cheap; people can easily write or type onto ditto or mimeo masters; it is often possible for members to leave a single copy of their piece where everyone else can read it carefully before class.

But reading out loud is good too. When you read your writing out loud, you often see things in it that you don't see any other way. Hearing your own words out loud gives you the vicarious experience of being someone else. Reading your words out loud stresses what is most important: writing is really a voice spread out over time, not marks spread out in space. The audience can't experience them all at once as they can a picture; they can only hear one instant at a time as with music. And there must be a voice in it.

Reading out loud also gives you a better idea of the effect of your words on an audience: they cannot go back to try to make sure their reactions are more "careful," "correct," or "objective." For example, someone may say "there were no details" when in fact there were quite a few, or "it doesn't have any organization so I felt lost," when in fact you had a careful structure. But this is good. You need to learn that the details or the structure didn't work for that reader. It's more important to learn what actually got through to a real reader than what might get through to an ideal reader. When a listener misinterprets something which he might have gotten right if he'd had a copy in his hands, his mistake is probably evidence of a real undertow in the writing. That undertow operates even on readers who have the paper in their hands and can read more carefully, but they often don't feel the undertow so they make you pay for it in more mysterious ways: more vague dissatisfactions and misinterpretations.

The nervousness you feel at reading out loud is part of your problem in writing. Even if you don't feel it *as you write*, that only means you've separated your experience of audience from your experience of writing. The fear of the audience is still affecting you somehow: it may be tying your tongue and clouding your mind when you sit down to write; or it may be closing off certain kinds of writing to you. Reading out loud brings the sense of audience back into your act of writing. This is a great source of power. Getting a sense of audience isn't just practice in feeling scared about how they might react. It also means learning how they *do* react. Most people are liberated by finally getting the reactions they fear most—usually extreme criticism or extreme praise. They discover the world doesn't fall apart.

When you read something out loud in class, however, always read it twice and allow at least a minute of silence after each reading for impressions to come clearer in your listeners.

Class Time

Find a regular time and stick to it. Otherwise you are asking for trouble.

As to how much time, fifteen to twenty minutes is sufficient for seven people to try to tell a writer how each of them perceived and experienced a short piece of writing. This means a class of eight people should get along with two to two-and-a-half hours a week. More time may be interesting and useful if people can spare it. But the essential process in this sort of class is to get what you can and then move on. You can never finish giving or getting the experience of a set of words. Instead of investing more and more minutes on one particular piece of writing, invest more and more weeks so everyone can begin to get good at this process. Keep the long haul in mind. Don't let the class take up so much time that people find it painful to keep coming. Besides, you usually can not make a significant improvement in your writing in less than two or three months no matter what kind of learning process you use. Learning to write is an exercise in slow, underground learning.

A Chairman

A chairman or leader can make things run more smoothly, keep an eye on the clock so that everyone's writing gets its fair share of time, help people overcome unproductive habits like talking too much or too little, and generally keep an eye out. This can make people feel more comfortable.

But it's possible to get along without a chairman too. It puts more of a burden on everyone, but it can also encourage everyone to take more responsibility for how the class goes. Whatever your decision, build in a procedure for periodic re-decision about whether to have one or who it should be.

Reactions to the Class Itself

Devote the last five minutes of each class to the class itself as though it were a piece of writing. How do the members perceive and experience that class meeting? The reactions can be communicated by speaking, or you can all do a five-minute freewriting exercise and pass them around. Don't think of this as a time for actually solving dissatisfactions. The same learning principles apply here as to writing: what is valuable is shared perception and experience, not advice about how to fix things. Problems will be solved gradually this way, but better.

Giving Movies of Your Mind

As a reader giving your reactions, keep in mind that you are not answering a timeless, theoretical question about the objective qualities of those words on that page. You are answering a time-bound, subjective but *factual* question: what happened in *you* when you read the words *this time*.

Pointing

Start by simply pointing to the words and phrases which most successfully penetrated your skull: perhaps they seemed loud or full of voice; or they seemed to have a lot of energy; or they somehow rang true; or they carried special conviction.

Any kind of getting through. If I have the piece of writing in my hand, I tend to put a line under such words and phrases (or longer passages) as I read. Later when telling my reactions, I can try to say which kind of getting through it was if I happen to remember. If I am listening to the piece read out loud, I simply wait till the end and see which words or phrases stick in my mind. I may jot them down as they come to me in the moments of silence after the readings.

Point also to any words or phrases which strike you as particularly weak or empty. Somehow they ring false, hollow, plastic. They bounced ineffectually off your skull. (I use a wavy line for these when I read with a pencil.)

Summarizing

Next summarize the writing:

a) First tell very quickly what you found to be the main points, main feelings, or centers of gravity. Just sort of say what comes to mind for fifteen seconds, for example, "Let's see, very sad; the death seemed to be the main event; um . . . but the joke she told was very prominent; lots of clothes."

b) Then summarize it into a single sentence.

c) Then choose *one word* from the writing which best summarizes it.

d) Then choose a word that isn't in the writing to summarize it.

Do this informally. Don't plan or think too much about it. The point is to show the writer what things he made stand out most in your head, what shape the thing takes in your consciousness. This isn't a test to see whether you got the words right. It's a test to see whether the words got you right. Be sure to use different language from the language of the writing. This insures that he is getting it filtered through your perception and experience—not just parroted. Also, try this test a week later: tell someone what you remember of his last week's piece.

Pointing and summarizing are not only the simplest ways to communicate your perception, but they are the most foolproof and the most useful. Always start with pointing and summarizing. If you want to play it safe and make sure your class is successful, or if you are terribly short of class time, or if your class is coming apart, try skipping all the following ways of giving feedback.

Telling

Simply tell the writer everything that happened to you as you tried to read his words carefully. It's usually easiest to tell it in the form of a story: first this happened, then this happened, then this happened, and so on. Here are two examples of telling (one concerning a story, the other a poem) from tape recordings of actual classes:

> I felt confused about the man in the gray suit and the men gathered around you. I suppose they're cops, and the escorts. Because I had first thought the gray suit was a cop, but then I thought he was a dignified person who got arrested. I was uncertain about it. And then you talked about the men gathered around at one point—fairly early. I felt like they were cops, and I wanted you to contrast them to the fantasies. There was one point where you talked about—I think you were going down the stairs—and I felt like that whole part with the father of the bride and the gown was like the flash a person has, supposedly, when he's going to drown and his whole life flows before him. I thought it was like an initiation of a girl—or a woman, particularly—out of her whole parental, social, ball-gown past into this new thing. And I was, I just, I was *surprised*. I didn't expect you to describe things that way. I was really happy. Then for some reason I felt like when you talked about the men who were gathered around—I felt like they were cops—and if I heard it again I might feel like I didn't need to have you say it, but at the time, as you said it, I wanted them to be blue suited or something contrasting. Perhaps that wouldn't be necessary for some other reader.
>
> I had a very sort of happy feeling when you went to drinking songs. But it felt like the whole history of someone's life from being a young bride to becoming an old fishwife. I felt like it was a social comment in a way. One gets brought up and goes from the ideal fantasies to being fat and drinking companion in pubs. And I was just very happy at that change in age. It seemed like the whole thing was—if it were a movie it would be going around like this—but the history of a whole person in a way retold in capsule form.

> I didn't get into it till the middle section with the "one-two"s. I think I'd read down through the first two stanzas and didn't, um, not very much happened. In fact I think I felt it a little bit purple, a little bit corny, a little bit saying to myself "well he's having those nice thoughts, these nice words, but I can't go along, I'm not there." But I think even on first reading, when I got to the "one-two" business, I immediately picked up. Those words somehow made me pay attention. They became quite loud, there was a lot of—they really got me. I really listened to it as an interrogation. But for me it wasn't—as Mary said a minute ago—a standing back from emotions and being logical. It's not that it was so logical. It was like an interrogation, sort of. Like putting your feelings into this funny, numerical, pseudo-logical form. But it's quite hammering. I wrote down "the language is very real." Somehow it's moving. I don't take it as logic. I take it as some very insistent hammering thing.
>
> And from then on I liked it. As I read down to the end I liked it fine. And when I got to the second page, I didn't even recognize that it was the same as the first page. I was starting to write down "I like this one much better," and

when I went back to the first page to compare, I found the two were the same thing. In other words, after the "one-two"s, this thing really worked for me, and I got into it; those words got into my head; although "water brothers for-ever"—I remain slightly unclear about what to do with that line although it's sort of evocative.

And then the last three lines. Different handwriting, different mode. Again it was a kind of hammering: "Do you *understand*." I didn't take it as something you were saying to a girl, I took it as something you were saying to yourself, or to the reader, or something. Sort of a kind of screaming. But screaming that works, not just screaming that's just sort of no good.

So then I went back. And when I saw that the first stanza was the same as the last stanza, I tried to figure out why I didn't like it so much the first time. And it was only then that I discovered that you had this great little device in the second stanza—repeating the first stanza with a new line interspersed every other line. I like that as an idea, but as far as the words go, they didn't work on me. I mean, once I perceived that pattern, I felt a kind of pleasure out of the pattern. I think patterns like that are fun. But I still couldn't like it as words. In particular the line "special cuz its hers": I didn't like it. I think part of it is that the abbreviation of 'because' into 'cuz' strikes me as corny and bothers me. It seems trivial but it's true. I don't know, I just didn't like it. "Seek and ye shall find" was maybe the one weak thing I didn't like in the "one-two" part. I ended up taking the whole thing very seriously as a poem.

The important thing in telling is not to get too far away from talking about the actual writing; people sometimes waste time talking only about themselves. But on the other hand, don't drift too far away from talking about yourself either, or else you are acting as though you are a perfectly objective, selfless critic.

To help you in telling, pretend that there is a whole set of instruments you have hooked up to yourself which record everything that occurs in you: not just pulse, blood pressure, EEG, and so on, but also ones which tell every image, feeling, thought, and word that happens in you. Pretend you have hooked them all up and now you are just reading off the print-out from the machines.

Showing

When you read something, you have *some* perceptions and reactions which you are not fully aware of and thus cannot "tell." Perhaps they are very faint, perhaps you do not have satisfactory language for them, or perhaps for some other reason you remain unconscious of them. But though you cannot tell these perceptions and reactions, you can *show* them if you are willing to use some of the metaphorical exercises listed below. These may seem strange and difficult at first, but if you use them consistently you will learn to tap knowledge which you have but which is usually unavailable to you.

1. Talk about the writing as though you were describing *voices:* for example, shouting, whining, whispering, lecturing sternly, droning, speaking abstractedly, and so forth. Try to apply such words not only to the whole thing but to different parts.

2. Talk about the writing as though you were talking about *weather:* for example, foggy, sunny, gusty, drizzling, cold, clear, crisp, muggy, and so forth. Not just to the whole thing but to different parts.

3. Talk about the writing as though you were talking about *motion* or *loco-motion:* for example, as marching, climbing, crawling, rolling along, tip-toeing, strolling, sprinting, and so forth.

4. *Clothing:* for example, jacket and tie, dungarees, dusty and sweaty shirt, miniskirt, hair all slicked down, etc.

5. *Terrain:* for example, hilly, desert, soft and grassy, forested, jungle, clearing in a forest, etc.

6. *Color:* what color is the whole? the parts?

7. *Shape.*

8. *Animals.*

9. *Vegetables.*

10. Musical instruments.

11. It is a *body:* what kind of body; which parts are feet, hands, heart, head, hair, etc.

12. Think of the piece of writing as having magically evolved out of a different piece of writing; and it will eventually evolve into some other piece of writing that again is different. Tell where it came from; where it is going.

13. Describe what you think was the writer's intention with this piece of writing. Then think of some crazy intention you think he might have had.

14. Assume that the writer wrote this *instead of* something very different that was really on his mind. Guess or fantasize what you think was really on his mind.

15. Assume that soon before he wrote this he did something very important or something very important happened to him—something that is not obvious from the writing. Say what you think it was.

16. Pretend this was written by someone you have never seen. Guess or fantasize what he or she is like.

17. The writing is a lump of workable clay. Tell what you would do with that clay.

18. Pretend to be someone else—someone who would have a very different response to the writing from what you had. Give this other person's perception and experience of the writing.

19. Quickly make the picture or doodle the writing inspires in you; pretend that the writing was received only by your arm with its pencil: now let them move.

20. Make the sound the writing inspires. Or imitate the sound of the writing. Different sounds for different parts.

21. Jabber it, that is, make the sound you would hear if someone was giving a somewhat exaggerated reading of it in the next room—in a language you had never heard (also compress it into 30 seconds or so).

22. Let your whole body make the movements inspired by the writing or different parts of it. Perhaps combine sounds and movements.

23. Do a ten-minute writing exercise on the writing and give it to the writer.

24. Meditate on the writing and try to tell him about what happened. Don't think about his writing. Try, even, to make your mind empty, but at the same time fully open to the writing. It's as though you don't chew and don't taste—just swallow it whole and noiselessly.

These showing procedures are not much use until you get over being afraid of them and unless you give two or three at a time. Therefore, I make it a rule that for your first four classes you make at least a couple of these oblique, metaphorical statements on each piece of writing. It may well feel strange and uncomfortable at first. Indeed, the reason I make this an explicit demand is that I have discovered that people in some trial teacherless classes were too timid to use them. In other classes where people did use them, almost everyone came to enjoy them and find them useful.

Don't struggle with them. Try to let the words just come. Say the thing that comes to mind even if it doesn't make any sense. And for the first few weeks, don't expect satisfactory results.

There's an easy way to think of the relation between telling and showing. Telling is like looking inside yourself to see what you can report. Showing is like installing a window in the top of your head and then taking a bow so the writer can see for himself. There's no need to try to remember what was happening as you read. Just bow. Showing conveys more information but in a more mixed and ambiguous form.

Further Advice to Readers

Make Sure You've Had a Good Chance to Read the Writing

Otherwise don't even start giving any reactions. If you read it silently in class, make sure you've had enough time to read it twice thoughtfully with a bit of time after each reading to let the words sink in and your impressions settle. *Don't let yourself be hurried.* If the writer reads it out loud, make sure he reads it twice and gives at least a whole minute of silence after each reading. And stop him whenever he reads too quickly or softly. A nervous writer may instinctively try to read it so no one can hear. Don't let him.

One Reader at a Time or All at Once?

There is a lot to be said for each reader giving full movies of his mind—pointing, summarizing, telling, and showing—before any other reader starts in. This gives the writer not just a big mixed pile of reactions but rather a sense of each reader's experience as a whole. But on the other hand, sometimes it is easier for readers, especially in the first few weeks, if they can throw out reactions helter-skelter all together. Or you might do all the pointings, then all the summarizings, and so forth. There is no right way. Keep trying different ways to find what works best for your class.

As long as you are careful to tell your original reaction, it is also good to tell later reactions that may be different. Someone else's report may remind you of a perception you were having too but didn't realize it. Report it briefly even if it's the same as his. The writer needs to know whether a reaction is common or rare. Also someone may convey a perception or experience *different* from yours, but once you hear it you start to share it very strongly. It may blot out or supersede yours. This is also important to tell.

Never Quarrel with Someone Else's Reaction

If someone reports something that seems crazy, listen to him openly. Try to have his experience. Maybe what you see is truly there and he's blind. But maybe what he sees is there too. Even if it contradicts what you see. It is common for words to carry contradictory meanings and effects. What he sees may not be the main thing in the words, but because of his particular mood, temperament, or experience, it drowns out for him what you are seeing. Your position may blind you to what he sees. Your only chance of trying to sharpen your eyesight is to take seriously his seeming craziness and try to see what he sees. This may similarly encourage *him* to try to share what you see and thereby help make him a better reader too.

Give Specific Reactions to Specific Parts

Not just general reactions to the whole thing. You may have to make a special effort to do this. If you have trouble, try to think back and simply notice which particular passages you remember most. Point them out. Try to tell why you remember them, why they stick out, how you perceive and experience them. Do showing exercises on them. When you tell what happened—for example, "first this happened, then that happened"—try to point to specific places in the writing.

No Kind of Reaction Is Wrong

Insufficient, perhaps, but not wrong. There are certain kinds of reaction that don't *in themselves* help the writer much. But they are helpful if seen as part of the larger picture—part of the whole story of what it was like to be you and read his words carefully. So never struggle to *omit* any kind of response; struggle to include more. If it happened, tell it. Here are some kinds of reactions that some class members thought they were supposed to leave out:

1. Some classes got the impression from earlier drafts of this material that it was their business to talk about "how a person wrote something" but not "what he wrote." Not at all. The job is to find out what his words do to real people: *what* he is saying all mixed in with how he is saying it. If you want to quarrel with something the writer says, tell him (but don't go on to *have* the quarrel with him). There's no need to unscramble "style" and "content." Just tell what happened.

2. Odd reactions. Don't try to filter out the nutty parts and give only the "sensible" reactions. In fact it helps if you slightly exaggerate the craziness. It helps the writer break his habit of listening to feedback as though he were listening to his teacher. It makes him automatically realize he's not listening to even-handed judgments, conclusions, and advice—just one unique person's perceptions and experience. And it automatically helps you realize you are not trying to be God or a more-competent-than-everyone-else critic—just one person giving a slant that probably no one else could give. Your odd reactions will also help other readers just be themselves.

3. Advice. It's not valuable *as advice*, but it's valuable as part of the picture of how you experienced his words. Don't look for advice or try to think it up, but if the interaction between you and his words produces the desire to give advice, that's something the writer should know about. Sometimes a piece of writing makes everyone want to give advice; whereas another piece of writing, though it's much less competent, doesn't inspire any advice at all. These are facts the writer needs to know.

   Let your advice lead you to the perception or experience behind it. I often find that a desire to advise some change in something I'm reading is my only clue that I'm experiencing those words in a certain way. If I ask myself *why* I want to make the change, I can lead myself back to an interesting and useful perception of the words.

4. Evaluation. Like advice, evaluation in itself has no value. Don't try to figure out an evaluation, but on the other hand don't waste any energy trying to stop yourself. Give it and make it lead you to the perception and experience behind it. For example a teacher after three days of paper-grading sometimes reaches the point where his only response to a paper is to know what grade he wants to give it. This doesn't mean (necessarily) that there aren't rich perceptions tucked away behind that B minus. If such a teacher

in such a state found himself in the teacherless writing class, he ought to start with the B minus and try to follow that string to find all the latent reactions behind it. What he should not do is to hide behind his evaluation and not tell his real experience.

Some people can't read without making judgments, other people seldom make any. The writer should get the feel of both kinds of reader. Even more interestingly, some pieces of writing somehow cry out for judgments—everyone's reaction is loud with them; whereas other pieces get themselves reacted to at great length with no evaluative talk at all.

One exception. I think it's worth banning negative judgments for the first three or four classes. When people get used to the class they can take the strongest kind of negative judgment in stride and learn from it without sweating it. But at the beginning people can be needlessly shaken. It's easy for four weeks simply to skip talking about what you didn't like.

5. Theories are less valuable than facts. But it's hard to keep the two apart. When you tell the writer what happened when you read his words, you are telling him a fact. If you tell him why it happened—why you were bored here or confused there—you are telling him a theory about how language works or how you work. Your facts are much more trustworthy. It's *not* true that tons of adjectives always make writing boring; it's *not* true that the passive voice is always weak; it's *not* true that abstractions are always vague; it's *not* true that examples always make things clearer. *In writing, anything can do anything.*

If *you* were bored by some adjectives, that's important; if *you* felt some particular passage as weak or vague, that's important; if *you* felt some example as helpful, that's important. Tell these things as happenings not theories. Your judgment about piles of adjectives in general, passive voice in general, abstractions in general, examples in general is not worth much, No one's is.

The trouble is that it is hard to keep theories apart from facts. Not only do some of your best facts only come when you uncork your dubious theories; *all* your facts are probably slightly polluted by your theories. If you think flowery writing is weak in general, you probably fool yourself into experiencing all flowery writing as weaker than you otherwise would. So you might as well let your theories show—so the writer can see how to distrust you. Here again, the moral is the same; your theories are not valuable in themselves, but they help give the writer a better sense of what it was like to be you as you read his words.

6. Seemingly irrelevant reactions. For example: "As I read it, all I could think about was what I'm going to do tomorrow" (or what I did yesterday, or how hot it is in here, or the fact that I'm bored by that subject). You might say these are not perceptions of the words at all but rather failures

to perceive them. Yet it is crucial to give this sort of reaction. The main thing is that these responses occurred when you read the words and your job is to tell what happened. Perhaps it's your "fault" that you didn't perceive them more, that you daydreamed. Perhaps you should try harder. But there's no way of figuring out whose fault it is. The main fact is that he put words on paper that were supposed to get into your head and they did not. Different readers often daydream at the same points in the writing—a clue that something funny is probably going on there.

There may be many such irrelevant reactions at the beginning of this kind of class. People are not used to giving reactions; they are self-conscious about it; they feel awkward trying to listen to something read out loud. Nevertheless, if it happened, tell it. This will free you to notice other perceptions that were hidden behind the irrelevant one.

But supposedly irrelevant reactions are not just good for their side-effects. In the majority of cases they are good feedback in themselves. *The basic fact about most verbal utterance is that it doesn't get through.* The main story of words interacting with people is the story of ideas and experiences falling useless on the ground or only faintly heard through the fog; people pretending they heard something when really they only saw someone's mouth moving and guessed what he was saying from the circumstances and the expression on his face. I've discovered that many classes try to ignore this primal fact. Readers try to tell the writer what they perceive or experience, but they are fishing and fumbling and making things up. They don't dare tell the most valuable reaction there is: "I didn't really hear a thing you said." It's no fun to get that reaction if you are the writer. But in the end it's a relief to have out on the table what you suspected was true all along.

Though No Reactions Are Wrong, You Still Have to Try to Read Well

The class is not an invitation to be merely lazy, sloppy, passive—a bad reader. In one of the teacherless classes I listened to on tape, one man said of a woman's essay, "I stopped reading after the first paragraph. I said the hell with it. It seemed to me like one of those essays in the *Sunday Times Magazine*. I figure if I want to read one of those things, I'll go read it in the *Sunday Times Magazine*." Now that's a good statement of *what happened* when he read the first paragraph. It's a useful thing to say (though not much fun to hear). He doesn't explain why he is so mad at the piece, but that's all right: it's not his job to psychoanalyze himself or to theorize about how words work. He localized his reaction to the first paragraph. That's good.

The trouble is he didn't read the rest. That's no fair. He should have kept reading. Perhaps his reactions would have changed. But even if they didn't, the perceptions of a hostile reader are useful.

When I took literature courses in college I remember that my main experience in reading was the feeling that I ought to have the right reactions. But I could never figure out what they were. I could scarcely think about what I was reading because I was always worrying about having the wrong reactions. This was no way to be a good reader. I had eventually to learn to be, *in a sense*, more passive and irresponsible—to relax and not worry and let the words do what they want to do. But that doesn't mean I can just sit back and be passive and wait for the words to pick me up and carry me. To be a good reader I must supply great effort, attention, and energy.

Sometimes You May Not Want To

If you sometimes find you simply don't want to give your reactions, and you don't know why but you just start to clam up and have nothing to say, respect these feelings. They are appropriate. To give movies of your mind is an act of extreme generosity, self-abnegation. You are making yourself a meter, a guinea pig, a laboratory. You're letting the writer use you as a tool for his own ends. For example, perhaps you think his piece is much too long and complicated. If, along with this opinion, you give him movies of your mind and tell him all the perceptions and feelings that are involved (that is, where did it start? were you actually perplexed or annoyed or just disapproving? and so on) you are giving him the opportunity to decide that length and complexity are not really the problem at all. By seeing your reactions more fully, he may even decide that he doesn't need to heed them. *And he may be right.* Yet he can't make this decision well unless you give him all your reactions and not just your conclusions. If you had told him *only* your judgment, you would have been invulnerable and he would have had to like it or lump it.

So it's no joke, this kind of feedback. You wouldn't be human if there weren't some occasions when you didn't feel like it. You might as well admit it. Even act on those feelings and don't tell your reactions. Say you are tired of it at the moment, you pass. This is much better than fooling yourself and going on to give responses that are really a smokescreen.

You Are Always Right and Always Wrong

You do your job as reader best in the light of this paradox.

You are always right in that no one is ever in a position to tell you what you perceive and experience. You must have a kind of faith or trust: not that your perception is always accurate, but that the greatest accuracy comes from using it more and listening to it better; and that the most valuable thing you can do for the writer is tell him what you really see and how you really react.

But you are always wrong in that you never see accurately enough, experience fully enough. There are always things in the words you cannot get. You must always put more energy into trying to have other people's perceptions and experiences—trying to make yourself more agile, more flexible, more refined. Don't stubbornly stay locked into your own impressions just because they are yours.

In short, you must be simultaneously sure of yourself and humble. Easier said than done. But it's worth the practice this class provides since it's just what's needed in countless other situations.

Advice to the Writer on Listening

Be Quiet and Listen

For many weeks you may have to bite your tongue. If you talk you'll keep readers from telling you important reactions. Don't give long introductions. In fact, you may learn more if the readers are a little uncertain what the writing is, what it is meant for, who it is aimed at. If they cannot comfortably pigeon-hole it, they may take less for granted and notice more.

You have to keep from making apologies or exlanations, for example, "I just wrote this last night, I didn't have much time and didn't revise it at all"; or "I'm really not satisfied with this"; or "I finally got this the way I want it, but I had to do four drafts." Above all, never say what you want your writing to do, how you want your readers to respond. You'll destroy any chance of getting trustworthy evidence of whether you did it. After you get your audience to tell you how they themselves perceived it, *then* you can ask them how they think some different audience might respond

As they are telling you their experience, you have to guard against being tricked into responding; that is, "What do you mean you were confused about the point of this paragraph? I wrote right in the first sentence that . . ." After the reactions are in, you can explain what you intended or what you think you've put in it. People will ask you questions: "Why did you do such and such?" "What did you mean here?" Don't answer till after you get their reactions, Get them to tell you what perception, feeling, or uncertainty made them ask. Such questions are often a clue to a reaction that the reader is not otherwise conscious of.

Don't Try to Understand What People Tell You

It will be a mess. Contradictory, incomplete, seemingly nonsensical. Just listen and take it all in. If you try to learn by understanding, you will cut yourself out of half the learning. Your organism as a whole is capable of benefitting from much more than you can understand.

But Do Try to Understand HOW They Tell It to You

You can't ask for all the useful information on a silver platter. Notice *how* people tell you about their experience of your words. Sometimes they aren't in a position to say, "Your words made me annoyed at you," but if you only listen you'll see that your words *did* annoy them. Or put them in a good mood. Or made them feel condescending. Or made them feel like not really taking your words seriously. Take it in.

Don't Reject What Readers Tell You

Listen to what they say *as though it were all true*. The way an owl eats a mouse. He takes it all in. He doesn't try to sort out the good parts from the bad. He trusts his organism to make use of what's good and get rid of what isn't. There are various ways in which a reader can be wrong in what he tells you; but still it pays you to accept it all:

1. If he gives you mere evaluations, advice about changes to make, or theories about writing, these are of no value to you in themselves. But don't try to stop him. It will just hang him up and prevent him from going on to tell you more about how he perceived and experienced your words. And besides, if you listen sensitively, you can feel *behind* his evaluation, advice, and theory what the rest of his reactions were like and what it was like to be him reading your words.

2. A reader *can* be mistaken about his own reactions. For example, someone can think he scorns a piece of writing or is bored by it or doesn't understand it when really he is threatened by it but won't let himself feel threatened. You can't eliminate this kind of error, only minimize it. The way to minimize it is to be as open and accepting a listener as possible in order to help the person hear and accept his real reactions.

3. If a reader fails to see or experience something that you are almost certain is in there, in this respect he is wrong. He is blind. He couldn't see something right there in front of his face. But don't make the mistake of concluding that he's therefore wrong about what he says he *does* see. Words usually contain many effects and even contrary meanings. The usefulness of the class is in bringing to light the whole range of possible effects and meanings in this set of words. There may be something very faintly in the words which this reader's situation makes him experience as dominant, but which none of the other readers can see. Of course it may *not* be there. But your only chance of benefiting is to take it in without trying to distinguish the wrong parts.

    In fact you should practice a kind of mystical discipline: assume the perceptions or experiences that seem most crazy are really most useful. Those perceptions you need most—that is, those you are least capable of having yourself because of your particular point of view—will naturally seem most crazy to you.

Don't Stop Them from Giving You Reactions

If you are not learning much about how they really reacted it is probably your fault. Not theirs. If you are too afraid of hearing how they really experience your words, that fear will come across and they will find some way of not telling you. Also if you don't really listen or take them seriously, that will get across and they will withhold reactions. If you oversimplify and pigeon-hole everybody—saying to yourself, "this is the grammar nut, this is the sentimental one, this is the overly logical one"—this too is a way of not really listening to them: defending yourself against really having their experience. They will feel it and hold back.

But Don't Be Tyrannized by What They Say

You've got to listen openly and take it in, but not be paralyzed or made helpless by it, Otherwise you will *scare* them into holding back. There's a kind of tacit agreement in any good feedback situation: they agree to transmit to you everything that happened *only if* they can see you won't be bamboozled by it.

Suppose they all agree that something you wrote is profoundly lousy. Be clear what that means. It means it didn't work for them. They couldn't get to it or it couldn't get to them. It *doesn't* necessarily mean it's lousy. It might be good. Some of the greatest pieces of writing are hated by most people. Don't look to your readers to find out whether your words are any good. Look to them to find out about what your words make happen in real consciousnesses. The better you get at feeling how your words affect consciousnesses, the better you will be at deciding *for yourself* whether your words are any good.

Suppose some readers think your writing is too sentimental (or too unclear, too intellectual, too ordinary, too whatever). What does this mean? It probably means they were bothered by the sentimentality. But you can bet they sometimes love things that are twice as sentimental (or unclear, etc.) The complaint might disappear entirely if you made some *other* change—perhaps something quite small that has nothing to do with sentimentality. That is why it is no use trying to figure it all out. Just take it all in. Assume that when you write something else—or rewrite this piece—your *own* choices about how to write it will organically benefit from hearing what they are now saying.

Remember who has what job. It's their job to give you their experience. It's your job to decide what to do next. If you start putting decision-making power into their hands, you push yourself out of the picture.

It's not their job to decide what's in your head or even on the page— merely what got into their heads. It's not their job to be fair. It's not their job to cushion you from harsh or incorrect perceptions. If they try to do that, they cannot do their main job of giving you their experience. It's not their job to play teacher or God and try to tell you what the words *might* do if this or that were different. If they get into the business of trying to tell you what other words *might* do, they'll lose their capacity to tell you what these words *did* do. (This is how teachers get into trouble.)

Ask for what you want, but don't play teacher with them. If there's some particular kind of feedback you find helpful, perhaps certain kinds of oblique, metaphorical statements from the "showing" list, ask them. Or ask them, if you wish, for their experience of some particular passage or aspect of your writing. Ask in such a way that they can decline.

But you will defeat yourself if you try to play teacher: asking them leading questions, helping them along, "conducting" them. If someone hasn't managed to give you movies of his mind, tell him. But don't try to tell him how to fix the situation. That's his job. He's the one who can find the best solution even though it might take a number of weeks.

You Are Always Right and Always Wrong

You, as writer, as well as reader, benefit most if you listen in the spirit of this paradox.

You are always right in that your decision about the writing is always final. They give you their experience, you decide what to do about it. You are in charge. You are the only one making decisions.

But you are always wrong in that you can never quarrel with their experience—never quarrel even with their report of their experience. And you must assume that you are never good enough at sharing their perception—shedding your blinders, getting into their shoes.

Like the reader, you must be simultaneously sure of yourself and humble.

The Class Process

I've been developing this kind of class over a long period; trying things out in my own classes; and listening to tapes of experimental teacherless classes which used earlier version of this material. Some classes went well, some adequately, and some pooped out.

Take what follows not as a satisfactory or sufficient map of the path ahead but rather as my attempt to tell you everything I know. You will still feel lost some of the time. It is how I often continue to feel when I participate in this kind of class.

Supplying the Ingredients

If you do the following things, you will prevent what I see as the most frequent problems:

Get a commitment from at least seven people for a ten-week stretch

Make sure everyone writes something every week

Make sure everything read out loud is read twice and given a minute's silence after each reading

Give pointing and summarizing responses to every piece of writing

Make sure everyone, for his first four classes, uses two showing exercises for transmitting his reactions

Do three ten-minute writing exercises each week

Use the last five minutes of each class for reactions to the class itself

Motivation

The main thing this class demands is that you really want to work on your writing. In a regular class you can play this kind of game with the teacher: "Please, teacher, I want to make my writing better. But I don't want to work. Please make me *want* to work. Or if you can't do that, at least *make* me work and let me resent you for it." People who are playing games with themselves may come to exploratory meetings but they won't commit themselves for ten weeks if you make the commitment clear. Soon you have a group of people who really mean business. It's a pleasure.

Down to Business

Business is a useful concept here. This class reminds some people of an encounter group because it makes such central use of the reactions of the members. But an encounter group has no business or agenda: whatever comes up in business; there is no such thing as wasting time. That's not true in the teacherless writing class. Here there is definite business. Each piece of writing must get reactions. The job to be done gives a kind of structure and solidity.

Patience

Though you have to want results and mean business, you can't be in a hurry. Improving your writing is necessarily gradual and erratic. The teacherless class isn't necessarily slower than a regular class but it usually *seems* slower. A teacher can give you something to do and someone to trust while waiting for the slow underground learning to take place. For example, he might tell you to stop using so many adjectives and long sentences, to start using more concrete details, and to give more unity to your paragraphs. Here's something to think about, something to try to do. In a sense it is good advice. You may even make progress toward these goals. By the fifth week you might be able to say to yourself, "Yes, I guess my writing isn't perfect yet, but at least I've gotten rid of some of the adjectives and long sentences, put in some concrete details and paragraph unity." This makes *everybody* feel much better. The trouble is your writing may actually be no better. In a sense worse. True, It's closer to someone's *model* of good

writing, but very likely it is no better at actually putting things inside real readers. Besides, these "improvements" probably stop when the course is over.[1] The
real process by which you generate words is probably unchanged. Writing is
probably harder, more painful and more confusing because you're now trying to
do certain new things yet your word-production process is unchanged. It's no
accident that many people stop writing when they start being taught how to write
better.

It takes a long time for the organism to learn new ways of generating
words—better ways to make words actually get through to other people. You
must be ready for long dry spells, setbacks, and spurts forward when you least
expect them. But remember what you often get from a teacher. He spurs and
encourages you: "Don't give up; I know you are discouraged, but keep it up,
things are going fine." He is someone to trust. And in some learning situations
he can force you to keep going. Learn here to get this support and encouragement—coercion if needs be—from yourself and from the others. It's harder, but
when you do it, there is great excitement because you have tapped a new energy
source that is extremely powerful and effective.

And while you are working at it, learn to have fun. Enjoy getting to
know the others well. Trying to see through their eyes is a good way. Enjoy,
almost as a game, the feedback process. Think of the class as a group of
amateur musicians who get together once a week to play for each other's
enjoyment.

A Different Style of Interaction

This class asks you to function with others in a way you are probably not used
to. Unless you can change a few crucial gears, the class will fold. I've seen it
happen in a number of experimental teacherless classes I've monitored. I can
specify better now what those gears are that you need to change.

In a sense it is simply a matter of not arguing. You can argue someone
out of an incorrect intellectual position (sometimes). But you can't argue
someone out of an incorrect perception or experience. He only discards one
when he already has another to replace it with. And the new one must be one
he is already having and believing, not one being rammed down his throat by
someone else. In short, if you want to improve someone's perception or
experience, you can't do it by arguing. The best you can do is persuade him
to share yours. The only way to do this, almost invariably, is to go over and
share his.

But there's something more central to focus on than arguing. It is the
cause of arguing: the impulse to *settle* things, *decide* things. When we are in
any class or meeting we tend to feel that the goal is to achieve agreement. We

1. This is one of the findings in *Themes, Theories, and Therapy,* the Report of the Dartmouth
Study of Student Writing, Albert Kitzhaber, McGraw Hill, 1963.

habitually feel frustrated if we have a discussion with great difference of opinion but no final agreement.

The teacherless class asks you to break out of this habit. It brings out the *maximum* differences but it asks you not to fight things out or try to settle on the truth. Only by inhibiting the compulsive urge to settle things can you bring out the maximum differences. The striking thing about most classes, meetings, and discussions—especially in comparison to a functioning teacherless class—is that there is usually such a *poverty* of difference, a poverty of disagreement. Who wants to ruffle things up when it is all for the purpose of having things smoothed down again in exactly fifty minutes? Who wants to play thesis or antithesis to someone's planned synthesis? And even when there is a heated fight, it is usually a fight between two polarized, narrow possibilities. A whole host of interesting points of view have never been raised because there is such an atmosphere of needing to settle things. It's only by tolerating *a lot* of ambiguity for a long time, by living with *a lot* of contradiction, and inhibiting the need to settle things too soon that you can get your hands on a decent array of data.

So keep two danger signals in mind: the two directions a class is apt to slide in when too many people can't handle their urge always to settle things.

1. *People persist in arguing.* They get mad and waste a lot of time trying to decide what is true. Or else they force themselves to stop overt arguments, but you can feel them still doing it underground. In their heads they're saying, "How can that idiot be so wrong, so blind? What's the matter with him? How come he doesn't admit he's wrong and agree with what I said? He's so *stupid!*" Such underground fuming is exhausting and wastes all available energy and the class breaks down.

2. *Or else people* don't *argue.* But stopping argument feels to them like a huge giving-in, capitulation. The wind has been taken out of their sails. It feels to them like a merely random, utterly relaxed, gutless activity: "Well, if we're not going to argue things out, if anyone can get away with saying anything he wants, if no one is going to stop people from shooting off their mouths with utter nonsense, then I'll just say what I want, the rest can say what they want. Who the hell cares." Because normal paths for energy are closed off, they withdraw all energy. The class is merely slack, relaxed, boring, unfocussed. It dies.

So the main thing I have finally been able to center on is the peculiar quality of energy and attention this class asks for. It's a great effort. But instead of being directed towards arguing and settling—toward closure—energy must be expended in the opposite direction of keeping oneself open, listening, trying to have other people's experiences—in a sense trying to *agree* with everyone at once. What it feels like, when it goes well, is a sense of attention, of tautness, of great energy invested into one's perceiving and experiencing muscles—all the while keeping the mind from making its instinctive clench.

Bravery

What I hear loudest in the tape of a good teacherless class is bravery. Willingness to risk. The teacherless class makes people nervous. They are on their own. There is no one there who has been there before to tell them when they are doing things right, to reassure them. It's almost as though I can hear someone saying to himself, "Well, it's no use waiting for someone else to do it for us. There's no one special to lead the way. I guess someone has to start. I'll give it a try." And he takes the risk of really sharing his perception and experience. It is a kind of ice-breaking operation that makes it possible for the others to follow. They discover that nothing terrible happens to the first person. When a class can't get itself going, what I feel is everyone hanging back, waiting for someone else.

This ice-breaking is not once-and-for-all. People don't plunge immediately into utter honesty. A successful class seems characterized by a series of small breakthroughs over a long time. By many increments, they work up to sharing fuller and fuller reactions to the words.

If you want to insure that a class gets going, try to find brave people to be in it: people who are willing to say what they see and feel, and not worry so much about how others will view it. Young children and useful members of a class.

Responsibility

In most regular classes you feel a responsibility toward the teacher, not toward the other members of the class. When you are wavering between going or not going, think how often the inner debate is in terms of "what will the teacher say or think if I don't come." All too often it is *only* the thought of the teacher that gets us to come to class.

With this background, it is hard to learn responsibility to peers. This is why I emphasize the commitment for ten weeks. It takes that long for most people to transfer their responsibility from a teacher to themselves and their peers—to feel and communicate that their learning depends on each other.

When a class works, you can feel people sticking up for themselves; making genuine demands and expectations of others that their time not be wasted, that they learn something. When a class fails, you can feel people failing to take responsibility for themselves. Saying, in effect, "What can I do; I'm helpless; my only choice is to quit."

Although you cannot entirely change the world or transform people at a stroke, this class makes it perfectly obvious that you *can* change instantaneously the way eight or ten people act toward you for a couple of hours a week. If a person has tendency to talk too much or be bossy, you cannot reverse his personality. But in this class you can stop him from cheating you with his talking and bossiness for a couple of hours a week. You have only to want it and stick up for yourself by insisting on it politely but firmly. The threatening thing about this class is that it faces people with the fact that they are not so helpless as they prefer to think. The idea that classes must always have teachers reinforces helplessness.

How to Destroy the Class Secretly

Here's the most common way this sort of class breaks down. Everyone is a bit nervous and even frightened because it's such a strange and unsettling enterprise. It's almost inevitable. In this situation, what's most soothing is to find someone who likes to talk: someone who likes to ramble on with personal anecdotes, someone who likes to make speeches, or someone who is nervous when there's a silence and just drones on to fill it up. From here it's easy. You just let him go. Encourage him, but not openly. Just let opportunities occur. And most of all, refrain from stopping him from boring you. Pretend you are extremely polite.

Everyone starts saying to himself, "Boy, what a drag this class is! That person just talks and talks. He's ruining it. I can't stand it much longer." This feeling gets in the air and then a couple of people sort of drop out. That is, they don't quite drop out so that you could ask them about it; it's just that important things somehow start coming up to conflict with class meetings. Then everyone can start saying, "Boy this class is discouraging! It feels like it's falling apart. Everyone is down. I'm really discouraged. By the way, I just remembered, I've got an important meeting I've got to go to when the class next meets."

Finally the class breaks up. Maybe you've already dropped out or maybe you're there at the end supposedly feeling bad and supposedly wondering why other people can't stick with something. And you can blame it all conveniently on the poor sucker you got to cooperate with you by being a bore when you invited him to. You couldn't stand letting others enjoy what was too scary for you so you helped destroy it—but secretly. Everyone blames him. He even blames himself. No one blames you.

The moral of the process is that you must take responsibility for what happens in class: if you don't really try to stop it, you must want it to happen.

Diversity

A functioning class exploits the differences *between* individuals to pry open more diversity *within* individuals. When everyone tries to have everyone else's perception and experience, richness is continually plowed back into the group. There is a constantly growing potential for diversity of experience.

But it is not foolproof. I'm sad to say I've seen one teacherless class drift in the opposite direction: toward a sense of conformity, group ideology. Watch out for any drift toward unspoken ideas that certain kinds of feeling or writing are more acceptable than others: for example, that simplicity is good and complexity is bad; that strong feelings are good and lack of strong feelings is bad; or that seriousness is good, frivolity is bad. It's simply wrong. It's a result of insecurity or fear. The whole usefulness of a group is to reinforce the only trustworthy theory about writing: anything is possible. It's what e. e. cummings meant by the old vaudeville line, "Would you hit a lady with a baby?" "If I had to, I'd hit her with a baseball bat!" In writing, anything can work and anything is right if you make it work.

19

Responding to Student Writing

Nancy Sommers

More than any other enterprise in the teaching of writing, responding to and commenting on student writing consumes the largest proportion of our time. Most teachers estimate that it takes them at least 20 to 40 minutes to comment on an individual student paper, and those 20 to 40 minutes times 20 students per class, times 8 papers, more or less, during the course of a semester add up to an enormous amount of time. With so much time and energy directed to a single activity, it is important for us to understand the nature of the enterprise. For it seems, paradoxically enough, that although commenting on student writing is the most widely used method for responding to student writing, it is the least understood. We do not know in any definitive way what constitutes thoughtful commentary or what effect, if any, our comments have on helping our students become more effective writers.

Theoretically, at least, we know that we comment on our students' writing for the same reasons professional editors comment on the work of professional writers or for the same reasons we ask our colleagues to read and respond to our own writing. As writers we need and want thoughtful commentary to show us when we have communicated our ideas and when not, raising questions from a reader's point of view that may not have occurred to us as writers. We want to know if our writing has communicated our intended meaning and, if not, what questions or discrepancies our readers sees that we, as writers, are blind to.

In commenting on our students' writing, however, we have an additional pedagogical purpose. As teachers, we know that most students find it difficult to imagine a reader's response in advance, and to use such responses as a guide in composing. Thus, we comment on student writing to dramatize the presence of a reader, to help our students to become that questioning reader themselves, because, ultimately, we believe that becoming such a reader will help them to evaluate what they have written and develop control over their writing.[1]

Even more specifically, however, we comment on student writing because we believe that it is necessary for us to offer assistance to student writers when they are in the process of composing a text, rather than after the text has been completed. Comments create the motive for doing something different in the next draft; thoughtful comments create the motive for revising. Without comments from their teachers or from their peers, student writers will revise in a consistently narrow and predictable way. Without comments from readers, students assume that their writing has communicated their meaning and perceive no need for revising the substance of their text.[2]

Yet as much as we as informed professionals believe in the soundness of this approach to responding to student writing, we also realize that we don't know how our theory squares with teachers' actual practice—do teachers comment and students revise as the theory predicts they should? For the past year my colleagues, Lil Brannon, Cyril Knoblach, and I have been researching this problem, attempting to discover not only what messages teachers give their students through their comments, but also what determines which of these comments the students choose to use or to ignore when revising. Our research has been entirely focused on comments teachers write to motivate revisions. We have studied the commenting styles of thirty-five teachers at New York University and the University of Oklahoma, studying the comments these teachers wrote on first and second drafts, and interviewing a representative number of these teachers and their students. All teachers also commented on the same set of three student essays. As an additional reference point, one of the student essays was typed into the computer that had been programed with the "Writer's Workbench," a package of twenty-three programs developed by Bell Laboratories to help computers and writers work together to improve a text rapidly. Within a few minutes, the computer delivered editorial comments on the student's text, identifying all spelling and punctuation errors, isolating problems with wordy or misused phrases, and suggesting alternatives, offering a stylistic analysis of sentence types, sentence beginnings, and sentence lengths, and finally, giving our freshman essay a Kincaid readability score of 8th grade which, as the computer program informed us, "is a low score for this type of document." The sharp contrast between the teachers' comments and those of the computer highlighted how arbitrary and idiosyncratic most of our teachers' comments are. Besides, the calm, reasonable language of the computer provided quite a contrast to the hostility and mean-spiritedness of most of the teachers' comments.

The first finding from our research on styles of commenting is that *teachers comments can take students' attention away from their own purposes in writing a particular text and focus that attention on the teachers' purpose in commenting*. The teacher appropriates the text from the student by confusing the student's purpose in writing the text with her own purpose in commenting. Students make the changes the teacher wants rather than those that the student perceives are necessary, since the teachers' concerns imposed on the text create the reasons for the subsequent changes. We have all heard our perplexed students say to us when confused by our comments: "I don't understand how you want me to change this" or "Tell me what you want me to do." In the beginning of the process there was the writer, her words, and her desire to communicate her ideas. But after the comments of the teacher are imposed on the first or second draft, the student's attention dramatically shifts from "This is what I want to say," to "This is what you the teacher are asking me to do."

This appropriation of the text by the teacher happens particularly when teachers identify errors in usage, diction, and style in a first draft and ask students to correct these errors when they revise; such comments give the student an impression of the importance of these errors that is all out of proportion to how they should view these errors at this point in the process. The comments create the concern that these "accidents of discourse" need to be attended to before the meaning of the text is attended to.

It would not be so bad if students were only commanded to correct errors, but, more often than not, students are given contradictory messages; they are commanded to edit a sentence to avoid an error or to condense a sentence to achieve greater brevity of style, and then told in the margins that the particular paragraph needs to be more specific or to be developed more. An example of this problem can be seen in the following student paragraph:

> *wordy - be precise*   *which*
> *Sunday?*   *comma needed*
> Every year[on one Sunday in the middle of January]tens of millions of
>
> *word choice*
> people cancel all events, plans or work to watch the Super Bowl. This
>
> *wordy*
> audience includes[little boys and girls, old people, and housewives and
>
> *Be specific - what reasons?*
> men.]Many reasons have been given to explain why the Super Bowl has
>
> *and why*   *what spots?)*
> become so popular that commercial (spots cost up to $100,000.00.
>
> *awkward*
> One explanation is that people like to take sides and root for a team.
>
> *another what?*   *spelling*
> Another is that some people like the pageantry and excitement of the
>
> *too colloquial*
> event. These reasons alone, however, do not explain a happening as big as
>
> the Super Bowl.

you need to do more research

This paragraph needs to be expanded in order to be more interesting to a reader.

In commenting on this draft, the teacher has shown the student how to edit the sentences, but then commands the student to expand the paragraph in order to make it more interesting to a reader. The interlinear comments and the marginal comments represent two separate tasks for this student; the interlinear comments encourage the student to see the text as a fixed piece, frozen in time, that just needs some editing. The marginal comments, however, suggest that the meaning of the text is not fixed, but rather that the student still needs to develop the meaning by doing some more research. Students are commanded to edit and develop at the same time; the remarkable contradiction of developing a paragraph after editing the sentences in it represents the confusion we encountered in our teachers' commenting styles. These different signals given to students, to edit and develop, to condense and elaborate, represent also the failure of teachers' comments to direct genuine revision of the text as a whole.

Moreover, the comments are worded in such a way that it is difficult for students to know what is the most important problem in the text and what problems are of lesser importance. No scale of concerns is offered to a student, with the result that a comment about spelling or a comment about an awkward sentence is given weight equal to a comment about organization or logic. The comment that seemed to represent this problem best was one teacher's command to his student: "Check your commas and semi-colons and think more about what you are thinking about." The language of the comments makes it difficult for a student to sort out and decide what is most important and what is least imporant.

When the teacher appropriates the text for the student in this way, students are encouraged to see their writing as a series of parts—words, sentences, paragraphs—and not as a whole discourse. The comments encourage students to believe that their first drafts are finished drafts, not invention drafts, and that all they need to do is patch and polish their writing. That is, teachers' comments do not provide their students with an inherent reason for revising the structure and meaning of their texts, since the comments suggest to students that the meaning of their text is already there, finished, produced, and all that is necessary is a better word or phrase. The processes of revising, editing, and proofreading are collapsed and reduced to a single trivial activity, and the students' misunderstanding of the revision process as a rewording activity is reinforced by their teachers' comments.

It is possible, and it quite often happens, that students follow every comment and fix their texts appropriately as requested, but their texts are not improved substantially, or, even worse, their revised drafts are inferior to their previous drafts. Since the teachers' comments take the students' attention away from their own original purposes, students concentrate more, as I have noted, on what the teachers commanded them to do than on what they are trying to say. Sometimes students do not understand the purpose behind their teachers' comments and take these comments very literally. At other times students understand the comments, but the teacher has misread the text and the comments, unfortunately, are not applicable. For instance, we repeatedly saw comments in which teachers commanded students to reduce and condense what was written, when in fact what the text really needed at this stage was to be expanded in conception and scope.

The process of revising always involves a risk. But, too often revision becomes a balancing act for students in which they make the changes that are requested but do not take the risk of changing anything that was not commented on, even if the students sense that other changes are needed. A more effective text does not often evolve from such changes alone, yet the student does not want to take the chance of reducing a finished, albeit inadequate, paragraph to chaos—to fragments—in order to rebuild it, if such changes have not been requested by the teacher.

The second finding from our study is that *most teachers' comments are not text-specific and could be interchanged, rubber-stamped, from text to text.* The comments are not anchored in the particulars of the students' texts, but rather are a series of vague directives that are not text-specific. Students are commanded to "Think more about [their] audience, avoid colloquial language, avoid the passive, avoid prepositions at the end of sentences or conjunctions at the beginning of sentences, be clear, be specific, be precise, but above all, think more about what [they] are thinking about." The comments on the following student paragraph illustrate this problem:

Begin by telling your reader what you are going to write about.

In the sixties it was drugs, in the seventies it was rock and roll. Now in

avoid - "one of the"

the eighties, one of the most controversial subjects is nuclear power. The

elaborate

United States is in great need of its own source of power. Because of

environmentalists, coal is not an acceptable source of energy. [Solar and

be specific

wind power have not yet received the technology necessary to use them.]

avoid - "it seems"

It seems that nuclear power is the only feasible means right now for ob-

taining self-sufficient power. However, too large a percentage of the

be precise

population are against nuclear power claiming it is unsafe. With as many

Think more about your reader.

problems as the United States is having concerning energy, it seems a

shame that the public is so quick to "can" a very feasible means of power.

Three sentences needed

Nuclear energy should not be given up on, but rather, more nuclear

plants should be built.

One could easily remove all the comments from this paragraph and rubber-stamp them on another student text, and they would make as much or as little sense on the second text as they do here.

We have observed an overwhelming similarity in the generalities and abstract commands given to students. There seems to be among teachers an accepted, albeit unwritten canon for commenting on student texts. This uniform code of commands, requests, and pleadings demonstrates that the teacher holds a license for vagueness while the student is commanded to be specific. The students we interviewed admitted to having great difficulty with these vague directives. The students stated that when a teacher writes in the margins or as an end comment, "choose precise language," or "think more about your audience," revising becomes a guessing game. In effect, the teacher is saying to the student, "Somewhere in this paper is imprecise language or lack of awareness of an audience and you must find it." The problem presented by these vague commands is compounded for the students when they are not offered any strategies for carrying out these commands. Students are told that they have done something wrong and that there is something in their text that needs to be fixed before the text is acceptable. But to tell students that they have done something wrong is not to tell them what to do about it. In order to offer a useful revision strategy to a student, the teacher must anchor that strategy in the specifies of the student's text. For instance, to tell our student, the author of the above paragraph, "to be specific," or "to elaborate," does not show our student what questions the reader has about the meaning of the text, or what breaks in logic exist, that could be resolved if the writer supplied specific information; nor is the student shown how to achieve the desired specificity.

Instead of offering strategies, the teachers offer what is interpreted by students as rules for composing; the comments suggest to students that writing is just a matter of following the rules. Indeed, the teachers seem to impose a series of abstract rules about written products even when some of them are not appropriate for the specific text the student is creating.[3] For instance, the student author of our sample paragraph presented above is commanded to follow the conventional rules for writing a five paragraph essay—to begin the introductory paragraph by telling his reader what he is going to say and to end the paragraph with a thesis sentence. Somehow these abstract rules about what five-paragraph products should look like do not seem applicable to the problems this student must confront when revising, not are the rules specific strategies he could use when revising. There are many inchoate ideas ready to be exploited in this paragraph, but the rules do not help the student to take stock of his (or her) ideas and use the opportunity he has, during revision, to develop those ideas.

The problem here is a confusion of process and product; what one has to say about the process is different from what one has to say about the product. Teachers who use this method of commenting are formulating their comments as if these drafts were finished drafts and were not going to be revised. Their commenting vocabularies have not been adapted to revision and they comment on first drafts as if they were justifying a grade or as if the first draft were the final draft.

Our summary finding, therefore, from this research on styles of commenting is that the news from the classroom is not good. For the most part, teachers do not respond to student writing with the kind of thoughtful commentary which will help students to engage with the issues they are writing about or which will help them think about their purposes and goals in writing a specific text. In defense of our teachers, however, they told us that responding to student writing was rarely stressed in their teacher-training or in writing workshops; they had been trained in various prewriting techniques, in constructing assignments, and in evaluating papers for grades, but rarely in the process of reading a student text for meaning or in offering commentary to motivate revision. The problem is that most of us as teachers of writing have been trained to read and interpret literary texts for meaning, but, unfortunately, we have not been trained to act upon the same set of assumptions in reading student texts as we follow in reading literary texts.[4] Thus, we read student texts with biases about what the writer should have said or about what he or she should have written, and our biases determine how we will comprehend the text. We read with our preconceptions and preoccupations, expecting to find errors, and the result is that we find errors and misread our students' texts.[5] We find what we look for; instead of reading and responding to the meaning of a text, we correct our students' writing. We need to reverse this approach. Instead of finding errors or showing students how to patch up parts of their texts, we need to sabotage our students' conviction that the drafts they have written are complete and coherent. Our comments need to offer students revision tasks of a different order of complexity and sophistication from the ones that they themselves identify, by forcing students back into the chaos, back to the point where they are shaping and restructuring their meaning.[6]

For if the content of a student text is lacking in substance and meaning, if the order of the parts must be rearranged significantly in the next draft, if paragraphs must be restructured for logic and clarity, then many sentences are likely to be changed or deleted anyway. There seems to be no point in having students correct usage errors or condense sentences that are likely to disappear before the next draft is completed. In fact, to identify such problems in a text at this early first draft stage, when such problems are likely to abound, can give a student a disproportionate sense of their importance at this stage in the writing process.[7] In responding to our students' writing, we should be guided by the recognition that it is not spelling or usage problems that we as writers first worry about when drafting and revising of our texts.

We need to develop an appropriate level of response for commenting on a first draft, and to differentiate that from the level suitable to a second or third draft. Our comments need to be suited to the draft we are reading. In a first or second draft, we need to respond as any reader would, registering questions, reflecting befuddlement, and noting places where we are puzzled about the meaning of the text. Comments should point to breaks in logic, disruptions in meaning, or missing information. Our goal in commenting on early drafts should be to engage students with the issues they are considering and help them clarify their purposes and reasons in writing their specific text.

For instance, the major rhetorical problem of the essay written by the student who wrote the second paragraph (the paragraph on nuclear power) quoted above was that the student had two principal arguments running through his text, each of which brought the other into question. On the one hand, he argued that we must use nuclear power, unpleasant as it is, because we have nothing else to use; though nuclear energy is a problematic source of energy, it is the best of a bad lot. On the other hand, he also argued that nuclear energy is really quite safe and therefore should be our primary resource. Comments on this student's first draft need to point out this break in logic and show the student that if we accept his first argument, then his second argument sounds fishy. But if we accept his second argument, his first argument sounds contradictory. The teacher's comments need to engage this student writer with this basic rhetorical and conceptual problem in his first draft rather than impose a series of abstract commands and rules upon his text.

Written comments need to be viewed not as an end in themselves—a way for teachers to satisfy themselves that they have done their jobs—but rather as a means for helping students to become more effective writers. As a means for helping students, they have limitations; they are, in fact, disembodied remarks—one absent writer responding to another absent writer. The key to successful commenting is to have what is said in the comments and what is done in the classroom mutually reinforce and enrich each other. Commenting on papers assists the writing course in achieving its purpose; classroom activities and the comments we write to our students need to be connected. Written comments need to be an extension of the teacher's voice—an extension of the teacher as reader. Exercises in such activities as revising a whole text or individual paragraphs together in class, noting how the sense of the whole dictates the smaller changes, looking at options, evaluating actual choices, and then discussing the effect of these changes on revised drafts—such exercises need to be designed to take students through the cycles of revising and to help them overcome their anxiety about revising: that anxiety we all feel at reducing what looks like a finished draft into fragments and chaos.

The challenge we face as teachers is to develop comments which will provide an inherent reason for students to revise; it is a sense of revision as discovery, as a repeated process of beginning again, as starting out new, that our students have not learned. We need to show our students how to seek, in the possibility of revision, the dissonances of discovery—to show them through our comments why new choices would positively change their texts, and thus to show them the potential for development implicit in their own writing.

Notes

1. C. H. Knoblach and Lil Brannon. 1981. "Teacher Commentary on Student Writing: The State of the Art." *Freshman English News*, 10 (Fall):1–3.

2. For an extended discussion of revision strategies of student writers see Nancy Sommers. "Revision Strategies of Student Writers and Experienced Adult Writers." 1980. *College Composition and Communication*, 31 (December):378–88.

3. Nancy Sommers and Ronald Schleifer. 1980. "Means and Ends: Some Assumptions of Student Writers." *Composition and Teaching*, 2 (December), 69–76.

4. Janet Emig and Robert P. Parker, Jr. Responding to Student Writing: Building a Theory of the Evaluating Process. Unpublished papers. Rutgers University.

5. For an extended discussion of this problem see Joseph Williams. 1981. "The Phenomenology of Error." *College Composition and Communication*, 32 (May): 152–68.

6. Ann Berthoff. 1981. *The Making of Meaning*. Portsmouth, NH: Boynton/Cook Publishers.

7. W. U. McDonald. 1978. "The Revising Process and the Marking of Student Papers." *College Composition and Communication*, 24 (May):167–70.

About the Author

Nancy Sommers, whose most recent essay in *CCC* appeared in the December, 1980, issue, is now a visiting assistant professor in the Graduate School of Education at Rutgers University. She is also director of RiverWind Writing Associates, a private consulting firm.

20

Responding to Texts

Facilitating Revision in the Writing Workshop

C. H. Knoblauch
Lil Brannon

There is a stock comic situation in which two people go through the motions of communicating but finally fail because each assumes that an idiosyncratic perspective is shared by the other when in fact it is not. A classic instance is the abortive conversation between Walter Shandy and Uncle Toby running through Sterne's marvelously madcap *Tristram Shandy*. Toby is preoccupied with his hobby-horse: he constructs models of famous battles as a means of making order out of the experiences that matter to him (the tentacles of modern rhetoric have a long reach). He employs a language, rich in military allusions and similes, that reflects his priorities, and he hears the remarks of others largely in terms of his own military interests. Walter, meanwhile, has a hobby-horse of his own, a fascination with the austere intellectual world of ancient logic, where presumably dispassionate rational analysis can get at the truth of things and inject coherence into human affairs. Since neither of these peculiar characters is prepared to take into account the viewpoint of the other, talk between them is hilariously oblique and unproductive. Walter's reference to a "train of ideas," for example, suggests to Uncle Toby a "train of artillery": on another occasion, mention of the "bridge" of Tristram's nose is misunderstood as a reference to the Marquis d'Hôpital's drawbridge; and elsewhere, Walter's elegant dissertation on the logical value of auxiliary verbs suggests nothing more to Toby and Corporal Trim than the auxiliary troops at the siege of Limerick. Each time these individuals attempt to converse, their hobby-horses interfere, extinguishing the hope that any constructive meeting of minds can result from acts of language.

The rhetorical principle violated in these abortive conversational efforts is one we have discussed often before now: people cannot communicate unless they first strive to accommodate each other's points of view and decide on a shared basis for talk. Human beings put the principle into practice many times every day in order to accomplish their purposes in both speaking and writing. Probably, the majority of writing teachers are sufficiently persuaded of the importance of audience expectation that they include lectures and exercises on the subject, or even "cases" that require students to anticipate different readers on different occasions. Presumably, these teachers understand quite clearly that communication entails a projecting from the self, a struggle to see things as others might see them, so that, by making connections between someone else's understanding and one's own, a strategy can evolve for making and sharing new meanings. What is peculiar, however, about the commitment of writing teachers to "audience" is the extent to which anticipating the perspectives of others is for them a one-way obligation. There's a curious disjunction between what these teachers tell students about projecting outward as the starting point of communication and what they do themselves as aspiring communicators. For in their ways of talking to students, and especially in their habits of responding to student writing, they tend, every bit as much as Uncle Toby does, to ride their own hobby-horses—sometimes to the extent that their students fail utterly to conceive what they might be talking about.

Too often, if not typically, when reading student writing, teachers ignore writers' intentions and meanings in favor of their own agendas, so that what students are attempting to say has remarkably little to do with what teachers are looking for, and therefore little bearing on what they say in comments on student texts. In the least subtle instances, while students are engaged in—let's say—describing personal experiences, their teacher is concentrating on the effective use of comparison or example; while they struggle dutifully to find significance in *KingLear*, the teacher is defending the imperiled constraints of a term paper or the canons of some, not necessarily announced, critical predisposition; while students are writing to understand the workings of a nuclear reactor, the teacher is enforcing detailed instructions of the assignment on "process analysis"; while they are locating personal meanings in public issues, the teacher is insuring that only the most orthodox opinions are appropriately paraded in all the tiresome pros and cons that arrange themselves repeatedly in school writing. Generally speaking, the hobby-horse of writing teachers is prose decorum, the propriety of discourse extending from its technical features to its formal appearances and even to its intellectual content as a display of approved ideas in conventional relationships to each other.[1] Their point of view largely determines what they talk about, even though it's a point of view that students barely comprehend or see the value of. To an extent, of course, by sheer power of position teachers can demand that students begin to pay attention to their pronouncements about structure and convention, enjoying the modest benefits of one-way conversation. But the question of *quid pro quo* seldom arises, that is, the value, for communication's sake, of paying attention to what matters most to writers by starting with their meanings instead of teacherly priorities when responding to their writing. And what is jeopardized as a consequence is the possibility of real communication, the chance to make intellectual progress through purposeful dialogue.[2]

Given the environment surrounding traditional instruction, it's perhaps not so surprising that teachers have missed the fact that responding to student writing is a species of communication, subject, therefore, to the same rhetorical principles that govern other situations. For communication, or dialogue, is a democratic act: both sides get to score points. Yet, the classic teacher-student relationship is defined, as we have suggested, in authoritarian terms, master and apprentice, knower and learner, talker and listener. In typical writing courses, students produce discourse not in order to be listened to but in order to give teachers something to talk about. Since the authority for judging pertinence, propriety, and effectiveness in writing rests with the teacher, then, paradoxically, the control of compositional choices ultimately belongs with the teacher as well. Could a more peculiar rhetorical situation possibly exist than one in which the person supposedly creating a text must yield control of its character and shape to the ostensible audience? Such is often the case in classrooms: the teacher's agenda is the one that matters, so the responsibility for anticipating expectations lies wholly with students. To the extent that the teacher's expectations are not satisfied, authority over the writing is stolen from the writer by means of comments, oral or written, that represent the teacher's agenda, whatever the writer's intentions may initially have been. A students task is to match an Ideal Text in the teacher's imagination which is insinuated through the teacher's commentary, not to pursue personal intentions according to the writer's own developing sense of what he or she wishes to say.[3] The student writer, in other words, is obliged to work diligently at locating a teacher's hobby-horse, experiencing some predictable frustration in the process, while the teacher is under no requirement to anticipate the writer's purposes before making comments on a text. The teacher's reading strategy is simply to apply his or her own inevitably reductive Ideal Text to students' actual writing, and to remark on discrepancies between the two, which the students are then called upon to reduce as the measure of their competences as writers.[4] It's the rare composition teacher who reads student writing with the assumption that composers legitimately control their own discourses, who accepts the possibility that student intentions matter more than teacher expectations as a starting-point for reading, and who recognizes that writers' choices are supposed to make sense mainly in terms of those intentions, not in proportion as they gratify a reader's view of what should have been said.

An experiment we have conducted suggests the pervasiveness of the concept of Ideal Text among writing teachers and the strength of their resistance to honoring writers' intentions when responding to their writing. We asked forty teachers to comment as they normally would on a particular student essay. The writer had studied the Lindbergh kidnapping trial and had produced a text simulating the closing argument of the prosecuting attorney. His text was heavily laden with emotional appeals to the jury because, he had told us, his intent was to create sympathy for the injured Lindberghs and revulsion against the accused. He believed that emotional language would be suited to this intent. Here is a portion of his writing:

> Ladies and gentlemen of the jury, I whole-heartedly believe that the evidence which has been presented before you has clearly shown that the man who is on trial here today is beyond a doubt guilty of murder of the darling, little, innocent Lindbergh baby.
>
> Sure, the defendant has stated his innocence. But who are we to believe? Do we believe the testimony of a man who has been previously convicted; in fact convicted to holding up innocent women wheeling baby carriages? Or do we believe the testimony of one of our nation's greatest heroes, Charles A. Lindbergh. Mr. Lindbergh believes the defendant is guilty. So do I.
>
> All I ask, ladies and gentlemen of the jury, is that you look at the evidence. . . .

When we asked teachers to read this text, but without benefit of the writer's explanation of intent (a disadvantage which did not, however, appear to bother them), they divided into two groups. One group felt that the emotional language showed the writer's immaturity and undeveloped rhetorical sense: their comments betrayed an Ideal Text featuring detached logical rigor and care for the details of evidence as the essential characteristics of a trial prosecutor's summation. The student's writing failed to anticipate these characteristics and therefore failed, in the eyes of one group of teachers, to demonstrate proficiency. The second group's conclusion was more interesting. Its members upheld the same Ideal Text, showed the same concern for logic and explanatory detail; but they reasoned that, since the writer could not possibly have been serious in resorting to blatant emotional appeals, the discourse must represent a wonderful spoof of the genre of "trial summation." Therefore, the writer must be unusually mature and the writing a clever demonstration of exceptional competence (though containing some technical flaws that could be corrected readily enough). The significant point here is that neither group stopped to consider the possibility that the student might have had a serious intent to use emotional appeal or that its use might constitute a plausible strategy in this situation. Instead, secure in their shared concept of an Ideal Text, both groups advanced without hesitation to precisely opposite conclusions about the merits of the writer's text and the ability of the writer himself.

Later, we showed these teachers both the student's description of intent and a transcript of portions of the actual summation delivered during the Lindbergh trial, which revealed the very emotional appeals to which the student writer had resorted, thereby suggesting the arbitrariness of the teachers' assumed Ideal Text:

> Why, men and women, if that little baby, if that little, curly-haired youngster were out in the grass in the jungle, breathing, just so long as it was breathing, any tiger, any lion, the most venomous snake would have passed that child without hurting a hair of its head.

Of course, the fact that the original attorney used such appeals does not imply that only one strategy exists for preparing trial summations. It only suggests that emotional appeals are no less legitimate than other strategies, so that the teachers' refusal to take the student writer's choices seriously, acknowledging the authority of that writer to choose in accordance with his own intentions, indicated the inappropriate tyranny of an Ideal Text over their commenting practices. The fact that their judgments were polarized, yet derived from a common prejudice, helps to make our point about Ideal Texts. But it would not be surprising if the student writer found either response puzzling since, in each case, the teachers were attending to their own predispositions and not to the student's effort to make meanings. The likelihood of serious, purposeful communication with that student would have to have been severely reduced.

The writing workshop depends on a style of response which differs altogether from that of traditional instruction because its concern is not merely to elicit writing in order to judge it, but to sustain writing through successive revisions in pursuit of richer insights and concurrently the maturation of competence. The workshop style assumes, above all, that, if teachers seriously aim to communicate with students about their writing and thereby affect students' performance, they must begin with what matters most to those writers, namely, the making of meaningful statements consistent with the writers' own purposes and their own estimations of how best to achieve them. In nearly every circumstance except the classical composition course, reading entails accepting a writer's authority to make precisely the choices that have been made in order to say precisely what the writer wishes to say. Readers seek gradually to understand and appreciate a writer's purposes by assessing the effects of textual choices on their way of seeing the subject. They suspend their own preconceptions, to a degree, in order to understand the writer's position, taking for granted the writer's capacity to make a position clear unless there is substantial reason to believe otherwise.[5] This seems a fair starting-point in responding to student writing as well, no matter how skeptical a teacher may be about a particular writer's ability to control choices. Instead of beginning with the supposition that the teacher-reader is rightfully in control rather than the writers, so that their discourses are valued only to the extent that they meet the teacher's preconceptions, the workshop reader begins—as most readers do— with an implicit trust in the writer's choice-making and with a concern to discover the writer's intentions rather than automatically preempting them with personal concerns. The main reason for returning to this normal reading habit is that the responders imply by doing so that they value writers' efforts to make meaning, thereby creating a powerful incentive to write. Conversely, the traditional tendency to preempt intentions diminishes incentive because it shows students that readers fail to value what they have to say.

What every teacher knows, of course, is that student writing does not always succeed in conveying or achieving its intentions. The workshop teacher knows this as well as anyone, but knows also that motivation to write depends crucially on the belief that the writing will be taken seriously—in other words, that the writer's authority to make statements in his or her own way will be respected. We are not recommending a suspension of the critical faculty in responding to student writing, but only an essentially receptive rather than essentially evaluative reading posture.[6] Rather than taking for granted a writer's proven or unproven ineptitude, which encourages the usurping of the writer's text as frequently as the teacher prefers, we suggest the normal posture of taking the writer's competence *generally* for granted, which encourages respecting the writer's choices as plausible alternatives as long as they appear to support his or her own purposes. When teachers begin reading student texts with the calculated (as opposed to naive) expectation that the writing is purposeful and suited to its own ends, their style of responding to it necessarily changes. Comments begin to register, not the discrepancy between a discourse and some teacher's personal Ideal Text, but rather the discrepancy between a writer's projected intentions and the effects of actual choices on an experienced reader's awareness of what the writer wishes to say. Any response will be designed to reveal the reader's uncertainties about the substance of the writer's communication, depending on a knowledge of the writer's purposes as the touchstone for recommending revisions. This reading posture is specially suited to the writing workshop because of its emphasis on revision as a natural feature of composing. The idea of response is to offer perceptions of uncertainty, incompleteness, unfulfilled promises, unrealized opportunities, as motivation for more writing and therefore more learning about a subject as well as more successful communication of whatever has been learned.

The relationship between response and revision is important. In traditional practice, commenting on student writing is essentially a product-centered, evaluative activity resembling literary criticism. Students write "papers" so that teachers can describe their strengths and weaknesses, grading them accordingly. The papers are then, often, simply retired and new ones composed, presumably under the influence of recollected judgments of the previous ones. The assumption has been that evaluating products of composing is equivalent to intervening in the process. Teachers have concentrated, therefore, on retrospective appraisals of "finished" discourses, where students either do no rewriting at all or perform superficial copy-editing exercises to make their discourses conform to a teacher's Ideal Text. This emphasis on product encourages a directive style of commentary, the function of which is either simply to label the errors in writing or to define restrictively what a student would (or will) have to do in order to perfect it in the teacher's eyes. The following response to a sample of student writing suggests the character of a directive commenting style. It may seem an exaggerated instance, and perhaps it is. But both the essay and the comments are genuine, coming from an actual first-year college writing class.

A lot of factors can contribute to the
rejection of a student by a college. It   *This is obvious-*
could be the student is not the type   *cut it out!*
of youngster that the college wants,
perhaps he/she did not do well on the
       ^ *or*
SATs or did not have a good high school

recommendation.

       No matter what the reason is, a
Unclear-
avoid "if" if   rejected student should never feel sad
you can   about it because being rejected is not
            as   *Proofread!*   ¶ *Start new paragraph with*
       that awful as people image. First of all   *this idea*
       ------ *avoid this - use many* ------
       all colleges are basically the same, but

       once you made a choice of a few, you have
       Don't use you in a formal essay - you started with
       kind of idealize it to be the kind of   *"student"*
                        a
       college which is perfect for you however

       it is not true! There are thousands of
Whew!
This should be   colleges throughout the country a lot
2 or 3   of them could be very suitable for you.
sentences.
       Therefore, do not intend to restrict
                        ^ *unnecessary- this weakens what*
       yourself, go reach out to more colleges   *you want to*
       and find a better one for yourself.   *say.*
                 ^"a more suitable one" Maybe?
            If the college of your choice is a
Use a
dictionary!   highly-reputed and you get rejected
                                        Do you really
rephrase -   by it do not worry. Find yourself a   *mean" Do not*
            second choice college   *worry?"*
       lower-ranked one and work hard in it,
                 often   a
       because it is easier to get high
RUN ON
SENTENCE   average in those schools, then you can
BREAK IT   always transfer back to some really   *your first choice*
UP!   *or perhaps*
       famous school, maybe you can go to their   *one of its*
       graduate schools later.

            anymore, it is not totally a bad idea,   *What?*
Unclear!   society is a wonderful college itself and
       once you come out to work, you acquire
       knowledge from it. You can also go back
                           like
       to evening school if you prefer to do so   */simplify!*
       after working for a while.
                 everybody has
            Finally, we all have disappointments
            life
       in our lives. Getting rejected by the
       college of your choice is only a minor

one, most people, including(me) have *keep yourself out of the essay.*

and should survive it and(take it *This is a formal essay.*

easy.)

Is this what you mean?

Your last ¶ should also restate that, as you have shown, there are good reasons not to despair about rejection. Use the last ¶ to tidy up the essay.

You're on the right track here, and your overall structure of developing new ideas in each paragraph is pretty good. But your writing becomes unhinged a bit within each ¶. You need to work on expressing your ideas as simply as possible — avoid unnecessary wording. (see my comments on your second sentence for example.)

Also, watch your tendency to write run-on sentences. For example, the second sentence of your second ¶ is quite a mouthful and goes zig-zag all over the place. Again, simplify!

Be sure you mean what you say. Don't use "it" if you can avoid it. Be more definite with your words.

Finally, proofread and use a dictionary if you are unsure of a spelling or word meaning. Errors in these areas are annoying and teachers will mark you down because of them.

Rewrite — be more careful, and good luck!

In the worst case, this essay with attached corrections would simply be put away and the student would be expected to move on to the next assignment with some memory of the mistakes committed earlier. But even if revision were required, the writer would mainly be obeying the teacher's prescriptions about structural and technical deficiencies, as though the text in its present form were a fixed entity and the revising only a matter of making the product as respectable as possible. Notice the authoritarian character of the teacher-critic's responses, aiming in effect to take control of the writer's discourse: "This is obvious—cut it out"; "don't use 'you' in a formal essay"; "start a new paragraph with this idea"; "simplify!" We could reconstruct this teacher's Ideal Text rather easily, but it's more important to note how uncommunicative and how unresponsive to the writer's perspective the teacher's comments are. Formal constraints, the teacher's hobby-horse, are far more important than the writer's concern to make a statement about being rejected by a college. Indeed, the first sentence of the teacher's end comment suggests that the "ideas" in the essay are adequate enough (which is really a way of dismissing them), and that the important matter is prose decorum. The teacher's confidence that this student somehow secretly understands the operative Ideal Text allows for comments such as "avoid unnecessary wording," "be sure you mean what you say," and "be more definite with your words," which are surely as incomprehensible to the student as Walter Shandy's discussion of auxiliary verbs was to Uncle Toby. An interesting question is, how much "better" would this writing be if all the local problems that bothered the teacher were removed? It seems to us that it would still be intellectually shallow and rhetorically immature, even if

How important are these factors? Do you imply that they are relative or that they don't always matter? Is your essay going to be about these factors?

A lot of factors can contribute to the rejection of a student by a college. It could be the student is not the type of youngster that the college wants, perhaps he/she did not do well on the SATs or did not have a good high school recommendation.

No matter what the reason is, a rejected student should never feel sad about it because being rejected is not that awful as people image. First of all, [all colleges are basically the same,] but once you made a choice of a few, you have kind of idealize it to the kind of college which is perfect for you however it is not true! [There are thousands of colleges throughout the country, a lot of them could be very suitable for you.] Therefore, do not intend to restrict yourself, go reach out to [more colleges] and find a better one for yourself.

What criteria lead you to decide this? Size? Location? Program offerings? the kind of student body?

But if all colleges are the same, then aren't all of them equally suitable? why only "a lot"? Do you really believe they are all suitable? What might determine suitability?

← any old college?

If the college of your choice is a highly-reputated and you get rejected by it, do not worry, Find yourself a [lower-ranked one] and work hard in it, because it is easier to get high average in those schools, then you can always transfer back to some [really famous school] maybe you can go to their graduate schools later.

If some are "lower ranked" then in what sense are they all "the same."

Is this a difference between colleges?

If you feel as bad after being rejected *are you saying that it doesn't really matter? Do you believe that?*

that you do not feel like going to college

anymore, it is not totally a bad idea,

society is a wonderful college itself

and once you come out to work, you

acquire knowledge from it. You can

also go back to evening school if you prefer

to do so after working for a while.

  Finally, we all have disappointments

for everyone? Would it be for you?

in our lives. Getting rejected by the *This sounds interesting, have you been rejected?*

college of your choice is (only a minor *Would it be worth talking about?*

one,) most people, including me, have and

should survive it and take it easy.

I can't tell whether your purpose here is just to make someone feel better or really to argue that all colleges are alike and that going or not going is an unimportant decision: in either case, do you really believe your statement? That is, would it make no difference if, for instance, you were forced to leave [the student's present school]? If so, why are you here now? Would you be just as happy at East Altuna Junior College in North Dakota? If you don't think you would, then do you think your reader would be consoled by what you say?

its newly polished surface covered the shallowness and immaturity with a somewhat more pleasing veneer. But the teacher's concern for a salvageable product rather than the writer's evolving meaning accounts for the directive preoccupation with veneer.

An alternative to directive commentary, a style that is valued in the writing workshop, is facilitative response, the purpose of which is to create motivation for immediate and substantive revision by describing a careful reader's uncertainties about what a writer intends to say. See the sample above of the same student text with responses that are facilitative rather than directive.

The comments of a facilitative reader are designed to preserve the writer's control of the discourse, while also registering uncertainty about what the writer wishes to communicate. The questions posed suggest the possibility of negotiation between writer and reader, leading to richer insights and more meaningful communication.[7] Negotiation assumes that the writer knows better than the reader the purposes involved, while the reader knows better than the writer the actual effects of authorial choices. The dialogue initiated by the comments (which may also be sustained by oral conversation) enables the writer to reflect on the connection between what was meant and what a reader has understood, using any difference between intent and effect as an incentive to test new choices. But importantly, the reader's engagement with the text is on a level similar to that of the writer's, namely, the level of meaning, line of reasoning, intellectual potentiality, thereby enabling dialogue and negotiation as opposed to editorial prescriptions. Emphasis is on the writer's developing understanding of the subject—in other words, the process of composing rather than the absolute quality of an achieved text. The comment on the writer's last sentence, for instance, concerning the somewhat veiled reference to a personal experience of rejection, suggests the possibility of a radically new focus to the writing, which the composer is free to consider though not constrained to adopt. Meanwhile, the end comment, which confesses the reader's uncertainty about the writer's purposes, suggests some of the problems of stance and intent which can lead to additional writing while avoiding the temptation to take control of choice-making from the writer by supplying a formula or direction for solving the problems. The writer and reader may, of course, discuss possibilities together, but the quality of a negotiated agreement to revise in one way as opposed to another depends on the teacher's skill at supporting the writer's exploration of alternatives while not directing its outcome.

Let's be clear about the difference between directive and facilitative commentary; it's not a difference between "form" response and "content" response, nor is it a difference between making statements about a text and just asking questions, nor is it a difference between being negative and being positive, that is, criticizing writers versus praising them. Responses to content can be as directive as responses to form: for instance, given the paper on college rejection, a teacher could say, "you need to give us an example of a college of high repute" or "colleges don't care about SATs, so omit the reference"—both plainly directive comments. Alternatively, facilitative responses can pertain to formal problems at times: for instance, "I can't tell what the 'it' in the second sentence of your second paragraph refers to, given the previous references to 'all colleges' and 'a few' colleges—are you thinking now of a single college?" Similarly, directive comments can take the shape of questions: "Is this a complete sentence?" means essentially "Change this into a complete sentence"; and facilitative comments can take the shape of assertions: "I don't see why you think being rejected by a college can be a beneficial experience." The distinction lies deeper than superficial comment form. Finally, criticism of what doesn't seem effective and support of what does can be found in both directive and facilitative commentary; they are equal parts of any healthy interaction between teachers and students, by no means parallel to the methodological distinction between giving directions in one style of commentary and characterizing a reader's uncertainties in the other. The essential difference between the two commenting styles is the degree of control over choices that the writer or the teacher retains. In directive commentary, the teacher says or implies, "Don't do it your way; do it this way." In facilitative commentary, the teacher says or implies, "Here's what your choices have caused me to think you're saying—if my response differs from your intent, how can you help me to see what you mean?" The essential difference—as is so often the case in the teaching alternatives we have been discussing—lies more in attitude and outlook than in perceivable changes of technique.

Of course, the majority of facilitative responses on the college rejection essay do take a question form and all of them happen to be "content" oriented. The tendency of a facilitative comment to take the form of a question is natural enough, since the reader's posture is probing and provocative, aimed at making a writer more reflective about the sufficiency of choices, rather than prescriptive about changes that must be made. But it's important to emphasize the posture beneath the surface appearance of a comment: attitude shapes practice, not the other way around. The content orientation is also natural, given the primitive, exploratory nature of the writing and given the priorities of the writing workshop—fluency, then clarity, then correctness. Doubtless, this writing has numerous formal and technical deficiencies: but it's also so far away from the copy-editing stage suggested by the comments of the teacher-critic that pointing out the deficiencies is superfluous. If the writer's ideas are not further developed, then none of the technical recommendations will make the writing any better than it is. On the other hand, if a next draft does substantially alter the writing in this earlier text, then many of the choices here will have been eliminated in the revision. We're not saying that form and technique are irrelevant and never to be responded to; we're only arguing that first things should come first, that a writer's on-going pursuit of meanings should be a teacher-reader's first consideration. As meanings emerge, as the relationship between intention and effect stabilizes, as successive revisions develop, narrower and more local concerns about structure and technical subtlety may well become appropriate. But the maturity of the writer and the intellectual/imaginative quality of his or her writing determine the usefulness of a more technical response: in general, the less real control of technique a writer possesses, the less intrusive should be the commentary on technical matters and the more conspicuous should be the response pertinent to emerging meanings.

The purpose, then, of facilitative commentary is to induce the reformulation of texts, the pursuit of new connections and the discovery of richer or more comprehensive meanings. By contrast, the main function of directive commentary is to make a given text look as good as it can. We would not suggest, however, that the mere presence of facilitative comments automatically leads to the substantive revision we have in mind. Without additional support, students will tend to make only the limited textual changes that directive responses elicit, even when the facilitative responses offer a fuller potential for new discovery. An inexperienced writer's natural tendency is to restrict revising to changes that minimally affect the plan and order of ideas with which she or he began, readily making only those adjustments that involve least pressure to reconceive or significantly extend the writing already done. This is not a matter simply of laziness. The resistance is normal, arising out of the anxiety that even experienced writers feel at having to reduce an achieved coherence, however inadequate, to the chaos of fragments and undeveloped insights from which they started. Practiced writers overcome their anxiety through habitual success in rewriting, but no such comforting pattern of successes exists to steady the resolve of the apprentice. Nor is this natural psychological resistance the only barrier to self-initiated revising. Another is the sheer difficulty of perceiving alternatives to the choices that have already been made, choices that lie reified as a document. The temptation is strong, even among experienced writers, to forget the arbitrariness of so many initial decisions about what to say, imagining in retrospect an inevitability about the patterns and connections that make up the existing discourse. Seeing through that apparent inevitability in order to recover additional options requires an intellectual discipline and a rhetorical awareness that unpracticed writers frequently have not acquired—indeed that they come to writing courses to develop.[8]

Perhaps the most concentrated effort in a writing workshop, therefore, is devoted to supporting substantive revision, for it is during revision that new learning is most likely to occur and competence most likely to develop. The first concern is to reveal to students, through the expectations implicit in facilitative responses, that "revision" does not mean copy-editing or, in general, making a given text more presentable. Nor does it mean superficial additions— "give more details," or subtractions—"this isn't relevant to your thesis," or redecorating—"move this paragraph to page 4." It means deeper intellectual penetration of a subject through additional composing, even to the point of repudiating earlier formulations altogether because subtler or more powerful insights have inspired new organizing principles and lines of reasoning. In-class writing to which students have not as yet committed major effort offers a good initial context for nurturing this view of revising. Making substantive changes is likely to entail less intimidation, less psychological resistance, when investment in a given text is still relatively small, as in the case of fifteen or twenty minutes of exploratory writing in class to be revised following comments from peers and the teacher-reader. Repeated short experiments in revision, with attentive teacher and peer support, can help create a willingness to try again, a strength of mind for reconceiving texts, which will carry over into larger-scale efforts. But encouragement remains equally necessary later, once students have become more willing to take chances, Writers need opportunities in workshop for discussing their rewriting plans with each other and with the teacher-reader. They need time to ask questions about responses and to test new choices on their readers. Less adventuresome or selfreliant students may need particular coaching—perhaps being encouraged to rewrite short statements with the instructor looking on and explaining his or her uncertainties about evolving meanings. Such activities are time-consuming, but there's no better way to spend the time. The revisions will be halting and inconsistently successful, especially at the start, but there's no more productive kind of failure, provided that what is emphasized is not the kinds and degree of failure but the glimmerings of communicative success.

Two awkward questions arise about the connection between facilitative commentary and the process of revision. Teachers naturally feel that their obligation in responding to writing is to locate the "major" problems or the most promising opportunities for change—hence, the first question: are there optimal responses that will help writers make the best possible revisions? At the same time, teachers often believe that the whole point of revision is to make texts better than they were in earlier versions—hence, the second question: shouldn't improvement from one draft to the next be expected as a sign both of commenting effectiveness and of writers' "progress" toward maturity? The insights of contemporary reader-response theory suggest some answers that will trouble teachers who expect the significant features of student writing and the degree of textual improvement to be readily and objectively verifiable. Louise Rosenblatt, first, and later Wolfgang Iser, David Bleich, and others,[9] have argued that all reading experiences entail transactions between reader and text, not a passive retrieval of meanings residing in the text and equally accessible to all careful observers, but an active creation of personal significances and impressions of quality based on individual responses. Readings are always, to a degree, idiosyncratic, dependent on the life-experiences, attitudes, feelings, beliefs, prejudices, which cause individuals to value different things and to construe in different ways. For reader-response theorists, therefore, the idea of a single "correct" or authoritative reading is problematic. Even highly experienced readers will view the same text differently, with dissimilar focuses of attention, various expectations, opposed notions about which textual cues are important or how they are important. The result is alternative but equally plausible transactions. Is there any reason to assume that responding to student writing entails more objectivity, less eccentricity, than responding to other texts? We think not.

So, our answer to the first question, in light of reader-response theory, is that there are no optimal responses, only more and less honest ones. Different readers find more or less meaning in different cues, and one teacher will view the potential in a student text differently from the way another does. Genuine personal reactions to a student's writing—for instance, the teacher's interest in the writer's own brush with disappointment in the college rejection essay—may not find duplication from reader to reader, but they are no less honest or potentially provocative for the writer's further efforts because of their individuality. Indeed, they are preferable to more formulaic, directive responses—for instance, to strike the reference to personal rejection as unsuited to the text's "main point"—which may well be dishonest in their overrestriction of valid lines of inquiry or development. Our answer to the second question is equally dependent on reader-response research: if different readers have alternative views of what is meaningful, valuable, interesting, or flawed in a text, then they will also have different notions about what would constitute "improvement" of that text. Teachers are sometimes tempted to correlate improvement with their personal preferences, to associate a student's willingness to follow directions with "better writing" on subsequent drafts. The chances are good, however, that no two teacher-readers will have the same opinion about how or why or the extent to which one draft of an essay is better than another. The perception of improvement in revised writing will always involve subjective, idiosyncratic judgments, even when the criteria for improvement include nothing subtler than avoiding surface errors and following teacher's directions about where or how to say things. Once richer criteria are also included, such as intellectual penetration of the subject, or quality of imaginative insight, or even closer proximity between intention and effect, the teacher's own consistency of judgment from student to student, essay to essay, is likely to deteriorate, let alone the consistency among different readers which would be required to assert an objective basis for evaluation. Since such a basis would be hard, if not impossible, to establish, teachers might be well-advised not to place such store in their powers of discernment as to expect that they can readily distinguish flawed from improved drafts. And if improvement is so difficult to perceive reliably, it seems pointless to depend on such a concept as the measure of commenting effectiveness. We would argue, instead, that once student writers have pursued worthwhile meanings through successive drafts, assisted by readers' personal reactions to the coherence, value, and communicative effectiveness of their developing discourses, their efforts have been successful by definition, because they serve the long-range goal of intellectual growth and the maturation of composing ability. Whether or not a second draft represents improvement over a first draft in some objective sense is not only extremely difficult to determine but is also irrelevant to the value of the process itself.

What follows is a student writer's revision of an earlier text in response to the facilitative commentary of a teacher-reader, illustrating our principal point that a writer's control of personal choices and opportunity to discover personal meanings are more important for growth than local textual "improvement," superficial or otherwise. Notice that the writer's basic strategy in her first attempt is to relate a particular, personal irritation—a roommate's smoking—to the general decline of morality in the world. It is this connection which the reader of her text will find not altogether plausible or rhetorically successful and which she will take greatest pains to reconceive in subsequent rewriting.

> There are no morals left in this world. People smoke, drink, abuse courtesy, cheat, marry and have sex as freely as they like. What happened to being ashamed of misdeeds? It has become a world of excuses. If a person knows or feels he/she has done something immoral then they will excuse it with some sweeping statement.

This is not a revolutionary idea but it has been brought to my mind most severely by a recent example. Unfortunately I live with this example everyday. It is my roommate and she smokes.

Of all things dear to me on this earth, the air I breathe is one and I simply can't tolerate cigarette smoke. It is one of the most offensive circumstances I could be amongst.

When I first found out she was a smoker I was aghast. I could not believe I was to live with such a monster when I had made it clear on my roommate questionnaire that I could not and would not live with a smoker. No way, absolutely not. What I had not accounted for was the trouble involved in switching rooms. Of course I didn't find out until a few days after I was well situated. By that time I was assured of the terrific personality of this girl and not thrilled with any of my other choices. In other words I didn't think I could find a nicer roommate and therefore relegated myself to living with the smoke.

The reason I find it immoral is because my roommate is a pre-med student. She studies nothing but chemistry and biology all day long. If anyone would be aware of smoking's hazards, she would. Yet time and time again she lights up in response to some nervous habit. In total disregard of herself and others. Her friends are the same and often congregate in her timy room filling it with a sickening haze of smoke. How can they live like this? They weren't born smoking. It's such an unnatural behavior—to inhale fumes and fire—that I don't see how it is even adopted. The mere thought of it, to me, is revolting. In fact I've never been confronted with it more in my life than since I moved to New York City. I had thought smoking was dying out. You carried a stigma if you smoked or at least I could say you were probably uncomfortable with your habit.

That is not the case in New York City. Here everyone smokes. No wonder you can't see the stars from the city. There's too much smog. And who creates that smog? the exact same people who smoke because it's chic and to calm themselves down. . . .

These people anger me that they are so selfish, but in this melting pot of immorality they find the word go. Someone even set fire accidently to a trash can in my dorm! It is absurd. . . . If someone as aware of life systems as a medical student is, smokes, then I think the morals of everything are deteriorating because it goes much deeper than that. Smoking is just another example that's indicative of the deterioration.

Perhaps the rules and standards become more lax as life itself toughens. That is not due cause though. Why doesn't everyone straighten up and try to be strong and individualistic about personal matters instead of throwing care to the wind? We have allowed ourselves to become a mass of contradictions.

Here's the teacher-reader's response, a single comment at the end of the writer's text. Notice that it probes the sufficiency of the writer's conclusions, her possibly overzalous connection of smoking to a general moral decline and her seeming self-righteousness in condemning the weaknesses of others. Naturally, the reader could have commented on any number of issues in the text; the response he chose to make is neither better nor worse than another in its focus, though it's a strategic response in its facilitative character, designed to keep the writer writing by drawing attention to something perceived as problematic in her argument.

> You seem to me to be saying that there's no more morality left in the world. You exemplify your belief with reference to your roommate's smoking. You seem to be puzzled about why anyone would pick up this immoral habit and thrust it upon innocent victims like yourself. You wonder why knowledgeable and bright people would even consider smoking.
>
> My central question is why do you link smoking with morality? Is smoking really a misdeed equivalent to illicit sex and cheating? Is smoking as terrible as stealing? If so, would you explain why? I have known some kind and generous people who happened to smoke. Should I consider them to be as terrible as rapists and wife-beaters?
>
> I can understand how your roommate mistreated you by smoking and allowing her friends to smoke in your room. But does this mean that the world is as bad as you say it is, that everything has gone to the dogs? I agree that smoking is unhealthy, but do you think your roommate is intentionally trying to poison herself and you? Have you considered the issue from her point of view, considering that it may not be a simple matter to quit? Would it be helpful to try to understand her motivation before abruptly condemning her behavior?

Since the writer had been encouraged to respond to the teacher's commentary if she wanted to, she offered the following statements along with her revision (the Pamela she refers to was a member of her class). Notice its tone: clearly, the writer believes that she remains in control of her own discourse and asserts responsibility for her authorial choices. She even feels free to fault the reader for defensiveness (presumably at the implied condemnation of his own smoking friends)!

> Thank you for your comments on my draft. Your comments combined with my group's were helpful. Pamela's reaction to my paper was unexpected. She thought that my emotions were overriding the theme of the work. She suggested that I remove the flaming comments directed towards my antismoking theme. So I put aside my personal feelings and concentrated on the event.
>
> But your reactions to my paper, defensive as they were, proved to me that it is impossible to divorce emotion from content. Now that I have finished the paper I believe it has lost some of the brimstone that I originally intended. So, Pamela's point of view does seem valid in lessening potential reader alienation.

Otherwise, any issue as to whether it is morally right or not, is beyond the intent of my paper and not within my grasp at this point. I would still appreciate your comments on my revised draft especially on those points which do not concern my views on smoking.

Here, finally, is the new text, in which the problematic connection between smoking and morality has given way before a new concern, which may or may not have arisen directly from the reader's response, for the writer's efforts to accommodate herself to a roommate whose smoking habit she finds distateful.

Moving away to school in a new city can involve many dramatic and new situations. I expected to be confronted by quite a few when I went away to college in New York City. Having always had trouble getting along with other people, I was told by many that I'd have to learn to bend and not be upset so easily. So I spent the months prior to moving away trying to prepare myself for the idiosyncrasies of a roommate or roommates that would greatly annoy me. I considered the roommate who would leave the room unlocked, the roommate who charged exorbitant long distance phone calls and the roommate who outright didn't like me. For all of these I had a solution, except, the roommate who smoked. For that, I was to learn, there is no resolve.

I first found out she was a smoker on moving-in-day, where I saw, amongst her possessions, an ashtray. I was aghast. I could not believe I was to live with such a monster when I had thought I made it absolutely clear on my roommate questionnaire that I could not and would not live with a smoke. Of all things dear to me on this earth, the air I breathe is one, and I simply can't tolerate cigarette smoke. I find it to be one of the most offensive mannerisms anyone can have and am immediately incensed by the presence of it.

Yet even though I hold a strong opinion against smoking, I am also too cowardly to tell most people. I am more likely to remain uncomfortable than complain to someone. But never in my wildest dreams, did I think I would actually have to live with a smoker every day for a year. Maybe if I had found out sooner, I could have made it my first opportunity to publicly voice my stand. As it happened though, I didn't find out she smoked until two hours after I had found a place for everything I had ever owned and given it a name too. That really threw water on my anti-smoking fire because if I wanted to change roommates, I would have to switch rooms entirely. According to the Housing Office, this was impossible. So I gritted my teeth and decided to stick it out.

Being stuck there didn't stop me from contriving plans to get my roommate to stop. I thought of everything from making her feel bad to threatening to tell her mother she smoked. I even considered a curfew prorated by half hours where I thought I might at least make some money from my suffering.

Eventually though, my roommate and I became very good friends, and I became concerned I would offend her by complaining. The smoking seemed trivial to her wonderful personality, and I was sure I couldn't have been placed with a better, more compatible roommate. As the semester progressed and the workload toughened, I noticed a dramatic increase in her smoking, especially when she was in large groups of people or friends. This was very upsetting for two reasons: (1) I didn't think I could tolerate it anymore and (2) because she rarely smoked when alone. Not only that, but she and her friends are all pre-med students. Of all people to smoke, why would those who study life and the body allow themselves to smoke? I found it very sad that they, in particular, smoke, because if they don't care, then why should anyone else care? It began to sadden me as well as anger me that she disregarded her own health and mine.

Smoking is more than just harmful; it's a selfish and filthy habit. Her friends often congregate in her tiny room, filling it with a sickening haze of smoke. Finding cigarette butts and ashes hidden among the dirt of your ficus tree can be infuriating. Watch smokers invent things to use as an ashtray, even themselves. Watch smokers try to carry something, get dressed, or eat with a cigarette in hand. They look absolutely foolish and act as if the cigarette is dearer than life itself. They'll even go so far as to hold hot ashes in their hands or burn holes in their clothes. For this, I say it is a selfish habit because it is self-satisfying that they allow the cigarettes to make fools of them.

Unfortunately, I can't change the world by myself. I can't stop everyone from smoking and a lot of people in New York smoke, so this isn't the place to start anyway. I also don't have the right to force my opinion upon another, only to present it.

Consequently, my schemes have been to no avail. My roommate still smokes at least a pack a day. Several days ago, I confided in an old friend who has a mother who smokes. I told him of my desire to end her vile habit. It seems I must continue to be upset by it because he bluntly told me to forget about trying. He spent eighteen years trying to convince his mother to stop and speaks from experience. So I too will end this crusade and hope that my roommate will at least exercise some courtesy in the future. But next year on moving day, I will ask before I unpack my bags.

In this instance, then, a writer has substantially altered a text in response to facilitative comments from a teacher-reader and fellow student. She has not followed directive instructions for "making her writing better" but has used a reader's reactions as the stimulus to look more deeply into issues she wishes to address. How confident could any teacher be, however, that the second text represents an "improvement" on the first? We asked a group of teachers to offer their impressions of the quality of the two essays and then give reasons for finding one better than the other. Here are some opinions. One reader said, "I like the first essay better —I'd give the student an A—it's entertaining and it makes the point from a very personal perspective about how a non-smoker feels about smoking. Essay 2 I'd give an A-. It's more factual and 'correct' in style and also gets the point across—but it lacks sparkle. I like pieces that entertain me as well as inform me." A second reader said, "The first essay contains fragmented ideas. In one part it speaks of immorality and in the next of the inability to tolerate cigarette smoke. The second essay systematically describes the writer's experience of leaving home and tolerating the idiosyncracies of a roommate. The first essay jumps around. The second flows nicely. Its theme develops consistently and the writer uses more complex sentences in a more coherent manner. Essay one—D, essay two—A." And a third reader said: "Essay one—C, essay two—B-. As a reader I am offended by the assumptions and assertions that create the context in the first essay. I feel insulted by the writer because she is asking me to take seriously totally unsubstantiated premises. Essay two has problems, particularly as far as sequencing goes, but the framework is legitimate. The writer is clearly engaged in this issue and I respect that effort." We could multiply these responses to show even more disagreement about grades (essay one: from D to A-; essay two: from C + to A), and about perceptions of superiority (from one is better than two, to one and two are about the same, to two is better than one), and about reasons for viewing each text one way as opposed to another. What matters, however, is not one person's estimate of improvement or degeneration, but the process of writing, responding, and writing again.

If the inescapable limitation of reader subjectivity serves to qualify the value of teacher's responses, it serves also to enhance the value of peer responses. In the writing workshop, the responsibility for facilitative response does not lie solely with the teacher. Peer response is fully as important, a crucial class activity. The concern in a workshop is to give writers access to the reactions of as many readers as possible, multiplying perspectives, introducing legitimate differences of opinion, and portraying the broadest possible range of effects that a given discourse can have on diverse readers. Writers confronted with these diverse reactions learn over time to gauge and anticipate the impact of their choices, forming in their own minds a Questioning Reader, comprised of recollections of all the actual responses they have experienced, which sharpens their critical sense and guides future composing. The style of facilitative commentary which a teacher-reader brings to student texts in the workshop serves also as a model for students' conversations among themselves about their writing. That is, peer groups discuss writing as an effort to make and communicate meanings. Members of a group identify and, when possible, explain for the writer's benefit the impact that a text has on their view of a subject and on their awareness of the writer's stance toward it. They discuss both the issues that a text raises and also the choices in the text that cause those issues to appear the way they do or to affect a reader in the way they do. Student-readers offer their opinions along with the teacher, collaborating to present the writer with a provocative range of responses from which to infer what else to say, what more to do, in order to convey personal intentions in satisfying ways.[10]

But two complaints frequently arise in connection with peer responses. The first is that, just as students lack the expertise to write effectively, so too they lack the expertise to comment on the writing of others. The second complaint, an extension of the first, is that not all the responses of group members have equal use or even equal validity and that the confusion sabotages instruction. To an extent, of course, students are inexpert at examining and communicating the impact a text has had on them. But the inexperience does not mean that students have no reactions to what they read or have the wrong reactions. Rather, students have typically had few opportunities to articulate their reactions or to discover that what they have to say might be valuable and pertinent. One reason for the denial of opportunity has been the assumption of teachers that "expertise" means knowledge of formal and technical conventions, rather than the more common sort of reader reaction focused on what a writer wishes to communicate and how the communication is affecting a particular individual. All readers, educated or not, technically conscious or not, respond to what they read and can, with opportunity and practice, articulate their response. Since facilitative commentary in the classroom parallels this common variety of reader interaction with a text, there's no more reason to assume students' inability to react usefully to each other's work than there is to assume that they do not have legitimate and meaningful experiences of literature or other kinds of reading. Granted, they require practice at conveying what a text has done to them, and a workshop strives to provide that experience. But with practice students become quite adept at characterizing their responses, though naturally the quality of response varies in proportion to their degrees of intellectual maturity. Not all students react subtly or richly, but their reactions are not for that reason false or unhelpful. Indeed, they may at times have more pertinence to the writer, who is after all another student, than the teacher's observations will have, being perhaps more sophisticated but also, often, less comprehensible.

The second objection—that students' responses disagree and are sometimes opposed to the teachers'—derives from the dubious assumption that teachers' judgments of texts are inevitably correct and may therefore serve as the measure of what else can legitimately be said. And this assumption derives in turn from teachers' experiences in traditional classrooms, where no one present has sufficient authority to challenge the master's pronouncements. If a group of teachers were to sit together in a peer discussion of the features and merits of a discourse, the likelihood of even rough agreement of views would be minimal, as we have shown in connection with the "smoking" essay. There would be argument, differing perspectives, even inaccuracy, personal prejudice, and obstinate refusals to hear alternative possibilities. Which of these peers has the "right" opinion? To answer "the most experienced one" is to invite more argument and more insistence on personal opinions. The fact is, no one has access to the Absolute Reading of a text, and everyone will occasionally err in voicing opinions even about technical matters, let alone the validity of a line of reasoning or the sufficiency of a manner of presentation. Students should learn to be as wary of teachers' comments as they are about those of other students, as willing to sort the useful from the frivolous, just as one experienced writer is invariably cautious about the opinions of another. Error surrounds all of us and all of us blunder into it. So, the first reason to tolerate student disagreement and even apparent mistakes of judgment is the humble realization that our own hobby-horses can interfere with clear perception too, that we are neither invariably right in what we say nor invariably right about whether our students are right. A second reason to tolerate it is the additional recognition that diversity is healthy and provocative, that the truth lies in negotiation, in compromise, in the mutual challenging of opinions, and in a willingness to concede that others will occasionally have insights superior to our own—even perhaps others with less experience.

Again, however, students require practice at articulating their own views because they are not, as a rule, accustomed to this degree of intellectual responsibility, or familiar with the possible varieties of response, or with the value that feedback can have for writers. At the start, therefore, peer reactions will often be formulaic ("I liked this"), traditional ("You need more details" or "This word is misspelled"), and rather stifled. A teacher who wishes to have students respond productively begins by dramatizing the style in her own talk while also encouraging students to trust that their reactions will be as valuable, as pertinent, as listened to, as her own. By modeling facilitative commentary in the workshop, she can lead students to adopt a similar style. Given an environment of mutual intellectual respect and encouragement, students will gradually overcome the reticence built up over years of enforced classroom silence. Here's an example of student interaction in a workshop where that supportive environment has been developed. The transcript below offers part of an extended conversation that members of a peer group in a college-level writing class carried on with the writer of the following short text. In the transcript, "W" refers to the writer, while "A," "B," and "C" refer to other participants in the conversation.[11]

Just a minute ago, I was in Gristede's buying a Coke when I saw a man taking a 7-Up from the refrigerator and putting it in his pocket. Then he was in front of me in line at the register and he paid for one 7-Up but the other was snuggled away. I could see into his jacket and the top of a little vodka bottle was peeking out. Those tariff labels are all the same. Then I saw him in the elevator and he was obviously very inebriated. He began to shout GOING UP! and he stood in the middle of the elevator with his feet in second position parallel trying to stabilize himself. I felt strange. Should I have said something at the store? I just winced when I saw him stick the soda in his pocket and I felt a flash flood of remorse, compassion, and anger. I fought the urge to be righteous. Am I a coward? Or am I just tired?

A: Was there only one incident like that? The first one you've ever had like that?

W: Yeah.

B: But did it occur to you that . . .

W: Yeah, right before class . . .

B: that the guy might be really poor?

W: Oh! Yeah, I thought about that too, but . . .

A: If you were revising that, would it be as spontaneous?

W: Well, I know what I'd do—I'd elaborate a lot. I'd describe what the man looked like; I'd change the tone and . . .

B: But what about the frantic thoughts, the moment, what was going through your head while it was happening. You weren't *thinking* about what he was wearing, were you?

W: No, that's true, but I . . .

A: Then, uh, your only impression was that he was being a thief?

B: What bothered you was that he stole it?

W: Not just that.

B: Didn't it bother you that he was an alcoholic?

W: Well, my concentration was on how I dealt with the man. My choices. I could have said something to the man at the cash register. But I didn't.

A: Would it have scared you to do that?

W: No, I've dealt with it before—people who've stolen. Like when I was in high school, these guys I knew, they were vandalizing and stealing stuff and I went and told them that I thought that was really crass and they were going "Oh, Maria, you think you're so righteous" and like that and so I talked to my teacher and he said he'd done something like that once—telling someone to stop ripping stuff off and the next day he got his tires slashed. But this thing—well, I could go at it a few ways . . .

B: You could dwell on the feeling.

C: What about the thing with the vandals in your school? Does that fit in somewhere? I thought that was interesting. But would it change the focus?

W: It would get back to—an open letter to myself about guilt and being cowardly and choice. That would be a fine approach except I don't like the idea that writing is self-referential. Do you know what I'm saying? All those papers that are just "I this" and "I that" and so on. It's so boring to read that sort of stuff.

B: The reader could learn a lot from your feelings. He can see how it is for others.

A: Yes. Everyone asks themselves the same question in that situation—should I? shouldn't I?

W: Yeah, I guess. Well, I have to think about it. I'm not real sure about how I want to do it yet.

These oral student responses are distinctive for their serious intellectual tone, suggesting the students' recognition that they have both the ability and the authority to help a writer discover ways to explore a subject further. The "rightness" or comprehensiveness or maturity of the responses is at most a subordinate issue: the writer must come to personal conclusions about what is helpful and what is not. From a teaching point of view, what matters is that the writer is privy to authentic and legitimate reactions of interested readers, which helps to clarify the sense of purpose and presentation with reference to questions and uncertainties those readers have seen fit to raise. Through dialogue, the writer can begin to develop an internal Questioning Reader, regardless of whether the responses of eighteen-year-olds are more or less expert than those of the teacher-reader (who will, in any case, have been responding also). Of course, student reactions can be written as well as oral, and can take place outside of classes as well as during the workshop. Here's an instance of written response, where students have broken into pairs in order to take turns in writer and reader roles. The student whose writing appears below appended to her complete first draft some personal estimates of what the choices in the text, paragraph by paragraph, were designed to achieve. What follows is, first, the entire draft, and then, the student's appraisal of her choices:[12]

As I started toward Beauty Therapy's door, the receptionist, Joan saw me and buzzed the door so I could open it. I pushed it open and as I walked in, I felt all eyes look up at me and all the girls left what they were doing to focus their attention on me.

I had just come from playing tennis so I was dressed in my white Tacchini warm-up suit with its navy and red stripes down the sides and my new Puma sneakers. My hair was up in a ponytail with a bandana tied under my bangs; I hate to sweat in my bangs.

I was wearing the usual thick mascara and lipstick. It was an ordinary Friday and everybody around was on display for each other as usual.

I hung up my Flatbush jacket and found an empty chair to sit in until Luda was ready to give me my manicure. I said hello to most of the girls who happened to be my friends or at least my acquaintances. After all, everybody in the community knows each other or at least who belongs to the community.

The women and younger girls were gossiping about the most important things in life; how many carats Mary's diamond ring is; Sally lost five pounds; Rochelle's outfit was seen in Bonwit Teller for $500; Denise and Robert were seen together three times which means that they must be getting engaged soon; and of course 134 is the prettiest nailpolish color for this time of year.

I thought the whole scene was amusing this Friday, while I had never before realized how trivial and silly the conversation really was. Luda called me to sit down and she began filing my nails.

My mind drifted for a while and I found myself wondering what it would be like living outside the community. I wouldn't be on display anywhere I went and I would have more privacy.

I would probably be close to my family like I am now, and we would probably live the same exact way. The difference would be that our lives wouldn't be open to all for discussion. We would still have a few select friends. The difference would be that everybody around wouldn't know what jewelry my mother owned or who I went out with.

But then who would I marry? My whole way of thinking is geared toward the family life available only in a close, tight-knit community. We are all similar to each other: religion-wise, financially, and most importantly, we want the same things out of life. Maybe that is why divorce is so uncommon in my community. No. I would never be able to live outside the community. I love it and need it too much; despite its faults. The farthest I'll ever get from the community will probably be living in the city my first year of marriage, and I'll probably come home to my mother's house for weekends then too.

I was unconsciously glancing at the various nailpolish colors deciding which to choose when I heard the door buzz. All eyes looked up to see who was entering the salon, what she was wearing, and waiting to hear what she had to say. Deep down inside, I was no different than the rest of the girls.

Paragraphs 1 and 2 I'm describing going to Beauty Therapy. The reader has no idea what it is except that there are girls there. They all looked up at me when I entered the place and I felt as if I was on display. I explain my routine tennis outfit to let the reader picture the scene and comment that although it was an ordinary Friday, I felt silly this week. The reader still doesn't know why I'm describing this, so they'll have to read on.

Paragraph 3 Beauty Therapy is apparently a manicure salon and I happened to know most of the girls there because they belong to my community. I am sarcastic about the fact that those in the community know who "belongs" in the community. I think the reader will wonder "What community"? But I hope that by reading on they'll find out.

Paragraphs 4 and 5 The girls were gossiping about other girls in the community and I was out of it. It all seemed so trivial to me and the reader can see why. The girls weren't talking about anything really significant. But the reader can see from these paragraphs that the girls know a lot about each other and it must be a tight-knit community. Who they are or where they come from, the reader still doesn't know.

Paragraph 6 I wondered what life would be like living outside the community and state that it would be much more private. I assume that I would still be close to my family. This is a normal assumption involving keeping some part of my present identity.

Paragraph 7 I'm finally asking the questions that a reader would ask. What is my community? Why do I live there? It sounds like a place where your life is an open book to all. I hope my reader will keep on and find out why I do live here.

Paragraph 8 I stop dreaming about life outside this (unknown) community. I claim that I will probably live there despite its disadvantages. The reader can easily see the disadvantages, but probably has no idea of what the community's assets are. What is the community? Who are these people? How many members? Where do they live? How did I become a part of the community? Why would I want to live there voluntarily? How long has the community been in this unknown place? What makes them a community? The reader doesn't know the answers to these questions. My advice to myself is to either get out of the community or come up with some good substantial reasons to stay there.

Paragraph 9 A girl walks into the place and all eyes look up to "check her out." I do the same. I realize that I am just like the rest of the girls in this community. A gossip! The community sounds really shallow in this paper and that's not what I intended.

The writer's text was then given to a student reader but without the writer's attached commentary. The reader was asked to estimate and characterize personal responses to the text, paragraph by paragraph, just as the writer had done. Here are the results:

Paragraph 1 Deborah walked into somewhere; place is not described. She is just starting her essay. I feel confused and must read on. I guess that's a normal feeling so far.

Paragraph 2 Deborah describes her outfit and appearance exactly and says that in this unknown place called Beauty Therapy, everyone is on display. Really, for all I know at this point, it could even be a house of prostitution. Why she explains her outfit in detail, I don't know.

Paragraph 3 Deborah now says that she's in a manicure place. Friends and acquaintances are there and now she hints that everyone knows each other in her community. This makes me think, are the friends the girls who are on display for each other? And what community? (even though I know). Still it's only the beginning of the essay, and it hasn't really gotten off the ground yet, so I'll wait and see what happens.

Paragraph 4   There's a hint of sarcasm here insinuating how shallow these friends and acquaintances are. I still am striving to understand what she's trying to say.

Paragraph 5   This is saying that the usual conversations that used to seem normal, now seem trivial. I am now starting to see the essay beginning to focus on something.

Paragraph 6   Deborah starts to think about what it would be like to live outside her community. It would mean having more privacy. All I know is that Deborah's community has no privacy and that people are on display, with their trivial conversations. This seems like a heck of a community. Poor Deborah— what a place to live. (Of course, I know she likes living there, so that means she's not letting her reader see the good side yet.)

Paragraph 7   Deborah assumes that her family life would stay the same. How does she know this? Also, she again says that lives wouldn't be open to all for discussion and everybody wouldn't know everything. All this community sounds like is a bunch of Rona Barretts gossiping all day long. What kind of horrible community is this, anyway?

Paragraph 8   Why is family available only in a tight-knit community? There is another assumption that's not backed up. Deborah says that the people/community are all similar and she loves it and could never live without it, despite its faults. Well, all I heard about this community in this essay so far is that they're close-knit and gossipers. What *are* the community's good points? How many people live there? Why are they called a community? The word community is used very often, but for all I know we could be talking about close-knit, gossipy werewolves.

Paragraph 9   Deborah uses a little example to show that she's just like the rest of the girls. Looking up and waiting to hear gossip in the manicure place.

Overall Response   Well, well. Deb—I think I know what you're trying to say and it's a great idea—but look what you make the community out to be! What is "community"? How can anyone *feel* anything for this when everything is so vague? If you were to build and zero in on your major ideas, not on what you're wearing, then the reader might catch on right away. What if you changed the beginning a little and said you walked into your usual manicure place and overheard two women gossiping about someone. If you really zero in on the trivial gossiping conversation you heard in detail, the reader could understand why you felt so annoyed. Then you could say something like how, even though the community is this and that (but you have to explain the community in detail so the reader can have something to hang on to), it's still a good place to live. You could explain that despite the pressure and the competition between people, we all help each other. You could tell how we built the center and the Hillel School—the good points. When you said you could never live without your community as a reader I had to say "why" because, based on what you'd said, I'd get out as fast as possible. But if you build up an impression of the community for the reader, then the whole thing will make more sense. I still don't see why you went to all the trouble to describe your outfit.

Notice how frequently the writer and reader raise similar questions about the text, suggesting points of agreement about where change might be desirable. Notice too where perceptions differ, creating the possibility of discussion and negotiation. Working together, the writer and reader compared their separate appraisals and talked over opportunities for revision. The writer then attempted a second draft in which she tried to make the purposes for writing more apparent in light of the student-reader's uncertainties. Here's that second draft.

> As I started toward Beauty Therapy's door, the receptionist, Joan, saw me and buzzed the door so I could open it. I pushed it open and as I walked in, I felt all eyes look up at me and all the girls left what they were doing to focus their attention on me.
>
> I had been too busy to get a manicure for weeks, but this week I managed to squeeze in the hour. I had just come from playing tennis, so I was dressed in my white Tacchini warm-up suit with its navy and red stripes down the sides and my new Puma sneakers. My hair was up in a ponytail with a white bandana tied under my bangs; I hate to sweat in my bangs. I was wearing the usual thick mascara and pink lipstick. It was an ordinary Friday and all the girls were on display for each other as usual. The difference was in me—I felt as if the whole scene was funny this week.
>
> I hung up my Flatbush jacket and found an empty chair to sit in until Luda was ready to give me my manicure. I said hello to most of the girls who happened to be my friends or at least my acquaintances. After all, everybody in the community knows each other or at least who belongs to the community.
>
> The women and younger girls were gossiping about the most important things in life: how many carats Mary's diamond ring is; Sally lost five pounds; Rochelle's outfit was seen in Bonwit Teller for $500. Denise and Robert were seen together three times which means that they must be getting engaged soon; and of course 134 is the prettiest nailpolish color for this time of year.
>
> I thought the whole scene was amusing this Friday, while I had never before realized how trivial and silly the conversation really was. Luda called me to sit down and she began filing my nails.
>
> My mind drifted for a while, and I found myself wondering what it would be like living outside the community. I wouldn't be on display anywhere I went

and I would have more privacy. I would probably be close to my family like I am now, and we would probably live in the same lifestyle. The difference would be that our lives wouldn't be open to all for discussion. We would still have a few select friends. However, I strongly doubt that everybody around would know what jewelry my mother owned or who I went out with.

I began to fancy the idea of living outside the community and I started getting worried. Wait a minute! Why is the community so great? Why does my family choose to live here rather than anywhere else in the world? My mind wandered back to the beginning.

The "community" started about seventy years ago when my grandparents, along with many other Syrian Jews, left Syria and immigrated into the United States. They all came penniless, since conditions were terrible in Syria at that time and they could rarely sell their homes or furniture if they were leaving the country. Many owned nothing but the shirts on their backs—literally.

These Syrian immigrants started their new lives in the lower East Side in New York. They began as peddlers of the textile industry—they sold linens, tablecloths, towels. Since they were very poor, most of the Syrians worked six days a week (they didn't work on Sabbath—the day of rest), from early in the morning until late at night. Their ambition, along with G-d's help, caused them to build up their financial status gradually. Soon these Syrian Jews were able to move to a nicer neighborhood in Brooklyn. Those Syrians who became wealthy invested or loaned their money to other Syrians. After many years of hard work, the Syrian "community" became very wealthy.

These nouveau riche people changed in certain ways, as would be expected, but they never forgot the important elements that kept them together. The synagogue never ceased to play a major role in the Syrians' lives—the Chief Rabbi married their children and he would teach and lecture the community about some new topic every Saturday in synagogue. The synagogue would hold drives every so often in order to raise money to build a yeshivah exclusively for the Syrian children. After much effort and money donations, Magen David Yeshivah was established. It is this school that ensured the educating of the youth in the manner desired. Basic tenets of Judaism were taught as well as Syrian customs. The Syrian method of praying differs from that of other Jews—in melody and even in the pronunciation of many of the Hebrew letters. Magen David helped keep many traditions that without it would definitely have disappeared.

The community continued to live in Brooklyn, except by now, many families were able to renovate or redecorate their homes, thus enhancing the beauty of the area.

The most important factor that kept the Syrians together was the shunning of intermarriage. According to Jewish law, a Jew can marry any Jew. The Syrians tend to take this law one step further. They even frown upon a Syrian marrying a Jew from outside the community. This may sound snobbish or narrow-minded, but this key factor seems necessary to maintain the

Syrian traditions and customs: the spicy food; the Syrian tradition of naming the first born son after the father's father and the first daughter after the father's mother; the phrases in Syrian that became part of their everyday conversations. All this sets the community apart from others.

Now, seventy years later, the community has grown tremendously. Approximately 35,000 people belong to the community. There are various new schools, synagogues, and Syrian stores to accommodate this quickly growing group. A recent addition is a Community Youth Sports Center—a new place for Syrian youth to congregate and meet.

The other day my sister Michele came running home from the center screaming, "Mom, I just met the most gorgeous hiloow (handsome; sweet) boy and he asked me out! His name is David Cohen. Can I go? Please?" At the mere mention of his name, my mother figured out who his family is. She teased my sister and said, "Is that the David Cohen who has two brothers, one sister, and he lives a couple of blocks away from us?" My mother knew more about the boy than Michele did herself. Of course, a Syrian girl must spend a great deal of time with a boy before she gets married, but a great advantage of the community is that it eliminates a lot of the preliminaries that other people must go through. There are usually no "deep dark secrets" that we find out about later. Maybe that is why divorce is so rare in the community.

I stopped myself and thought—how can I have ever doubted the community? This is the only place I know of where I would want to raise a family. We are protective of one another. I love the community and need it too much; despite its faults. My G-d! With so many women living so close to each other, who know so much about one another, how can there not be gossip? As of now, I think that the farthest I'll ever get from the community will probably be living in the City my first year of marriage, and I'll probably come home to my mother's house for weekends then too.

I was unconsciously glancing at the various nailpolish colors, deciding which to choose, when I heard the door buzz. I watched all eyes look up to see who was entering the salon, what she was wearing, and waiting to hear what she had to say. Deep down inside I was no different than the rest of the girls because I too looked up.

In response to the reader's observations, the writer has included a lengthy passage on the "community" mentioned rather mysteriously in draft one, feeling the necessity to elaborate on her desire to remain a member despite its faults. At the same time, however, she does not regard the reader's comments as instructions for change: she retains her description of the tennis outfit, for example, despite the reader's confusion about it. The point is, a student-reader has responded facilitatively and productively to a writer's effort, enhancing the writer's awareness of opportunities for deeper understanding and for sharpened clarity of intention. When this support is supplemented by the responses of a teacher-reader, still further possibilities for development are likely to emerge. There are certainly many other ways of enabling students to join with teachers in the process of responding to texts in order to promote additional writing. We are content to leave methodological variation to the imaginations of teachers who accept and wish to proceed from the philosophical premises we have introduced. Methods are important, but attitudes are more important. The teacher who devises a check-list of critical items—"is the introduction interesting?"; "does every paragraph have a single idea?"—and who distributes the list to peer groups so that students can mechanically evaluate each other's writing according to the teacher's Ideal Text has altogether missed our point. Making students accomplices in a traditional instructional activity is not equivalent to leading them toward intellectual freedom and responsibility. The philosophical attitude governing *any* method restricts that method within the limitations of that perspective.

Notes

1. A recent study has shown that more than half of the teachers it surveyed restricted their commentary on student writing to narrowly technical corrections, while practically no teachers offered substantive responses intended to encourage revision. See Dennis Searle and David Dillon. 1980. "The Message of Marking: Teacher Written Responses to Student Writing at Intermediate Grade Levels." *Research in the Teaching of English*, 14 (October): 233–42. On the limitations of technical correction, see W. U. McDonald. 1978. "The Revising Process and the Marking of Student Papers," *College Composition and Communication*, 24 (May): 167–70.

2. Nancy Sommers has pointed out the uncommunicative nature of typical responses to student writing in "Responding to Student Writing." *College Composition and Communication,* 33 (May 1982): 148–56.

3. The concept of Ideal Text, and the argument related to the Lindbergh essay, are developed in Lil Brannon and C.H. Knoblauch, "On Students' Rights to Their Own Texts: A Model of Teacher Response," *College Composition and Communication*, 33 (May 1982): 157–66.

4. Study after study has shown the futility of this method of responding to writing, students' subsequent efforts revealing little or no change as a result of the commentary. See, for instance, in addition to Searle and Dillon, R. J. Marzano and S. Arthur, "Teacher Comments on Student Essays: It Doesn't Matter What You Say," a study conducted at the University of Colorado, Denver, in 1977 (ERIC ED 147864). For a review of several studies, all reporting negative results, and an argument for the reasons, see C. H. Knoblauch and Lil Brannon, "Teacher Commentary on Student Writing: The State of the Art," *Freshman English News*, 10 (Fall 1981): 3–4.

5. "Ethos" is, of course, an ancient concept—see Aristotle, *Rhetoric*, 1356a2. When readers accept writers' authority, and usually they do at least at the start of reading, they work at understanding what the writer intends to say. I. A. Richards has noted the power of authority in *Practical Criticism* (New York: Harcourt, Brace. 1929, 297). The mere name of a well-known poet is enough to insure attentive reading of a mediocre work,

yet a perfectly fine example of student writing will be criticized and subordinated to an Ideal Text, whatever its merits.

6. This reading posture is perhaps a version of Peter Elbow's "believing game." See *Writing Without Teachers* (New York: Oxford University Press. 1973, 169 ff).

7. Donald Murray has shown how oral facilitative response, not just written, can help students become wise questioners of their own texts by first hearing the supportive questions of teachers. See "Teaching the Other Self: The Writer's First Reader," *College Composition and Communication*, 33 (May 1982): 140–47.

8. Several studies of the revision process of less experienced writers illustrate this point. See Nancy Sommers, "Revision Strategies of Student Writers and Experienced Adult Writers," *College Composition and Communication*, 31 (December 1980), 378–88; Lester Faigley and Stephen Witte, "Analyzing Revision," *College Composition and Communication*, 32 (December 1981), 400–414; Richard Beach, "Self-Evaluation Strategies of Extensive Revisers and Non-Revisers," *College Composition and Communication*, 27 (1976), 160–64; Richard Beach, "The Effects of Between-Draft Teacher Evaluation Versus Student Self-Evaluation on High School Students' Revising of Rough Drafts," *Research in the Teaching of English*, 13 (1979), 111–19; and Lillian S. Bridwell, "Revising Strategies in Twelfth Grade Students' Transactional Writing," *Research in the Teaching of English,* 14 (October 1980), 197–222.

9. Louise Rosenblatt first explored the active behaviors of readers in *Literature as Exploration* (New York: Noble and Noble, 1938), and later in *The Reader, the Text, the Poem: The Transactional Theory of the Literary Work* (Carbondale: Southern Illinois University Press, 1978). For the work of various reader-response theorists, see Jane Tompkins, ed., *Reader Response Criticism: From Formalism to Post-Structuralism* (Baltimore: Johns Hopkins, 1980) and Susan R. Suleiman and Inge Crosman, eds., *The Reader in the Text: Essays on Audience and Interpretation* (Princeton: Princeton University Press, 1980).

10. John Clifford in "Composing in Stages: The Effects of a Collaborative Pedagogy," *Research in the Teaching of English*, 15 (February 1981), 37–53 and Douglas Barnes and Frankie Todd in *Communication and Learning in Small Groups* (London: Routledge and Kegan Paul, 1977) demonstrate the effectiveness of peer group interaction in the writing workshop. Douglas Barnes in *From Communication to Curriculm* (Harmondsworth, England: Penguin, 1976); Nancy Martin, *et al.*, in *Understanding Children Talking* (Penguin, 1976); B. M. Kroll and R. J. Vann, eds., in *Exploring Speaking-Writing Relationships; Connections and Contrasts* (Urbana, IL: NCTE, 1981); and Douglas Barnes, James Britton, and Harold Rosen in *Language, the Learner and the School* (Penguin, 1971) all argue for the connections between talk and learning and between talk and writing.

11. The student text and responses cited here are from a textbook by Lil Brannon, Melinda Knight, and Vara Neverow-Turk, *Writers Writing* (Portsmouth, NH: Boynton/Cook, 1982, 120–24). The book can be useful to teachers interested in setting up peer groups and encouraging peer response.

12. *Writers Writing*, pp. 111–19.

21

Enlisting the Writer's Participation in the Evaluation Process

Jeffrey Sommers

All writing courses eventually reach the moment of truth when the instructor turns judge and must pass sentence on her students' work. However, as our understanding of the role of revision in the composing process has grown, many instructors, even entire writing programs, have come to rely upon a method of evaluation called "semester grading" or "portfolio grading." In such a scheme of evaluation, the student writer submits her work to the instructor and receives, instead of a grade, suggestions about how to improve the writing through rewriting. These suggestions may take the form of written comments, tape-recorded advice, or one-to-one conferences with the instructor or one's peers in class. At the end of the course, the portfolio is submitted for a grade with the writer selecting her most effective revised pieces of writing for evaluation.

This approach to evaluation reinforces the value of revision as an integral part of writing because submitted work is treated as drafts in progress rather than as finished essays—at least until the writer identifies the drafts as finished. Additionally, a more productive relationship is established between student and teacher, who are no longer defendant and judge but instead writer and editor.[1]

But a problem exists for the instructor-turned-editor functioning in a course which employs semester grading since the role of an editor is a more challenging one than that of a judge who merely voices an opinion and explains it briefly. The instructor's editorial function requires her to make intelligent and useful comments so that students can actually work to improve their writing. Nancy Sommers has reported that "teachers' comments can take students' attention away from their own purposes in writing a particular text and focus that attention on the teachers' purposes in commenting" (149). Can composition instructors read as "dumb readers," in Walker Gibson's apt phrase, ignorant of the intent of their student writers, and still hope to avoid making the kinds of inappropriate comments Sommers describes? Can an instructor "be a guide who doesn't lead so much as stand behind the young explorer [the student writer], pointing out alternatives only at the moment of panic" (Murray 142) if the writer's initial intent remains buried in a heap of impenetrable freshman prose? Will students take advantage of the revision opportunities in a semester-grading situation if the instructor's comments are too directive or too obtuse? Lil Brannon and C. H. Knoblauch argue that "it is precisely the chance to accomplish one's own purpose by controlling one's own choices that creates incentive to write" (159) and further argue that student writers ought to be consulted about their texts before the editor comments. Brannon and Knoblauch are concerned with the students' right to their texts, but the issue also extends to students' right to have their texts evaluated fairly. That editor will eventually metamorphose into a judge. If the suggestions the editor has been making are not useful, they may lead the student writer to inferior revision which may subsequently lead to lower evaluations (i.e. "bad grades"), making the instructor complicitous in bringing about that poor evaluation. The question then is how can instructors know their students' intentions before commenting on their drafts, and the answer is to enlist the participation of their students in the responding process.

The student-teacher memo is one method of enlisting that participation. In this approach, the instructor makes an assignment for writing and simultaneously makes an assignment for a student-teacher memo: a brief, informal not-to-be-graded communication written to the instructor by the student who comments on the draft in question. Although the students have the option to write these memos in any form they choose, the instructor makes the assignment in the form of a series of open-ended questions such as "Who is your audience in this piece of writing?" "How did that audience affect what you have written?" "What do you want the audience to get out of this piece of writing?" "Which parts of the essay seem to be the least successful in achieving your goals? Why?" "Which parts were most successful? Why?" "What do you want me to comment on in particular in the paper?"

With the information provided by the student, the instructor need no longer be a "dumb reader." The instructor becomes less likely to push the student into writing an essay the instructor wants instead of writing what the student wants. I would like to examine a student draft, its accompanying memo, and the subsequent final draft of the paper to illustrate how the student-teacher memo can help instructors respond to student work effectively and subsequently evaluate it fairly.

The only stipulation for this assignment was that the students were to write an expository paper. Lori, a first semester college freshman, submitted the following first draft:

High Quality Education

As a student attending Central High, the quality of my high school education was not one of my major concerns. However, after attending Miami University for several weeks, the matter strikes me in an entirely different perspective. I have found myself inadequately prepared for college and feel that I can offer useful insight and suggestions to help other students have opportunities that I did not have.

Typically a teenager is not likely to exert any more effort than he needs. In all probability he is not going to consider the fact that eventually he may seek a post high school education and that the education he receives during high school will largely determine his success. A typical teenager needs to be guided in the right direction. Many times during high school, I received little or no direction. Basically I registered for classes and was permitted to take whatever courses I wanted regardless of what value they did or did not serve me.

I have spoken with other students at Miami and have learned many useful ideas utilized by other high school guidance counselors. For instance, several students felt that questionnaires concerning post high school plans, interests, and possible career interests were very useful in choosing classes particularly when their guidance counselors helped them to choose classes in relation to their answers on the questionnaires. Also many students had participated in a job simulation program which allowed them an opportunity to consider their interests and skills. Most students had taken an aptitude test designed to evaluate their skills and interests. These programs allowed the students to take classes that held some value for them. The majority of the students with whom I spoke felt that the programs were very helpful to them.

Under-qualified teachers is another area with which we should be concerned. For instance, when questioning the proper usage of the pronouns who and whom, one of my English teachers once told me not to worry about it because she had never really understood how to use them herself. In an algebra course I took, we couldn't complete our lessons trying to compete with the chaos in the classroom. The teacher simply had no control. I have also had teachers who displayed flirtatious and highly unprofessional behavior in the classroom; I do not feel that such actions are condusive to learning.

Perhaps the requirements for teachers at Central High are too lenient. A strict screening committee or a strict personal evaluation of the teachers would help. Also increased classroom observations by administrators could check the problem.

The final area which concerns me is low graduation requirements. The requirements at Central High include one year of math, three years of English, one semester of health, one year of physical education, two years of social studies, one year of science. I do not feel that these requirements create a well-rounded individual. Students who I have spoken with were surprised at such lax standards. Most were required two or more years of math, four years of English, three years of social studies, and two years of science. Such standards not only benefit college bound students but also help to create more responsible citizens.

I feel that these areas deserve genuine consideration. New programs need to be started and old ones need to be updated. These actions will help many people.

If I had to comment on this paper without benefit of the accompanying memo, I would focus on my uncertainty about its intended audience and the problems that creates in the voice of the paper. The opening paragraph, especially the final sentence, led me to infer that Lori was writing to her fellow students in our class. However, in the fifth and sixth paragraphs she focuses her criticism squarely on her own high school, a matter hardly of interest to the majority of her classmates who did not attend Central High. In fact, her conclusion is vague enough to leave unclear whether she wants to assist her poor former classmates still languishing at Central High or whether she wants to assist other "inadequately prepared" students at the University. Also puzzling is that when she sketches out alternative programs that might remedy some of the problems she has identified, she presents her ideas too off-handedly. At this point she also seems to be addressing an audience powerful enough to implement those programs. Her classmates would hardly have that power. Finally, who is the other party in the "we" she uses in paragraph 4: her current classmates, her former Central High classmates, some third unidentified group?

Since Lori seems most concerned with her own high school and with improving the quality of education it offers, I would have suggested that she make her criticisms more pointed (what was the "highly unprofessional behavior" cited in paragraph 4, for instance?) and that she become more vigorously persuasive about her proposed solutions.

However, I did not actually make these comments because Lori also submitted a student-teacher memo with the draft. She chose to use the questions I had asked as a launching pad for a free-form response. Here is what she wrote.

> In this paper I want the reader to realize that Central doesn't have good guidance counselors; Central doesn't have high enough graduation standards; Central doesn't have very strict requirements for their teachers. However, I kept in mind that this letter is supposedly to my former high school principal and therefore, I wasn't as forceful as I really felt I should be or could be. I wanted my voice to be constructive not demanding. I'm not finished working on this—I still feel that I'm not really creating the picture I want the way that I want. One problem I see with my paper is that I could have used my examples more effectively and I did not. The actual writing of the paper isn't giving problems—the ideas are basically there, they simply aren't in a finished form yet. Tell me what you feel when you read this paper. Do I sound as if I'm pointing a finger? If you were my high school principal would you take offense? Am I being argumentative enough? Can I take a stronger stand without creating the wrong impression? Sometimes I think this memo helps me as much as it helps you. This paper has been easier than the rest, but I have

that feeling that it's just not finished yet. If I didn't get to rewrite it again, I still probably would because I think it can be done better.

In her very first sentence Lori has answered one of my central questions by identifying her purpose; her interest, she says, lies in focusing on Central High School's deficiencies. Her following comment, however, may be the most significant one in the memo; it came as a surprise to me that she had been writing this paper as a letter to her former principal. I now understood the "we" in paragraph 4 of the draft; I understood her recommending specific programs for implementation; I also understood why she had not presented her proposals more vigorously. Lori had been quite sensitive to her audience, as the rest of her memo illustrates when she attempts to cast me in the role of the principal in order to receive the feedback she needs, guiding my responses by asking me specific questions. I did feel that she was pointing a finger, especially in paragraph 5 as she oversimplifies the complexities of teacher evaluation; I also felt that the principal would be likely to take offense. Her final two questions were more difficult to answer. I could not be sure. When I actually commented on the paper, I made certain to address these concerns of Lori's. I told her my reactions as a pretend principal of Central High, including my uncertainty about her final two questions. I did not, however, advise her to make her criticism more pointed nor her proposals more persuasive.[2] Lori then went back and reworked her paper, later submitting a final version in her portfolio which I was to grade:

High Quality Education

In college, I find myself repeatedly experiencing the same sort of difficulty in many of my courses. I am continually grasping to learn the fundamentals of a given course while the majority of the class has already learned or at least been exposed to that material during high school. Therefore, I feel that a great deal of my difficulty stems directly from specific deficiencies in the educational process at Central High School.

For one thing, Central is not particularly strong in its sciences. Being a nursing student, I need a great deal of science courses. Some of my college class requirements include zoology and chemistry. Central, unfortunately, does not offer either of these sciences. I now struggle a great deal with the basics which most other students learned in their high school science courses. These students can devote their time to the more complex aspects of zoology and chemistry while I attempt to grasp both the simpler as well as the more difficult ones.

In addition, many courses that I did take did not cover a great deal of the material for which I am now responsible. When I registered for my college classes in August, I consulted the placement guide in the University Catalog. "One year high school algebra . . . MTH 101–102." I chose to take Math 101 and, indeed, that was a wise decision. I would have been entirely lost in Math 102—I was in Math 101. The first class meeting, the professor simply reviewed. His review, however, included things that, up to that point, I had yet to "view." Most of the students who I spoke with after class were familiar with the material that the professor had covered. My high school algebra course had covered only a small portion of the material that the professor expected me to know. And then there is my English course. I am doing fairly well except I must spend too much time checking and rechecking grammatical points when I could be writing or revising. My high school English teacher was not concerned with grammar. In fact, she totally dismissed the importance of learning the proper usage of the pronouns who and whom. She said that she had difficulty understanding them herself and did not want to bother trying to teach them to someone else. And so I find myself spending time with certain fundamentals, such as grammar, that most other students learned in high school.

Finally, Central did offer some courses that might have been beneficial to me in college but that, unfortunately, I did not take. This is basically a result of poor guidance counseling. Teenagers cannot be expected to make class choices on their own. When I was in high school the only criteria I considered before taking a class was would it be fun or was Kim taking it. Guidance counselors go to college and receive degrees so that they will be educated in helping students make the right class choices. Rarely, if ever, did a guidance counselor offer any assistance or advice in choosing classes which would be helpful later. For instance, Central offered a course on study skills for college. I should have taken it but it certainly did not seem like an enjoyable class to me so I did not take it. Some person should stress the importance of taking a given course and insist that you take it. From the title, I would assume that person to be the guidance counselor.

Ultimately, I feel that college would have been easier for me had my high school education been more helpful. My courses would not be nearly so difficult. And I could devote my time to the major concerns of most of my courses instead of worrying with minor ones.

Here Lori has clearly abandoned the principal as her audience; she has decided against trying to reform the system at Central High, and instead has decided that her strong feelings of frustration should be the focus of her essay. In her opening paragraph she now identifies the nature of her problems, which she makes a recurrent theme throughout the paper, returning to it in each of the subsequent paragraphs. The hesitating, weak voice of her first draft—caused by her concern at offending her principal—has been replaced by a more natural voice, an authentic voice, one even able to be humorous about the situation as her play on the words "review" and "view" in paragraph 3 illustrates. She has pruned out the accusations of "unprofessional behavior" and instead concentrated on the inadequacies of the actual instruction in her high school. And she is confident enough to show her anger at the do-nothing guidance counselors while being mature enough to acknowledge that she is in part to blame for her problems by not selecting the proper courses (paragraph 4).

My point is not at all to argue that Lori's final version of "High Quality Education" deserves an A or a B or even a C; my argument instead is that without having enlisted Lori's assistance in commenting on her paper, I would have been urging her to make her first draft more consistent in addressing its implied audience: someone with the authority to change things at Central High. In other words, I would have been pushing her to keep the essay in the form of a letter to her principal without even being aware that that was what I was doing. Instead Lori guided me so that I could respond to what she felt was significant, allowing her to clarify for herself the best approach to her material. There is no question in my mind that her second paper is better, but there is also no question in my mind that she never would have written it if I had made the comments which I had originally planned to offer.

Where then would that have left Lori? She would have been struggling with the paper I wanted her to write instead of the one *she* wanted to write. She would have submitted "High Quality Education" for a grade, and I might possibly have graded it lower than I would have the second version which I have reproduced here.

Brannon and Knoblauch conclude their discussion of students' rights to their texts by observing that evaluation is the "natural conclusion of the process of response and negotiation, carried through successive drafts," stressing that when the teacher responds appropriately, he can foster incentive in the student to re-write her paper meaningfully. They add,

> By negotiating those changes rather than dictating them, the teacher returns control of the writing to the student. And by evaluating, the teacher gives the student writer an estimate of how well the teacher thinks the student's revisions have brought actual effects into line with stated intentions. By looking first to those intentions, both in responding and in evaluating, we show students that we take their writing seriously and that we assume they are responsible for communicating what they wish to say. (166)

By looking first at students' intentions, instructors also demonstrate that *they* are responsible evaluators, that they plan to judge the student's ability to write rather than her ability to please. Perhaps the worst comment instructors of composition can hear from their students upon returning graded papers is, "Well, I didn't know what you wanted." The student-teacher memo allows instructors to ward off such comments by providing the insights necessary to offer useful commentary on student writing. Actually, as readers of student texts, writing instructors could just as often say to their students, "I didn't know what you wanted me to respond to." For equitable and meaningful evaluation of student writing, this mutual guesswork at intentions must be replaced with genuine communication about that writing. If Brannon and Knoblauch have convincingly answered the question "*Why* is student participation in the process of response and evaluation vital?" the student-teacher memo is an equally convincing answer to the corollary question, "*How* can we enlist that vital student participation?"

About the Author

An Assistant Professor of English, Jeffrey Sommers teaches writing courses at the Middletown Campus of Miami University (Middletown, Ohio).

Notes

1. Nancy Sommers comments that "Theoretically, at least, we know that we comment on our students' writing for the same reasons professional editors comment on the work of professional writers or for the same reasons we ask our colleagues to read and respond to our own writing." (148).

2. To support my hypothetical response: I used this essay in a workshop I ran with two colleagues, Donald A. Daiker and Mary F. Hayes, at a conference on composition pedagogy. After the workshop participants had read the first draft, without seeing the memo, they discussed their likely responses to the student. They made the same sorts of comments I have sketched out here. After supplying them with the memo, I then led a second discussion about the paper; it showed the same shift in focus of the response that I have described here.

References

Brannon, Lil, and C. H. Knoblauch. 1982. "Students' Rights to Their Own Texts." *College Composition and Communication* 33: 157–75.

Murray, Donald M. 1982. "Teaching the Other Self: The Writer's First Reader." *College Composition and Communication* 33: 140–56.

Sommers, Nancy, 1982. "Responding to Student Writing." *College Composition and Communication* 33: 148–56.

22

Teacher Response as Conversation

More Than Casual Talk, an Exploration

Richard Straub

It has become a commonplace in scholarship on teacher response: viewing comments as a dialogue between teacher and student, an ongoing discussion between the teacher reader and the student writer, a conversation. Erika Lindemann advises teachers to make comments that "create a kind of dialogue" between teacher and student and "keep the lines of communication open" (216). Chris Anson encourages teachers to write comments that are "more casual than formal, as if rhetorically sitting next to the writer, collaborating, suggesting, guiding, modeling" (352–53). Nina Ziv asserts that comments "can only be helpful if teachers respond to student writing as part of an ongoing dialogue between themselves and their students" (376). Comments that create real dialogue on the page, these authors suggest, allow students to see value in what they have to say and assume greater control over their own writing choices. Peter Elbow, explaining his reasons for framing his comments as a letter to the student, says: "When I write in the form of a letter I feel I am engaged in a writerly *conversation*—I am *talking* to the student—rather than trying to 'mark' or 'edit' or 'correct' the paper" (10). In an essay devoted to the subject, "The Voice in the Margins: Paper-Marking as Conversation," M. Francine Danis describes the benefits of looking at teacher commentary as similar to a "good talk with a friend." Viewing comments as a conversation, she says, "encourages me to regard myself in a positive light and to work toward an image of myself that I would want to write for. I would rather think of myself as a collaborator—a midwife, a coach—than a ruthless judge. So I'm faced with the challenge of responding in such a way that students will hear in my comments the kind of voice that I'm trying to project" (19).[1]

This metaphor of response as conversation has come about as a corrective to the traditional use of comments simply to label errors and mark problems. C. H. Knoblauch and Lil Brannon, reacting to the absence of anything approaching communication in most teacher commentary, argue that all too typically teachers are so concerned with their own agendas when they read student texts that they fail miserably at adapting their own writing, their written comments, to the rhetorical situation in front of them:

> There's a curious disjunction between what . . . teachers tell students about projecting outward as the starting point of communication and what they do themselves as aspiring communicators. For in their ways of talking to students, and especially in their habits of responding to student writing, they tend . . . to ride their own hobby-horses—sometimes to the extent that their students fail utterly to conceive what they might be talking about. . . .
> (*Rhetorical Traditions* 119)

Such responders establish a one-way line of communication, dictating changes to be made and robbing students of the opportunity to make decisions about their own meanings and purposes. Instead, Knoblauch and Brannon advise teachers to adopt the role of helpful readers and to see in their responses "the possibility of real communication, the chance to make intellectual progress through purposeful dialogue" (*Rhetorical Traditions* 119).

But what does it mean to treat teacher commentary as a dialogue? What makes teacher comments "conversational"? And how do such comments initiate revision and help students develop as writers? In this essay I define the basic features of conversational response and, then, working within and against this popular notion, develop a more rigorous definition of response as conversation. I suggest how the metaphor may be used more productively to help teachers make responses that turn students back into the chaos of revision, foster independent, substantive thought in their writing, and engage students in learning how writers and readers work intersubjectively through texts to achieve understanding.

In a way, we can tell pretty easily when a set of comments is conversational. Take a look, for instance, at the following sample comments, made in response to a rough draft by a first-year college writer. The essay, titled "Attention: Bass Fishermen," was handed in for an assignment that asked students to explain an idea or activity they are knowledgeable about to readers who are not as knowledgeable about the subject.[2] The draft frequently shifts from an expository account to a narrative of personal experience, as in the following passage:

> Lake Ivenho is unique because the only thing between you and the fish are the occasional patches of lillypads. The best solution to this problem is to work a top-water buzz bait in the early morning or late afternoon. I have hooked some big bass using this technique, but if the bass is big enough to give a good long fight it can be very difficult to get it through the lillypads. After fishing the lillypads that morning my next move was to work a plastic worm under the giant oak trees that hang out over much of Lake Ivenho. Bass like to hang out in these shady areas during the heat of the day so they can

better spot unsuspecting prey swimming by. This didn't produce the monster bass I was looking for so my next move was to work a spinner-bait along the southeast bank of the lake.

All six of the teachers' responses appear as end notes, either after the essay or on a separate page[3]:

Sample Responses to "Attention: Bass Fishermen"

1.   The fine details convey a real sense of what fishing is like. But the paper keeps shifting in mode: sometimes it is simply descriptive, sometimes a personal narrative of the day. The best tone for this assignment is the one you set in your opening paragraph, in which the details show what is special for you about fishing. Hold onto this perspective all the way through in your revision. (EW)

2.   Your choice of subject is a good one. You do, apparently, have considerable knowledge of it, and that was a requirement for the topic. Now, what must you do to make succeeding drafts of this paper better? First, you're going to have to focus on the assignment. This is not a personal experience essay. Too much of your paper is given over to your love of fishing for bass in Orlando and an account of one day's fishing on Lake Ivenhoe. After you've announced the prey, large mouth bass, you should immediately begin with your discussion of habitat. After that, talk about equipment. You also move, without transitions, from a semi-abstract discussion of bass fishing to references to a particular day's fishing. A reader can get confused by that kind of maneuver. Remember: your *first* obligation is to tell the reader where the fish are, what to use, and how to catch them. Having established that structure for the paper, you can put in the necessary details and then end with your zinger: the story of the big bass you caught. (DS)

3.   Well, let's take a look at your second draft of the newspaper piece here. . . . Ok, let's see. Let me give you some impressions I had of the draft first and try to raise some questions for you to think about, ok? Um, first of all, one thing . . . is this question of how much "you" you want here and how much you want to, uh, well essentially how much of yourself and your impressions and experiences you want to be in this piece. . . . And I think that's a judgment call. . . . Um, what you could do is go through your paper and strip out everything about yourself and there wouldn't be much left but it would be purely informational—for example, "all these were formed by sink-holes thousands of years ago." That's purely informational and not really . . . you're doing a kind of encyclopedic writing there. And then at the other extreme, when you say, "During my early childhood the first fun thing that I was taught to do by my grandfather was fish for bluegill," which is a purely personal, narrative style of writing. And the two of them are really mixed together, which happens a lot in this kind of writing. So I would encourage you to think about how much you want of yourself and

your experiences, and . . . how much straight information you want to provide. (CA)

4. Your choice of topic is excellent because you clearly know a great deal about bass fishing. Your description of Orlando's lakes and of Lake Ivenho in particular gives me a real feeling for the place and for fishing there—because you include so many concrete examples and details, but these accounts also raise some problems. When you begin to recount specific experiences they tend to take over. Instead of explaining fishing you move into a narrative of one event. This is particularly true beginning in the middle of page 2 with the section that begins "After fishing the lillypads that morning. . . ." This account leads into the narrative that closes the paper. By concentrating on this event you abandon your role as expert explaining bass fishing. As you revise this essay try to concentrate on explaining bass fishing rather than telling the story of one fishing trip. You can certainly draw on your own experiences to illustrate points you make, but try to prevent the narrative from taking over. (AG)

5. I like the feel of this draft. You've captured something of the pleasure and skill involved in bass fishing. Details like using top-water buzz bait in patches of lillypads will make your readers want to buy some waders and head on out to Ivenho. In your next draft, keep those wonderful details, but pay attention as well to how you can make this more an expository essay than a personal experience piece. If I had to pick a title for this draft, it would be something like: "The Day I Caught My Monster Bass." What would you need to do to your paper to make the following title fit it: "Fishing in the Lakes of Central Orlando." (GH)

6. I felt something interesting going on here. Seemed as though you had the assignment in mind (don't just tell a story of your experiences but explain a subject)—for awhile—but then gradually forgot about it as you got sucked into telling about your particular day of fishing. (You'll see my wiggly lines of slight bafflement as this story begins to creep in.) The trouble is I like your stories/moments. My preference would be not to drop them ("Shame on you—telling stories for an expository essay") but to search around for some way to save it/them as part of a piece that does what the assignment calls for. Not sure how to do it. Break it up into bits to be scattered here and there? Or leave it a longer story but have material before and after to make it a means of *explaining your subject?* Not sure; tricky problem. But worth trying to pull off. Good writers often get lots of narrative and descriptive bits into expository writing. (PE)

All six sets of comments are thoughtful and well-crafted. They offer the student useful ideas about how the essay might be improved, in ways he would be able to understand. All of them, in fact, were made by teachers who are well informed about recent composition studies and have contributed to

the scholarship on evaluating and responding to student writing: Edward
White (set 1), Donald Stewart (set 2), Chris Anson (set 3), Anne Gere (set 4),
Glynda Hull (set 5), and Peter Elbow (set 6).[4] But not all of these responses
are "conversational."

Intuitively, it seems to me, the last four sets of comments have the feel of
conversations: They simply have the sound of someone talking with someone
else. It is this quality that would lead us to see the third set of comments as the
most conversational in the list. With good reason. The response is an excerpt of
Anson's tape-recorded message to the student. The first two sets of comments,
by contrast, are more autonomous and discursive, more authoritative. What is it,
though, that makes some responses, and not others, take on this sense of talk, the
feel of an implicit dialogue with the student? On closer inspection, the last four
responses display certain fundamental characteristics of conversational response,
features that make them, in the popular sense of the term, "conversational."

The Basic Features of Conversational Response

First of all, the last four end notes have an informal, spoken voice. They talk
with the student rather than talk to him or speak down at him. At its most ele-
mental level, of course, achieving a conversational style of response means
just this: getting the gestures, tone of voice, and sense of speech in one's written comments. As Danis notes, picturing response as conversation "does for us
as teachers what our advice about picturing an audience is meant to do for our
students: it concretizes the awareness that we're communicating *with someone*" (19). The following comments in particular have this spoken quality:

- Well, let's take a look at your second draft of the newspaper piece here.
  (Response 3)

- Your description of Orlando's lakes and of Lake Ivenho in particular gives
  me a real feeling for the place and for fishing there. . . . (Response 4)

- I like the feel of this draft. (Response 5)

- Not sure how to do it. Break it up into bits to be scattered here and there?
  (Response 6)

Much of this informality is achieved through the teacher's simple word
choice. The last four sets of commentary are marked by a minimal use of
technical language and teacher talk. They rely instead on a common, everyday language:

- One thing . . . is this question of how much "you" you want here and how
  much you want to, uh, well essentially how much of yourself and your
  impressions and experiences you want to be in this piece. (Response 3)

- You can certainly draw on your own experiences to illustrate points you
  make, but try to prevent the narrative from taking over. (Response 4)

- If I had to pick a title for this draft, it would be something like "The Day I Caught My Monster Bass." (Response 5)
- Seemed as though you had the assignment in mind (don't just tell a story of your experiences but explain a subject)—for awhile—but then gradually forgot about it as you got sucked into telling about your particular day of fishing. (Response 6)

The first two sets of comments, by White and Stewart, do not have a lot of teacher talk. But they have more of it than the others: "the fine details"; "the best tone"; "the paper keeps shifting in tone"; "This is not a personal experience essay"; "You also move, without transitions, from a semi-abstract discussion of bass fishing to references to a particular day's fishing."[5]

Less obviously, the last four sets of comments make frequent use of text-specific language—language that, in Nancy Sommers' phrase, is "anchored in the particulars of the students' texts" (152) and that is specific and precise, as in the following comments:

- What you could do is go through your paper and strip out everything about yourself and there wouldn't be much left but it would be purely informational—for example, "all these were formed by sink-holes thousands of years ago."
- Instead of explaining fishing you move into a narrative of one event. This is particularly true beginning in the middle of page 2 with the section that begins "After fishing the lillypads that morning. . . ." (Response 4)
- Details like using top-water buzz bait in patches of lillypads will make your readers want to buy some waders and head on out to Ivenho. (Response 5)

By dealing in the actual words of the student's text, these responders establish a common ground with the writer, showing that they have come to terms with what he has to say and giving their comments a local habitation and a familiar name. White and Stewart are clear and precise about what they expect the student to do by way of revision. Stewart also goes into specific detail about what he'd like to see revised. But their comments are cast in the teacher's language, not the language of the student's text. White does not ground his statement about how the essay shifts from a "simply descriptive" account to "a personal narrative" in the student's text. Stewart casts almost all of his comments in his own terms: "announced the prey," "habitat," "semi-abstract discussion of bass fishing," "that kind of maneuver," "the necessary details." He does little to link his guidelines for revision to the student's own language and meanings.[6]

The last four sets of comments also display one other feature that is central to an effective conversational style, in the conventional sense of the term: They all focus on what the writer has to say and engage him in a discussion of his ideas and purposes.[7] As Knoblauch and Brannon point out, "if teachers seriously aim to communicate with students about their writing and thereby affect students' performance, they must begin with what matters most to those writers, namely, the making of meaningful statements consistent with the writers' own purposes and their own estimations of how best to achieve them" (*Rhetorical Traditions* 122). All four of these teachers go out of their way to understand and appreciate the writer's intentions and to play back their way of interpreting the text. Anson plays back his sense of where the writing gets "informational" and where it gets "personal." Gere gives her reading of how the writer's experiences begin to take over the paper and points out specific passages where she sees the shift occur. Hull praises the writer's success at capturing "the pleasure and skill involved in bass fishing" and makes special note of one particularly effective detail. Elbow presents less specific playback than the others, but he makes a point of providing his gloss on the writing before getting into his ideas about revision.

The first two readers focus on the overall purpose of the writing, but they do less by way of playing back their reading of the text. White praises the paper for conveying "a sense of what fishing is like," but his reading stops here, at this general level. Stewart indicates that he has closely read the writing, but he frames his reading as criticism: "Too much of your paper is given over to your love of fishing for bass in Orlando and an account of one day's fishing on Lake Ivanhoe." Such comments create White and Stewart as critics or editors, while the last four sets of comments create the teachers as readers first and critics, teachers, advisers, facilitators, and mentors only second, after they have completed this central task of showing that they have tried to understand what the writer is saying. To be a conversational responder is to be, first of all, a reader—one who listens to what the writer says and lets him know what she has heard.

Teachers who make comments that are conversational in this popular sense of the term, then, employ three basic strategies:

1. **They create an informal, spoken voice, using everyday language.**

2. **They tie their commentary back to the student's own language on the page, in text-specific comments.**

3. **They focus on the writer's evolving meanings and play back their way of understanding the text.**

Together, these qualities enable responders to meet what Danis calls one of the greatest challenges facing most student writers, the effort "to imagine the receiver, to compensate for that person's physical absence" (19), and what Sommers calls the key purpose of commenting on student writing, "to dramatize the presence of a reader" (148).

But it seems to me that these last four teachers are doing more than just creating a conversation in this basic sense of the term. Moreover, the three features identified above seem to capture only part of what the term may more productively come to mean. Because our talk about conversational response has emerged from a rejection of prescriptive commentary, we have come too quickly to associate this concrete, talkative style of response with casual, facilitative commentary. The idea of response as a *conversation* has become a catch-all for any teacher response that is informal, positive, and nurturing, or even for any response that is nonprescriptive.[8] The term has come to refer to any response that puts the teacher in the role of reader or coach rather than the role of critic or judge. It has consequently come to have the sound of other concepts in composition that have become hard to speak against and even more difficult to pin down, like "writing as process" and, more recently, "writing in community" and "writing as collaboration." When we think of response that is "conversational," we think of comments that are easy, gentle, and friendly, comments that, from another perspective, may be too readily dismissed as "soft."[9]

We would do well, of course, to be more casual and friendly in our comments, especially given teachers' historically bad reputation as harsh critics. Comments that have a spoken, casual quality help open lines of communication between teacher and student, and they are more likely to get read. But comments may be friendly and "conversational" without being facile and nonchalant, and they have to be more than informal, specific, and friendly if they are to accomplish the large goals we have come to expect of them. An easy, informal voice and an emphasis on playing back the text as a reader are important to any concept of response as conversation, but they alone will not make comments into productive conversations.

The Features of Conversational Response as an Exploration

If we look more closely at the last four sets of comments, it is clear that they do more than carry on an informal chat with the student. More than sounding casual or friendly, more than taking on the role of a reader, facilitator, or coach, these responders make comments that are tough, incisive, and critical. They are not only friendly and helpful; they are also expectant and probing. They engage in conversations with the student, but they are conversations that are at once relaxed *and* serious. They turn their comments into an inquiry into the writing, an exploration of the text and the student behind the text. The meaning I have in mind is suggested in Boswell's *Life*, where Johnson, after a time spent involved in what Boswell too casually calls "a *conversation*," proclaims: "No, sir . . . we had talk enough, but no conversation; there was nothing *discussed*."[10] Here conversation is defined not so much by its casualness as by its engagement with a subject and a real exchange between two parties. In this sense response becomes a conversation when the teacher makes her comments into a give-and-take discussion with the student—an exchange that defines both parties as investigators and that may lead to a richer understanding of the subject and to more productive writing, reading, revision, and learning.

What do the last four sets of teacher comments do that makes them conversational in this richer sense of the term? How do they create such inquiries on the page? In addition to simply making use of concrete language and a talk-ative style, these responders practice three strategies that help turn their comments into examinations of the subject, real conversations:

4. **They make critical comments but cast them in the larger context of help or guidance.**

5. **They provide direction for the student's revision, but they do not take control over the writing or establish a strict agenda for that revision.**

6. **They elaborate on the key statements of their responses.**

Beyond assuming the role of reader or coach, the last four responders take on the roles of teacher, demanding reader, and co-investigator. This interplay of roles is created through, and reflected in, the modes of response these teachers employ—that is, the ways they frame their comments and in doing so establish various relationships with the student. White's and Stewart's endnotes are dominated by directive commentary, in which the teacher, adopting the stance of a critic or judge, takes control over the writing and lays out what is not working and what should be changed:

- The paper keeps shifting in mode: sometimes it is simply descriptive, sometimes a personal narrative of the day. The best tone for this assignment is the one you set in your opening paragraph, in which the details show what is special for you about fishing. Hold onto this perspective all the way through in your revision. (Response 1)

- First, you're going to have to focus on the assignment. This is not a personal experience essay. Too much of your paper is given over to your love of fishing for bass in Orlando and an account of one day's fishing on Lake Iveohoe. After you've announced the prey, large mouth bass, you should immediately begin with your discussion of habitat. After that, talk about equipment. . . . (Response 2)

Anson, Gere, Hull, and Elbow, on the other hand, make *some* use of these directive modes, but it is limited and moderate. They all present evaluations of the writing and indicate how the student might take up changes in his revision. But the control they exert over the student is tempered by the content, voice, and form of these directive comments. Instead of presenting outright criticisms, they present *qualified evaluations*:

- When you begin to recount specific experiences, they tend to take over. (Response 4)

- Seemed as though you had the assignment in mind (don't just tell a story of your experiences but explain a subject)—for awhile—but then gradually forgot about it as you got sucked into telling about your particular day of fishing. (Response 6)

Instead of requesting changes, they offer *advice*:

- So I would encourage you to think about how much you want of yourself and your experiences, and . . . how much straight information you want to provide. (Response 3)

- You can certainly draw on your own experiences to illustrate points you make, but try to prevent the narrative from taking over. (Response 4)

- In your next draft, keep those wonderful details, but pay attention as well to how you can make this more an expository essay than a personal experience piece. (Response 5)

- My preference would be not to drop them . . . but to search around for some way to save it/them as part of a piece that does what the assignment calls for. (Response 6)

These moderate modes give these evaluations and directives the feel of helpful, constructive criticism.[11]

The last four responders further temper their control and make their commentary interactive by surrounding the critical, directive comments they do make with a variety of nonjudgmental comments. They play back their reading of the text in interpretive comments, offer additional advice and questions for the student to consider, and provide examples and explanations of their responses. In doing so, they create a sense of mutual exchange between reader and writer, teacher and student, and turn their commentary into conversations in this richer sense of the term. It is not the case, then, that conversational comments cannot employ criticism or calls for revision. They can. In fact, they must, if they are to probe into the writing and push the writer to engage in richer pursuits of meaning. They just cannot have so much directive commentary—or so much directive commentary left unmodified by nondirective comments— that they define the teacher predominantly as a critic or a judge over the role of reader, adviser, facilitator, or mentor.

What most makes the last three sets of comments conversational in the more encompassing sense of the term is the depth of the responses: the extent to which these teachers give substance to and elaborate on their primary comments. It is obvious that Gere, Hull, and Elbow simply have *more* to say in their comments. But it is what they do in these additional comments that makes these responses distinctive. They don't just provide more comments or cover more ground; they deal more fully with the issues they take up. White's and Stewart's comments are one-dimensional. They make a statement and directly move on to another statement at the same level of generality.[12] The comments are listed, not developed. By contrast, the last three sets of comments are layered; they have a rich texture. One statement leads into, and is enriched by, another.

Early in her response, for instance, Gere elaborates on her main criticism of the essay, about how the writer's experiences dominate the writing:

[1] When you begin to recount specific experiences they tend to take over.

[2] Instead of explaining fishing you move into a narrative of one event.

The second statement goes back over the ground of her initial statement, adding to it, explaining it. She then follows up on this statement. She grounds it in the student's text and clarifies it—and then, further, explains the consequences of this decision. As she clarifies the problem for herself, she also draws the student into her way of seeing the paper and clarifies the problem for him:

[1] When you begin to recount specific experiences they lend to take over.

[2] Instead of explaining fishing you move into a narrative of one event.

[3] This is particularly true beginning in the middle of page 2 with the section that begins "After fishing the lillypads that morning. . . ."

[4] This account leads into the narrative that closes the paper.

[5] By concentrating on this event you abandon your role as expert explaining bass fishing.

The response moves from a qualified evaluation expressing her concern about the mixed genres to four follow-up comments—all of them nondirective—that serve to explain and work out the primary comment. By leading the student deliberately across the path of her thinking, she leads him to take up a like-minded investigation of these issues. In the process her comments model a writer using writing as a way of thinking.

To get a better appreciation of Gere's use of elaboration in her response, all we have to do is consider the comments as they would appear if she simply presented her general criticisms of the writing and her calls for revision by themselves, without any elaboration:

Your choice of topic is excellent because you clearly know a great deal about bass fishing. You include so many concrete examples and details, but these accounts also raise some problems. When you begin to recount specific experiences they tend to take over. As you revise this essay try to concentrate on explaining bass fishing rather than telling the story of one fishing trip.

By going back over the ground of these general comments, elaborating on them at a more specific level, working directly with the words of the student's text, and framing her comments in interactive modes, Gere is able to pursue her thoughts about the paper and turn them simultaneously into a conversation and an inquiry. She gets engaged in the subject, explores the issues that are raised for her, and initiates a real, open exchange with the subject and the writer. The student is called to consider how to integrate his personal experiences with his advice about bass fishing, but he is also left to decide what specifically to do with them on his own.

The same kind of strategies for developing comments may be found in Hull's response. Generally, Hull says nothing more than she likes the draft but wants the writer to make it more fully into an expository essay. But instead of saying this and this alone, she defines what she likes about the writing and considers how it may be revised. Here is the response, again set off in levels to highlight the relationships among the individual comments:

¹ I like the feel of this draft.

² You've captured something of the pleasure and skill involved in bass fishing.

³ Details like using top-water buzz bait in patches of lillypads will make your readers want to buy some waders and head on out to Ivenho.

⁴ In your next draft, keep those wonderful details, but pay attention as well to how you can make this more an expository essay than a personal experience piece.

⁵ If I had to pick a title for this draft, it would be something like: "The Day I Caught My Monster Bass."

⁶ What would you need to do to your paper to make the following title fit it: "Fishing in the Lakes of Central Orlando."

Hull revisits each of her two general comments and, reaching to see better what she means, specifies what she has in mind. Notably, the comments she adds by way of elaboration are cast in interactive modes. She uses an explanatory comment and an example to give substance to her opening statement about what is captivating about the piece, and she adds an interpretive comment and an open question to talk more explicitly about how the writer might attend to making the piece into more of an expository essay. Even as she adds to her comments, she does not add to her control as a responder. She shares responsibility with the student, allowing him to decide what to do by way of revision. Now that the teacher has said what she has to say, the student is invited to have his turn at speaking.[13]

Similarly, Elbow follows up briefly on each of his main comments. Instead of telling the student what to do or laying out specific changes, he thinks out loud about how the student might find a way to keep the personal anecdotes in the revised essay:

¹ Not sure how to do it.

² Break it up into bits to be scattered here and there?

³ Or leave it a longer story but have material before and after to make it a means of *explaining* your *subject*?

⁴ Not sure; tricky problem. But worth trying to pull off.

⁵ Good writers often get lots of narrative and descriptive bits into expository writing.

His comments present one side of what is clearly intended as a two-sided investigation into the subject of how this writing may be improved. Like Gere and
Hull, even as he elaborates his primary comments, Elbow allows the student to
retain a good measure of control over the writing. Will the student decide to scatter these moments from his experience across the essay? Will he try to find a way
to use this long account of his own day at the lake? Given these constraints—
and this direction—he is left to take up the investigation for himself.

It is this kind of elaborating, more than anything else, that makes Gere's,
Hull's, and Elbow's commentary more than simply talkative. They seem to
imagine their comments as a kind of essay in its own right, an attempt to get
at in their own minds, in their own words, a teacher's reading of the writing.
What is the essay saying? Where does it work well and where can it be made
to work better? How can it be turned into an occasion for learning? We can see
just how important elaboration—and, in particular, elaboration cast in interactive modes—is to this richer sense of conversational response by comparing
Anson's and Stewart's responses to "Attention: Bass Fishermen"—this time,
using the fuller versions of what they said to this writer.[14]

In his original response, Anson follows his opening comments with a
number of more specific, exploratory comments (in boldface), all of them
designed to follow up on his advice that the student "think about how much
you want of yourself and your experiences, and . . . how much straight information you want to provide":

> Now, my impression right now, and well see how the others react, is that
> you're probably a little bit over toward the extreme of personal memory as
> opposed to the informational. So that there are some places where you might
> try out the "so what" test: **"I grew up on them and I know most of the hid-
> den underwater structures, like fallen trees." Ok, if somebody's inter-
> ested in perhaps going to Orlando to fish, . . . knowing that you know
> where all the hidden structures are isn't going to be useful information,
> if you see what I mean. Useful in a narrative about your childhood,
> maybe, but not, um, you know, for an article on these great fishing spots.
> Something that would be useful to know is that this lake, Ivanho (is that
> spelled like the novel, maybe?)—that this lake is a great fishing lake. And
> the information that you then go into here on, uh, that the lake is fishable
> from the shoreline and so on, would be appropriate.**
>
> Um, so. So one big issue to think about for revision, then, is how much
> information you want to take out which might not be of great interest to the
> reader and then what other sorts of information they might want to know.[15]

Anson uses five comments to develop his basic comments. He points to a specific example from the text and illustrates, through two explanatory comments,
how one might go about deciding what to keep and what to omit by considering the needs of a prospective reader. He then goes on to suggest, in two additional comments, the kind of information that might be helpful. The added

commentary is probing and reflective, creating the sense of someone working alongside the writer, looking to see what might be done to pursue these ideas and form them into a more thoughtful, focused piece of writing. In the process Anson offers more lines of thought to consider, more direction for the student, yet also manages to exert only a moderate control over the text. Notably, these additions are nondirective: They do not lay out a plan for revision so much as they consider an issue the student would do well to think about. The comments do not emphasize informal talk at the expense of exploring ideas for revision, and they do not emphasize exploration at the expense of communicating easily with the student. They demonstrate how the best conversational responses integrate informal dialogue *and* serious inquiry.

While elaboration usually helps make a set of responses less directive, not all elaboration necessarily leads to conversation. Stewart's fuller original response is a case in point. Following his opening comments, where he presents in no uncertain terms his concern about the writer's failure to fulfill the expository aims of the assignment, Stewart adds nine comments by way of elaboration (in bold):

> Too much of your paper is given over to your love of fishing for bass in Orlando and an account of one day's fishing on Lake Ivenhoe. . . . While your personal experience can certainly be incorporated into this kind of paper, it's not what the editor of *Field and Stream* wants. After you've announced the prey, large mouth bass, you should immediately begin with your discussion of habitat. **This is the place to bring in the information you have provided in your narrative about the habits of the bass, under differing conditions.** After that, talk about equipment. **You mention two types of lures, but you never tell us what kind of rod you use, how to cast for bass, and what motions to impart to the lure to attract bass.** You also move, without transitions, from a semi-abstract discussion of bass fishing to references to a particular day's fishing. A reader can get confused by that kind of maneuver. **Remember: your *first* obligation is to tell the reader where the fish are, what to use, and how to catch them. When those are your emphases, you can work in the other material. For example, you could say that bass prefer certain kinds of lakes at certain temperatures with certain kinds of hiding places and certain kinds of food.**
>
> **After that you can tell us that the particular lake you like meets these qualifications superbly. Having established that structure for the paper, you can put in the necessary details and then end with your zinger: the story of the big bass you caught. In this paper, you give us only two sentences after hooking it. That's not enough. The reader wants a longer report of the battle you had landing this big fish. Otherwise, the paper ends on a terribly abrupt and anticlimactic note.**[16]

All nine of these comments, however, are framed in authoritative modes: four as unqualified criticisms, five as requests for specific changes. In contrast to

Anson's commentary, none of these follow-up comments is presented as an explanation, an option, or a question. None of them explores the subject or examines possible alternatives the student may consider. Instead, they are presented as a kind of blueprint for revision. Adopting the role of editor, Stewart sets out his own rather rigid agenda for revision. He does not open up an inquiry or engage in a give-and-take exchange with the student, and as a result his comments fall well short of creating a conversation.[17] While Stewart's commentary, then, is detailed and specific, it is not exploratory. Only by elaborating one's comments in a way that opens up the matters under discussion for a mutual investigation by writer and reader can a teacher make his comments conversational in the sense I am pursuing here.[18]

In summary, then, Anson, Gere, Hull, and Elbow put into practice a number of responding strategies that turn their conversations into explorations:

1. **They create an informal, spoken voice, using everyday language.**

2. **They tie their commentary back to the student's own language on the page, in text-specific comments.**

3. **They focus on the writer's evolving meanings and play back their way of understanding the text.**

4. **They make critical comments but cast them in the larger context of help or guidance.**

5. **They provide direction for the student's revision, but they do not take control over the writing or establish a strict agenda for that revision.**

6. **They elaborate on the key statements of their responses.**

All six of these strategies are important to conversational response in this richer, exploratory sense of the term. The first three strategies help create the sense of someone talking with someone else on the page and develop a sense of exchange between teacher and student. The last three strategies are the keys to creating responses that are discussions and explorations.[19]

Anson, Gere, Hull, and Elbow are not intent simply on exchanging informal talk with the student or communicating their views about the writing to the writer. Their attention is not fixed above all other concerns on turning their comments into a kind of informal reader-based prose. These responders seem to concentrate on the subject at hand, not on the student reading the comments, and engage the writing in a way that they hope will engage the writer. By constructing themselves as investigators, the teachers implicitly construct the student writer as an investigator. By treating the issues raised in the writing as real issues, real matters to be discussed and considered, they accept the student as someone who has something to say, something well worth exploring. By talking about the text as an act of writing and reading, they create the student as someone who is both capable of, and interested in, working through these issues of writing and improving himself as a writer. The more they delve into their responses, the more they establish their roles as writers and readers in an intersubjective dialogue, as partners in an ongoing conversation, and the more likely they may bring the student both to participate further in the conversation and learn something more about the ways writers and readers share understanding through texts.

What makes response to student writing "conversational" in this rich, Johnsonian sense of the term is the teacher's double focus: On the one hand, she is trying to talk with the writer about what he has to say; on the other, she is trying to explore and exploit the possibilities in the writing, to suggest what else might be done with it *and* what else might be learned about how writers and readers use texts to come together and make meaning.[20] Because the comments are written in a casual manner and are more detailed, they are engaging and understandable. Because they are searching and provisional, they challenge and encourage the student to explore his options as a writer. Because they are interactive and open-ended, they allow the teacher to negotiate two contrary but equally necessary strategies of teacher response: They give the student more help and direction, yet they keep a good deal of control and responsibility in his hands. The comments do not lay out an agenda for revision so much as they dramatize the act of reading the text and push the student back into the writing, calling on him to consider the sufficiency of his choices and possibilities for further development in this text and in his overall work as a developing writer and reader.

Viewing response as both a conversation and an exploration encourages teachers to avoid making comments that are cryptic, anonymous, and overly directive. It encourages them to write comments that dramatize the presence of a reader, keep a good deal of control over the writing in the hands of the writer, and lead students back into the chaos of revision—three goals that have come to dominate our talk about responding to student writing.[21] But the metaphor of response as conversation goes beyond these goals. It emphasizes, in addition, the importance of making judgments about the content of student writing, offering students direction, and pushing them to reach for more to say in their writing. The conversational responders whose work is reviewed here do not eschew all forms of directive and evaluative response; in fact, their commentary in many ways is shaped around such commentary. But their evaluative and directive comments are used selectively, and the ones that are presented are augmented by an array of interactive responses. Since their comments are designed to promote richer inquiry, they provide more direction and exert greater control over student writing than recent models of teacher response seem to recommend.

Viewing response as a conversation also encourages teachers to adopt a reader's perspective and play back for students how well they are communicating their intentions to an audience. As Knoblauch and Brannon remind us: "we comment on student essays to dramatize the presence of a reader who depends on the writer's choices in order to perceive the intent of a discourse. Thoughtful commentary describes when communication has occurred and when it has not, raising questions that the writer may never have considered from a reader's point of view" ("Teacher Commentary" 1). But the metaphor of response as conversation asks teachers to do more than assume the role of a target audience; it urges them, in addition, to create themselves as demanding, expectant readers and lead students to look for more from their writing than clear communication alone. Writing itself, the metaphor reminds us, is a searching, a shaping, an interchange of ideas. It suggests that teachers would do well to strive toward a Burkean identification with students in their comments and construct themselves and their students as fellow inquirers. If teachers respond as interested *and* expectant readers, looking to promote richer inquiry and not just writing that is better formed, students will exert more effort at constructing something worthwhile to say and finding ways to share this understanding more fully with others.[22]

The metaphor of response as conversation also dramatizes the processes by which writers and readers come together intersubjectively through a text to coconstruct meaning. The rich interaction that conversational response creates between writer and reader promotes what Deborah Brandt sees as the key knowledge of literate development: "knowing how people read and write, how they do the work of it" (6):

> Writers and readers in action are deeply embedded in an immediate working context of aims, plans, trials, and constructions. . . . The language that they write and read finds meaning only in relationship to this ongoing context—a context more of work than of words. Further, reference in literate language is also contextbound and essentially deictic, pointing not in at internal relations of a text but out to the developing here-and-now relationship of writer and reader at work. Texts talk incessantly about the acts of writing and reading in progress. No matter what their ostensible topic, written texts are primarily about the writing and reading of them. What they refer to is not an explicit message but the implicit process by which intersubjective understanding is getting accomplished. That is what you have to know in order to read and write. (4)

When teachers treat their response as a conversation—not just feedback—they model for students how readers and writers muster and manage language, metacommunicative cues, and context in order to create meaning. They provide the kind of knowledge about texts and text-making that Brandt finds crucial to literacy learning, by giving students "not merely experience with texts but ample access to other people who read and write and who will show you why and how they do it" (6). Teachers who make their comments part of a larger conversation with the student do not view the text as an autonomous artifact; they view the text as a meeting place for writers and readers, a "public social reality," a means for intersubjective dialogue. Their comments say, here's how I understand what you are saying, here's what I'm thinking about it, and here's what you might consider if you want me to meet you somewhere further along in this discussion. Conversational comments bring the meaning a reader creates from the text back out, through the reader's comments, into the arena of social exchange, where meaning may be refined, redirected, and developed. Writing is reciprocated with writing, exchange with both an exchange and an invitation to further writing and inquiry. Because writers and readers do not merely have to keep a message going but also have to keep a whole process going, any response that promotes a detailed, honest interaction about a piece of writing will contribute to the student's work in revision and her ongoing development as a writer.

Conversational Response: Theory into Practice

Looking at the length and involvement of these sample comments, many teachers will think that, sure, conversational response may be a viable option for that small cluster of teacher-theorists who teach just one or two writing classes a year and who have the luxury of giving such attention to their comments on student writing, but they are not for me. Faced with the baffling prospect of teaching three or four sections of writing with 20–30 students per section, these teachers may wonder about the feasibility of a method of response that asks even more of them as teachers than they are already getting worn out trying to do. They may wonder how they could give more time and attend more fully to the content and thought of student writing in the ways we see here. And with good reason. The fact is, they will not be able to write these kind of involved comments in the time they could spend dealing with the traditional, formalistic concerns of student writing, in a traditional, editorial way.

Nevertheless, teachers can somehow adopt the principles of conversational response without spending any more time than they now spend in responding to student writing. They can focus more of their comments on the ideas of the student's writing and find ways to condense the commentary they make on matters of style and correctness. They can limit their comments to one or two issues per paper—and concentrate on only two or three places where these issues arise. They can deal extensively with the content and thought of their students' writing in the first half of the course and hold off on doing more with sentence structure and correctness until the second half. They can concentrate on writing fewer but fuller marginal comments and write only brief overview comments at the end of a paper. Several well-developed marginal comments will take less time than a full endnote, yet they can go far toward leading the student back into the writing.[23] Teachers can also respond more fully at the start of the course and, as the course progresses, place more and more responsibility on students to respond to one another's writing. They can even give more or less involved comments alternately to various groups of students, rotating the groups across the term.

With only a little more time to respond to each set of papers, teachers can make a practice of clarifying and extending some of the key comments they do make. In fact, by making their comments exploratory and conversational, they will more than likely make much better use of the time they do spend on responding to student writing and reap better dividends for their efforts. Much of the time teachers devote now to their comments, the research suggests, is wasted. I suspect this is true—not because teacher comments are not useful but because the ways we have come to make comments on student writing are unconsidered. Our comments fall on deaf ears or simply do not get read, I suspect, largely because they do not deal with what the student has to say or might say in a piece of writing and because they are written in a language and style that, far from inviting interest, thwart the student from reading what we have to say. By engaging ourselves in what our students have to say and inviting them to read what we have to say in response—and by making response a significant matter for the larger classroom conversation—we may make whatever time we do spend on responding to student writing truly worthwhile. Comments that are shaped into a real conversation blur the lines between writing and reading, and allow teachers to actively model and encourage acts of making meaning. They create a shared responsibility for writing and revision and enable a real *discussion*, a two-way conversation, to take place between reader and writer, teacher and student. Such conversational responses will engage students in looking again into their writing and challenge them to take up their part of the dialogue, continue the discussion, and continue their work as writers.

Notes

1. I would like to thank Peter Elbow and David Foster (*RR* peer reviewers), whose responses on the drafts of this essay took on all the marks of both a conversation with me and an exploration into the ideas presented here. I am grateful for their helpful, challenging commentary.

2. The essay and the assignment are presented in a book-length study of teacher response coauthored by Ronald F. Lunsford and me, *Twelve Readers Reading: Responding to College Student Writing* (Cresskill, NJ: Hampton, 1995).

3. These six sets of teachers' comments are taken from *Twelve Readers Reading*, which examines the responding styles of 12 well-recognized composition teachers. Several sets of these comments—namely, sets 1, 2, 4, and 6—include several additional comments in the margins of the student text, not represented here.

4. Stewart's (set 2), Anson's (set 3), and Elbow's (set 6) endnotes are not presented in their entirety—in part, due to space considerations, since each of their comments runs to at least twice the length of the excerpt.

5. The following sample endnotes, taken from a study of another group of teachers, present more obvious examples of language that is technical and teacherly and responses that are not conversational:

> 1. You need to work on your tenses, your clarity of sentence structure and paragraph structure. You jump around with your thoughts. They are not in order. You also need to explain some terms.

> 2. You need work on paragraphing. All of the ideas are put into just two paragraphs. There needs to be better organization. A paragraph needs to have a topic

sentence, and all of the information in it needs to be on that particular topic. Think about organization. Plus the paper needs a better focus. Concentrate on topics.

3. After you discuss the advantages of Lake Ivenho, your paper digresses from its controlling idea about the lakes of central Orlando being the greatest natural fishing holes. The paper, it this point, becomes a narration/process paper about fishing this particular lake. You seem to lose sight of your purpose. You need to reevaluate your purpose and revise to create a *unified* paper. Do you want to write about the good bass fishing in the Orlando lakes, or do you want to write about a fishing experience on Lake Ivenho?

6. The other responders might also do well to write more of their comments in the language of the student's text—especially in those comments where they are giving their reading of the writing. Elbow's commentary, in particular, could use more text-specific commentary. He *indicates* ideas, and passages he is referring to, but he does not *use* any of the actual words from the student's text.

7. The more a teacher tries to cover a full range of concerns, including sentence structure, paragraphing, arrangement, and correctness, and makes no distinctions about which is more important than others, the more difficult it is to make those comments conversational. Of course, teachers *may* take up a number of concerns and turn them into a conversation, as long as they are willing to make longer responses and deal principally with what the writer has to say. See, for example, Chris Anson's responses in *Twelve Readers Reading.*

8. One doesn't have to look long or hard to find the association of conversational comments with friendly or nurturing commentary. In pointing to the benefits of response as conversation, Danis, for example, writes: "First, and perhaps most importantly, thinking of paper-marking as conversation helps me enjoy myself as I respond to papers. A good talk with a friend or two is a pleasure: I like hearing other people's views and ways of putting things, and of course I enjoy sharing my own thoughts and feelings, especially when I know that someone is really interested" (19).

9. That we've come to associate conversational response with easygoing facilitiative response is easily illustrated by the fact that we would very likely hesitate to call the following response conversational: "Listen, Steve, you may have a few pretty good lines here about bass fishing and this day spent fishing the Orlando lakes, but it's just not anywhere near where it needs to be yet. It's too scattered and unfocused. I mean, page two is full of quick stops and turns. There's no way a reader'll be able to keep up with the way you constantly shift from one thing to another." Although the response has a conversational tone, it simply too critical to be considered "conversational" in the way we have come to use the term.

10. The nature of "conversation" is a subject that frequently arises in Boswell's biography—and not always only with this meaning.

11. Notably, all six responders make a point of praising something in the student's work. The last three responders, though, devote more of their response to acknowledging what this student did well in the draft. Gere praises the writer's choice of topic and his description of the Orlando lakes; she goes on to explain what accounts for these positive reactions: his use of concrete examples and detail. Hull gives half of her comments to expressing how the detail engages her in the writing. In the excerpt here and

in the rest of his response, Elbow makes no fewer than four comments that praise the writing: "I enjoyed reading your piece"; "I even enjoyed the metaphor of setting a fish on the hook—and then realized it's merely the conventional term"; "What I like is your voice and presence and the sense of immediacy through lots of detail. I marked places that I especially liked"; and "The trouble is I like your stories/moments." It is not the case that these responders balance positive and negative comments; the point is that they make sure to acknowledge what is working well and give substance to their praise. It seems that once they have played back their reading of the text and pointed to what works in the piece, they feel as though they are in a better position to call on the student to look back on the writing and make revisions. This observation would confirm the many studies calling for greater use of praise in teacher commentary. It would also urge teachers to employ, in particular, genuine praise.

12. I am relying here on Francis Christensen's concept of "levels of generality" and his "generative rhetoric" of the paragraph, where sentences in a sequence of sentences are seen in relation to other surrounding sentences. See his *Notes Toward a New Rhetoric*. I should note here also that I have modified Stewart's and Anson's responses to this essay in order to dramatize certain characteristics of their responding styles.

13. I am reminded of a talk I heard by Nancy McCracken at a 1993 NCTE preconvention workshop in Pittsburgh, in which she examined teacher response in relation to Mary Louise Pratt's speech-act theory.

14. By adding these comments to the pared-down versions I presented earlier, I hope to dramatize more fully the effect of these follow-up comments.

15. Here is the original, full version of the first half of Anson's commentary, which makes up half of his overall response. Anson assumes that the writer has already received peer responses in small groups and has submitted his own tape-recorded concerns about the writing to Anson with his draft. His basic comments are in regular type; the rest (in boldface) elaborate on these comments:

> Hi, Steve. Well, let's take a look at your second draft of the newspaper piece here. . . . Ok, let's see. Let me give you some impressions I had of the draft first and try to raise some questions for you to think about, ok? Um, first of all, one thing . . . is this question of how much "you" you want here and how much you want to, uh, well essentially how much of yourself and your impressions and experiences you want to be in this piece. . . . And I think that's a judgment call, **because the *Trib* article you attached to your tape is obviously, um, a good example of how somebody can provide information . . . to readers who might be interested in getting that information and yet do so from a, uh, a kind of narrative perspective, uh, where in addition to saying, "Here are some places to go and here's, you know, this is a good restaurant, and don't try skiing too late in the spring, and try the fondu here or here's a great little place to get wine and cheese"— in addition to giving that sort of information, he's also sharing, speaking from experience and sharing some of those experiences: "We liked the food at 'Le Petit Cafe' at the foot of Zermatt," or "we were simply appalled at the cost for a lift up to the top of the Matterhorn," or whatever. And I think the two of them can go together just fine; otherwise it comes off like,**

**um, you know, so purely informational that the reader might not trust
the writer for making certain judgments.**

But I think it's really a question of balance. Um, what you could do is
go through your paper and strip out everything about yourself and there
wouldn't be much left but it would be purely informational—**for example,
"all these were formed by sink-holes thousands of years ago." That's
purely informational and not really . . . you're doing a kind of encyclopedic writing there.** And then at the other extreme **when you say,
"During my early childhood the first fun thing that I was taught to do
by my grandfather was fish for bluegill,"** which is a purely personal, narrative style of writing. **And the two of them are really mixed together,
which happens a lot in this kind of writing.** So I would encourage you to
think about how much you want of yourself and your experiences, and . . .
how much straight information you want to provide. Now, my impression
right now, and we'll see how the others react, is that you're probably a little
bit over toward the extreme of personal memory as opposed to the informational. So that there are some places where you might try out the "so what"
test: **"I grew up on them and I know most of the hidden underwater
structures, like fallen trees." Ok, if somebody's interested in perhaps
going to Orlando to fish, . . . this might be useful information. But
knowing that you know where all the hidden structures are isn't going
to be useful information, if you see what I mean. Useful in a narrative
about your childhood, maybe, but not, um, you know, for an article on
these great fishing spots. Something that would be useful to know is
that this lake, Ivanho (is that spelled like the novel, maybe?) that this
lake is a great fishing lake. And the information that you then go into
here on, uh, that the lake is fishable from the shoreline and so on,
would be appropriate.** Um, so. So one big issue to think about for revision, then, is how much information you want to take out which might not
be of great interest to the reader and then what other sorts of information
they might want to know.

16. Stewart's excerpt here makes up about two-thirds of his overall response. The rest
of the endnote deals with a few editorial problems.

17. Some teachers, like While and Stewart, might take exception to such a view of conversational response because they feel it is too open-ended and does not provide enough
direction to students. These teachers probably emphasize the written product and expect
their comments to lead students to produce formally complete writing. Other teachers,
like Brannon and Knoblauch, might say that this view of conversational response may
take too much control out of the hands of the writer. They are probably committed to
either a process or a collaborative view of writing instruction, and believe that the more
students are left to experience and assess their own writing and reading processes, with
less teacher intervention, the more proficient they will become. The view of conversational response developed here works in between these two views of writing instruction.
It looks to exploit the possibilities in the developing draft and lead the writer to produce
fuller and more thoughtful texts, yet it also strives to keep the student in control of his
own ideas and tries to attend to the student's gradual development as a writer. Teachers
and students alike have come to prefer the outward forms of writing, the obvious features

of the formal text, to the less tangible domain of thought. But, as James Moffett reminds us, "teachers have no business preferring either and have no choice but to work *in the gap* between thought and speech," between, that is, the student's ways of thinking and the manifestation of that thought in a text.

18. Notice how the tone of the following end note changes—and becomes more conversational in the sense I am pursuing here—when such open-ended elaboration (in boldface) is added to the basic comments of the response:

> It is difficult to determine exactly what you are writing about—is it the lakes of Orlando or a particular fishing trip or how to catch fish? At times I get the feeling that it's one, but then I think it's another. While your paper has possibility, you need to reorganize and decide exactly what you are trying to relate. I wonder what you could do to help me out. **Maybe you could cut your personal anecdotes and focus on presenting your advice on bass fishing. (How important is it that we know that you know where all these "underground structures" are? Would it be important to know this story about your day fishing?) Or maybe you could work your personal experiences into an essay that is mostly about how to fish for bass—for instance, by just making brief mention of them to illustrate your advice.**

19. The concept of response as conversation that I develop here goes beyond the one Ronald F. Lunsford and I present in *Twelve Readers Reading* (Chapter 5). Our use of the term in the book is consistent with the generally accepted understanding, which emphasizes the teacher-student relationship and interpersonal communication. In this essay I am pursuing a more specific and potentially more useful definition of the term, which emphasizes the teacher-text relationship and exploration.

20. Those who have championed the idea of response as an informal dialogue, like Danis and Knoblauch and Brannon, might say that pushing students to explore their ideas further might work against the basic goal of conversational response—to establish an informal, cooperative relationship between teacher and student, one that minimizes the teacher's authority as a responder and emphasizes the teacher's role as a supportive reader. Of course, teachers would do well to look to their comments, first of all, to open up an informal, cooperative dialogue with their students. But, having achieved such a give-and-take relationship, they might take a greater initiative in leading students to develop the thought of their writing and push themselves as developing writers.

21. See, for example, the pioneering articles by Nancy Sommers, and Lil Brannon and C. H. Knoblauch, "Responding to Student Writing" and "On Students' Rights to Their Own Texts: A Model of Teacher Response."

22. It is important to note that looking at response as both a conversation and an exploration does not assume any one particular theory of teaching writing. It may be used by teachers who base their classes on a social constructionist approach, a process approach, a rhetorical approach, a cognitive approach, or an expressivist approach. Looking at commentary as a conversation allows teachers to emphasize the particular concerns of these various approaches even as it allows them to attend more fully to the content and thought of student writing.

23. Although a conversational style is most readily achieved in endnotes or in letters, it can also be achieved in marginal comments. The key to making such comments in

the margins lies in making use of text-specific combination comments, where the teacher presents two or more comments on a given area of the writing. Beyond simply making evaluations or presenting advice or commands, the responder plays back the text, raises questions for the student to consider, and offers explanations, all the while trying to maintain an open-ended discussion with the writer, as in the following comments:

> I see you moving here from talk about bass fishing to a specific account of one day's fishing at Lake Ivanhoe. I think it might help to stick with explaining the delights of bass fishing in Orlando rather than telling about a specific day of fishing—or perhaps to find a better way to use this one experience to illustrate how to fish for bass in these Orlando lakes.
>
> This is useful information about fishing around lily pads. Do you fish during the early morning and late afternoon because those are the times when bass would be feeding here? I wonder if all good fishermen have a knack for where to fish at what times and when to move on to new locations.
>
> Okay, so you're real familiar with these lakes. What can you tell us about how you determine the best places to fish there? Do you go to different areas depending on the time of day, the type of weather, or the time of the year?
>
> Finding out about how bass hang out around shady areas during the day and how they react to changes in barometric pressure teaches me a lot about bass fishing. Id like to hear even more of this detailed insider knowledge.

Ultimately, it is of little consequence whether the comments appear in the margins of the text or in an end note. What *is* important is that the teacher speak in specific terms about the content of the writing and use those comments to create a give-and-take discussion with the student—a conversation that is informal and expectant, one that is geared toward turning students back into their texts and their thinking.

References

Anson, Chris. 1989. "Response Styles and Ways of Knowing." *Writing and Response: Theory, Practice, Research:* 332–66. Urbana, IL: NCTE.

Boswell, James. 1904. *Life of Johnson,* edited by R.W. Chapman. Oxford: Oxford University Press.

Brandt, Deborah. 1990. *Literacy as Involvement: The Acts of Writers, Readers, and Text.* Carbondale: Southern Illinois University Press.

Brannon, Lil, and C. H. Knoblauch. 1982. "On Students' Rights to Their Own Texts: A Model of Teacher Response." *College Composition and Communication* 32: 157–66.

Christensen, Francis. 1967. *Notes Toward a New Rhetoric.* New York: Harper.

Danis, M. Francine. 1987. "The Voice in the Margins: Paper-Marking as Conversation." *Freshman English News* 15: 18–20.

Elbow, Peter. 1995. "Principles That Underlie My Teaching." Unpublished material submitted to Richard Straub and Ronald F. Lunsford's *Twelve Readers Reading: Responding to College Student Writing.* Cresskill, NJ: Hampton.

Knoblauch, C. H., and Lil Brannon. 1984. *Rhetorical Traditions and the Teaching of Writing.* Portsmouth, NH: Boynton/Cook.

———. 1981. "Teacher Commentary on Student Writing: The State of the Art." *Freshman English News* 10: 1–4.

Lindemann, Erika. 1987. *A Rhetoric for Writing Teachers.* 2nd ed. New York: Oxford University Press.

Moffett, James. 1981. "Integrity in the Teaching of Writing." *Coming on Center.* Portsmouth, NH: Boynton/Cook.

Sommers, Nancy. 1982. "Responding to Student Writing." *College Composition and Communication* 32: 148–56.

Straub, Richard, and Ronald F. Lunsford. 1995. *Twelve Readers Reading: Responding to College Student Writing.* Cresskill, NJ: Hampton.

Ziv, Nina. 1984. "The Effect of Teacher Comments on the Writing of Four College Freshmen." In *New Directions in Composition Research*, edited by Richard Beach and Lillian Bridwell, 362–80. New York: Guilford.

23

Reflective Reading

Developing Thoughtful Ways to Respond to Students' Writing

Chris M. Anson

Writers improve by *being read*. Hearing other people's response to their work helps writers to develop a kind of internal monitor, a "reading self," that informs their decisions as they enter new and more sophisticated worlds of writing. By experiencing a range of responses to their work—from teachers, peers, and others—young writers gain a sense of their own authorship, learn how their composing choices affect their readers, and become more able to assess the effectiveness of their syntax, diction, and organization.

Early research and scholarship on response to student writing aimed to develop principles and methods that teachers could use more or less uniformly to help students improve their writing in different settings. However, more recent scholarship, which is well demonstrated in the contributions to this collection, has been exploring response and evaluation in complex and multifaceted ways that take into account issues of gender, culture, and personality (see also Elbow 1993; Hake 1986; Sperling 1993; Straub and Lunsford 1995; McCracken 1993). In practice, as much of this work suggests, response to writing is richly complex, highly context-dependent, and widely varied in method, style, and focus both within and across classrooms. Our stated beliefs about teaching and our descriptions of our response styles are not always reflected in what we write on students' papers, which may vary depending on our mood, context, or knowledge of specific students and their writing. In many cases, such variation takes place so tacitly that we may not be aware of the differences between our beliefs and the different roles we play as readers (see Purves

Chris M. Anson, "Reflective Reading: Developing Thoughtful Ways to Respond to Students' Writing," from *Evaluating Writing* by Charles R. Cooper and Lee Odel, eds. Copyright © 1999 by the National Council of Teachers of English. Reprinted with permission.

1984). The self-confessed grammarian, for example, finds himself so thoroughly engaged in a paper that he stops reading with, as Mina Shaughnessy put it, "a lawyer's eyes, searching for flaws" (1977, 7). He unconsciously overlooks several errors that he would have identified for a student with less engaging material. The response or evaluation then displays a greater enthusiasm for the captivating material, and the proportion of identified errors goes down. Similarly, a teacher who claims that she always tries to render her comments as questions for revision might become so frustrated with a student who changes very little between drafts that she starts writing specific, controlling directions. Her response might look authoritative (and certainly inconsistent) next to her stated practices, but she is using her best intuitions as a teacher to guide this particular student.

Faced with discrepancies in our response practices, many teachers become frustrated or anxious, as if we have been made aware of some small but annoying hypocrisy. We don't like to think of ourselves reading students' writing subjectively, messily. The hope for uniformity and consensus becomes a way to remove such feelings of instability or inconsistency. In the practice of response to student writing, we like to think that if we can discover some key method, informed by theory and predictable in outcome, its application will lessen some of the bewildering complexity that reading students' work inevitably calls into play.

But given the influence of context on our responses, we need to reconsider this prevailing attitude toward inconsistency. As Straub and Lunsford (1995) have shown in their study of the differences in response styles among twelve "expert" composition scholar-teachers, it seems problematic to develop a unified set of practices for responding to students' writing. Response is so rooted in context and human temperament that accepting diverse and even contradictory approaches or rhetorical styles may be more useful than searching for a single method supported by empirical research. It may be entirely appropriate, in other words, to use quite different response strategies as long as we know how to choose and apply them constructively. This is not to suggest that we don't bring to our responses an overarching disposition or educational theory that guides our choices and sometimes makes us do similar things with different pieces of writing. But it allows us to admit some flexibility with which we can make informed choices about the strategies to employ for a specific piece of writing.

Such a shift in priorities mirrors new theories of teaching effectiveness which place the locus of teachers' improvement not on the accumulation of research findings but on developing a higher consciousness, a kind of "thoughtfulness," often captured in the phrase "reflective practice" (Schön 1983, 1987). In the area of response to writing, such an approach assumes that developing a greater awareness of how our context influences the way we read students' writing can help us to make more informed decisions—and to become more able to adapt our responses to specific situations.

This chapter looks first at an interesting and troubling student essay in order to describe some of the contextual factors that influence our response practices in classroom settings. What external conditions shape our responses? How might situations change the way we look at a piece of student writing? The chapter then turns to some practical ways in which we can become more thoughtful readers of students' writing, developing the strategic knowledge that allows us to adapt our response methods to various students, classrooms, and institutions in educationally productive ways.

Some Varieties of Response and Their Possible Sources

As an illustration of how we might begin to explore the ways in which our responses may be contextually influenced, consider an unusual essay, written by Leang, a young Cambodian refugee who was a first-year college student enrolled in a regular section of an introductory composition course.[1]

My Message

Thanks God for let me have my life still, also thanks for let me have my little brother too, plus my older one and sisters. But I still can't forget my others, My parents and the people of Cambodia. What a past! I miss my family so very much and my country too. I wished I had my family back. The family of ten brothers and sisters stood side by side with my parents plus my nieces, nephews and grand nephews running all over the house. What had happened to my family and every family in the whole country? Who had created that problem???

April, 17, 1975, It was the day that Cambodia had collapsed into communism. In that day every thing in my country had changed. It was the disastrous day for my people. All school, hospitals, shops and markets and any business were closed. A lot of city people were killed by communist sodiers. And the rest were force to leave the cities to the country side. The jungle where no one live before. There was no more freedom. It was "THE COMMUNISM." The regime that all the properties were belong to the government alone. That was under the leader of Pol Pot. Imagine, Phenom Phen, the capital city of Cambodia used to be noisy with the sound of cars, trucks, radio, T.V., school children and everything, had been turned into the city of graveyard. The new rules and regulation had been set to people by the communist. It said "There are no more rich, no more people. We are all equal. No more religion, and no more believe in anything, but there is one to believe in "FARMING". My family the same as the rest of the city people were forced to leave the city with bare

---

1. Leang graciously allowed me to use his essay in faculty workshops as well as to reproduce and comment on it here. Because his essay is so much a part of this chapter, I offered him an honorarium for his contribution and invited him to write a response to be included in the chapter, but he declined both, simply glad, he said, that his essay was being put to use.

hands to work in the farm. Over there, there were no buildings, no houses, no street-shops or market, but there were trees, forest far away in the country side. At first, my dad had started with to cut the trees branches and leaves to make hut ourselve. We ran out of food, medicine clothing and lack of others consumer goods that we needed. Because the fierce Government would not let us so. The communists starved to give people very little of food, almost nothing day by day. But, they forced us to work so damn hard, at list 12 to 16 hours every day. We worked like slave. We worked without enough food. When we got sick, the fierce communists ignored us and gave us no medicine. They used the forces on people. They said all kind of bad words and even killed someone just to show the rest net to do the same. "You'll must work in the farm! You'll must obey the communist's Rules! And must do whatever the communists have said, other wise, you people are known as the enemy of the communist Government! The enemy must dead!!!" The rule had set.

Three years and eight months living in communism was a trash. Life was really a tragic. In my family alone, first one of my sisters was dead, six months later, one of my brother was dead. Then my Aunts, uncles, nieces, nephews, my other brothers plus sister-in-laws. And at last when the communist ground our people so bad, my parents passed away. My parents died only one week apart. My family, my people, the whole couple millions of cambodian died one after others because of the starvation and the killing. I still remembered how my dad died. He died because he was sick. He could not go to work for them (communist Government) and they starved him for weeks to die. My mom too, if they kindly gave my mom only a tea spoon of sugar to make home made medicine, probably she still suvive till today. I had seen every movement of my parents before they died because I was living with them.

In communism, actually we lived separately in the group of age. Children must lived differented from adults, adults lived differently from older adults and elderly. The reason that I could live with my parents and my four years old brother because I took a risk of my own life. I ran away from my group. There was nothing hurt more than seeing family, parents and a little brother laying sick side by side on a dirty mat at home with out food, medicine and water and had not a thing around. At that time I was about 12 years old, I myself was so weak too because I had malaria for months. I was so skinny with all my body turned pale; my eyes was kind of blue and yellow. But I had no more thinking of myself. I had tried all my best to find out the things that my family needed. I was became a thief. I stole foods from people. I disobeyed the rules of the communism and running around to find helps. I even prayed to God to take my life or killed me first before he took my parents and my little brother. But that was impossible, not very long later my parents died. God did not accepted my pray neither. Any way. I still have my mom's last words before she died. Her word remind me all the time I think of them. She said in a very weak sound that she wanted me to stay alive; do not give up no matter what. She wanted me grown up to be a man with mercy. A man that knew right and wrong. A man that knew clearly between war-killing and peace. A man that knew the difference between communism and freedom. And before she met the end of her life she called me in name, wispered and looked at me in the eyes and turned to look at my ennicent brother sitting quietly on the dirty clothe near the fire wood that I had made. My mom's eyes were full of tear. It seem like she had million of words to say. Then she passed away and left us behind in the middle of no where.

When I think of "The War" I always think of my country, my family and my people. I think the way they were destroyed........then, I turned to get angry, sad and even more frustrate. I still miss my family and country so much. I love them always, I used to live with comfortable when they're around.

After reading this essay, many teachers have strong feelings. The content moves some to tears. Others are shocked to think the student is enrolled in a standard first-year college composition course. Still others become immersed in the underlying politics of Leang's "message," and reflect on their attitudes toward communism, human rights, the Vietnam War, or whether Leang should be more radical and proactive than his essay suggests. The variety of readings prompted by this essay whenever it is presented without any context—and the even greater range of suggestions about what we might say to Leang about his writing—illustrate some of the many sources of our response practices.

The Influence of Curricular Timing

Our choice of what to say to a student about his or her writing is heavily influenced by the point at which we read the writing in its development. Before the process movement began to pressure more traditional teaching practices, response was heavily evaluative; it was almost entirely summative, measuring the student's text against some established standards. Comments aimed at improving the writing (or the writer) looked toward the next occasion for practice; but comments on the next paper were again judgmental, coming from sometimes new and different sets of standards.

In the contemporary, process-oriented classroom, response may vary depending on when it is given in the development of a piece of writing. In such classes, response typically serves to motivate revisions (and encourage learning and further writing practice). A common response to Leang's essay, for example, locates the paper early in the process and treats it as a draft:

> Leang's story is *so* dramatic that it would be a great piece of writing if he could reorganize it, cut some material, expand some material, and clean up all the errors, I'd put him to work identifying as much of this as he could so that he could end up with a really first-rate paper.

Implied in this response is a vision of the classroom as a workshop, but one still very much focused on finished products. For both teacher and student, success is measured by the number of good papers produced, and the very best quality control (instruction, response, and evaluation) yields papers that can even be circulated or entered into contests. Although revision may play an important role in the course, it is directed toward the improvement of specific papers, without being generalized as a set of strategies for other and perhaps quite different tasks.

Some newer curricular approaches offer interesting and complicated varieties of this focus on the production of polished texts, requiring an even greater repertoire of response strategies. In some courses, a greater focus on the student shifts attention away from products alone and toward their writers, who will eventually move from site to site (into, say, a biology class or, later, a corporation or small business). In other courses in which students create portfolios of their work (see Belanoff and Dickson 1991), teachers may comment on students' in-process writing by playing the role of a (later) evaluator. This strategy involves first reading from the perspective of some institutionalized standards for the portfolio assessment, and then translating this reading into comments that recognize the progress of the student's work and its improvement. Some teachers who use a portfolio method, for example, would advise Leang that his narrative comes nowhere near the portfolio standards already established. The result may be a comment that invokes both the evaluator's and the teacher's different roles:

> I think as this essay stands that it won't be judged as ready for entry into Leang's portfolio. But I find it a really moving and interesting narrative, one that with some more revision and editing might just get there. I would say so to Leang, and then suggest that we sit down together so I can explain in more detail what he needs to do to get this ready for the portfolio assessment.

Some teachers may also be mindful of the entire process a student goes through in readying a piece for an external assessment; the response given on one occasion, then, plays a role in a later assessment of the student's overall performance on a writing project or in a course.

These potentially complicated readings of student writing suggest the need to identify and refine response strategies that are sensitive to issues of *timing and purpose.* While it may seem obvious that a response to a draft-in-progress will not look like a response to a final, graded paper, we must become more aware of how our choice of comments affects students at various points during this process. A teacher who "reads for meaning, not for errors," might not see the need to switch strategies between an in-progress draft and a final text submitted for a grade. But unless we are subverting an institutional grading system, differences must exist between these two occasions—differences in our roles as guides and coaches vs. gatekeepers and evaluators. Knowing what these differences are, and how they govern our choice of strategies, offers us the kind of higher-level knowledge that leads to more principled practice.

The Influence of Institutional Standards

As Mina Shaughnessy suggested in her discussion of the reaction to open admissions policies in the late 1960s at CUNY (1977), one response to students who don't seem to exhibit the appropriate skills necessary to survive in an academic setting is to quietly eliminate those students through failure. This strategy almost always involves a sorting and ranking process. Typically, a teacher will make expert decisions about a student's ability relative to the available program of instruction:

> It's clear that Leang is misplaced. Something went wrong in the diagnostic or advising system. He belongs in an ESL class, where he would get the kind of help he needs as a non-native speaker, especially with the surface mechanics and grammar.

This has traditionally been called text-based response because it measures the student's writing against a preexisting, often institutionalized standard. Such response strategies involve at least some gatekeeping: The student's paper is "owned" by the system, rather than by the student (cf. Knoblauch and Brannon 1982). The teacher's role—often requiring considerable training, expertise, and knowledge of alternative curricula available in the system—is to accurately assess ability against the standards set at the gate.

Standards for judging the quality of writing come to us from many sources at many levels—cultural, institutional, disciplinary, departmental, and personal (Anson and Brown 1991, 257–66). At the highest level, a "cultural ideology" of writing often influences how we think about and respond to students' work. Schools, while maintaining their autonomy and academic freedom within the larger culture, often reflect and amplify "larger sets of social and cultural values in the emphases they give to kinds and ways of knowing" (Piché 1977, 17). Nationally sponsored "writing report cards," speeches by the secretary of education or other high-ranking officials, reportage and editorials in newspapers and periodicals, and other commentaries on the state of education all subtly influence our values. Some teachers confess to using response practices that invoke much tougher standards in the wake of such commentaries, which may leave some students confused or frustrated as they try to figure out why there has been a sudden shift in the language or focus of the response.

In the case of recommending Leang to a different curriculum, the ranking takes place at an *institutional* level that focuses on the necessary skills and preparation of a college student, ignoring the kind of intellectual and emotional "preparation" that Leang brings into that setting from a regime in which he experienced atrocities that many American students can hardly imagine. Teachers comfortable with such an institutionalized ranking system will not feel as conflicted in their responses as those who may be opposed to it; but it is the very relationship between the two systems—institution and classroom—that guides our responses (see, for example, Mary Traschel's [1992] study of the role of college entrance examinations in the teaching of English).

Discipline-specific norms and standards may also influence our response to students' writing. When students enter an academic discipline as novices or outsiders, they may not be familiar with these norms. In such contexts, it is important for teachers to learn how to respond both as a representative of the discipline (gatekeeper) and as one who helps students to learn the information and strategies needed to pass through the gate. A response from the former position alone may be entirely unhelpful in encultuvating students into the field.

Occasionally an individual *department* may have collective practices that are somewhat different from those expected professionally. Teachers in technical or scientific fields who tolerate or even encourage students to write from a highly subjective position may respond in ways antithetical to the goals of more traditional colleagues. In such situations, response to writing might come entwined with commentary about the discipline's received paradigm; "I really like the way you've placed yourself at the center of your case study, Peter. You know, of course, that many scientists would insist on a kind of clinical objectivity that your paper resists."

Some teachers may entirely avoid imposing institutional standards on students in a particular class, perhaps because they have more context-specific goals for their instruction than those that are generally expected across the campus. For example, in dislodging the emphasis on error hunting or pushing student writing into the synthetic mold of the five-paragraph theme, reader-response advocates have for several decades championed a less criterion-based way of responding to students' writing that deliberately avoids the didactic effluence of the red pen. This practice, in its further extension, may downplay the role of response and evaluation: the writing is produced in what Peter Elbow calls an "evaluation-free zone" (1993). The following often-heard reaction to Leang's essay illustrates this approach to the issue of standards:

> I'm incredibly moved by this account. In fact, the story is so authentic that cleaning up the errors makes it too Anglo, too fake. There is something compelling about the voice, the voice of a real refugee. I want to react in all my original horror, to be moved, because the story is moving and Leang should know it.

The strategy implied by such a response is to help Leang develop by focusing on function and meaning—a strategy strongly and elegantly advocated in much of the work of Russell Hunt (see Hunt 1986 and 1989 for representative accounts). Theoretically, literate activities are by nature purposeful, meaning-rich, and contextual (Bleich 1989; Brandt 1991). It follows that literacy improves mainly through meaningful literate experiences, not the practice of isolated skills or the production of artificial, readerless texts.

Yet approaches that deliberately avoid error hunts or red-ink corrections may seem puzzling to students who are already socialized into a system where their lived experience is subjugated to the goal of perfecting the linguistic features of their writing. From the student's perspective, this strategic withholding of response often appears deliberately, sometimes playfully, sometimes even unfairly evasive—the teacher's attempt to push the relativism of multiple rhetorical choices (see Perr 1970; Anson 1989a). After working so hard to acquire English, Leang may be fully expecting to have his errors identified even in the context of so moving a personal account. An important strategy is knowing in advance when a student is ready for what may be an unfamiliar kind of response.

An extension of this meaning-focused response relates readerly reactions more closely to the process of revision:

> I wouldn't grade Leang's paper or invoke any kind of textual standards whatsoever. What he doesn't need right now are criteria; he needs a real, natural, reader-based response, one that can connect with him on the basis of his meaning. I'd say how moved I was. I'd also indicate some places where I was confused or wanted more information, or where I stumbled over his expression. But I'd keep the focus pretty much on Leang's experience and my experience, and hope that my reaction would lead him to identify places he could improve.

Here, the goal is to use the reading process (usually characterized as "natural") to encourage the student to explore other options. It relies, in other words, on the social construction of meaning to create the dissonance that will lead to revision.

While reader-based response supports a purposeful, meaning-centered curriculum, it is wrong to assume that such reading is any more "natural" than hunting for errors. It is, after all, a kind of pedagogical strategy. Our position as educators is already inscribed by our context. Behind the apparently simple donning of an armchair-reader's perspective lies an elaborate set of theories about what might help students to develop their writing in just a few weeks. That development is not purely rhetorical and linguistic; it involves creating in students' own thinking the same underlying beliefs about writing being modeled in our response. (Much of the literature on peer groups suggests that students can learn to respond to each other's writing as we do, even though the conditions of their response are altogether different from ours.)

The Influence of Personal Belief

What specific beliefs do we bring to our reading, relative to its content, that might influence our response? Teachers reading Leang's essay sometimes respond in ways apparently designed to pressure him into thinking about the underlying political implications of his autobiographical account. When they take the form of typical academic consciousness-raising, such responses may place the teacher in a fairly neutral position, perhaps by invoking a reader who

might not agree with the writer. When they take the form of a more direct challenge, however, such comments demonstrate a political critique designed to
make the student intellectually uncomfortable. At its strongest, "contestatory"
response admits that all texts (and all reactions to them) must be political and
ideological. Instead of veiling this fact beneath the discourse of feigned neu-
trality, contestatory response tries to pressure students into becoming more
aware of their political and personal conditions and how their writing and the
writing of their culture can either reveal or hide such realities. As illustrated in
the following paraphrase, the teacher can use this strategy to reflect a particular bias or position, very strongly deciding for the writer what intellectual jour-
ney he or she should travel:

> I don't think Leang goes far enough in trying to understand what
> Communism is, so he ends up simply endorsing (by default) an American
> system that has its own share of atrocities both national and international. He
> is almost blind to the ways in which he has been oppressed twice, and the
> second case is in some ways more insidious than the first because the oppres-
> sion is less visible. I'd want to tell him so, and get him to critique his mater-
> ial conditions now, to examine what has really changed, and who is really in
> control in the midst of his newfound freedom.

Because it is sometimes emotionally charged, such a response strategy
can be very difficult to apply. Unconsciously, we may praise some students for
making assertions with which we agree, but then engage our strategy of con-
testation for students whose thinking we want to reform. The former students
remain complacent in their views while the latter are challenged.

At a time when many teachers are actively challenging students' attitudinal
complacencies, understanding the relationship between response, personal
belief, and the development of writing abilities has never been more important.
Many tensions now arising between teachers and students owe to mismatches of
political and cultural attitudes expressed in student writing and teachers' own
often strongly held beliefs. Better awareness of the sometimes tacit ways in
which belief systems influence response can help us to develop strategies that do
not condemn while they contest, strategies that are sensitive to the goals of particular courses, as well as the backgrounds and dispositions of particular students and their own intentions for their papers. We can then more ably translate
personal reactions into the kinds of comments that help students to see multiple
perspectives and not feel as if they are being forced to accept particular views.

The Influence of Rhetorical and Situational Goals

Knowledge of the complicated relationships between the rhetorical goals of an
assignment and the student's interpretation of those goals in her own rhetorical
plans can strongly influence our response. Typically, response is shaped by the
extent to which a paper (as a text) conforms to the implicit rhetorical standards

of the assignment. Yet students' own goals and plans offer a rich source of information about a piece of writing that can completely change a teacher's response strategy. Jeffrey Sommers (1989), for example, has described a technique in which students write a memo about their paper to help their teacher decide how to respond. The response is shaped by the student's own expressed needs. Similar strategies involve short, tape-recorded narrative commentaries from the student describing his or her goals for a paper and calling attention to things the student wants to work on. In collections of students' work, the reflective "cover statement" accomplishes a similar objective—to provide teachers with the student's own "review and consideration and narration and analysis and exploration of what learning is occurring in writing" (Yancey 1992, 16). Response that expects students to articulate their own intentions, as illustrated in the following paraphrase, also helps to move students beyond what Sharon Crowley calls the "distressing fact that students' intentions may amount to little more than getting a passing grade on an assignment, or pleasing us by demonstrating their ability to observe the formal strictures we have laid down in class" (1989, 108):

> My response would be a set of questions to Leang. I want to know what he wants to do with this paper, who he's talking to, what his purpose is in sharing this piece. Does he want us to think differently about refugees or Cambodians? Does he want us to feel the tension between his love of his country and people and his hatred of the oppressive regime under which he suffered? Or is this therapeutic, a venting of his life woes, a completely self-directed text shared with us only through his educational circumstances?

Here the teacher is simply unable to talk to Leang without more complete knowledge of his purposes. Extended a bit further, this response can become a nonresponse, not in the sense of an "evaluation-free zone" (Elbow 1993), but an inability to respond until the student himself has helped the teacher to choose the most useful strategy for the student's needs.

Sometimes response may be influenced by imagined situational goals that extend beyond students' expressed needs, as shown in the following comment which has surfaced in discussions of Leang's paper at several schools:

> I've seen this sort of paper before. Such papers are all too common to people who work in writing labs. While I don't doubt the authenticity of Leang's account, many students who have had shocking experiences in other countries try to use these to get an emotional response from a teacher, softening the grammatical blow. Sometimes they'll use the same paper or experience several times because they know it works. It's a kind of unsinister ploy. I wouldn't play into it.

This response practice tries to take into account the student's subsidiary motives for choice of topic, writing style, or use of detail. It may come from thinking about the circumstances of the student's writing beyond the classroom (that the student is on an athletic team, or is trying to get into law school, or is the daughter of the department chair) or from imagining more general aspects of student "underlife" to which most of us have little direct access (see Brooke 1987; Anderson et al. 1990). Attitudes toward students in general or toward the particular kinds of students that attend our school can profoundly influence our response. In this case, the teacher simply guesses, perhaps in a less than charitable way, what nonnative speakers like Leang try to do with their writing.

In the absence of information from students about their intentions, we usually invoke instructional goals often deeply embedded in our teaching, such as the need to avoid generalizations, entertain a reader, or give evidence for assertions:

> I assume that in this kind of writing it is always important to use details and images to embellish and support more general claims. Under these circumstances, I would want Leang to go back over the piece and identify places where he could add detail or sharpen our image of the events.

This response practice comes from a more highly goal-driven pedagogy: specific papers are occasions to learn specific skills, sometimes in isolation. Narratives, for example, are used to work on "showing versus telling"; or five-paragraph themes are used to practice logical and argumentative structures. Such practices often owe to what Peter Mosenthal calls a "utilitarian ideology" that stresses the nature of tasks and the passing on of knowledge necessary to survive in real-world settings (1983, 40). Tasks are often organized in increasing complexity, using writing for their practice and acquisition. Assuming that Leang's assignment is designed to help students practice effective paragraphing techniques, the teacher might focus on various moments in his essay where such technique is lacking.

Bringing students' needs together with implied and expressed goals of particular assignments can lead to a more strategic, tailored response. The decision to focus on a particular rhetorical issue such as paragraph development, for example, can also be informed by a higher sense of what is appropriate given the content of the text, as well as Leang's personality, his interaction in class and in small groups, his office visits, the nature of his previous writing, and the amount of time already spent in class working on the skills being applied. Without knowledge of these often intricate details, we have no basis on which to cast a negative judgment on a response that puts aside Leang's meaning in favor, for this moment, of calling attention to errors.

The Influence of Readers' Circumstances

Most of the time, we respond to writing without reflecting consciously on the influence of our personal circumstances. We may be aware that we read four (of twenty-five) student papers early in the morning on a train or bus, ten more later in our office (with coffee), three during the evening news, and the final eight late at night after a long day. While such considerations may seem trivial, developing strategies for response in quite different circumstances can help us to avoid trying to use the wrong strategy at the wrong time. Some teachers aware of this issue split their response process into different readings. "First reading" can be done anywhere—it is an occasion to get a holistic impression of an entire text. "Second reading," however, is accompanied by careful response and must be done without distraction and in time blocks conducive to reflection.

Another external circumstance is the order in which papers are read. Most of us have experienced the curious phenomenon of searching for the paper of a "good" student when we are tired and want to respond just to one or two more pieces of writing. In such cases, we may be choosing a different strategy for response, one that acknowledges our readings of students' past work or class performance. The reading may seem easier because we expect fewer errors, organizational problems, or weaknesses in content. Our focus shifts to other, more meaning-centered issues, issues that may require less translation of our reactions into directed commentary for revision or assessment. Similarly, one paper in a group of essays may influence our subsequent judgments. Six papers all displaying the same lack of paragraph development may have a profound effect on the reading of the seventh, which is judged to be very strong when it might have been judged problematic if preceded by six superb essays. In Leang's case, the content of the essay may be so rich and culturally interesting on the heels of half a dozen bland accounts of minor car accidents and summer jobs that its quality improves by virtue of its location in a string of essays.

The "pace" or "tempo" of reading students' work can also influence the nature and focus of the response (see Himley 1989). Reading students' writing first requires a complicated, rich internal response, much of it never shared with the writer. Of this response, we then select relevant ideas and translate them into an external commentary, using appropriate, student-centered language. In most cases, the internal response is more elaborate and less strictly pedagogical than external response. Good teaching requires a highly complex process as we read, collect impressions, formulate an internal response, choose which of the many impressions and ideas the student should receive, and then decide what form the commentary should take, how long it should be, and what language and style it should be rendered in.

Developing expertise in response relies on a higher awareness of the "tempo" of this translation. Novice teachers sometimes experience little lag time between an internal reaction and an external written comment, time when a more experienced teacher might pause to reflect on the internal reaction and translate it into a comment that will carry more weight or be more instructive. Unable to slow their reading to the molasses-like pace that could yield a really full response for each of fifty (or 150) student papers, expert teachers learn to trade off external response time (marginal comments) against time to reflect internally, knowing that a single well-chosen and articulated comment can ripple through an entire paper and, for the right student, harvest a major and fortuitous revision. In other words, the teacher writes less but says more.

There are several reasons for disparities in the amount of reflection between internal and external response. Newer teachers often feel that quantity shows diligence: The more they can say or write, the more their students will improve. Some teachers may also suffer from conditions that work against reflection—150 papers begging for response, or large classes of blurred faces in a mechanical curriculum. Under these less-than-ideal circumstances, however, a changed tempo and a more reflective response may actually lessen a teacher's burden and offer students more useful feedback. Furthermore, some kinds of writing may require less time for reflection and translation of internal response than others. If a teacher is modeling the process of reading, then writing down internal responses as they occur may be more appropriate than reading the entire text, reflecting on it, and translating and distilling many impressions into a carefully worded summary.

Many other dimensions of our situations as educators affect our response to students' writing. The few I have touched on here represent some useful starting points for discussions of what we do when we respond and, given the great variety in our focus and styles, how we can make the best use of these in particular circumstances. Doing so, as I have argued, is helped by reflection—by sharing strategies and by developing as much consciousness of our practices as we can. The next section considers some of the ways in which, as teachers, we can practice such reflection, both individually and collectively.

Toward Reflective Practice in Response and Evaluation

As a kind of discourse, response to students' writing is carried out in an often-personal domain between teacher and student—necessarily personal, we might argue, because of the expert-novice relationship that ensues in most educational settings. Yet this privacy not only blocks the chance for collaborative inquiry into our practices, but, perhaps as a result, relegates response to a more tacit domain of instruction, unexamined and undiscussed. Unlike the course syllabus, which teachers develop with conscious attention to various educational principles and which is often seen and even responded to by other colleagues, response remains curiously shielded from collective view (Anson 1989b). Clearly, we need more effective approaches for drawing to the surface, in both personally meaningful and collectively useful ways, the complexities involved in reading, responding to, and evaluating students' writing. Several such approaches—including "authentic" faculty-development workshops, teaching portfolios, and deep cases—are promising ways to begin such individual and collaborative reflections on response.

Authentic Workshops on Response

In spite of the ultimately personal nature of response, the most productive methods for improving this area of teaching take place, not surprisingly, in collaborative settings involving sustained dialogue and exchanges among trusting peers. While any such group activities must adjust to local circumstances, they offer participants the chance to share and study the complex interactions between teachers and individual students.

Samples of students' work, such as the essay written by Leang, can help us to talk about and analyze our methods for response and evaluation. While the resulting discussion can be enlightening, most of the time it is set in motion by generalized "response schemas" based on typical educational settings. The discussion may also lead to remarks *about* the essay, not comments directed to the student who wrote it.

More useful for developing response strategies are workshops that invite participants to bring in actual samples of students' writing from their own classes, on which they have made either formative or summative evaluative comments. In such "authentic" workshops, teachers can take turns describing the context of the paper(s) they have brought, which inevitably calls into play descriptions of the student, assignment, curriculum, preceding classroom work, school, and other important information. Once the context of the writing is clear, the group can discuss the teacher's commentary in detail, focusing on the appropriateness of the remarks, their style, focus, length, and effectiveness. Reflection can be prompted by comparisons of the teacher's and other participants' internal responses; by careful analyses of the language the teacher chose, relative to his or her purposes in the context described; by discussions of the participants' impressions of specific comments, especially their attempts to understand the teacher's underlying purpose or rationale for the comment and its placement; and by conclusions about the relationship between the teacher's system of beliefs and the response he or she made. Sharing such reflections not only exposes us to different response strategies (perhaps ones we have never used or seen used), but also helps us to formulate theoretical and practical justifications for the decisions we make. What results from such discussions is at once a larger repertoire of response strategies and a clearer, more informed understanding of how to use such strategies in the classroom.

Teacher Portfolios as a Context for Reflection

Workshops that bring teachers together to share their ideas, observations, and practices provide a social context for faculty development, but individual teachers need time to reflect on their instruction and then try out new methods in their classrooms. As Centra (1993) points out, teachers "become experts in part by the lessons they learn through their own inquiries and insights" (111). The "teaching portfolio," a widely heralded method for instructional development, is ideally suited for encouraging such reflective inquiry.

Teaching portfolios have gained national attention, especially in higher education, as useful tools both for improving teaching through greater reflection and for evaluating teaching effectiveness through richer forms of documentation than student evaluations or peer-review notes (see Anson 1994; Edgerton, Hutchings, and Quinlan 1991; Seldin 1991). As repositories of documents that demonstrate sustained reflection on important teaching issues, portfolios give us a space in which to examine critically our own response practices and develop new strategies.

Portfolio entries to be shared in draft form during inservice meetings or faculty workshops could reflect on specific features of response, such as the balance of positive, negative, and constructive commentary, or even on the definition of such terms as "positive," "negative," and "constructive." In development programs for preservice teachers or teaching assistants, participants might work through several such features of response, each in a different portfolio entry (choice of language; choice of focus; clarity of explanations; amount of annotation; percentage of questions vs. command statements; balance of comments on surface features vs. matters of meaning; and so on). Teachers with more background in rhetoric or composition research could supplement their discussions with references to the theories that inform their practices. Over time, teachers could revisit samples of writing to which they responded years before and chart the course of their own development as readers of students' writing, along the lines of various developmental schema of teaching (e.g., Shaughnessy 1976; Anson 1989b).

"Deep Cases" of Response

In the absence of real samples of students' writing, "deep cases" may give enough context to enrich group discussions of student writing. Deep cases are real or highly realistic scenarios that invite readers to imagine themselves in the situation and often pose some problem or set of problems to solve. Such cases often take the form of narratives with various characters—teacher, students, supervisors, colleagues—and involve complicated, unresolved conflicts that lead teachers into long, involved conversations about the issues, problems, and potential solutions or courses of action in the case. Cases of student writing, for example, could offer rich, detailed background information about many of the factors that we have already examined in this chapter. Participants could then respond to the writing (in its draft or final form) and discuss, analyze, or rationalize their commentary in light of the deep background information provided. Cases could be created to highlight certain aspects of the response process or the teaching situation (see Anson et al. 1993; Hutchings 1993).

Collaborative Teaching

As teachers we should be actively experimenting with response methodology and sharing the results with colleagues. Portfolio programs for student writing, for example, have led to creative new teaching situations involving multiple readings of students' work (see Elbow and Belanoff 1986). Several experiments in which teachers team up to offer the same version of a course, but read and anonymously grade the work of each other's students, have offered interesting anecdotal information about the interpersonal dynamics of response (in one case, for example, students felt hopelessly cheated because their evaluator was not privy to their visible hard work and earnestness in the classroom—aspects of response and evaluation that beg for much more exploration).

Various institutionally sponsored initiatives can encourage teachers to pair or team up in ways that directly affect the way they respond to students' writing. Linked courses, for example, can bring teachers of English or writing together with teachers in discipline-specific courses such as psychology, history or science to create joint-enrollment courses. Teachers linked in such ways can design writing assignments together and then work out creative ways to read and respond to them. Constantly comparing their impressions and judgments can help them to reflect on the relationship between the students' work and the many other contextual issues influencing their decisions.

New Media for Response

In light of the electronic revolutions taking place in education at all levels, we must begin to explore more fully various alternative media for response. Although tape-recorded responses have been discussed in the literature sporadically for decades, few scholars or teachers have looked carefully into this alternative to handwritten marginalia (see Anson 1997). Computer programs are now available that allow teachers to deposit icons in the margins of their students' on-screen work; these icons turn on a computer tape recorder to record the teacher's verbal comments. A second click of the icon turns off the recording device until the next comment is desired. The student, opening her paper on her own computer screen later on, can click on the marginal icons and hear her teacher's voice commenting on her text. Such programs were once thought futuristic, but now they are being supplemented by video boxes that appear in the corner of the screen to give the verbal message a visual accompaniment.

Interactive computer technology, e-mail response, chat lines, virtual writing labs with tutors who telecommute, programs that pretend to read and analyze texts—all such systems and more will characterize the response environment of the next few decades. While many such alternatives seem exciting and novel, we must also be prepared to assess them from the perspective of the new awareness encouraged by deeper thought about our more conventional, traditional methods.

Response in Classroom-Based Research

Most of us have little occasion to study the effects of our response and evaluative practices on our students or to test out new strategies. Such information usually comes to us in the form of successful or unsuccessful revisions of drafts on which we have commented, or when students are puzzled or upset by what we write or say about their work. A more systematic investigation of response and evaluation, however, can lead to many new insights about the teaching and learning processes. Questions teachers can explore without the need for much sophisticated apparatus or complicated research designs might include these:

1. What sorts of responses do students like and dislike the most, and why?
2. Which forms of response do they find most helpful? How are they judging what is "helpful"? What kinds of revision are prompted by the response?
3. How do the conditions of our response affect us?
4. What do we typically do with student writing when we respond to it?
5. How do we respond to different kinds of writing (short or long, basic or advanced) or by different kinds of students (men or women, native or non-native speakers, majors or nonmajors, upper- or working-class)?
6. How do we vary our responses in light of our knowledge about the writer or the circumstances of the writing?
7. How do we change our response between in-progress work and final texts?
8. How do institutional or departmental standards affect our practices?

Studying such questions in the context of our own teaching not only forms higher-level awareness of our practices but also encourages improvement by giving us at least some quasi-empirical basis for our understandings and beliefs.

In this chapter I have claimed that multiple strategies for response may be more instructionally useful to us than aiming for a single, unified method. My belief is supported by my faith in the power of reflection to help us understand and justify our diverse practices, so that we do not fall into the trap that Richard Fulkerson (1979) documented in his analysis of unprincipled shifts in response styles. To adapt our practices to meet our increasingly diverse educational settings, we must become more reflective of the many complicated influences on our behavior. Those reflections, finally, will lead us to educational practices that are informed by thoughtfulness, balance, and clarity of method.

Yet, clearly, much more inquiry is needed into the relationship between teacher reflection and the practice of responding to students' writing. We do not know, for example, what effects a strong focus on reflective practice could have on the success of teachers' responses. Furthermore, the focus of reflective practice has remained steadily on teachers, largely ignoring the ways in which students' own reflections might provide information that facilitates both learning and teaching in specific classrooms. We need much more inquiry into what students bring to the response process—how they read our comments, and how, in turn, they develop new ways of reading their own and others' writing. In an interesting analysis of students reading and commenting on each other's writing, Lee Odell (1989) asks a number of questions about how students develop the ability to respond to other people's texts and to interpret the responses they receive. In addition to developing strategies for responding to students' writing based on fuller analyses of our situations, we need to be investigating and reflecting on how students interpret and act on these responses.

With the new knowledge such investigations yield, and with more attention to the ways in which we can think about and develop our teaching and responding methods, we will be in a better position to play out our roles as expert readers in a context where many people are growing in different ways.

References

Anderson, Worth, Cynthia Best, Alycia Black, John Hurst, Brandt Miller, and Susan Miller. 1990. "Cross-Curricular Underlife: A Collaborative Report on Ways with Academic Words." *College Composition and Communication* 41: 11–36.

Anson, Chris M. 1989a. "Response Styles and Ways of Knowing." In *Writing and Response: Theory, Practice, and Research,* edited by Chris M. Anson, 332–66. Urbana, IL: National Council of Teachers of English.

———. 1989b. "Response to Writing and the Paradox of Uncertainty." In *Writing and Response: Theory, Practice, and Research,* edited by Chris M. Anson, 1–11. Urbana, IL: National Council of Teachers of English.

———. 1994. "Portfolios for Teachers: Writing Our Way to Reflective Practice." In *New Directions in Portfolio Assessment: Reflective Practice, Critical Theory, and Large-Scale Scoring,* edited by Laurel Black, Donald Daiker, Jeffrey Sommers, and Gail Stygall, 185–210. Portsmouth, NH: Boynton/Cook-Heinemann.

———. 1997. "In Our Own Voices: Using Tape-Recorded Commentary to Respond to Student Writing." In *Assigning and Responding to Writing in the Disciplines,* edited by Peter Elbow and Mary Deane Sorcinelli, 105–13. San Francisco: Jossey-Bass.

Anson, Chris M., and Robert L. Brown, Jr. 1991. "Large-Scale Portfolio Assessment: Ideological Sensitivity and Institutional Change." In *Portfolios: Process and Product,* edited by Pat Belanoff and Marcia Dickson, 248–69. Portsmouth, NH: Boynton/Cook-Heinemann.

Anson, Chris M., Joan Graham, David A. Jolliffe, Nancy Shapiro, and Carolyn Smith. 1993. *Scenarios for Teaching Writing: Contexts for Discussion and Reflective Practice.* Urbana, IL: National Council of Teachers of English.

Belanoff, Pat, and Marcia Dickson, eds. 1991. *Portfolios: Process and Product.* Portsmouth, NH: Boynton/Cook-Heinemann.

Bleich, David. 1989. "Reconceiving Literacy: Language Use and Social Relations." In *Writing and Response: Theory, Practice, and Research,* edited by Chris M. Anson, 15–36. Urbana, IL: National Council of Teachers of English.

Brandt, Deborah. 1991. *Literacy as Involvement: The Acts of Readers, Writers, and Texts.* Carbondale: Southern Illinois University Press.

Brooke, Robert. 1987. "Underlife and Writing Instruction." *College Composition and Communication* 38: 141–53.

Centra, John A. 1993. *Reflective Faculty Evaluation: Enhancing Teaching and Determining Faculty Effectiveness*. San Francisco: Jossey-Bass.

Cooper, Charles R. 1977. "Holistic Evaluation of Writing." In *Evaluating Writing: Describing, Measuring, Judging*, edited by Charles R. Cooper and Lee Odell, 3–32. Urbana, IL: National Council of Teachers of English.

Crowley, Sharon. 1989. "On Intention in Student Texts." In *Encountering Student Texts: Interpretive Issues in Reading Student Writing*, edited by Bruce Lawson, Susan Sterr Ryan, and W. Ross Winterowd, 99–110. Urbana, IL: National Council of Teachers of English.

Edgerton, Russell, Patricia Hutchings, and Kathleen Quinlan. 1991. *The Teaching Portfolio: Capturing the Scholarship in Teaching*. Washington, DC: American Association for Higher Education.

Elbow, Peter, 1993. "Ranking, Evaluating, and Liking." *College English* 55: 187–206.

Elbow, Peter, and Pat Belanoff. 1986. "Portfolios as a Substitute for Proficiency Examinations." *College Composition and Communication* 37: 336–39.

Fulkerson, Richard P. 1979. "Four Philosophies of Composition." *College Composition and Communication* 30: 43–56.

Hake, Rosemary. 1986. "How Do We Judge What They Write?" In *Writing Assessment: Issues and Strategies*, edited by Karen L. Greenberg, Harvey S. Wiener, and Richard A. Donovan, 153–67. White Plains, NY: Longman.

Himley, Margaret. 1989. "A Reflective Conversation: 'Tempos of Meaning.'" In *Encountering Student Texts: Interpretive Issues in Reading Student Writing*, edited by Bruce Lawson, Susan Sterr Ryan, and W. Ross Winterowd, 5–19. Urbana, IL: National Council of Teachers of English.

Hunt, Russell A. 1986. "Could You Put in a Lot of Holes? Modes of Response to Writing." *Language Arts* 64: 229–32.

———. 1989. "A Horse Named Hans, a Boy Named Shawn: The Herr von Osten Theory of Response to Writing." In *Writing and Response: Theory, Practice, and Research*, edited by Chris M. Anson, 80–110. Urbana, IL: National Council of Teachers of English.

Hutchings, Pat. 1993. *Using Cases to Improve College Teaching: A Guide to More Reflective Practice*. Washington, DC: American Association of Higher Education.

Knoblauch, Cy, and Lil Brannon. 1982. "On Students' Rights to Their Own Texts: A Model of Teacher Response." *College Composition and Communication* 33: 157–66.

Lees, E. O. 1979. "Evaluating Student Writing." *College Composition and Communication* 30: 370–74.

McCracken, Nancy. 1993 (November). "Toward a Conversational Theory of Response." Paper presented at the Annual Convention of the National Council of Teachers of English, Pittsburgh, PA.

Mosenthal, Peter. 1983. "On Defining Writing and Classroom Writing Competence." in *Research on Writing: Principles and Methods*, edited by Peter Mosenthal, Lynne Tamor, and Sean S. Walmsley, 26–71. New York: Longman.

Murray, Patricia Y. 1989. "Teachers as Readers, Readers as Teachers." In *Encouraging Student Texts: Interpretive Issues in Reading Student Writing,* edited by Bruce Lawson, Susan Sterr Ryan, and W. Ross Winterowd, 73–85. Urbana, IL: National Council of Teachers of English.

Odell, Lee. 1989. "Responding to Responses: Good News, Bad News, and Unanswered Questions." In *Encountering Student Texts: Interpretive Issues in Reading Student Writing,* edited by Bruce Lawson, Susan Sterr Ryan, and W. Ross Winterowd, 221–34. Urbana, IL: National Council of Teachers of English.

Perr, William G., Jr. 1970. *Forms of Intellectual and Ethical Development in the College Years: A Scheme.* New York: Holt, Rinehart & Winston.

Piché, Gene L. 1977. "Class and Culture in the Development of the High School Curriculum, 1880–1900." *Research in the Teaching of English* 11: 17–27.

Polanyi, Michael. 1966. *The Tacit Dimension.* Garden City, NY: Doubleday.

Purves, Alan C. 1984. "The Teacher as Reader: An Anatomy." *College English* 46: 259–65.

Schön, Donald A. 1983. *The Reflective Practitioner: How Professionals Think in Action.* New York: Basic.

———. 1987. *Educating the Reflective Practitioner.* San Francisco: Jossey-Bass.

Seldin, Peter. 1991. *The Teaching Portfolio.* Boston: Ankara.

Shaughnessy, Mina P. 1976. "Diving In: An Introduction to Basic Writing." *College Composition and Communication* 27: 234–39.

———. 1977. *Errors and Expectations: A Guide for the Teacher of Basic Writing.* New York: Oxford University Press.

Sommers, Jeffrey. 1989. "The Writer's Memo: Collaboration, Response, and Development." In *Writing and Response: Theory, Practice, and Research,* edited by Chris M. Anson, 174–86. Urbana, IL: National Council of Teachers of English.

Sperling, Melanie. 1993 (November). Response to Writing Multiply Construed. Paper presented at the Annual Convention of the National Council of Teachers of English, Pittsburgh, PA.

Straub, Richard, and Ronald F. Lunsford. 1995. *Twelve Readers Reading.* Cresskill, NJ: Hampton Press.

Traschel, Mary. 1992. *Institutionalizing Literacy: The Historical Role of College Entrance Examinations in English.* Carbondale: Southern Illinois University Press.

Yancey, Kathleen Blake. 1992. "Teachers' Stories: Notes Toward a Portfolio Pedagogy." In *Portfolios in the Writing Classroom,* edited by Kathleen Blake Yancey, 12–19. Urbana, IL: National Council of Teachers of English.

About the Author

Chris M. Anson, a professor at the University of Minnesota, has focused on teacher responses to student writing in much of his scholarship, including *Writing and Response: Theory, Practice, and Research* and *Scenarios for Teaching Writing:*

Contexts for Discussion and Reflective Practice. In this 1999 article first published in Charles Cooper and Lee Odell's *Evaluating Writing: The Role of Teachers' Knowledge About Text, Learning, and Culture,* Anson describes many of the circumstances that can affect a teacher's response to a paper, from the teacher's pedagogical goals, personal beliefs, and knowledge of the student to the teacher's mood and the time of day. Anson's article hopes to help teachers comment more reflectively on student writing, with greater awareness of how circumstances affect their responses and of how students respond to their responses.

Continued from page iv

"Teacher Commentary on Student Writing: The State of the Art" by C. H. Knoblauch and Lil Brannon. From *Freshman English News*, Vol. 10, No. 2, Fall 1981. Copyright © 1981. Reprinted with permission.

"The Interaction of Instruction, Teacher Comment, and Revision in Teaching the Composing Process" by George Hillocks, Jr. From *Research in the Teaching of English*, 16.3. Copyright © 1982 by the National Council of Teachers of English. Reprinted with permission.

"The Effect of Teacher Comments on the Writing of Four College Freshmen" by Nina D. Ziv from *New Directions in Composition Research,* edited by Birhard Beach and Lillian S. Bridwell. Copyright © 1984. Published by Guilford Press. Reprinted by permission.

"A Good Girl Writes Like a Good Girl" by Melanie Sperling and Sarah Warshauer Freedman. From *Written Communication*, Vol. 4, No. 4, October 1987. Copyright © 1987 by Sage Publications, Inc. Reprinted by permission of Sage Publications, Inc.

"Teachers' Rhetorical Comments on Student Papers" by Robert J. Connors and Andrea A. Lunsford. From *College Composition and Communication*, 44.2. Copyright © 1993 by the National Council of Teachers of English. Reprinted with permission.

Excerpts from "Twelve Readers Reading: A Survey of Contemporary Teachers' Commenting Strategies" by Ronald Lunsford and Richard Straub. From *Twelve Readers Reading: Responding to College Student Writing (Written Language)*. Copyright © 1995. Reprinted by permission of Hampton Press, Inc.

"Listening to Students: Contextualizing Response to Student Writing" by Peggy O'Neill and Jane Mathison Fife. From *Composition Studies*, 27, Fall 1999. Copyright © 1999. Reprinted by permission.

"Some Semantic Implications of Theme Correction" by William J. Dusel. From *English Journal*, Vol. XLIV, No. 7, Oct. 1955. Copyright © 1955 by the National Council of Teachers of English. Reprinted with permission.

"In Praise of Praise" by Paul B. Diederich. From *NEA Journal*, LII, Sept. 1963. Copyright © 1963. Reprinted with permission.

"Two Types of Grading" by W. S. Ward, ed. From *Principles and Standards in Composition*, *Kentucky English Bulletin*, Vol. 6, No. 1, Fall 1956. Copyright © 1956. Reprinted with permission.

"Learning to Write by Writing" by James Moffett. From *Papers of the Yale Conference on English*. Copyright © 1967 by the Office of Teacher Training, Yale University. Reprinted courtesy of Yale University.

"The Art of Writing Evaluative Comments on Student Themes" by D. G. Kehl. From *English Journal*, 59.7. Copyright © 1970 by the National Council of Teachers of English. Reprinted with permission.

"The Teacherless Writing Class" by Peter Elbow. From *Writing Without Teachers*. Copyright © 1973. Reprinted by permission of Oxford University Press, Inc.

"Responding to Student Writing" by Nancy Sommers. From *College Composition and Communication*, 33.2. Copyright © 1982 by the National Council of Teachers of English. Reprinted with permission.

Excerpts from *Rhetorical Traditions and the Teaching of Writing* by Cy Knoblauch and Lil Brannon. Copyright © 1984. Published by Boynton/Cook. Reprinted by permission.

"Enlisting the Writer's Participation in the Evaluation Process" by Jeffrey Sommers. From *Journal of Teaching Writing*, Vol. 4, No. 1, Spring 1985. Copyright © 1985. Reprinted with permission.

"Teacher Response as Conversation: More Than Casual Talk, an Exploration" by Richard Straub. From *Rhetoric Review*, Vol. 14, No. 2, Spring 1996. Copyright © 1996. Reprinted by permission of Lawrence Erlbaum Associates, Inc.

"Reflective Reading: Developing Thoughtful Ways to Respond to Students' Writing" by Chris M. Anson. From *BOOK: Evaluating Writing: The Role of Teachers' Knowledge About Text, Learning, and Culture*. Copyright © 1999 by the National Council of Teachers of English. Reprinted with permission.